The Editors

PETER HULME is Emeritus Professor in Literature at the University of Essex. His recent books include *Cuba's Wild East: A Literary Geography of Oriente* (2011) and *The Dinner at Gonfarone's: Salomón de la Selva and His Pan-American Project in Nueva York, 1915–1919* (2019).

WILLIAM H. SHERMAN is Director of the Warburg Institute in the University of London's School of Advanced Study. He served for many years as Associate Editor of *Shakespeare Quarterly* and has published widely on the history of books and readers and the plays of Shakespeare and his contemporaries.

HULME and SHERMAN have also edited *"The Tempest" and Its Travels* (2000).

NORTON CRITICAL EDITIONS
SHAKESPEARE

ANTONY AND CLEOPATRA
AS YOU LIKE IT
HAMLET
1 HENRY IV
JULIUS CAESAR
KING LEAR
MACBETH
MEASURE FOR MEASURE
THE MERCHANT OF VENICE
A MIDSUMMER NIGHT'S DREAM
OTHELLO
RICHARD III
ROMEO AND JULIET
THE TAMING OF THE SHREW
THE TEMPEST

For a complete list of Norton Critical Editions, visit
wwnorton.com/nortoncriticals

A NORTON CRITICAL EDITION

William Shakespeare
THE TEMPEST

AN AUTHORITATIVE TEXT
SOURCES AND CONTEXTS
CRITICISM
REWRITINGS AND APPROPRIATIONS

SECOND EDITION

Edited by

PETER HULME
UNIVERSITY OF ESSEX

AND

WILLIAM H. SHERMAN
WARBURG INSTITUTE

W · W · NORTON & COMPANY · *New York* · *London*

W. W. Norton & Company has been independent since its founding in 1923, when William Warder Norton and Mary D. Herter Norton first published lectures delivered at the People's Institute, the adult education division of New York City's Cooper Union. The firm soon expanded its program beyond the Institute, publishing books by celebrated academics from America and abroad. By midcentury, the two major pillars of Norton's publishing program—trade books and college texts—were firmly established. In the 1950s the Norton family transferred control of the company to its employees, and today—with a staff of four hundred and a comparable number of trade, college, and professional titles published each year—W. W. Norton & Company stands as the largest and oldest publishing house owned wholly by its employees.

Manufacturing by Maple Press
Book design by Antonina Krass
Production manager: Stephen Sajdak

Library of Congress Cataloging-in-Publication Data

Names: Shakespeare, William, 1564–1616, author. | Hulme, Peter, editor. |
    Sherman, William H. (William Howard) editor.
Title: The tempest : an authoritative text, sources and contexts, criticism,
    rewritings and appropriations / William Shakespeare ; edited by Peter
    Hulme, University of Essex and William H. Sherman, Warburg Institute.
Description: Second edition. | New York : W. W. Norton & Cimpany, 2019. |
    Series: A Norton critical edition | Includes bibliographical references.
Identifiers: LCCN 2018044651 | **ISBN 9780393265422 (pbk.)**
Subjects: LCSH: Fathers and daughters—Drama. | Political refugees—
    Drama. | Shipwreck victims—Drama. | Magicians—Drama. | Islands—
    Drama. | Spirits—Drama. | Shakespeare, William, 1564–1616. Tempest.
Classification: LCC PR2833.A2 H85 2019 | DDC 822.3/3—dc23 LC record
    available at https://lccn.loc.gov/2018044651

W. W. Norton & Company, Inc., 500 Fifth Avenue, New York, N.Y. 10110
            www.wwnorton.com
W. W. Norton & Company Ltd., 15 Carlisle Street, London W1D 3BS

5   6   7   8   9   0

Contents

Preface

The earliest recorded performance of *The Tempest* was at court, before King James, on "Hallomas nyght" (November 1), 1611. A year and a half later, on May 20, 1613, the play was performed again for the king, during the festivities leading up to the marriage of his daughter. The play was probably also performed for a wider public by the company formed under the patronage of King James, the "King's Men"—either indoors at the Blackfriars Theatre or outdoors at The Globe. But the text's first appearance in print (as with roughly half of Shakespeare's plays) had to wait until seven years after Shakespeare's death, when it was published as the opening title in the First Folio of 1623.

This privileged position has given weight to *The Tempest*'s status as Shakespeare's swan song. While Shakespeare had a hand in at least two plays after this one (*Henry VIII* and *The Two Noble Kinsmen*), and while scholars now tend to be suspicious of simplistic identifications between Prospero and Shakespeare (making the former's renunciation of illusions and charms the latter's farewell to the stage), the play's position as both a crowning achievement and an inaugural work is entirely appropriate. *The Tempest* offers some of Shakespeare's most profound meditations on the cycles of life, shuttling between a sense of an ending and a sense of a beginning, and culminating in a potent (and potentially unstable) mixture of death and regeneration, bondage and release.

The editors of the First Folio divided Shakespeare's plays into three generic groupings—comedies, histories, and tragedies. They placed *The Tempest* in the first of these categories, but few modern readers have been entirely content to leave it there. The play shares some of the otherworldly setting and romantic playfulness of *A Midsummer Night's Dream*, and it moves, like other Shakespearean comedies, toward reconciliation and marriage; but the seriousness of its tone, the suffering experienced by all of the play's characters, and the presence of themes such as exile, enslavement, and mortality have led many modern critics to label it a "tragicomedy" or to group it with Shakespeare's other late plays in a special category called the "romances" or the "problem plays."

In most of Shakespeare's plays the plot is adapted from readily identifiable historical or literary texts. No such source has been identified for *The Tempest*; but the search has turned up references and even quotations from a wide range of texts, including Virgil's *Aeneid*, Ovid's *Metamorphoses*, Montaigne's essay "Of the Cannibals," and one or more contemporary accounts of the shipwreck of the *Sea Venture* on the coast of Bermuda in July 1609. The only accepted source for a name in the play is Caliban's "dam's god Setebos" (1.2.372), who is borrowed from Antonio Pigafetta's account of Ferdinand Magellan's circumnavigation of the world, where "Setebos" is named as a Patagonian devil. But echoes have been heard from the Bible (particularly Isaiah XXIX), earlier plays featuring magicians (especially *Friar Bacon and Friar Bungay* and *Doctor Faustus*), histories of Renaissance Italy, and prose romances from Italy, France, and Spain (which often featured shipwrecks, sorcerers, monsters, and long-deferred marriages between knights and maidens).

Similarly, alongside the explicit responses to and rewritings of *The Tempest* featured in a special section of this Norton Critical Edition, a number of texts written by Shakespeare's contemporaries seem to contain echoes of the play, as when Samuel Purchas writes in the 1620s about the native conspiracies against the English colonists in Virginia or Gabriel Naudé in the 1630s about the theatrical exercise of political power. A selection of these materials—few of which can count as indisputable sources, but all of which cast light on the play—is featured in "Sources and Contexts," providing some sense of the contemporary discourses by which *The Tempest* was informed (and which it, in turn, helped to shape). These texts are here divided into three overlapping subsections: "Magic and Witchcraft," "Politics and Religion," and "Geography and Travel."

It is the last of these that is immediately invoked by the play's title and opening scene, and that accounts for some of its exploratory themes and nautical language: the plot of *The Tempest* begins with a dramatic storm that wrecks a ship off the coast of an "uninhabited island." We find out in 1.2 that the island is, in fact, inhabited by as strange a cast of characters as can be found in any Renaissance play. Some twelve years before the play begins, the Italian magician Prospero had been the legitimate Duke of Milan; but by withdrawing into his studies and turning over the ducal duties to his ambitious brother Antonio, he lost power in a coup d'état—the reversal of which provides the central plot for the play. Prospero was put to sea with his young daughter Miranda, some basic provisions, and at least some of the books from his precious library ("volumes that / I prize above my dukedom"). Their little boat took them to the island where the play is set, and which the geographical references in the text seem to place in both the Mediterranean and the Atlantic: the course being followed by the entourage of Alonso after the celebration of his daughter Claribel's wedding to the King of Tunis is back across the Mediterranean toward his kingdom of Naples, but Ariel refers to the Bermudas and the word *Setebos* comes from Patagonia.

Prospero and Miranda are attended by two characters who were already on the island when they arrived—their servant Caliban and the spirit Ariel. We are told by Prospero and Ariel that Caliban had been brought to the island by his now-dead mother, the Algerian witch Sycorax, who had herself been exiled to the island (spared from execution because of her pregnancy) and, after an attempted rape of Miranda, had been confined to a rock and forced to gather fuel for Prospero's fire. Caliban's appearance in 1.2 is one of the most enigmatic aspects of the play: in this and the following scenes he is described by various characters as "earth," "tortoise," "hagseed," "fish," "monster," "moon-calf," "puppy-headed," "misshapen," and a "thing of darkness," but he also speaks some of the most beautiful lines in the play and in several places is acknowledged as having human features, feelings, and aspirations. Ariel is also in the service of Prospero, who freed him from the tree he was imprisoned in by Sycorax. Prospero has promised him (or her, as Ariel is often played) that if he performs all of his magical commands for the duration of the play, he will earn his freedom and return to the elements.

If Prospero's books are the cause of his banishment, they are also the source of the power he uses to overcome it: he raises the storm in order to bring to the island the Italian noblemen who had deposed him and forced him from Milan. The first member of the wedding party encountered by Prospero and Miranda is Alonso's son Ferdinand, the young prince of Naples, who believes himself to be the sole survivor of the shipwreck. According to Prospero's plan, he falls in love with Miranda at first sight. One plotline follows their brief courtship (in the play's central scene, 3.1), and the action of the play is brought to a climax with their betrothal in 4.1 and presentation to Alonso and the other courtiers in 5.1.

In 2.1 we are introduced to the rest of the wedding party—notably Gonzalo (the old and noble councillor), Antonio (Prospero's usurping brother), and Sebastian (Alonso's younger brother). While the exhausted king and courtiers sleep, Antonio tries to persuade Sebastian to murder the king and, like himself, take over his brother's role—but Prospero, through Ariel, prevents this first of two conspiracies in the play. The other conspiracy is hatched by Caliban, who (in 2.2 and 3.2) encourages the jester Trinculo and the butler Stefano to seize control of the island from Prospero, killing the magical tyrant, burning his books, and taking his daughter as their queen. For their parts, Stefano and Trinculo are more interested in the alcohol they have managed to rescue from the ship, and their mock-conspiracy (along with Caliban's dreams of freedom) degenerates into drunken banter. In 3.2 they are led off by an invisible Ariel and his music.

In 3.3 the busy Ariel arranges for an edifying (and mystifying) dumb show, which presents the hungry wedding party with the image of a feast before snatching it away and chastising them for their wrongs. While they are wandering in despair, Prospero (in 4.1) unites Miranda and Ferdinand and celebrates their engagement with a masque featuring the goddesses Iris, Juno, and Ceres. Suddenly remembering the threat of Caliban and his co-conspirators, Prospero breaks off the show and delivers the play's most famous speech ("Our revels now are ended").

Having foiled Caliban's conspiracy by tempting Trinculo and Stefano with gaudy clothing, Ariel and his spirits chase them through a filthy swamp. In the play's final act, Prospero resolves to give up his magic and grant Ariel his freedom and turn his own thoughts to preparing for death. The king and his courtiers are reunited with Ferdinand and his future princess—and queen—Miranda. Ariel returns the ship and the mariners, miraculously restored, and after general statements of apology and forgiveness, the Italians prepare for their departure while Prospero (in a brief epilogue) asks for the audience's applause.

The Tempest is, after The Comedy of Errors, Shakespeare's shortest play, and it is full of loose ends and open questions. Where (indeed, what) is the island on which the play is set? How are we supposed to feel toward Caliban? What are we to make of the play's absent women? What happens to the balance of power at the end of the play, as the ship prepares to return to Milan? And what is the source of Prospero's power? Does it derive from his study of the "liberal arts" and the books from his library that he took into exile? From his magical book, robe, and staff, and the assistance of Ariel and other supernatural spirits? From his ability (like Shakespeare himself) to enchant an audience with words and images? Or from his tyrannical control over those he has placed in a position of weakness?

The range and openness of these questions has guaranteed a long and lively critical history, reflected in the section called "Criticism," which contains material from four centuries and includes such notable literary figures as Dryden, Coleridge, and Henry James. Over the last sixty years The Tempest has been at the heart of critical debates about matters as diverse as postcolonialism, textual editing, and Renaissance magic, all of which are discussed in the latter part of the "Criticism" section. The play's adaptability has given it a rich

performance history, the last century of which is briefly indicated in
a short essay entitled "Performances and Productions," describing
some of its transformations into dance, opera, and film.

The universality of *The Tempest*'s relationships (father and daughter,
husband and wife, older brother and younger brother, king and subject, master and servant, colonizer and colonized) has helped make it
one of the most adaptable texts of the entire literary canon, and it has
been reread and rewritten more radically than any of Shakespeare's
other works. The play has in fact been adapted from the outset, and
the text as we now know it has only been used on stage for just over
half of its existence. The section "Rewritings and Appropriations"
offers extracts from some of the earliest theatrical responses by Shakespeare's contemporaries or near-contemporaries that imitate or parody
aspects of *The Tempest*, as well as from Dryden and Davenant's 1667
adaptation for the Restoration theater, *The Enchanted Island*, which
displaced the version printed in Shakespeare's First Folio (and itself
became the subject of parody); and from one representative example of
the astonishing array of altered forms—including comic opera, bur-
lesque, and pantomime—in which the play continued to appear
throughout the nineteenth century (even after the production of 1838
that restored the original text to the stage).

As a play that foregrounds the power of books, *The Tempest* has
also been an enduring source of inspiration and provocation to contemporary writers working in a wide range of genres and styles. Novels and longer narrative poems are difficult to excerpt, so here we
merely gesture toward them with the opening and closing sections
of Robert Browning's "Caliban upon Setebos"; but within the lyric
tradition Shelley, Rilke, and many others have given new voice to the
play's characters in their meditations on the music of the theatrical
island, the power of language, and the ends of art. Contemporary
authors have been drawn less to Prospero than to Ariel and Caliban;
and some—like contemporary critics—have also been fascinated by
the shadowy presence of Sycorax, Claribel, and Setebos, who never
appear on stage. This section includes one poem from Ted Hughes's
coruscating use of the whole range of the play's characters to relate
the story of his marriage.

In the critical essays, quotations from *The Tempest* come from a
variety of editions. These have not been amended, but the line number references have been changed to correspond with those in this
Norton Critical Edition.

The editors would like to thank the authors of several of the pieces
included in this volume for either suggesting ways of editing their

material or allowing the editors a free hand in doing so. We would also like to express our appreciation of the sterling contribution of Thea Goodrich in obtaining the necessary permissions. We regret that the exorbitant fees requested by some publishers put some crucial essays and rewritings out of our (and your) reach.

The Text of
THE TEMPEST

PROSPERO, the right Duke of Milan
MIRANDA, daughter to Prospero
ANTONIO, his brother, the usurping Duke of Milan

ALONSO, King of Naples
SEBASTIAN, his brother   5
FERDINAND, son to Alonso

GONZALO, an honest old councillor
ADRIAN and FRANCISCO, lords

ARIEL, an airy spirit
CALIBAN, a savage and deformed slave   10

TRINCULO, a jester
STEFANO, a drunken butler

MASTER of a ship
BOATSWAIN
MARINERS   15

SPIRITS *appearing as*
IRIS
CERES
JUNO
Nymphs   20
Reapers

THE SCENE: *An uninhabited island.*

1. **Prospero:** An Italian word meaning favorable or propitious. Prospero is the *right*, that is legitimate, Duke of Milan (pronounced throughout the play with the accent on the first syllable). Milan was one of the most powerful states in Renaissance Italy, but was taken over first by France and then by Spain.
2. **Miranda:** A word derived from the Latin verb *miror*, meaning "she who is to be wondered at or admired." She is next in line to Prospero's dukedom.
3. **Antonio:** As Prospero explains in 1.2, Antonio had usurped Prospero's dukedom twelve years earlier.
4. **Alonso:** As King of Naples, he controls the large area of southern Italy that in Shakespeare's time was under Spanish rule.
5. **Sebastian:** Second in line to the throne of Naples after Ferdinand.
6. **Ferdinand:** Heir to the throne of Naples.
7. **Gonzalo:** Gives advice (counsel) to his king.
9. **Ariel:** A word glossed in the Geneva Bible as "lion of God," but probably just denotes "airiness."
10. **Caliban:** Often considered an anagram of "canibal."
11. **Trinculo:** Probably derived from the Italian *trincare*, to drink. He is a *jester*, a fool employed by the royal house for entertainment.
13. **Master:** Captain.
14. **Boatswain:** Pronounced "bosun"; in charge of the ship's rigging and anchors, and acts as intermediary between the Master and the sailors.
22. **uninhabited:** having no permanent human occupation.

1.1

A tempestuous noise of thunder and lightning heard.
Enter a ship['s] MASTER *and a* BOATSWAIN.

MASTER   Boatswain!

BOATSWAIN   Here, Master. What cheer?

MASTER   Good, speak to th' mariners. Fall to't yarely, or we
run ourselves aground. Bestir, bestir!   *Exit.*
   Enter MARINERS.

BOATSWAIN   Heigh, my hearts! Cheerly, cheerly, my hearts!   5
Yare, yare! Take in the topsail. Tend to th' Master's whistle.
[*to the storm*] Blow till thou burst thy wind, if room enough!
   Enter ALONSO, SEBASTIAN, ANTONIO, FERDINAND,
   GONZALO, *and others.*

ALONSO   Good Boatswain, have care. Where's the Master?
[*to the* MARINERS] Play the men!

BOATSWAIN   I pray now, keep below.   10

ANTONIO   Where is the Master, Boatswain?

BOATSWAIN   Do you not hear him? You mar our labor. Keep
your cabins: you do assist the storm!

GONZALO   Nay, good, be patient.

BOATSWAIN   When the sea is. Hence! What cares these roarers   15
for the name of king? To cabin! Silence! Trouble us not.

GONZALO   Good, yet remember whom thou hast aboard.

BOATSWAIN   None that I more love than myself. You are a
councillor: if you can command these elements to silence and
work the peace of the present, we will not hand a rope more.   20
Use your authority! If you cannot, give thanks you have lived
so long, and make yourself ready in your cabin for the mischance of the hour, if it so hap. [*to the* MARINERS] Cheerly,
good hearts! [*to* GONZALO] Out of our way, I say!

Exit [BOATSWAIN *with* MARINERS].

3. **Good:** Good fellow; **yarely:** quickly.
5. **hearts:** hearties.
6. **Take . . . topsail:** The first stage in reducing the ship's speed; **Tend:** Attend. Both
    Master and Boatswain would convey orders by means of a whistle.
7. **Blow . . . enough:** Blow as hard as you like, as long as we have room between ship
    and rocks. Winds were often pictured as faces with puffed cheeks.
9. **Play the men!:** Either (to the Mariners) "Act like men!" or (to the Boatswain) "Ply the
    men!"—that is, put them to work.
14. **good:** my good man; **patient:** composed.
15. **cares:** A plural subject with a singular form of the verb was a common formulation in
    the period; **roarers:** Roaring winds and waves, with a metaphoric link to social disor-
    der ("roaring boys" were riotous young men).
19. **councillor:** member of the king's council; advisor.
20. **work . . . present:** bring peace to the present turmoil; **hand:** handle.
23. **hap:** happen.

GONZALO   I have great comfort from this fellow. Methinks he   25
hath no drowning mark upon him; his complexion is
perfect gallows. Stand fast, good Fate, to his hanging; make
the rope of his destiny our cable, for our own doth little
advantage. If he be not born to be hanged, our case is
miserable.   30

                       Exeunt [GONZALO, ALONSO, SEBASTIAN,
                               ANTONIO, *and* FERDINAND].

     Enter BOATSWAIN.

BOATSWAIN   Down with the topmast! Yare! Lower, lower! Bring
her to try with main-course. (*A cry within.*) A plague upon
this howling! They are louder than the weather or our office.

     Enter SEBASTIAN, ANTONIO, *and* GONZALO.

Yet again? What do you here? Shall we give o'er and drown?
Have you a mind to sink?   35

SEBASTIAN   A pox o' your throat, you bawling, blasphemous,
incharitable dog!

BOATSWAIN   Work you, then.

ANTONIO   Hang, cur! Hang, you whoreson insolent noise-
maker! We are less afraid to be drowned than thou art.   40

GONZALO   I'll warrant him from drowning, though the ship
were no stronger than a nutshell and as leaky as an
unstanched wench.

BOATSWAIN   Lay her a-hold, a-hold! Set her two courses! Off
to sea again! Lay her off!   45

     Enter MARINERS, *wet.*

MARINERS   All lost! To prayers, to prayers! All lost!

                           [*Exeunt* MARINERS.]

BOATSWAIN   What, must our mouths be cold?

GONZALO   The King and Prince at prayers! Let's assist them,
for our case is as theirs.

---

25. **Methinks:** It seems to me.
25–27. **he . . . gallows:** The proverb was, "He that is born to be hanged will never be
    drowned."
26. **complexion:** appearance; temperament.
28–29. **doth little advantage:** is of little use.
31–32. **Bring . . . try:** Move forward tentatively under minimum sail.
32. **main-course:** mainsail.
33. **our office:** (the noise we make at) our work.
34. **give o'er:** stop working.
36. **blasphemous:** Unless some original blasphemy was cut from the Boatswain's speech,
    this word simply implies "abusive" or "disrespectful."
41. **warrant . . . drowning:** guarantee he'll never drown.
42–43. **leaky . . . wench:** The phrase may refer to a menstruating woman, with the flow
    of blood unstopped; but "leaky" could also mean sexually insatiable.
44–45. **Lay . . . off:** Bring the ship close to the wind by setting foresail and mainsail (the
    "two courses"), then take her out to sea.
47. **must . . . cold?:** must we die?

SEBASTIAN   I'm out of patience.   50
ANTONIO   We are merely cheated of our lives by drunkards.
    This wide-chopped rascal—would thou mightst lie drowning
    the washing of ten tides!
GONZALO   He'll be hanged yet, though every drop of water
    swear against it and gape at widest to glut him.   55
        A confused noise within.
MARINERS [*within*]   Mercy on us! We split, we split! Farewell,
    my wife and children! Farewell, brother! We split, we split,
    we split!

                                              [*Exit* BOATSWAIN.]
ANTONIO   Let's all sink wi'th' King.
SEBASTIAN   Let's take leave of him.   *Exit* [*with* ANTONIO].   60
GONZALO   Now would I give a thousand furlongs of sea for an
    acre of barren ground: long heath, brown furze, anything.
    The wills above be done, but I would fain die a dry death.

                                                              Exit.

                              1.2
            Enter PROSPERO *and* MIRANDA.
MIRANDA   If by your art, my dearest father, you have
    Put the wild waters in this roar, allay them.
    The sky, it seems, would pour down stinking pitch
    But that the sea, mounting to th' welkin's cheek,
    Dashes the fire out. Oh, I have suffered   5
    With those that I saw suffer: a brave vessel—
    Who had, no doubt, some noble creature in her—
    Dashed all to pieces! Oh, the cry did knock
    Against my very heart! Poor souls, they perished.
    Had I been any god of power, I would   10
    Have sunk the sea within the earth or ere

---

51. **merely:** completely, utterly.
52. **wide-chopped:** big-mouthed.
53. **the . . . tides:** An exaggerated form of the sentence passed on pirates, who were
    hanged on the shore at low-water mark and left there until three tides had flowed.
55. **glut:** swallow.
61. **furlong:** 220 yards.
62. **heath:** heather; **furze:** gorse. Both grow in poor soil.
63. **fain:** gladly.
1. **art:** learning; magic powers.
2. **allay:** set to rest.
3. **pitch:** tar.
4. **welkin's cheek:** face of the sky.
6. **brave:** fine, noble.
11. **or ere:** before.

It should the good ship so have swallowed and
The fraughting souls within her.
PROSPERO   Be collected.
No more amazement. Tell your piteous heart
There's no harm done.
MIRANDA   Oh, woe the day!
PROSPERO   No harm.   15
I have done nothing but in care of thee—
Of thee, my dear one, thee, my daughter—who
Art ignorant of what thou art, naught knowing
Of whence I am, nor that I am more better
Than Prospero, master of a full poor cell   20
And thy no greater father.
MIRANDA   More to know
Did never meddle with my thoughts.
PROSPERO   'Tis time
I should inform thee farther. Lend thy hand
And pluck my magic garment from me.—
   [*She helps him remove the cloak, and he puts it aside.*]
                                             —So,
Lie there, my art. —Wipe thou thine eyes; have comfort.   25
The direful spectacle of the wreck, which touched
The very virtue of compassion in thee,
I have with such provision in mine art
So safely ordered that there is no soul—
No, not so much perdition as an hair   30
Betid to any creature in the vessel
Which thou heard'st cry, which thou saw'st sink. Sit down,
For thou must now know farther.
MIRANDA   You have often
Begun to tell me what I am, but stopped
And left me to a bootless inquisition,   35
Concluding, "Stay: not yet."
PROSPERO   The hour's now come;
The very minute bids thee ope thine ear.

---

13. **fraughting souls:** people who were the cargo; **Be collected:** Compose yourself.
14. **amazement:** bewilderment; anguish; **piteous:** pitying.
19. **whence I am:** where I came from; **more better:** higher in rank.
20. **full poor cell:** small, humble dwelling (with a monastic overtone).
21. **no greater:** of no higher status than the dwelling suggests.
22. **meddle with:** intrude upon.
25. **my art:** That is, the cloak.
26. **direful:** having dire consequences; **wreck:** shipwreck.
27. **virtue:** essence.
28. **provision:** foresight.
30. **perdition:** loss.
31. **Betid:** Happened.
35. **bootless inquisition:** fruitless inquiry.

Obey, and be attentive. Canst thou remember
A time before we came unto this cell?
I do not think thou canst, for then thou wast not   40
Out three years old.

MIRANDA   Certainly, sir, I can.

PROSPERO   By what? By any other house or person?
Of anything the image tell me that
Hath kept with thy remembrance.

MIRANDA   'Tis far off,
And rather like a dream than an assurance   45
That my remembrance warrants. Had I not
Four or five women once that tended me?

PROSPERO   Thou hadst, and more, Miranda. But how is it
That this lives in thy mind? What seest thou else
In the dark backward and abysm of time?   50
If thou rememb'rest aught ere thou cam'st here,
How thou cam'st here thou mayst.

MIRANDA   But that I do not.

PROSPERO   Twelve year since, Miranda, twelve year since,
Thy father was the Duke of Milan and
A prince of power.

MIRANDA   Sir, are not you my father?   55

PROSPERO   Thy mother was a piece of virtue, and
She said thou wast my daughter, and thy father
Was Duke of Milan, and his only heir
And princess no worse issued.

MIRANDA   O the heavens!
What foul play had we that we came from thence?   60
Or blessèd was't we did?

PROSPERO   Both, both, my girl.
By foul play, as thou say'st, were we heaved thence,
But blessedly holp hither.

MIRANDA   Oh, my heart bleeds
To think o'th' teen that I have turned you to,
Which is from my remembrance! Please you, farther.   65

PROSPERO   My brother and thy uncle, called Antonio—

---

41. **Out:** Fully; that is, not yet three years old.
44. **with thy remembrance:** within thy memory.
46. **warrants:** guarantees as true.
50. **abysm:** abyss, chasm.
51. **aught:** anything.
56. **piece:** model.
59. **no worse issued:** of no less noble birth (than her father).
61. **blessèd:** providential.
63. **holp:** helped.
64. **teen . . . to:** trouble I've been to you.
65. **from:** not present in.

I pray thee mark me, that a brother should
Be so perfidious!—he whom next thyself
Of all the world I loved, and to him put
The manage of my state, as at that time   70
Through all the signories it was the first
And Prospero the prime duke, being so reputed
In dignity, and for the liberal arts
Without a parallel. Those being all my study,
The government I cast upon my brother   75
And to my state grew stranger, being transported
And rapt in secret studies. Thy false uncle—
Dost thou attend me?

MIRANDA   Sir, most heedfully.

PROSPERO   Being once perfected how to grant suits,
How to deny them, who t'advance, and who   80
To trash for overtopping, new created
The creatures that were mine, I say, or changed 'em,
Or else new formed 'em; having both the key
Of officer and office, set all hearts i'th' state
To what tune pleased his ear, that now he was   85
The ivy which had hid my princely trunk
And sucked my verdure out on't. Thou attend'st not.

MIRANDA   O good sir, I do.

PROSPERO   I pray thee, mark me.
I, thus neglecting worldly ends, all dedicated
To closeness and the bettering of my mind   90
With that which, but by being so retired,
O'er-prized all popular rate, in my false brother
Awaked an evil nature; and my trust,
Like a good parent, did beget of him
A falsehood in its contrary as great   95
As my trust was, which had indeed no limit,

---

70. **manage**: administration.
71. **signories**: lordships; territories.
72. **prime**: senior.
73. **liberal arts**: The arts and sciences studied at universities, specifically, grammar, logic, and rhetoric (the trivium), and arithmetic, geometry, music, and astronomy (the quadrivium).
76. **transported**: carried away.
79. **perfected**: completely versed in; **suits**: petitions.
81. **trash for overtopping**: check (as in the training of hounds) for undue ambition.
82. **or**: either.
83–84. **key . . . office**: control over positions and those who held them.
85. **that**: so that.
87. **verdure**: vitality, therefore power; **on't**: of it.
90. **closeness**: privacy.
91–92. **With . . . rate**: With studies that were more valuable than public appreciation, except that they withdrew me from the people.

A confidence sans bound. He being thus lorded
Not only with what my revenue yielded,
But what my power might else exact, like one
Who, having into truth by telling of it,   100
Made such a sinner of his memory
To credit his own lie, he did believe
He was indeed the duke, out o'th' substitution
And executing th'outward face of royalty
With all prerogative. Hence his ambition growing—   105
Dost thou hear?

MIRANDA   Your tale, sir, would cure deafness.

PROSPERO   To have no screen between this part he played
And him he played it for, he needs will be
Absolute Milan. Me, poor man, my library
Was dukedom large enough. Of temporal royalties   110
He thinks me now incapable; confederates,
So dry he was for sway, wi'th' King of Naples
To give him annual tribute, do him homage,
Subject his coronet to his crown, and bend
The dukedom yet unbowed—alas, poor Milan!—   115
To most ignoble stooping.

MIRANDA   O the heavens!

PROSPERO   Mark his condition and th'event; then tell me
If this might be a brother.

MIRANDA   I should sin
To think but nobly of my grandmother.
Good wombs have borne bad sons.

PROSPERO   Now the condition.   120
This King of Naples, being an enemy
To me inveterate, hearkens my brother's suit;
Which was that he, in lieu o'th' premises

---

97.   **sans bound:** without limit; **lorded:** made a lord.
100. **into:** unto or against; **it:** That is, his own lie.
103. **out o'th' substitution:** by virtue of having taken my place.
105. **prerogative:** privileges of office.
107–09. **part . . . Milan:** The distinction is between Antonio playing the part of duke on
      behalf of Prospero ("him he played it for") and becoming the real duke ("Absolute
      Milan").
110. **temporal royalties:** secular power.
111. **confederates:** allies; conspires.
112. **dry:** thirsty, hence eager; **sway:** power.
114. **Subject . . . crown:** Antonio conspires to make the dukedom of Milan, symbolized
      by the coronet, subject to the control of the crown of Naples.
115. **yet:** hitherto.
117. **his condition . . . th'event:** the terms of his agreement with Naples and its
      outcome.
119. **but:** other than.
122. **hearkens:** listens attentively to.
123. **in lieu . . . premises:** in return for the conditions.

Of homage and I know not how much tribute,
Should presently extirpate me and mine   125
Out of the dukedom and confer fair Milan,
With all the honors, on my brother. Whereon,
A treacherous army levied, one midnight
Fated to th' purpose did Antonio open
The gates of Milan, and i'th' dead of darkness,   130
The ministers for th' purpose hurried thence
Me and thy crying self.
MIRANDA   Alack, for pity!
  I, not remembering how I cried out then,
  Will cry it o'er again; it is a hint
  That wrings mine eyes to't.
PROSPERO   Hear a little further,   135
  And then I'll bring thee to the present business
  Which now's upon's, without the which this story
  Were most impertinent.
MIRANDA   Wherefore did they not
  That hour destroy us?
PROSPERO   Well demanded, wench:
  My tale provokes that question. Dear, they durst not,   140
  So dear the love my people bore me, nor set
  A mark so bloody on the business, but
  With colors fairer painted their foul ends.
  In few, they hurried us aboard a bark,
  Bore us some leagues to sea, where they prepared   145
  A rotten carcass of a butt, not rigged,
  Nor tackle, sail, nor mast—the very rats
  Instinctively have quit it. There they hoist us
  To cry to th' sea that roared to us; to sigh
  To th' winds, whose pity, sighing back again,   150
  Did us but loving wrong.
MIRANDA   Alack, what trouble
  Was I then to you!

125. **presently:** immediately; **extirpate:** literally, to pull up by the roots, therefore to drive out.
129. **Fated:** Appointed by fate.
131. **ministers:** agents.
134. **hint:** occasion.
137. **the which:** That is, the present business.
138. **impertinent:** irrelevant; **Wherefore:** Why.
139. **demanded:** asked; **wench:** young girl; term of endearment.
144. **In few:** In short; **bark:** small boat.
145. **leagues:** A league is three miles.
146. **butt,** literally, a barrel or tub.
151. **Did . . . wrong:** Responding sympathetically, only blew us farther out to sea.

PROSPERO   Oh, a cherubin
Thou wast that did preserve me. Thou didst smile,
Infusèd with a fortitude from heaven,
When I have decked the sea with drops full salt,   155
Under my burden groaned, which raised in me
An undergoing stomach to bear up
Against what should ensue.
MIRANDA   How came we ashore?
PROSPERO   By Providence divine.
Some food we had and some fresh water that   160
A noble Neapolitan, Gonzalo,
Out of his charity—who being then appointed
Master of this design—did give us, with
Rich garments, linens, stuffs, and necessaries,
Which since have steaded much. So, of his gentleness,   165
Knowing I loved my books, he furnished me
From mine own library with volumes that
I prize above my dukedom.
MIRANDA   Would I might
But ever see that man.
PROSPERO   Now I arise.
Sit still, and hear the last of our sea-sorrow.   170
Here in this island we arrived, and here
Have I, thy schoolmaster, made thee more profit
Than other princes can, that have more time
For vainer hours, and tutors not so careful.
MIRANDA   Heavens thank you for't. And now I pray you, sir,   175
For still 'tis beating in my mind, your reason
For raising this sea-storm?
PROSPERO   Know thus far forth:
By accident most strange, bountiful Fortune,
Now my dear lady, hath mine enemies
Brought to this shore; and by my prescience   180
I find my zenith doth depend upon

152. cherubin: The plural of cherub (angel) could be used as a singular form.
155. decked: adorned.
156. which: That is, your smile.
157. undergoing stomach: determination to persevere.
164. stuffs: utensils or fabrics.
165. steaded: been useful; gentleness: kindness; nobility.
168–69. Would . . . ever: I wish that some day I might.
169. Now I arise: Either an implicit stage direction or an allusion to Prospero's rising
    fortunes.
172. made . . . profit: provided a better education.
173. can: that is, can gain; princes: a generic term for royal children of either sex.
174. careful: caring, attentive.
181. my zenith: the highest point (in my fortunes).

A most auspicious star, whose influence
If now I court not but omit, my fortunes
Will ever after droop. Here cease more questions.
Thou art inclined to sleep. 'Tis a good dullness,   185
And give it way. I know thou canst not choose.
    [MIRANDA *sleeps.*]
[*to* ARIEL] Come away, servant, come! I am ready now.
Approach, my Ariel. Come!
    Enter ARIEL.
ARIEL   All hail, great master; grave sir, hail! I come
To answer thy best pleasure, be't to fly,   190
To swim, to dive into the fire, to ride
On the curled clouds. To thy strong bidding task
Ariel and all his quality.
PROSPERO   Hast thou, spirit,
Performed to point the tempest that I bade thee?
ARIEL   To every article.   195
I boarded the King's ship. Now on the beak,
Now in the waist, the deck, in every cabin,
I flamed amazement. Sometimes I'd divide
And burn in many places; on the topmast,
The yards, and bowsprit would I flame distinctly,   200
Then meet and join. Jove's lightning, the precursors
O'th' dreadful thunderclaps, more momentary
And sight-outrunning were not. The fire and cracks
Of sulfurous roaring the most mighty Neptune
Seem to besiege and make his bold waves tremble,   205
Yea, his dread trident shake.
PROSPERO   My brave spirit!
Who was so firm, so constant, that this coil
Would not infect his reason?

---

182. **influence:** astrological power.
183. **omit:** disregard.
185. **dullness:** drowsiness.
186. **give it way:** give in to it.
192. **task:** set tasks for; test.
193. **quality:** skills; fellow spirits.
194. **to point:** exactly.
196. **beak:** prow.
197. **in the waist:** amidships.
198. **flamed amazement:** appeared as terrifying fire, as in the marine phenomenon of St. Elmo's fire.
200. **yards:** crossbars on masts; **bowsprit:** pole to which the lower part of the sail is fastened, **distinctly:** separately.
201. **Jove:** The most powerful of the Roman gods, traditionally armed with lightning bolts.
202. **momentary:** transitory.
203. **sight-outrunning:** faster than the eye could follow.
204. **Neptune:** Roman god of the sea, usually pictured with his trident.
207. **coil:** tumult.

ARIEL   Not a soul
  But felt a fever of the mad and played
  Some tricks of desperation. All but mariners   210
  Plunged in the foaming brine and quit the vessel,
  Then all afire with me; the King's son Ferdinand,
  With hair upstaring—then like reeds, not hair—
  Was the first man that leapt, cried, "Hell is empty,
  And all the devils are here!"
PROSPERO   Why, that's my spirit.   215
  But was not this nigh shore?
ARIEL   Close by, my master.
PROSPERO   But are they, Ariel, safe?
ARIEL   Not a hair perished.
  On their sustaining garments not a blemish,
  But fresher than before; and, as thou bad'st me,
  In troops I have dispersed them 'bout the isle.   220
  The King's son have I landed by himself,
  Whom I left cooling of the air with sighs
  In an odd angle of the isle, and sitting,
  His arms in this sad knot.
PROSPERO   Of the King's ship,
  The mariners, say how thou hast disposed,   225
  And all the rest o'th' fleet.
ARIEL   Safely in harbor
  Is the King's ship; in the deep nook where once
  Thou called'st me up at midnight to fetch dew
  From the still-vexed Bermudas, there she's hid;
  The mariners all under hatches stowed,   230
  Who, with a charm joined to their suffered labor,
  I have left asleep; and for the rest o'th' fleet,
  Which I dispersed, they all have met again
  And are upon the Mediterranean float,
  Bound sadly home for Naples,   235
  Supposing that they saw the King's ship wrecked
  And his great person perish.

209. **of the mad:** of the kind suffered by lunatics.
213. **upstaring:** standing on end.
219. **bad'st:** commanded.
220. **troops:** groups (actually, one group and three separate individuals).
223. **angle:** corner.
224. **in . . . knot:** folded, a conventional sign of melancholy.
229. **still-vexed:** always troubled by storms; **Bermudas:** In Shakespeare's time, a group of
     uninhabited Atlantic islands feared for their dangerous reefs and ferocious storms.
230. **under hatches:** below deck.
231. **with a charm joined to:** by virtue of a charm as well as; **suffered labor:** exertions
     during the storm.
234. **float:** sea.

PROSPERO   Ariel, thy charge
 Exactly is performed; but there's more work.
 What is the time o'th' day?
ARIEL   Past the mid-season.
PROSPERO   At least two glasses. The time twixt six and now   240
 Must by us both be spent most preciously.
ARIEL   Is there more toil? Since thou dost give me pains,
 Let me remember thee what thou hast promised,
 Which is not yet performed me.
PROSPERO   How now? Moody?
 What is't thou canst demand?
ARIEL   My liberty.   245
PROSPERO   Before the time be out? No more.
ARIEL   I prithee,
 Remember I have done thee worthy service,
 Told thee no lies, made no mistakings, served
 Without or grudge or grumblings. Thou did promise
 To bate me a full year.
PROSPERO   Dost thou forget   250
 From what a torment I did free thee?
ARIEL   No.
PROSPERO   Thou dost, and think'st it much to tread the ooze
 Of the salt deep,
 To run upon the sharp wind of the north,
 To do me business in the veins o'th' earth   255
 When it is baked with frost.
ARIEL   I do not, sir.
PROSPERO   Thou liest, malignant thing! Hast thou forgot
 The foul witch Sycorax, who with age and envy
 Was grown into a hoop? Hast thou forgot her?
ARIEL   No, sir.
PROSPERO   Thou hast. Where was she born? Speak. Tell me.   260
ARIEL   Sir, in Algiers.
PROSPERO   Oh, was she so? I must
 Once in a month recount what thou hast been,

239. **mid-season:** noon.
240. **two glasses:** two hours.
241. **preciously:** valuably, carefully.
242. **pains:** tasks; troubles.
243. **remember:** remind.
244. **Moody:** Stubborn; sullen.
249. **or . . . or:** either . . . or.
250. **bate me:** deduct from the period of my servitude.
252. **ooze:** muddy bottom.
253. **salt deep:** sea.
255. **veins:** channels; seams of metal.
256. **baked:** hardened.
258. **envy:** malice.

Which thou forgett'st. This damned witch Sycorax,
For mischiefs manifold and sorceries terrible
To enter human hearing, from Algiers,   265
Thou know'st, was banished. For one thing she did
They would not take her life. Is not this true?

ARIEL   Ay, sir.

PROSPERO   This blue-eyed hag was hither brought with child
And here was left by th' sailors. Thou, my slave,   270
As thou report'st thyself, was then her servant;
And for thou wast a spirit too delicate
To act her earthy and abhorred commands,
Refusing her grand hests, she did confine thee,
By help of her more potent ministers,   275
And in her most unmitigable rage,
Into a cloven pine; within which rift
Imprisoned thou didst painfully remain
A dozen years, within which space she died
And left thee there, where thou didst vent thy groans   280
As fast as millwheels strike. Then was this island—
Save for the son that she did litter here,
A freckled whelp, hag-born—not honored with
A human shape.

ARIEL   Yes, Caliban her son.

PROSPERO   Dull thing, I say so: he, that Caliban   285
Whom now I keep in service. Thou best know'st
What torment I did find thee in: thy groans
Did make wolves howl, and penetrate the breasts
Of ever-angry bears. It was a torment
To lay upon the damned, which Sycorax   290
Could not again undo. It was mine art,
When I arrived and heard thee, that made gape
The pine and let thee out.

ARIEL   I thank thee, master.

PROSPERO   If thou more murmur'st, I will rend an oak
And peg thee in his knotty entrails till   295

---

266. **one thing:** generally assumed to be her pregnancy.
269. **blue-eyed:** Blue eyelids were associated with pregnancy, but also with malevolent
     women; the epithet also suggests that Sycorax would be an unusual figure in Algiers
     where dark eyes would be the norm; **hag:** witch.
272. **for:** because.
274. **hests:** commands.
275. **ministers:** agents.
280. **vent:** emit.
281. **as . . . strike:** as the blades of water-wheels strike the water.
282. **litter:** Give birth to: a term usually associated with animal births.
292. **made gape:** opened up.
294. **murmur'st:** complain.

Thou hast howled away twelve winters.
ARIEL   Pardon, master.
    I will be correspondent to command
    And do my spriting gently.
PROSPERO   Do so, and after two days
    I will discharge thee.
ARIEL   That's my noble master!
    What shall I do? Say what, what shall I do?   300
PROSPERO   Go make thyself like a nymph o'th' sea. Be subject
    To no sight but thine and mine, invisible
    To every eyeball else. Go, take this shape
    And hither come in't. Go! Hence with diligence.
                              Exit [ARIEL].
    [*to* MIRANDA] Awake, dear heart, awake! Thou hast slept well.   305
    Awake.
MIRANDA   The strangeness of your story put
    Heaviness in me.
PROSPERO   Shake it off. Come on;
    We'll visit Caliban, my slave, who never
    Yields us kind answer.
MIRANDA   'Tis a villain, sir,
    I do not love to look on.
PROSPERO   But, as 'tis,   310
    We cannot miss him. He does make our fire,
    Fetch in our wood, and serves in offices
    That profit us. What ho! Slave! Caliban!
    Thou earth, thou: speak!
CALIBAN (*within*)   There's wood enough within.
PROSPERO   Come forth, I say! There's other business for thee.   315
    Come, thou tortoise! When?
        Enter ARIEL *like a water nymph.*
    —Fine apparition! My quaint Ariel,
    Hark in thine ear.
       [*He whispers.*]
ARIEL   My lord, it shall be done.   *Exit.*
PROSPERO   Thou poisonous slave, got by the devil himself
    Upon thy wicked dam, come forth!   320
        Enter CALIBAN.

297. **correspondent:** compliant.
303. **shape:** appearance.
307. **Heaviness:** Drowsiness.
309. **villain:** evil or low-born person.
311. **miss:** do without.
312. **offices:** tasks.
317. **Fine:** Exquisitely fashioned; **quaint:** skillfull.
319. **got:** begot.

CALIBAN   As wicked dew as e'er my mother brushed
    With raven's feather from unwholesome fen
    Drop on you both! A southwest blow on ye
    And blister you all o'er!
PROSPERO   For this, be sure, tonight thou shalt have cramps,   325
    Side-stitches that shall pen thy breath up; urchins
    Shall forth at vast of night that they may work
    All exercise on thee; thou shalt be pinched
    As thick as honeycomb, each pinch more stinging
    Than bees that made 'em.
CALIBAN   I must eat my dinner.   330
    This island's mine by Sycorax my mother,
    Which thou tak'st from me. When thou cam'st first
    Thou strok'st me and made much of me; wouldst give me
    Water with berries in't, and teach me how
    To name the bigger light and how the less   335
    That burn by day and night. And then I loved thee
    And showed thee all the qualities o'th' isle:
    The fresh springs, brine-pits, barren place and fertile.
    Cursèd be I that did so! All the charms
    Of Sycorax—toads, beetles, bats—light on you!   340
    For I am all the subjects that you have,
    Which first was mine own king; and here you sty me
    In this hard rock whiles you do keep from me
    The rest o'th' island.
PROSPERO   Thou most lying slave,
    Whom stripes may move, not kindness. I have used thee,   345
    Filth as thou art, with humane care, and lodged thee
    In mine own cell till thou didst seek to violate
    The honor of my child.
CALIBAN   Oh ho, oh ho! Would't had been done!
    Thou didst prevent me; I had peopled else
    This isle with Calibans.
MIRANDA   Abhorrèd slave,   350
    Which any print of goodness wilt not take,
    Being capable of all ill. I pitied thee,

323. **southwest:** Winds from the southwest brought warm and damp air, and were there-
    fore considered unwholesome.
326. **pen . . . up:** stop you breathing; **urchins:** goblins in the form of hedgehogs.
327. **at vast of:** during the boundless.
328–29. **pinched . . . honeycomb:** pinched with as many holes as a honeycomb has cells.
337. **qualities:** characteristics.
339. **charms:** spells.
342. **sty:** confine (as with swine).
345. **stripes:** strokes of the whip.
349. **Thou . . . else:** Had you not prevented me, I would have populated.
351. **print:** imprint.

Took pains to make thee speak, taught thee each hour
One thing or other. When thou didst not, savage,
Know thine own meaning but wouldst gabble like   355
A thing most brutish, I endowed thy purposes
With words that made them known. But thy vile race,
Though thou didst learn, had that in't which good natures
Could not abide to be with; therefore wast thou
Deservedly confined into this rock,   360
Who hadst deserved more than a prison.
CALIBAN   You taught me language, and my profit on't
Is I know how to curse. The red plague rid you
For learning me your language!
PROSPERO   Hag-seed, hence!
Fetch us in fuel; and be quick, thou'rt best,   365
To answer other business. Shrugg'st thou, malice?
If thou neglect'st or dost unwillingly
What I command, I'll rack thee with old cramps,
Fill all thy bones with aches, make thee roar,
That beasts shall tremble at thy din.
CALIBAN   No, pray thee.   370
[aside] I must obey. His art is of such power
It would control my dam's god Setebos
And make a vassal of him.
PROSPERO   So, slave, hence.   Exit CALIBAN.
        Enter FERDINAND, and ARIEL, invisible, playing
        and singing.
ARIEL [sings]   Come unto these yellow sands,
                And then take hands.   375
                Curtsied when you have, and kissed,
                The wild waves whist.
                Foot it featly here and there,
                And sweet sprites bear
                The burden.   380
SPIRITS [within, sing the] (burden dispersedly)
                Hark, hark! Bow-wow!
                The watch-dogs bark: bow-wow!

357. race: natural or inherited disposition.
364. learning: teaching; Hag-seed: Offspring of a witch.
366. answer other business: perform other tasks.
368. old cramps: the cramps of old age.
372. Setebos: A devil of the Patagonian natives, according to Richard Eden's 1555 trans-
     lation of Antonio Pigafetta's account of Magellan's circumnavigatory expedition.
373. SD. playing: Probably a lute.
377. whist: becoming silent.
378. featly: nimbly.
380. burden: refrain.
381. SD. Here, as in 395 SD and 402 SD, the Folio adds the direction "dispersedly," not
     in unison.

ARIEL   Hark, hark. I hear
               The strain of strutting Chanticleer
               Cry cock-a-diddle-dow.   385
FERDINAND   Where should this music be? I'th' air or th'earth?
    It sounds no more; and sure it waits upon
    Some god o'th' island. Sitting on a bank,
    Weeping again the King my father's wreck,
    This music crept by me upon the waters,   390
    Allaying both their fury and my passion
    With its sweet air. Thence I have followed it,
    Or it hath drawn me rather; but 'tis gone.
    No, it begins again.
ARIEL [sings]   Full fathom five thy father lies;   395
               Of his bones are coral made;
               Those are pearls that were his eyes;
               Nothing of him that doth fade,
               But doth suffer a sea-change
               Into something rich and strange.   400
               Sea-nymphs hourly ring his knell.
SPIRITS [within, sing the] (burden)   Ding dong.
ARIEL   Hark, now I hear them.
SPIRITS [within]   Ding dong, bell.
FERDINAND   The ditty does remember my drowned father.
    This is no mortal business, nor no sound   405
    That the earth owes. I hear it now above me.
PROSPERO [to MIRANDA]   The fringèd curtains of thine eye
    advance
    And say what thou seest yond.
MIRANDA   What is't? A spirit?
    Lord, how it looks about. Believe me, sir,
    It carries a brave form. But 'tis a spirit.   410
PROSPERO   No, wench, it eats and sleeps and hath such senses
    As we have—such. This gallant which thou seest
    Was in the wreck; and but he's something stained

384. strain: song; Chanticleer: Rooster.
387. waits upon: attends.
391. passion: literally, suffering.
395. Full fathom five: A fathom—the nautical measure of the depth of the sea—is about
    six feet, so five full fathoms is around thirty feet.
398. fade: decay.
399. suffer: undergo.
404. ditty does remember: song commemorates.
405. mortal: earthly.
406. owes: owns.
407. advance: raise.
408. yond: yonder.
410. brave: handsome.
412. gallant: fine gentleman (perhaps spoken ironically).
413. but: except for the fact that; something: somewhat.

With grief—that's beauty's canker—thou mightst call him
A goodly person. He hath lost his fellows   415
And strays about to find 'em.
MIRANDA   I might call him
A thing divine, for nothing natural
I ever saw so noble.
PROSPERO [aside]   It goes on, I see,
As my soul prompts it. [to ARIEL] Spirit, fine spirit, I'll free thee
Within two days for this.
FERDINAND   Most sure, the goddess   420
On whom these airs attend! Vouchsafe my prayer
May know if you remain upon this island,
And that you will some good instruction give
How I may bear me here. My prime request,
Which I do last pronounce, is—O you wonder!—   425
If you be maid or no?
MIRANDA   No wonder, sir,
But certainly a maid.
FERDINAND   My language? Heavens!
I am the best of them that speak this speech,
Were I but where 'tis spoken.
PROSPERO   How? The best?
What wert thou if the King of Naples heard thee?   430
FERDINAND   A single thing, as I am now, that wonders
To hear thee speak of Naples. He does hear me,
And that he does I weep. Myself am Naples,
Who with mine eyes, never since at ebb, beheld
The King my father wrecked.
MIRANDA   Alack, for mercy!   435
FERDINAND   Yes, faith, and all his lords, the Duke of Milan
And his brave son being twain.
PROSPERO [aside]   The Duke of Milan
And his more braver daughter could control thee

414. **canker**: something that corrodes or consumes.
418. **It**: That is, my plan.
419. **As . . . it**: According to the direction of Prospero's intellectual power.
420–21. **Most . . . attend**: This sentence recall Aeneas's phrase in the *Aeneid* when he meets his mother, Venus, disguised as a huntress: *O dea certe* (Oh, surely the goddess).
421. **airs**: Ariel's songs; **Vouchsafe**: Grant.
422. **May know**: That I may know; **remain**: live.
424. **bear me**: conduct myself; **prime**: most important.
426. **maid**: a girl, as opposed to either a goddess or a married woman.
431. **A single thing**: Without family; unmarried; weak.
432–33. Because Ferdinand believes his father to have drowned, he thinks of himself as (King of) Naples; so "he" (the King) and "me" are for Ferdinand the same person.
434. **at ebb**: at low tide, that is, the tears have never since stopped.
437. **his brave son**: the only reference in the play to Antonio's son; **twain**: two of them.
438. **more braver**: worthier; **control**: contradict.

If now 'twere fit to do't. At the first sight
They have changed eyes. [*to* ARIEL] Delicate Ariel,   440
I'll set thee free for this! [*to* FERDINAND] A word, good sir.
I fear you have done yourself some wrong. A word.
MIRANDA   Why speaks my father so ungently? This
    Is the third man that e'er I saw, the first
    That e'er I sighed for. Pity move my father   445
    To be inclined my way.
FERDINAND   Oh, if a virgin,
    And your affection not gone forth, I'll make you
    The Queen of Naples.
PROSPERO   Soft, sir! One word more.
    [*aside*] They are both in either's powers. But this swift business
    I must uneasy make, lest too light winning   450
    Make the prize light. [*to* FERDINAND] One word more! I
        charge thee
    That thou attend me. Thou dost here usurp
    The name thou ow'st not, and hast put thyself
    Upon this island as a spy to win it
    From me, the lord on't.
FERDINAND   No, as I am a man.   455
MIRANDA   There's nothing ill can dwell in such a temple.
    If the ill spirit have so fair a house,
    Good things will strive to dwell with't.
PROSPERO [*to* FERDINAND]   Follow me.
    [*to* MIRANDA] Speak not you for him: he's a traitor. [*to*
        FERDINAND] Come!
    I'll manacle thy neck and feet together.   460
    Sea-water shalt thou drink; thy food shall be
    The fresh-brook mussels, withered roots, and husks
    Wherein the acorn cradled. Follow!
FERDINAND   No.
    I will resist such entertainment till
    Mine enemy has more power.
        He draws [*his sword*], *and is charmed from moving.*
MIRANDA   O dear father,   465

440. **changed eyes:** exchanged glances, with the implication of falling in love; **Delicate:**
    Artful.
442. **you:** Ferdinand; **yourself:** the King of Naples.
445. **Pity:** Let pity.
447. **gone forth:** given over to someone else.
450. **uneasy:** difficult.
450–51. **light . . . light:** easy . . . cheap.
451. **charge:** command.
453. **ow'st:** owns.
462. **fresh-brook mussels:** These are inedible.
464. **entertainment:** treatment.

Make not too rash a trial of him, for
He's gentle and not fearful.
PROSPERO   What, I say,
  My foot my tutor? [*to* FERDINAND] Put thy sword up, traitor,
  Who mak'st a show but dar'st not strike, thy conscience
  Is so possessed with guilt. Come from thy ward,   170
  For I can here disarm thee with this stick
  And make thy weapon drop.
MIRANDA   Beseech you, father—
PROSPERO   Hence! Hang not on my garments.
MIRANDA   Sir, have pity.
  I'll be his surety.
PROSPERO   Silence! One word more
  Shall make me chide thee, if not hate thee. What,   475
  An advocate for an imposter? Hush!
  Thou think'st there is no more such shapes as he,
  Having seen but him and Caliban. Foolish wench,
  To th' most of men this is a Caliban,
  And they to him are angels.
MIRANDA   My affections   480
  Are then most humble. I have no ambition
  To see a goodlier man.
PROSPERO [*to* FERDINAND]   Come on, obey.
  Thy nerves are in their infancy again,
  And have no vigor in them.
FERDINAND   So they are.
  My spirits, as in a dream, are all bound up.   485
  My father's loss, the weakness which I feel,
  The wreck of all my friends, nor this man's threats
  To whom I am subdued, are but light to me,
  Might I but through my prison once a day
  Behold this maid. All corners else o'th' earth   490
  Let liberty make use of; space enough
  Have I in such a prison.
PROSPERO [*aside*]   It works. [*to* FERDINAND] Come on!
  [*to* ARIEL] Thou hast done well, fine Ariel. [*to* FERDINAND]
      Follow me.

466. **rash:** hasty.
467. **not fearful:** not a cause of fear; not afraid.
470. **Come . . . ward:** Give up your defensive stance.
471. **this stick:** Prospero's magic wand or staff.
479. **To:** Compared to.
483. **nerves:** sinews.
488. **light:** minor burdens.
490. **All corners else:** All other corners.

[*to* ARIEL] Hark what thou else shalt do me.

MIRANDA [*to* FERDINAND]   Be of comfort;
  My father's of a better nature, sir,   495
  Than he appears by speech. This is unwonted
  Which now came from him.

PROSPERO [*to* ARIEL]   Thou shalt be as free
  As mountain winds; but then exactly do
  All points of my command.

ARIEL   To th' syllable.

PROSPERO [*to* FERDINAND]   Come, follow. [*to* MIRANDA] Speak   500
  not for him.   *Exeunt.*

2.1

Enter ALONSO, SEBASTIAN, ANTONIO, GONZALO,
ADRIAN, *and* FRANCISCO.

GONZALO   Beseech you, sir, be merry. You have cause—
  So have we all—of joy; for our escape
  Is much beyond our loss. Our hint of woe
  Is common: every day some sailor's wife,
  The masters of some merchant, and the merchant   5
  Have just our theme of woe. But for the miracle—
  I mean our preservation—few in millions
  Can speak like us. Then wisely, good sir, weigh
  Our sorrow with our comfort.

ALONSO   Prithee, peace.

SEBASTIAN [*to* ANTONIO]   He receives comfort like cold porridge.   10

ANTONIO [*to* SEBASTIAN]   The visitor will not give him o'er so.

SEBASTIAN   Look, he's winding up the watch of his wit; by
  and by it will strike.

GONZALO   [*to* ALONSO]   Sir—

SEBASTIAN   One. Tell.   15

GONZALO   When every grief is entertained that's offered,
  comes to th'entertainer—

---

494. do me: do for me.
496. unwonted: unusual.
498. then: That is, in order to be free.
3.   **hint:** occasion.
5.   **merchant . . . merchant:** trading ship . . . ship-owner.
6.   **just:** exactly.
9.   **with:** against.
10. **porridge:** pottage, sometimes made of peas, therefore a pun on "peace."
11. **visitor:** one taking comfort to the sick, as Gonzalo is doing; **give him o'er:** abandon
    him.
15. **Tell:** Keep count.
16. **entertained:** accepted.
17. **th'entertainer:** the recipient.

SEBASTIAN   A dollar.

GONZALO   Dolor comes to him, indeed. You have spoken truer
than you purposed.   20

SEBASTIAN   You have taken it wiselier than I meant you should.

GONZALO [*to* ALONSO]   Therefore, my lord—

ANTONIO   Fie, what a spendthrift is he of his tongue!

ALONSO   I prithee, spare.

GONZALO   Well, I have done. But yet—   25

SEBASTIAN   He will be talking.

ANTONIO   Which of he or Adrian, for a good wager, first
begins to crow?

SEBASTIAN   The old cock.

ANTONIO   The cockerel.   30

SEBASTIAN   Done. The wager?

ANTONIO   A laughter.

SEBASTIAN   A match.

ADRIAN   Though this island seem to be desert—

ANTONIO   Ha, ha, ha!   35

SEBASTIAN   So, you're paid.

ADRIAN   Uninhabitable and almost inaccessible—

SEBASTIAN   Yet—

ADRIAN   Yet—

ANTONIO   He could not miss't.   40

ADRIAN   It must needs be of subtle, tender, and delicate
temperance.

ANTONIO   Temperance was a delicate wench.

SEBASTIAN   Ay, and a subtle, as he most learnedly delivered.

ADRIAN   The air breathes upon us here most sweetly.   45

SEBASTIAN   As if it had lungs, and rotten ones.

ANTONIO   Or as 'twere perfumed by a fen.

GONZALO   Here is everything advantageous to life.

ANTONIO   True, save means to live.

---

18. **dollar:** At this time, a German or Spanish coin in wide circulation.
19. **dolor:** grief.
20. **purposed:** intended.
24. **spare:** stop.
28. **crow:** speak.
29. **old cock:** That is, Gonzalo.
30. **cockerel:** That is, Adrian.
33. **A match:** Agreed.
34. **desert:** uninhabited.
40. **miss't:** avoid saying "yet"; miss the island.
41. **must needs be:** has to be; **subtle:** delicate; **delicate:** pleasant.
42. **temperance:** mildness of climate.
43. **Temperance:** A girls' name; **delicate:** voluptuous.
44. **subtle:** crafty; **delivered:** uttered.
49. **save:** except.

SEBASTIAN   Of that there's none, or little.   50

GONZALO   How lush and lusty the grass looks! How green!

ANTONIO   The ground indeed is tawny.

SEBASTIAN   With an eye of green in't.

ANTONIO   He misses not much.

SEBASTIAN   No, he doth but mistake the truth totally.   55

GONZALO   But the rarity of it is, which is indeed almost beyond
credit—

SEBASTIAN   As many vouched rarities are.

GONZALO   That our garments being, as they were, drenched
in the sea, hold notwithstanding their freshness and gloss,   60
being rather new-dyed than stained with salt water.

ANTONIO   If but one of his pockets could speak, would it not
say he lies?

SEBASTIAN   Ay, or very falsely pocket up his report.

GONZALO   Methinks our garments are now as fresh as when   65
we put them on first in Africa, at the marriage of the King's
fair daughter Claribel to the King of Tunis.

SEBASTIAN   'Twas a sweet marriage, and we prosper well in
our return.

ADRIAN   Tunis was never graced before with such a paragon   70
to their queen.

GONZALO   Not since widow Dido's time.

ANTONIO   Widow? A pox o' that! How came that "widow" in?
Widow Dido!

SEBASTIAN   What if he had said "widower Aeneas" too? Good   75
Lord, how you take it!

ADRIAN   "Widow Dido," said you? You make me study of that:
she was of Carthage, not of Tunis.

GONZALO   This Tunis, sir, was Carthage.

ADRIAN   Carthage?   80

GONZALO   I assure you, Carthage.

ANTONIO   His word is more than the miraculous harp.

---

51. lush: tender; **lusty:** vigorous.
52. tawny: yellowish brown.
53. eye: tinge.
55. but: merely.
58. vouched rarities: strange phenomena accepted as true.
62–63. would . . . lies: That is, because it would still be holding water.
64. pocket up: conceal.
71. to: for.
74. Widow Dido!: In Virgil's version of the story in the *Aeneid*, Dido, founder and queen
of Carthage, was already a widow when Aeneas met her; however, Antonio takes Gonzalo's use of the term as an overdelicate way to describe a woman deserted by her
lover.
76. take: interpret.
77. study of: think about.
82. miraculous harp: the mythical harp of Amphion, which raised the walls of Thebes,
while Gonzalo's error has created a whole new city.

SEBASTIAN   He hath raised the wall, and houses too.

ANTONIO   What impossible matter will he make easy next?

SEBASTIAN   I think he will carry this island home in his   85
    pocket and give it his son for an apple.

ANTONIO   And sowing the kernels of it in the sea, bring forth
    more islands.

GONZALO   Ay.

ANTONIO   Why, in good time.   90

GONZALO [to ALONSO]   Sir, we were talking, that our garments
    seem now as fresh as when we were at Tunis at the marriage
    of your daughter, who is now queen.

ANTONIO   And the rarest that e'er came there.

SEBASTIAN   Bate, I beseech you, widow Dido.   95

ANTONIO   Oh, widow Dido? Ay, widow Dido.

GONZALO   Is not, sir, my doublet as fresh as the first day I
    wore it? I mean, in a sort.

ANTONIO   That "sort" was well fished for.

GONZALO   When I wore it at your daughter's marriage.   100

ALONSO   You cram these words into mine ears against
    The stomach of my sense. Would I had never
    Married my daughter there; for coming thence
    My son is lost, and, in my rate, she too,
    Who is so far from Italy removed   105
    I ne'er again shall see her. O thou mine heir
    Of Naples and of Milan, what strange fish
    Hath made his meal on thee?

FRANCISCO   Sir, he may live.
    I saw him beat the surges under him
    And ride upon their backs. He trod the water   110
    Whose enmity he flung aside, and breasted
    The surge, most swol'n, that met him. His bold head
    'Bove the contentious waves he kept, and oared
    Himself with his good arms in lusty stroke
    To th' shore, that o'er his wave-worn basis bowed,   115
    As stooping to relieve him. I not doubt
    He came alive to land.

ALONSO   No, no, he's gone.

SEBASTIAN   Sir, you may thank yourself for this great loss,

95.   **Bate:** Except.
97.   **doublet:** close-fitting jacket.
98.   **in a sort:** in a way.
102.   **stomach of my sense:** appetite for listening to them.
104.   **rate:** opinion.
109.   **surges:** waves.
115.   **o'er . . . bowed:** the cliff, eroded by waves, projected outward.
116.   **As:** As if.

That would not bless our Europe with your daughter,
But rather loose her to an African,   120
Where she, at least, is banished from your eye,
Who hath cause to set the grief on't.
ALONSO   Prithee, peace.
SEBASTIAN   You were kneeled to and importuned otherwise
By all of us; and the fair soul herself
Weighed, between loathness and obedience, at   125
Which end o'th' beam should bow. We have lost your son,
I fear, forever. Milan and Naples have
More widows in them of this business' making
Than we bring men to comfort them. The fault's
Your own.
ALONSO   So is the dearest o'th' loss.   130
GONZALO   My lord Sebastian,
The truth you speak doth lack some gentleness,
And time to speak it in. You rub the sore
When you should bring the plaster.
SEBASTIAN   Very well.
ANTONIO   And most chirurgeonly.   135
GONZALO [to ALONSO]   It is foul weather in us all, good sir,
When you are cloudy.
SEBASTIAN   Foul weather?
ANTONIO   Very foul.
GONZALO   Had I plantation of this isle, my lord—
ANTONIO   He'd sow't with nettle-seed.
SEBASTIAN   Or docks, or mallows.
GONZALO   And were the king on't, what would I do?   140
SEBASTIAN   Scape being drunk for want of wine.
GONZALO   I'th' commonwealth I would by contraries
Execute all things. For no kind of traffic
Would I admit; no name of magistrate;
Letters should not be known; riches, poverty,   145
And use of service, none; contract, succession,
Bourn, bound of land, tilth, vineyard, none;

119. **That:** You who.
122. **Who:** That is, Claribel.
123. **importuned:** begged.
126. **Which . . . bow:** Which end of the scales should lower.
130. **dearest:** heaviest.
135. **chirurgeonly:** like a surgeon.
138. **plantation:** colonization.
139. **docks . . . mallows:** weeds used to rub on nettle stings.
140. **on't:** of it.
141. **want:** lack.
142. **by contraries:** opposite to customary practice.
143. **traffic:** trade.
145. **Letters:** Literature.
147. **Bourn . . . tilth:** Boundaries, property limits, tillage.

No use of metal, corn, or wine, or oil;
No occupation, all men idle, all;
And women too, but innocent and pure;   150
No sovereignty—

SEBASTIAN   Yet he would be king on't.

ANTONIO The latter end of his commonwealth forgets the
beginning.

GONZALO —All things in common nature should produce
Without sweat or endeavor. Treason, felony,   155
Sword, pike, knife, gun, or need of any engine
Would I not have; but nature should bring forth
Of its own kind, all foison, all abundance,
To feed my innocent people.

SEBASTIAN   No marrying 'mong his subjects?   160

ANTONIO   None, man, all idle: whores and knaves.

GONZALO   I would with such perfection govern, sir,
T'excel the golden age.

SEBASTIAN   Save his majesty!

ANTONIO   Long live Gonzalo!

GONZALO   And do you mark me, sir?   165

ALONSO   Prithee, no more. Thou dost talk nothing to me.

GONZALO   I do well believe your highness, and did it to minister
occasion to these gentlemen, who are of such sensible and
nimble lungs that they always use to laugh at nothing.

ANTONIO   'Twas you we laughed at.   170

GONZALO   Who in this kind of merry fooling am nothing to
you. So you may continue, and laugh at nothing still.

ANTONIO   What a blow was there given!

SEBASTIAN   An it had not fallen flatlong.

GONZALO   You are gentlemen of brave mettle; you would lift   175
the moon out of her sphere if she would continue in it five
weeks without changing.

Enter ARIEL *[invisible,] playing solemn music.*

SEBASTIAN   We would so, and then go a-bat-fowling.

ANTONIO   Nay, good my lord, be not angry.

148. **corn:** grain.
154. **in common:** for communal use.
156. **engine:** machine used in warfare.
158. **foison:** plenty.
163. **Save:** God save.
167–68. **minister occasion:** provide the opportunity.
168. **sensible:** sensitive.
169. **use:** are accustomed.
174. **An:** If; **flatlong:** with the flat of the blade.
175. **mettle:** spirit.
176. **sphere:** orbit.
178. **a-bat-fowling:** hunting birds with a stick.

GONZALO   No, I warrant you, I will not adventure my discretion   180
   so weakly. Will you laugh me asleep, for I am very heavy?
ANTONIO   Go sleep, and hear us.
           [*All sleep, except* ALONSO, SEBASTIAN, *and* ANTONIO.]
ALONSO   What, all so soon asleep? I wish mine eyes
   Would, with themselves, shut up my thoughts. I find
   They are inclined to do so.
SEBASTIAN   Please you, sir,   185
   Do not omit the heavy offer of it.
   It seldom visits sorrow; when it doth,
   It is a comforter.
ANTONIO   We two, my lord,
   Will guard your person while you take your rest,
   And watch your safety.
ALONSO   Thank you. Wondrous heavy.   190
                      [ALONSO *sleeps. Exit* ARIEL.]
SEBASTIAN   What a strange drowsiness possesses them!
ANTONIO   It is the quality o'th' climate.
SEBASTIAN   Why
   Doth it not then our eyelids sink? I find
   Not myself disposed to sleep.
ANTONIO   Nor I: my spirits are nimble.   195
   They fell together all as by consent;
   They dropped, as by a thunderstroke. What might,
   Worthy Sebastian, oh, what might—? No more.
   And yet methinks I see it in thy face
   What thou shouldst be. Th'occasion speaks thee, and   200
   My strong imagination sees a crown
   Dropping upon thy head.
SEBASTIAN   What? Art thou waking?
ANTONIO   Do you not hear me speak?
SEBASTIAN   I do, and surely
   It is a sleepy language, and thou speak'st
   Out of thy sleep. What is it thou didst say?   205
   This is a strange repose, to be asleep
   With eyes wide open; standing, speaking, moving,
   And yet so fast asleep.
ANTONIO   Noble Sebastian,
   Thou lett'st thy fortune sleep—die rather; wink'st

---

180. warrant: promise.
180–81. adventure . . . weakly: risk my reputation for discretion for so weak a cause.
181. heavy: sleepy.
186. omit: refuse; heavy offer: chance to sleep.
196. consent: agreement.
200. Th'occasion speaks thee: The opportunity calls upon you.
209. wink'st: (you) shut your eyes.

Whiles thou art waking.

SEBASTIAN   Thou dost snore distinctly;   210
There's meaning in thy snores.

ANTONIO   I am more serious than my custom. You
Must be so too, if heed me; which to do
Trebles thee o'er.

SEBASTIAN   Well, I am standing water.

ANTONIO   I'll teach you how to flow.

SEBASTIAN   Do so. To ebb   215
Hereditary sloth instructs me.

ANTONIO   Oh!
If you but knew how you the purpose cherish
Whiles thus you mock it; how in stripping it
You more invest it. Ebbing men, indeed,
Most often do so near the bottom run   220
By their own fear or sloth.

SEBASTIAN   Prithee, say on.
The setting of thine eye and cheek proclaim
A matter from thee; and a birth, indeed,
Which throes thee much to yield.

ANTONIO   Thus, sir:
[*indicating* GONZALO] Although this lord of weak   225
    remembrance, this,
Who shall be of as little memory
When he is earthed, hath here almost persuaded—
For he's a spirit of persuasion, only
Professes to persuade—the King his son's alive,
'Tis as impossible that he's undrowned   230
As he that sleeps here swims.

SEBASTIAN   I have no hope
That he's undrowned.

---

213. **if heed me:** if you are to heed me.
214. **Trebles thee o'er:** Makes you three times as important; **standing water:** That is, at
    a standstill.
215. **ebb:** decline.
216. **Hereditary sloth:** That is, idleness imposed on Sebastian by his position as younger
    brother.
217–18. **If . . . mock it:** If only you realized how in mocking your indolence you in fact
    show how you desire to embrace my plan.
218–19. **how in . . . invest it:** how in attacking it you show its value.
220. **bottom:** That is, where they might miss the turning tide of fortune.
222. **setting:** fixed expression.
223. **matter:** matter of importance.
224. **throes . . . yield:** causes you pain to say it.
225. **this lord:** Gonzalo; **weak remembrance:** poor memory.
226. **little memory:** little remembered.
227. **earthed:** buried.
228. **spirit:** embodiment (as a councillor).

ANTONIO   Oh, out of that no hope
  What great hope have you! No hope that way is
  Another way so high a hope that even
  Ambition cannot pierce a wink beyond,   235
  But doubt discovery there. Will you grant with me
  That Ferdinand is drowned?
SEBASTIAN   He's gone.
ANTONIO   Then tell me,
  Who's the next heir of Naples?
SEBASTIAN   Claribel.
ANTONIO She that is Queen of Tunis; she that dwells
  Ten leagues beyond man's life; she that from Naples   240
  Can have no note, unless the sun were post—
  The man i'th' moon's too slow—till newborn chins
  Be rough and razorable; she that from whom
  We all were sea-swallowed, though some cast again,
  And by that destiny to perform an act   245
  Whereof what's past is prologue, what to come
  In yours and my discharge.
SEBASTIAN   What stuff is this? How say you?
  'Tis true my brother's daughter's Queen of Tunis;
  So is she heir of Naples, twixt which regions
  There is some space.
ANTONIO   A space whose ev'ry cubit   250
  Seems to cry out, "How shall that Claribel
  Measure us back to Naples? Keep in Tunis,
  And let Sebastian wake." Say this were death
  That now hath seized them: why, they were no worse
  Than now they are. There be that can rule Naples   255
  As well as he that sleeps; lords that can prate
  As amply and unnecessarily
  As this Gonzalo; I myself could make
  A chough of as deep chat. Oh, that you bore
  The mind that I do! What a sleep were this   260
  For your advancement! Do you understand me?
SEBASTIAN Methinks I do.

235. **wink:** glimpse.
240. **Ten leagues . . . life:** That is, beyond the journey of a lifetime.
241. **note:** news; **post:** messenger.
243. **from:** coming from.
244. **cast:** disgorged.
247. **discharge:** responsibility.
250. **cubit:** old unit of measurement, about twenty inches.
252. **Measure:** Retrace; **Keep:** Stay.
255. **There be:** There are those.
256. **prate:** speak foolishly.
258–59. **make . . . chat:** teach a jackdaw to speak as profoundly.

ANTONIO   And how does your content
  Tender your own good fortune?
SEBASTIAN   I remember
  You did supplant your brother Prospero.
ANTONIO   True:
  And look how well my garments sit upon me,   265
  Much feater than before. My brother's servants
  Were then my fellows; now they are my men.
SEBASTIAN   But for your conscience?
ANTONIO   Ay, sir, where lies that? If 'twere a kibe,
  'Twould put me to my slipper; but I feel not   270
  This deity in my bosom. Twenty consciences
  That stand twixt me and Milan, candied be they,
  And melt ere they molest. Here lies your brother,
  No better than the earth he lies upon
  If he were that which now he's like—that's dead—   275
  Whom I with this obedient steel, three inches of it,
  Can lay to bed forever; whiles you, doing thus,
  To the perpetual wink for aye might put
  This ancient morsel, this Sir Prudence, who
  Should not upbraid our course. For all the rest,   280
  They'll take suggestion as a cat laps milk;
  They'll tell the clock to any business that
  We say befits the hour.
SEBASTIAN   Thy case, dear friend,
  Shall be my precedent. As thou gott'st Milan,
  I'll come by Naples. Draw thy sword: one stroke   285
  Shall free thee from the tribute which thou payest,
  And I the King shall love thee.
ANTONIO   Draw together;
  And when I rear my hand, do you the like
  To fall it on Gonzalo.
SEBASTIAN   Oh, but one word.
Enter ARIEL, [*invisible,*] *with music and song.*
ARIEL   My master through his art foresees the danger   290

262. **content:** inclination.
263. **tender:** regard.
266. **feater:** more fittingly.
269. **kibe:** chilblain.
270. **put me to:** make me wear.
271. **This deity:** That is, conscience.
272. **candied:** crystallized in sugar; **be they:** may they be.
273. **molest:** interfere.
278. **perpetual wink:** everlasting sleep; **for aye:** forever.
280. **Should not:** Could not then; **upbraid:** criticize.
281. **suggestion:** prompting.
282. **tell the clock to:** agree with.
289. **fall it:** let it fall.

That you his friend are in, and sends me forth—
For else his project dies—to keep them living.
                    [*He*] *sings in Gonzalo's ear.*
                    While you here do snoring lie,
                    Open-eyed conspiracy
                    His time doth take.   295
                    If of life you keep a care,
                    Shake off slumber and beware.
                    Awake, awake!
ANTONIO   Then let us both be sudden.
          [ANTONIO *and* SEBASTIAN *draw their swords.*]
GONZALO [*waking*]   Now, good angels preserve the King.   300
          [*He wakes* ALONSO.]
ALONSO   Why, how now? Ho! Awake! Why are you drawn?
     Wherefore this ghastly looking?
GONZALO   What's the matter?
SEBASTIAN   Whiles we stood here securing your repose,
     Even now we heard a hollow burst of bellowing,
     Like bulls, or rather lions. Did't not wake you?   305
     It struck mine ear most terribly.
ALONSO   I heard nothing.
ANTONIO   Oh, 'twas a din to fright a monster's ear,
     To make an earthquake: sure it was the roar
     Of a whole herd of lions.
ALONSO   Heard you this, Gonzalo?
GONZALO   Upon mine honor, sir, I heard a humming,   310
     And that a strange one too, which did awake me.
     I shaked you, sir, and cried. As mine eyes opened,
     I saw their weapons drawn. There was a noise,
     That's verily. 'Tis best we stand upon our guard,
     Or that we quit this place. Let's draw our weapons.   315
ALONSO   Lead off this ground, and let's make further search
     For my poor son.
GONZALO   Heavens keep him from these beasts,
     For he is sure i'th' island.
ALONSO   Lead away.
ARIEL   Prospero my lord shall know what I have done.
     So, King, go safely on to seek thy son.   *Exeunt.*   320

292. **for else:** otherwise.
295. **time:** chance.
299. **sudden:** quick.
312. **cried:** called out.
314. **verily:** true.

2.2

Enter CALIBAN *with a burden of wood.*

CALIBAN All the infections that the sun sucks up
From bogs, fens, flats, on Prosper fall, and make him
By inchmeal a disease!

A noise of thunder heard.

                              His spirits hear me,
And yet I needs must curse. But they'll nor pinch,
Fright me with urchin-shows, pitch me i'th' mire,   5
Nor lead me like a firebrand in the dark
Out of my way, unless he bid 'em. But
For every trifle are they set upon me;
Sometime like apes that mow and chatter at me
And after bite me; then like hedgehogs, which   10
Lie tumbling in my barefoot way and mount
Their pricks at my footfall; sometime am I
All wound with adders, who with cloven tongues
Do hiss me into madness.

            Enter TRINCULO.

                              Lo, now, lo!
Here comes a spirit of his, and to torment me   15
For bringing wood in slowly. I'll fall flat.
Perchance he will not mind me.

TRINCULO Here's neither bush nor scrub to bear off any
weather at all, and another storm brewing: I hear it sing i'th'
wind. Yond same black cloud, yond huge one, looks like a foul   20
bombard that would shed his liquor. If it should thunder as it
did before, I know not where to hide my head. Yond same
cloud cannot choose but fall by pailfuls. [*He sees* CALIBAN.]
What have we here? A man or a fish? Dead or alive? A fish:
he smells like a fish; a very ancient and fishlike smell; a   25
kind of not-of-the-newest poor john. A strange fish. Were I in
England now, as once I was, and had but this fish painted,
not a holiday fool there but would give a piece of silver. There
would this monster make a man; any strange beast there

---

2. **flats:** swamps.
3. **inchmeal:** inch by inch.
4. **needs must:** have to; **nor:** neither.
5. **urchin-shows:** goblin-shows.
6. **firebrand:** burning piece of wood.
9. **mow:** grimace.
13. **wound with:** entwined by.
17. **mind:** notice.
18. **bear off:** ward off.
21. **bombard:** leather jug.
26. **poor-John:** salted fish.
27. **painted:** That is, on a sign outside a booth.
29. **make a man:** make a man rich.

makes a man. When they will not give a doit to relieve a lame   30
beggar, they will lay out ten to see a dead Indian. Legged like
a man, and his fins like arms. Warm, o'my troth! I do now let
loose my opinion, hold it no longer: this is no fish, but an
islander that hath lately suffered by a thunderbolt. [*Thunder.*]
Alas, the storm is come again. My best way is to creep under   35
his gaberdine; there is no other shelter hereabout. Misery
acquaints a man with strange bedfellows. I will here shroud
till the dregs of the storm be past.
          [*He crawls under Caliban's cloak.*]
          Enter STEFANO *singing.*
STEFANO   I shall no more to sea, to sea,
               Here shall I die ashore.   40
This is a very scurvy tune to sing at a man's funeral. Well,
here's my comfort.
          [*He*] *drinks* [*and*] *sings.*
               The master, the swabber, the boatswain and I,
               The gunner and his mate,
               Loved Moll, Meg, and Marian, and Margery,   45
               But none of us cared for Kate.
               For she had a tongue with a tang,
               Would cry to a sailor, "Go hang!"
               She loved not the savor of tar nor of pitch,
               Yet a tailor might scratch her where'er she did itch. 50
               Then to sea, boys, and let her go hang!
This is a scurvy tune, too; but here's my comfort.
          [*He*] *drinks.*
CALIBAN   Do not torment me! Oh!
STEFANO   What's the matter? Have we devils here? Do you
put tricks upon 's with savages and men of Ind? Ha? I have   55
not scaped drowning to be afeared now of your four legs;
for it hath been said, "As proper a man as ever went on four
legs cannot make him give ground"; and it shall be said so
again, while Stefano breathes at' nostrils.
CALIBAN   The spirit torments me! Oh!   60
STEFANO   This is some monster of the isle with four legs who

---

30. **doit:** small coin.
32. **o'my troth:** upon my faith.
36. **gaberdine:** cloak.
37. **shroud:** take shelter.
41. **scurvy:** worthless.
43. **swabber:** seaman who washes down the decks.
47. **tang:** sting.
49. **savor:** smell.
55. **Ind:** The Indies.

hath got, as I take it, an ague. Where the devil should he learn our language? I will give him some relief if it be but for that. If I can recover him and keep him tame and get to Naples with him, he's a present for any emperor that ever trod on neat's leather. 65

CALIBAN Do not torment me, prithee! I'll bring my wood home faster.

STEFANO He's in his fit now, and does not talk after the wisest. He shall taste of my bottle. If he have never drunk wine afore, it will go near to remove his fit. If I can recover him and keep him tame, I will not take too much for him. He shall pay for him that hath him, and that soundly. 70

CALIBAN Thou dost me yet but little hurt; thou wilt anon, I know it by thy trembling. Now Prosper works upon thee. 75

STEFANO Come on your ways. Open your mouth: here is that which will give language to you, cat. Open your mouth: this will shake your shaking, I can tell you, and that soundly. [CALIBAN drinks.] You cannot tell who's your friend. Open your chaps again. 80

TRINCULO I should know that voice. It should be—but he is drowned, and these are devils. Oh, defend me!

STEFANO Four legs and two voices: a most delicate monster! His forward voice now is to speak well of his friend; his backward voice is to utter foul speeches and to detract. If all the wine in my bottle will recover him, I will help his ague. Come. [CALIBAN drinks.] Amen. I will pour some in thy other mouth. 85

TRINCULO Stefano!

STEFANO Doth thy other mouth call me? Mercy, mercy! This is a devil and no monster. I will leave him; I have no long spoon. 90

TRINCULO Stefano? If thou beest Stefano, touch me and speak to me, for I am Trinculo—be not afeard—thy good friend Trinculo. 95

---

62. **ague:** fever.
62–63. **should he learn:** could he have learned.
64. **for that:** That is, for speaking our language.
66. **neat's leather:** cowhide.
69–70. **after the wisest:** in the wisest manner.
71. **afore:** before.
73. **hath:** That is, buys.
74. **anon:** soon.
76. **on your ways:** That is, come here.
80. **chaps:** jaws.
85. **detract:** make scornful remarks.
86. **help:** cure.
91–92. **long spoon:** Playing on the proverb "He must have a long spoon that will sup with the devil."

STEFANO   If thou beest Trinculo, come forth: I'll pull thee by
the lesser legs. If any be Trinculo's legs, these are they. [*He
pulls him out.*] Thou art very Trinculo indeed! How cam'st
thou to be the siege of this mooncalf? Can he vent Trinculos?

TRINCULO   I took him to be killed with a thunderstroke. But   100
art thou not drowned, Stefano? I hope now thou art not
drowned. Is the storm overblown? I hid me under the dead
mooncalf's gaberdine, for fear of the storm. And art thou
living, Stefano? O Stefano, two Neapolitans scaped!

STEFANO   Prithee, do not turn me about, my stomach is not   105
constant.

CALIBAN [*aside*]   These be fine things, an if they be not
sprites. That's a brave god, and bears celestial liquor. I will
kneel to him.

STEFANO   How didst thou scape? How cam'st thou hither?   110
Swear by this bottle how thou cam'st hither. I escaped upon
a butt of sack which the sailors heaved o'erboard, by this
bottle, which I made of the bark of a tree, with mine own
hands, since I was cast ashore.

CALIBAN   I'll swear upon that bottle to be thy true subject,   115
for the liquor is not earthly.

STEFANO   Here. Swear then how thou escaped'st.

TRINCULO   Swum ashore, man, like a duck. I can swim like a
duck, I'll be sworn.

STEFANO [*giving* TRINCULO *the bottle*]   Here, kiss the Book.   120
Though thou canst swim like a duck, thou art made like a
goose.

TRINCULO   O Stefano, hast any more of this?

STEFANO   The whole butt, man. My cellar is in a rock by the
seaside, where my wine is hid. [*to* CALIBAN] How now,   125
mooncalf, how does thine ague?

CALIBAN   Hast thou not dropped from heaven?

STEFANO   Out o'th' moon I do assure thee. I was the man
i'th' moon, when time was.

CALIBAN   I have seen thee in her, and I do adore thee. My   130
mistress showed me thee, and thy dog, and thy bush.

---

98.   **very**: the real.
99.   **siege**: excrement; **mooncalf**: misshapen creature; **vent**: expel, that is, defecate.
105–06. **not constant**: unsettled.
107. **an if**: if.
108. **brave**: fine; **bears**: he carries.
112. **butt**: cask; **sack**: Canary wine (a sweet white wine from the Canary Islands).
114. **since**: after.
129. **when time was**: once upon a time .
131. **thy dog, and thy bush**: By tradition, the Man in the Moon has with him a dog and a
       thornbush.

STEFANO [*giving the bottle to* CALIBAN]   Come, swear to that:
 kiss the Book. I will furnish it anon with new contents.
 Swear.
TRINCULO   By this good light, this is a very shallow monster.   135
 I afeared of him? A very weak monster. The man i'th' moon?
 A most poor credulous monster. Well drawn, monster, in
 good sooth.
CALIBAN   I'll show thee every fertile inch o'th' island, and I
 will kiss thy foot. I prithee, be my god.   140
TRINCULO   By this light, a most perfidious and drunken
 monster! When's god's asleep he'll rob his bottle.
CALIBAN   I'll kiss thy foot. I'll swear myself thy subject.
STEFANO   Come on, then: down and swear.
TRINCULO   I shall laugh myself to death at this puppy-headed   145
 monster. A most scurvy monster. I could find in my heart to
 beat him—
STEFANO [*to* CALIBAN]   Come, kiss.
TRINCULO   —but that the poor monster's in drink. An abomi-
 nable monster.   150
CALIBAN   I'll show thee the best springs; I'll pluck thee berries;
 I'll fish for thee, and get thee wood enough.
 A plague upon the tyrant that I serve!
 I'll bear him no more sticks but follow thee,
 Thou wondrous man.   155
TRINCULO   A most ridiculous monster, to make a wonder of a
 poor drunkard.
CALIBAN   I prithee, let me bring thee where crabs grow;
 And I with my long nails will dig thee pig-nuts,
 Show thee a jay's nest, and instruct thee how   160
 To snare the nimble marmoset. I'll bring thee
 To clust'ring filberts, and sometimes I'll get thee
 Young scamels from the rock. Wilt thou go with me?
STEFANO   I prithee now lead the way without any more talking.
 Trinculo, the King and all our company else being drowned,   165
 we will inherit here. [*to* CALIBAN] Here, bear my bottle.
 —Fellow Trinculo, we'll fill him by and by again.
CALIBAN (*sings drunkenly*)   Farewell, master; farewell, farewell.

137. **drawn:** pulled (on the bottle).
137–38. **in good sooth:** indeed.
149. **in drink:** drunk.
159. **pig-nuts:** edible wild tubers.
161. **marmoset:** small monkey.
162. **filberts:** hazelnuts.
163. **scamels:** possibly sea-mews, a seabird; possibly a lost dialect word for a kind of
     mollusk.
165. **else:** apart from us

TRINCULO   A howling monster, a drunken monster.

CALIBAN [*continuing to sing*]   No more dams I'll make for fish,   170
        Nor fetch in firing
        At requiring,
        Nor scrape trencher, nor wash dish,
        'Ban, 'Ban, Ca-Caliban
        Has a new master: get a new man.   175
  Freedom, high-day; high-day, freedom; freedom, high-day,
    freedom!

STEFANO   O brave monster, lead the way!   *Exeunt.*

3.1

Enter FERDINAND, *bearing a log.*

FERDINAND   There be some sports are painful, and their labor
Delight in them sets off. Some kinds of baseness
Are nobly undergone, and most poor matters
Point to rich ends. This my mean task
Would be as heavy to me as odious, but   5
The mistress which I serve quickens what's dead
And makes my labors pleasures. Oh, she is
Ten times more gentle than her father's crabbed,
And he's composed of harshness. I must remove
Some thousands of these logs and pile them up,   10
Upon a sore injunction. My sweet mistress
Weeps when she sees me work and says such baseness
Had never like executor. I forget;
But these sweet thoughts do even refresh my labors,
Most busil'est, when I do it.

Enter MIRANDA, *and* PROSPERO [*unseen*].

MIRANDA   Alas now, pray you,   15
  Work not so hard. I would the lightning had
Burnt up those logs that you are enjoined to pile.
Pray set it down and rest you. When this burns

171. **firing:** firewood.
172. **At requiring:** On demand.
173. **trencher:** wooden plate.
176. **high-day:** holiday.
1.   **sports:** activities, physical exertions.
2.   **sets off:** compensates; **baseness:** degradation.
3.   **undergone:** undertaken.
4.   **mean:** lowly.
5.   **but:** except that.
6.   **quickens:** gives life to.
8.   **crabbed:** sour.
11. **sore injunction:** harsh order.
13. **Had . . . executor:** Was never undertaken by such a person; **I forget:** That is, to work.
14. **Most . . . it:** When I am busiest at my work.
18. **this:** That is, the log.

'Twill weep for having wearied you. My father
Is hard at study. Pray now, rest yourself.   20
He's safe for these three hours.

FERDINAND   O most dear mistress,
   The sun will set before I shall discharge
   What I must strive to do.

MIRANDA   If you'll sit down
   I'll bear your logs the while. Pray give me that:
   I'll carry it to the pile.

FERDINAND   No, precious creature,   25
   I had rather crack my sinews, break my back,
   Than you should such dishonor undergo
   While I sit lazy by.

MIRANDA   It would become me
   As well as it does you; and I should do it
   With much more ease, for my goodwill is to it,   30
   And yours it is against.

PROSPERO [aside]   Poor worm, thou art infected:
   This visitation shows it.

MIRANDA   You look wearily.

FERDINAND   No, noble mistress, 'tis fresh morning with me
   When you are by at night. I do beseech you,
   Chiefly that I may set it in my prayers,   35
   What is your name?

MIRANDA   Miranda. —O my father,
   I have broke your hest to say so!

FERDINAND   Admired Miranda!
   Indeed the top of admiration, worth
   What's dearest to the world. Full many a lady
   I have eyed with best regard, and many a time   40
   Th' harmony of their tongues hath into bondage
   Brought my too diligent ear. For several virtues
   Have I liked several women; never any
   With so full soul but some defect in her
   Did quarrel with the noblest grace she owed   45
   And put it to the foil. But you, O you,

19. **weep**: exude resin, that is, tears.
21. **safe**: withdrawn.
22. **discharge**: complete.
34. **by**: nearby.
35. **Chiefly**: Principally.
37. **hest**: command.
39. **dearest**: most valuable.
40. **eyed . . . regard**: held in highest esteem.
42. **diligent**: attentive.
45. **owed**: owned.
46. **put it to the foil**: foiled it.

So perfect and so peerless, are created
Of every creature's best.

MIRANDA   I do not know
One of my sex; no woman's face remember
Save, from my glass, mine own. Nor have I seen   50
More that I may call men than you, good friend,
And my dear father. How features are abroad
I am skilless of; but by my modesty,
The jewel in my dower, I would not wish
Any companion in the world but you,   55
Nor can imagination form a shape
Besides yourself to like of. But I prattle
Something too wildly, and my father's precepts
I therein do forget.

FERDINAND   I am in my condition
A prince, Miranda; I do think a king—   60
I would not so!—and would no more endure
This wooden slavery than to suffer
The flesh fly blow my mouth. Hear my soul speak:
The very instant that I saw you did
My heart fly to your service, there resides   65
To make me slave to it, and for your sake
Am I this patient log-man.

MIRANDA   Do you love me?

FERDINAND   O heaven, O earth, bear witness to this sound,
And crown what I profess with kind event
If I speak true! If hollowly, invert   70
What best is boded me to mischief! I,
Beyond all limit of what else i'th' world,
Do love, prize, honor you.

MIRANDA   I am a fool
To weep at what I am glad of.

PROSPERO [aside]   Fair encounter
Of two most rare affections. Heavens rain grace   75
On that which breeds between 'em.

48. **Of:** Out of.
50. **glass:** mirror.
52. **How . . . abroad:** What people elsewhere look like.
53. **skilless:** ignorant; **modesty:** chastity.
54. **dower:** dowry
57. **like of:** be fond of.
58. **Something:** Somewhat.
59. **condition:** rank.
63. **flesh fly:** insect that lays eggs in dead flesh; **blow my mouth:** lay its eggs in my mouth.
69. **kind event:** happy outcome.
70. **hollowly:** insincerely; **invert:** turn.
71. **boded:** in store for; **mischief:** harm.
72. **what:** whatever.

FERDINAND   Wherefore weep you?
MIRANDA At mine unworthiness, that dare not offer
  What I desire to give, and much less take
  What I shall die to want. But this is trifling,
  And all the more it seeks to hide itself   80
  The bigger bulk it shows. Hence, bashful cunning,
  And prompt me, plain and holy innocence!
  I am your wife if you'll marry me;
  If not, I'll die your maid. To be your fellow
  You may deny me, but I'll be your servant   85
  Whether you will or no.
FERDINAND   My mistress, dearest,
  And I thus humble ever.
MIRANDA My husband, then?
FERDINAND   Ay, with a heart as willing
  As bondage e'er of freedom. Here's my hand.
MIRANDA And mine, with my heart in't. And now farewell   90
  Till half an hour hence.
FERDINAND   A thousand thousand!
        Exeunt [FERDINAND *and* MIRANDA, *separately*].
PROSPERO So glad of this as they I cannot be,
  Who are surprised withal; but my rejoicing
  At nothing can be more. I'll to my book,
  For yet ere suppertime must I perform   95
  Much business appertaining.   *Exit.*

3.2

Enter CALIBAN, STEFANO, *and* TRINCULO.
STEFANO Tell not me. When the butt is out we will drink
  water, not a drop before. Therefore bear up and board 'em.
  —Servant monster, drink to me!
TRINCULO "Servant monster"? The folly of this island! They
  say there's but five upon this isle. We are three of them; if   5
  th'other two be brained like us, the state totters.

79. **to want:** if I lack it.
84. **maid:** servant and unmarried; **fellow:** bedfellow.
86. **will or no:** want it or not; **My mistress:** That is, the woman I serve.
88–89. **willing . . . freedom:** desirous as slaves always are to be free.
91. **thousand thousand:** That is, farewells.
93. **withal:** by everything that happens
94. **book:** That is, book of magic.
96. **appertaining:** related to this.
1.   **out:** empty.
2.   **bear . . . 'em:** approach and attack (the language of naval battles used to refer to their
     assault on the alcohol).
6.   **be brained like us:** have brains in a condition like ours.

STEFANO   Drink, servant monster, when I bid thee. Thy eyes
are almost set in thy head.

TRINCULO   Where should they be set else? He were a brave
monster indeed if they were set in his tail.   10

STEFANO   My man-monster hath drowned his tongue in sack.
For my part, the sea cannot drown me. I swam, ere I could
recover the shore, five and thirty leagues, off and on. By this
light, thou shalt be my lieutenant, monster, or my standard.

TRINCULO   Your lieutenant, if you list; he's no standard.   15

STEFANO   We'll not run, Monsieur Monster.

TRINCULO   Nor go neither, but you'll lie like dogs and yet say
nothing neither.

STEFANO   Mooncalf, speak once in thy life, if thou beest a
good mooncalf.   20

CALIBAN   How does thy honor? Let me lick thy shoe.
I'll not serve him; he is not valiant.

TRINCULO   Thou liest, most ignorant monster; I am in case
to jostle a constable. Why, thou debauched fish thou, was
there ever man a coward that hath drunk so much sack as I   25
do today? Wilt thou tell a monstrous lie, being but half a
fish and half a monster?

CALIBAN   Lo, how he mocks me. Wilt thou let him, my lord?

TRINCULO   "Lord," quoth he? That a monster should be such
a natural!   30

CALIBAN   Lo, lo again! Bite him to death, I prithee.

STEFANO   Trinculo, keep a good tongue in your head. If you
prove a mutineer, the next tree! The poor monster's my
subject, and he shall not suffer indignity.

CALIBAN   I thank my noble lord. Wilt thou be pleased   35
To hearken once again to the suit I made to thee?

STEFANO   Marry, will I. Kneel and repeat it. I will stand, and
so shall Trinculo.

Enter ARIEL *invisible.*

8. **set:** sunk.
9. **set:** placed.
13. **recover:** reach; **leagues:** That is, about a hundred miles; **off and on:** in fits and starts.
13–14. **By this light:** An oath.
14. **standard:** standard-bearer.
15. **list:** like; **no standard:** That is, not standing up.
17. **go:** walk; **lie:** lie down; tell lies.
23. **in case:** in a condition to.
24. **constable:** officer of the law; **debauched:** seduced away from proper allegiance.
26. **monstrous:** enormous lie; told by a monster.
30. **natural:** idiot.
33. **the next tree:** That is, you will hang from the next tree.
37. **Marry:** Indeed; originally "by the Virgin Mary."

CALIBAN   As I told thee before, I am subject to a tyrant,
　A sorcerer, that by his cunning hath   40
　Cheated me of the island.
ARIEL   Thou liest.
CALIBAN [to TRINCULO]   Thou liest, thou jesting monkey, thou!
　I would my valiant master would destroy thee.
　I do not lie.
STEFANO   Trinculo, if you trouble him any more in 's tale, by   45
　this hand, I will supplant some of your teeth.
TRINCULO   Why, I said nothing.
STEFANO   Mum, then, and no more. —Proceed.
CALIBAN   I say by sorcery he got this isle;
　From me he got it. If thy greatness will   50
　Revenge it on him—for I know thou dar'st,
　But this thing dare not—
STEFANO   That's most certain.
CALIBAN   Thou shalt be lord of it, and I'll serve thee,
STEFANO   How now shall this be compassed? Canst thou bring   55
　me to the party?
CALIBAN   Yea, yea, my lord. I'll yield him thee asleep,
　Where thou mayst knock a nail into his head.
ARIEL   Thou liest; thou canst not.
CALIBAN   What a pied ninny's this! Thou scurvy patch!   60
　I do beseech thy greatness give him blows
　And take his bottle from him. When that's gone,
　He shall drink naught but brine, for I'll not show him
　Where the quick freshes are.
STEFANO   Trinculo, run into no further danger. Interrupt the   65
　monster one word further and, by this hand, I'll turn my
　mercy out o'doors and make a stockfish of thee.
TRINCULO   Why, what did I? I did nothing. I'll go farther off.
STEFANO   Didst thou not say he lied?
ARIEL   Thou liest.   70
STEFANO   Do I so?
　　　　　　[He beats TRINCULO.]

---

43. **valiant master:** That is, Stefano.
46. **supplant:** displace.
48. **Mum:** Keep quiet.
50. **thy greatness:** That is, Stefano.
52. **this thing:** That is, Trinculo.
55. **compassed:** accomplished.
56. **party:** the person you're talking about, that is, Prospero.
60. **pied ninny:** jester in a motley costume; **patch:** fool.
64. **quick freshes:** running springs.
67. **stockfish:** saltfish, beaten before cooking.
68. **off:** away.

Take thou that! As you like this, give me the lie another time.

TRINCULO I did not give the lie! Out o'your wits, and hearing
too? A pox o'your bottle. This can sack and drinking do. A
murrain on your monster, and the devil take your fingers!   75

CALIBAN Ha, ha, ha!

STEFANO Now forward with your tale. —Prithee stand further off.

CALIBAN Beat him enough. After a little time I'll beat him too.

STEFANO Stand farther. —Come, proceed.   80

CALIBAN Why, as I told thee, 'tis a custom with him
I'th' afternoon to sleep. There thou mayst brain him,
Having first seized his books; or with a log
Batter his skull, or paunch him with a stake,
Or cut his weasand with thy knife. Remember   85
First to possess his books, for without them
He's but a sot as I am, nor hath not
One spirit to command—they all do hate him
As rootedly as I. Burn but his books.
He has brave utensils, for so he calls them,   90
Which, when he has a house, he'll deck withal.
And that most deeply to consider is
The beauty of his daughter. He himself
Calls her a nonpareil. I never saw a woman
But only Sycorax my dam and she;   95
But she as far surpasseth Sycorax
As great'st does least.

STEFANO   Is it so brave a lass?

CALIBAN Ay, lord. She will become thy bed, I warrant,
And bring thee forth brave brood.

STEFANO Monster, I will kill this man. His daughter and I will   100
be king and queen—save our graces—and Trinculo and
thyself shall be viceroys. Dost thou like the plot, Trinculo?

TRINCULO Excellent.

STEFANO Give me thy hand. I am sorry I beat thee. But while
thou liv'st, keep a good tongue in thy head.   105

---

72. **give me the lie:** call me a liar.
75. **murrain:** plague.
84. **paunch:** stab in the belly.
85. **weasand:** windpipe.
87. **sot:** fool.
89. **but:** only.
90. **brave:** splendid.
91. **deck withal:** furnish it with.
94. **nonpareil:** That is, without equal.
97. **brave:** fine.
98. **become:** suit.
101. **save:** God save.

CALIBAN Within this half hour will he be asleep.
  Wilt thou destroy him then?
STEFANO   Ay, on mine honor.
ARIEL [*aside*] This will I tell my master.
CALIBAN Thou mak'st me merry. I am full of pleasure;
  Let us be jocund. Will you troll the catch   110
  You taught me but whilere?
STEFANO At thy request, monster, I will do reason, any reason.
  Come on, Trinculo, let us sing.
  (*Sings.*)   Flout 'em, and scout 'em
                  And scout 'em, and flout 'em.   115
                  Thought is free.
CALIBAN That's not the tune.
          ARIEL *plays the tune on a tabor and pipe.*
STEFANO What is this same?
TRINCULO This is the tune of our catch, played by the picture
  of Nobody.   120
STEFANO If thou beest a man, show thyself in thy likeness. If
  thou beest a devil, take't as thou list.
TRINCULO Oh, forgive me my sins!
STEFANO He that dies pays all debts. I defy thee! Mercy
  upon us!   125
CALIBAN Art thou afeard?
STEFANO No, monster, not I.
CALIBAN Be not afeard: the isle is full of noises,
  Sounds and sweet airs that give delight and hurt not.
  Sometimes a thousand twangling instruments   130
  Will hum about mine ears; and sometimes voices,
  That, if I then had waked after long sleep,
  Will make me sleep again; and then, in dreaming,
  The clouds methought would open and show riches
  Ready to drop upon me, that when I waked   135
  I cried to dream again.
STEFANO This will prove a brave kingdom to me, where I
  shall have my music for nothing.
CALIBAN When Prospero is destroyed.
STEFANO That shall be by and by: I remember the story.   140
                    [*Exit* ARIEL *playing music.*]

110. **jocund:** jolly; **troll the catch:** sing the round.
111. **but whilere:** just a short time ago.
112. **reason, any reason:** anything reasonable.
114. **flout:** mock; **scout:** deride.
117 **SD. tabor:** small drum.
119–20. **picture of Nobody:** allusion to a figure with limbs but no body.
122. **as thou list:** however you want to.
129. **airs:** tunes.
140. **by and by:** in good time.

TRINCULO   The sound is going away; let's follow it, and after
do our work.

STEFANO   Lead, monster, we'll follow. I would I could see
this taborer: he lays it on.

TRINCULO [*to* CALIBAN]   Wilt come? I'll follow Stefano.   145

Exeunt.

3.3

Enter ALONSO, SEBASTIAN, ANTONIO, GONZALO,
ADRIAN, *and* FRANCISCO.

GONZALO   By'r lakin, I can go no further, sir.
My old bones aches. Here's a maze trod indeed
Through forthrights and meanders. By your patience,
I needs must rest me.

ALONSO   Old lord, I cannot blame thee,
Who am myself attached with weariness   5
To th' dulling of my spirits. Sit down and rest.
Even here I will put off my hope, and keep it
No longer for my flatterer: he is drowned
Whom thus we stray to find, and the sea mocks
Our frustrate search on land. Well, let him go.   10

ANTONIO [*aside to* SEBASTIAN]   I am right glad that he's so out
of hope.
Do not, for one repulse, forgo the purpose
That you resolved t'effect.

SEBASTIAN [*aside to* ANTONIO]   The next advantage
Will we take throughly.

ANTONIO [*aside to* SEBASTIAN]   Let it be tonight;
For now they are oppressed with travail, they   15
Will not nor cannot use such vigilance
As when they are fresh.

SEBASTIAN [*aside to* ANTONIO]   I say tonight: no more.

---

144. **lays it on:** bangs it vigorously.
1.   **By'r lakin:** By our ladykin (Our Lady).
3.   **forthrights and meanders:** straight and crooked paths; **By your patience:** With
       your permission.
4.   **needs must:** need to.
5.   **attached:** seized.
6.   **To . . . spirits:** To the point of being dispirited.
8.   **for:** as.
10.   **frustrate:** frustrated.
11.   **right:** very.
12.   **for:** on account of; **repulse:** setback.
13.   **advantage:** opportunity.
14.   **throughly:** thoroughly.
15.   **now:** now that.

Solemn and strange music. [Enter] PROSPERO *on the
top, invisible.*

ALONSO   What harmony is this? My good friends, hark!

GONZALO   Marvelous sweet music.   20

*Enter several strange shapes, bringing a banquet;
and dance about it with gentle actions of salutations,
and inviting the King etc. to eat, they depart.*

ALONSO   Give us kind keepers, heavens! What were these?

SEBASTIAN   A living drollery. Now I will believe
That there are unicorns; that in Arabia
There is one tree, the phoenix' throne, one phoenix
At this hour reigning there.

ANTONIO   I'll believe both;   25
And what does else want credit, come to me,
And I'll be sworn 'tis true. Travelers ne'er did lie,
Though fools at home condemn 'em.

GONZALO   If in Naples
I should report this now, would they believe me?
If I should say I saw such islanders—   30
For certes these are people of the island—
Who, though they are of monstrous shape, yet note
Their manners are more gentle, kind, than of
Our human generation you shall find
Many, nay, almost any.

PROSPERO [*aside*]   Honest lord,   35
Thou hast said well; for some of you there present
Are worse than devils.

ALONSO   I cannot too much muse
Such shapes, such gesture, and such sound, expressing—
Although they want the use of tongue—a kind
Of excellent dumb discourse.

PROSPERO [*aside*]   Praise in departing.   40

FRANCISCO   They vanished strangely.

SEBASTIAN   No matter, since
They have left their viands behind; for we have stomachs.
Wilt please you taste of what is here?

ALONSO   Not I.

---

18 SD. **on the top**: on a third level above the gallery.
21. **kind keepers**: guardian angels.
22. **living drollery**: comic picture come to life.
24. **phoenix**: Mythical Arabian bird, of which only one is alive at any one time, said to
     reproduce itself every five hundred years by dying in flames and being renewed.
26. **what**: whatever; **want credit**: lacks credibility.
31. **certes**: certainly.
37. **muse**: wonder at.
39. **want**: lack.
40. **Praise in departing**: Keep your praise till it finishes.
42. **viands**: food; **stomachs**: appetites.

GONZALO   Faith, sir, you need not fear. When we were boys,
　　Who would believe that there were mountaineers,   45
　　Dewlapped like bulls, whose throats had hanging at 'em
　　Wallets of flesh? Or that there were such men
　　Whose heads stood in their breasts? Which now we find
　　Each putter-out of five for one will bring us
　　Good warrant of.

ALONSO　　　　　　　I will stand to and feed;   50
　　Although my last, no matter, since I feel
　　The best is past. Brother, my lord the duke,
　　Stand to and do as we.

　　　　　　[ALONSO, SEBASTIAN, *and* ANTONIO *approach the table.*]
　　　　　　Thunder and lightning.
　　　　　　Enter ARIEL, *like a harpy; claps his wings upon*
　　　　　　the table, and with a quaint device the banquet
　　　　　　vanishes.

ARIEL   You are three men of sin, whom destiny—
　　That hath to instrument this lower world   55
　　And what is in't—the never-surfeited sea
　　Hath caused to belch up you, and on this island,
　　Where man doth not inhabit—you 'mongst men
　　Being most unfit to live. I have made you mad;
　　And even with suchlike valor men hang and drown   60
　　Their proper selves.

　　　　　　[ALONSO, SEBASTIAN, *and* ANTONIO *draw their*
　　　　　　swords.]
　　　　　　　　　　　You fools, I and my fellows
　　Are ministers of fate. The elements
　　Of whom your swords are tempered may as well
　　Wound the loud winds, or with bemocked-at stabs
　　Kill the still-closing waters, as diminish   65

---

45. mountaineers: mountain dwellers.
46. Dewlapped: With a fold of skin hanging from the neck, like cattle.
48. heads . . . breasts: One of the classical and medieval monstrous races, also referred
　　to in *Othello*: "men whose heads / Do grow beneath their shoulders" (1.3.144–45).
49. putter-out of five for one: Traveler who deposited a sum money with an underwriter
　　before a journey that, if successfully completed, would net him five times the deposit.
50. warrant: proof; **stand to:** set to work.
51. Although my last: Even if it turns out to be my last meal.
53 SD. harpy: mythical creature with the face and breasts of a woman and the body of a
　　vulture, an instrument of divine vengeance; **quaint:** ingenious.
55. instrument: control.
57. up you: you up.
60. suchlike valor: the bravado of the mad.
61. proper: own.
62. ministers: agents.
63. whom: which.
64. bemocked-at: scorned.
65. still-closing: always closing again when parted.

One dowl that's in my plume. My fellow ministers
Are like invulnerable. If you could hurt,
Your swords are now too massy for your strengths
And will not be uplifted. But remember—
For that's my business to you—that you three   70
From Milan did supplant good Prospero;
Exposed unto the sea, which hath requit it,
Him and his innocent child; for which foul deed
The powers, delaying not forgetting, have
Incensed the seas and shores—yea, all the creatures—   75
Against your peace. Thee of thy son, Alonso,
They have bereft; and do pronounce by me
Ling'ring perdition—worse than any death
Can be at once—shall step by step attend
You and your ways; whose wraths to guard you from,   80
Which here in this most desolate isle else falls
Upon your heads, is nothing but heart's sorrow
And a clear life ensuing.
            He vanishes in thunder; then, to soft music, enter the
            shapes again, and dance with mocks and mows, and
            [*then exeunt*], *carrying out the table.*
PROSPERO [*aside*]   Bravely the figure of this harpy hast thou
Performed, my Ariel; a grace it had, devouring.   85
Of my instruction hast thou nothing bated
In what thou hadst to say. So with good life
And observation strange my meaner ministers
Their several kinds have done. My high charms work,
And these mine enemies are all knit up   90
In their distractions. They now are in my power;
And in these fits I leave them, while I visit
Young Ferdinand, whom they suppose is drowned,
And his and mine loved darling.   [*Exit.*]

66. **dowl**: feather.
67. **like**: similarly; **If**: Even if.
68. **massy**: heavy.
70. **business**: message.
72. **requit it**: repaid the deed.
77. **bereft**: deprived.
78. **perdition**: ruin.
80. **whose**: That is, the heavenly powers'.
81. **else**: otherwise.
82. **is nothing**: there is no option.
83. **clear**: unblemished.
83 **SD. mocks and mows**: mocking gestures and grimaces.
85. **a grace . . . devouring**: you gracefully made the food disappear.
86. **bated**: omitted.
87. **So**: Similarly; **good life**: lifelike actions.
88. **observation strange**: exceptional care; **meaner**: lesser.
89. **several . . . done**: various parts have played.
91. **distractions**: confusions.

GONZALO   I'th' name of something holy, sir, why stand you   95
  In this strange stare?
ALONSO   Oh, it is monstrous, monstrous!
  Methought the billows spoke and told me of it,
  The winds did sing it to me, and the thunder,
  That deep and dreadful organ pipe, pronounced
  The name of Prosper. It did bass my trespass.   100
  Therefore my son i'th' ooze is bedded, and
  I'll seek him deeper than e'er plummet sounded,
  And with him there lie mudded.   [*Exit.*]
SEBASTIAN   But one fiend at a time,
  I'll fight their legions o'er!
ANTONIO   I'll be thy second.
                              Exeunt [SEBASTIAN *and* ANTONIO].
GONZALO   All three of them are desperate: their great guilt,   105
  Like poison given to work a great time after,
  Now gins to bite the spirits. I do beseech you
  That are of suppler joints, follow them swiftly,
  And hinder them from what this ecstasy
  May now provoke them to.
ADRIAN   Follow, I pray you.   *Exeunt.*   110

                              4.1
                Enter PROSPERO, FERDINAND, *and* MIRANDA.
PROSPERO [*to* FERDINAND]   If I have too austerely punished you,
  Your compensation makes amends, for I
  Have given you here a third of mine own life—
  Or that for which I live—who once again
  I tender to thy hand. All thy vexations   5
  Were but my trials of thy love, and thou
  Hast strangely stood the test. Here, afore heaven,
  I ratify this my rich gift. O Ferdinand,

97.   **billows:** waves; **it:** That is, my sin.
100. **bass my trespass:** proclaim my guilt in a bass voice.
101. **Therefore:** For that reason.
102. **plummet:** lead weight (to measure depth of water); **sounded:** tested.
103–04. **But . . . o'er:** If the fiends come one at a time, I'll fight all of them.
104. **second:** assistant.
105. **desperate:** in despair; reckless.
107. **gins:** begins; **bite:** sap.
109. **ecstasy:** frenzy.
1.   **austerely:** severely.
3.   **a third . . . life:** That is, Miranda. It is not clear whether Prospero means she repre-
      sents a large part of what he cares about, or whether he has devoted a third of his life
      to her upbringing.
5.   **tender:** offer.
7.   **strangely:** wonderfully.
8.   **ratify:** confirm.

Do not smile at me that I boast her off,
For thou shalt find she will outstrip all praise   10
And make it halt behind her.

FERDINAND   I do believe it against an oracle.

PROSPERO   Then, as my guest, and thine own acquisition
Worthily purchased, take my daughter. But
If thou dost break her virgin-knot before   15
All sanctimonious ceremonies may
With full and holy rite be ministered,
No sweet aspersion shall the heavens let fall
To make this contract grow; but barren hate,
Sour-eyed disdain, and discord shall bestrew   20
The union of your bed with weeds so loathly
That you shall hate it both. Therefore take heed,
As Hymen's lamps shall light you.

FERDINAND   As I hope
For quiet days, fair issue, and long life,
With such love as 'tis now, the murkiest den,   25
The most opportune place, the strong'st suggestion
Our worser genius can, shall never melt
Mine honor into lust, to take away
The edge of that day's celebration
When I shall think or Phoebus' steeds are foundered,   30
Or night kept chained below.

PROSPERO   Fairly spoke.
Sit then and talk with her: she is thine own.
—What, Ariel! My industrious servant, Ariel!

          Enter ARIEL.

ARIEL   What would my potent master? Here I am.

PROSPERO   Thou and thy meaner fellows your last service   35
Did worthily perform, and I must use you

---

9. **boast her off:** That is, boast of her.
11. **halt:** limp.
13. **against an oracle:** even if an oracle should pronounce otherwise.
14. **purchased:** earned.
16. **sanctimonious:** sacred.
18. **aspersion:** sprinkling of water.
23. **Hymen's lamps:** Wedding torches (Hymen was the Roman god of marriage); **shall light you:** If the torches burned brightly, it was a good omen for a happy marriage: Prospero warns them not to behave in a way that will jeopardize their good fortune.
24. **fair issue:** beautiful children.
26. **suggestion:** temptation.
27. **worser genius:** evil attendant spirit; **can:** That is, can make.
29. **edge:** sharpness of appetite or pleasure.
30-31. **or . . . Or:** either . . . or
30. **Phoebus' . . . foundered:** The sun god's horses are made lame (that is, he will be kept waiting for the wedding night).
35. **meaner fellows:** lesser spirits.

In such another trick. Go bring the rabble
O'er whom I give thee pow'r here to this place.
Incite them to quick motion, for I must
Bestow upon the eyes of this young couple   40
Some vanity of mine art. It is my promise,
And they expect it from me.

ARIEL   Presently?

PROSPERO   Ay, with a twink.

ARIEL   Before you can say "come" and "go,"
And breathe twice and cry "so, so,"   45
Each one tripping on his toe,
Will be here with mop and mow.
Do you love me, master? No?

PROSPERO   Dearly, my delicate Ariel. Do not approach
Till thou dost hear me call.

ARIEL   Well; I conceive.   *Exit.*   50

PROSPERO [*to* FERDINAND]   Look thou be true; do not give
    dalliance
Too much the rein. The strongest oaths are straw
To th' fire i'th' blood. Be more abstemious,
Or else good night your vow.

FERDINAND   I warrant you, sir,
The white cold virgin snow upon my heart   55
Abates the ardor of my liver.

PROSPERO   Well.
—Now come, my Ariel: bring a corollary
Rather than want a spirit. Appear, and pertly.
        Soft music.
No tongue, all eyes! Be silent!
        Enter IRIS.

IRIS   Ceres, most bounteous lady, thy rich leas   60
Of wheat, rye, barley, vetches, oats, and peas;

---

37. **trick:** ingenious device; theatrical performance; **rabble:** That is, the spirits, not the
    courtiers.
41. **vanity:** trifle, minor display.
42. **Presently:** Immediately.
43. **with a twink:** in the time it takes to wink.
47. **mop and mow:** grimaces.
50. **conceive:** understand.
51. **true:** steadfast, true to your word.
51–52. **do not . . . rein:** do not give flirtation too much freedom.
54. **Or . . . vow:** Or else say "good night" to your promise; **warrant:** assure.
55–56. **The . . . liver:** That is, keeping his or Miranda's chastity (pure and cold as snow)
    in his heart will balance his hot passions (thought to have their seat in the liver).
57–58. **bring . . . spirit:** bring one too many spirits rather than lack enough; **pertly:**
    briskly.
59. **No tongue:** That is, no speaking.
60. **Ceres:** Goddess of the earth; **leas:** meadows.
61. **vetches:** tares, weedy plants grown for fodder.

Thy turfy mountains where live nibbling sheep,
And flat meads thatched with stover, them to keep;
Thy banks with pionèd and twillèd brims,
Which spongy April at thy hest betrims   65
To make cold nymphs chaste crowns; and thy broom-groves,
Whose shadow the dismissèd bachelor loves,
Being lass-lorn; thy poll-clipped vineyard,
And thy sea-marge, sterile and rocky-hard,
Where thou thyself dost air—the queen o'th' sky,   70
Whose wat'ry arch and messenger am I,
Bids thee leave these, and with her sovereign grace,
Here on this grass-plot, in this very place
To come and sport. Her peacocks fly amain.
Approach, rich Ceres, her to entertain.   75
   Enter CERES.
CERES Hail, many-colored messenger, that ne'er
Dost disobey the wife of Jupiter;
Who with thy saffron wings upon my flowers
Diffusest honey-drops, refreshing showers,
And with each end of thy blue bow dost crown   80
My bosky acres and my unshrubbed down,
Rich scarf to my proud earth. Why hath thy queen
Summoned me hither to this short-grassed green?
IRIS A contract of true love to celebrate
And some donation freely to estate   85
On the blessed lovers.
CERES   Tell me, heavenly bow,
If Venus or her son, as thou dost know,
Do now attend the Queen? Since they did plot
The means that dusky Dis my daughter got,

---

63. **thatched with stover:** meadows covered with winter forage.
64. **pionèd:** dug out; **twillèd:** braided (perhaps suggesting the use of woven foliage to prevent erosion from the current).
65. **spongy:** wet; **hest:** behest.
66. **cold:** chaste; **broom-groves:** clumps of broom or gorse (thorny shrubs with yellow flowers).
68. **poll-clipped:** pruned.
69. **sea-marge:** shore.
70. **queen o'th' sky:** That is, Juno.
71. **wat'ry arch:** rainbow.
74. **peacocks:** the sacred birds that pull Juno's chariot; **amain:** quickly.
75. **entertain:** greet.
81. **bosky:** covered with bushes; **unshrubbed down:** bare hills.
82. **Rich scarf:** That is, the rainbow.
85. **estate:** bestow.
87. **son:** That is, Cupid; **as:** as far as.
88–89. **they . . . got:** According to Ovid, Venus (goddess of love) and Cupid (god of desire; son of Venus and Mars, the god of war) arranged for Proserpina (daughter of Ceres) to be abducted by dark Pluto ("dusky Dis," god of the underworld).

Her and her blind boy's scandaled company   90
I have forsworn.
IRIS   Of her society
Be not afraid. I met her deity
Cutting the clouds towards Paphos, and her son
Dove-drawn with her. Here thought they to have done
Some wanton charm upon this man and maid,   95
Whose vows are that no bed-right shall be paid
Till Hymen's torch be lighted; but in vain.
Mars's hot minion is returned again;
Her waspish-headed son has broke his arrows,
Swears he will shoot no more but play with sparrows,   100
And be a boy right out.
         JUNO *descends.*
CERES   Highest queen of state,
Great Juno comes; I know her by her gait.
JUNO   How does my bounteous sister? Go with me
To bless this twain that they may prosperous be
And honored in their issue.   105
         [JUNO *and* CERES] *sing.*
                    Honor, riches, marriage-blessing,
                    Long continuance and increasing,
                    Hourly joys be still upon you,
                    Juno sings her blessings on you.
CERES   Earth's increase and foison plenty, 110
                    Barns and garners never empty,
                    Vines with clust'ring bunches growing,
                    Plants with goodly burden bowing;
                    Spring come to you at the farthest,
                    In the very end of harvest.   115
                    Scarcity and want shall shun you,
                    Ceres' blessing so is on you.
FERDINAND   This is a most majestic vision, and

---

90. **blind:** Cupid was traditionally pictured with a blindfold (to suggest that "love is
     blind").
91. **society:** company.
93. **Paphos:** A city in Cyprus, sacred to Venus and her followers.
94. **Dove-drawn:** Venus's chariot was pulled by doves.
95. **wanton:** lewd.
97. **Hymen's . . . lighted:** Until they have been married.
98. **Mars's hot minion:** That is, Venus, lover of Mars.
99. **waspish-headed:** referring to the sting both of his arrows and of his personality.
101. **right out:** simply.
108. **still:** always.
110. **foison:** abundance.
111. **garners:** granaries.
114–15. **Spring . . . harvest:** May spring follow the harvest (so that there will be no
     winter).

Harmonious charmingly. May I be bold
To think these spirits?

PROSPERO   Spirits, which by mine art   120
I have from their confines called to enact
My present fancies.

FERDINAND   Let me live here ever!
So rare a wondered father and a wise
Makes this place paradise.

          JUNO *and* CERES *whisper, and send* IRIS *on*
          employment.

PROSPERO   Sweet now, silence.
Juno and Ceres whisper seriously.   125
There's something else to do. Hush and be mute,
Or else our spell is marred.

IRIS   You nymphs called naiads of the wind'ring brooks,
With your sedged crowns and ever-harmless looks,
Leave your crisp channels, and on this green land   130
Answer your summons; Juno does command.
Come, temperate nymphs, and help to celebrate
A contract of true love. Be not too late.

          Enter certain Nymphs.

—You sunburned sicklemen of August weary,
Come hither from the furrow and be merry;   135
Make holiday; your rye-straw hats put on,
And these fresh nymphs encounter every one
In country footing.

          Enter certain Reapers, properly habited. They join
          with the Nymphs in a graceful dance, towards the
          end whereof PROSPERO *starts suddenly and speaks,*
          after which, to a strange, hollow, and confused noise,
          they heavily vanish.

PROSPERO   I had forgot that foul conspiracy
Of the beast Caliban and his confederates   140
Against my life. The minute of their plot
Is almost come. [*to the Spirits*] Well done. Avoid, no more!

FERDINAND   This is strange: your father's in some passion

---

122. **fancies:** illusions; whims.
123. **wondered:** wondrous; full of wonders.
128. **nymphs:** the female spirits who peopled the countryside; **naiads:** spirits associated
     with water; **wind'ring:** The only known use of this word, which may combine the
     senses of wandering and winding.
129. **sedged crowns:** garlands made from sedges (rushlike plants growing at the edges of
     rivers).
137–38. **encounter . . . footing:** join in a rustic dance.
138 **SD. habited:** dressed.
142. **Avoid:** Leave.

That works him strongly.
MIRANDA   Never till this day
Saw I him touched with anger so distempered.   145
PROSPERO   You do look, my son, in a movèd sort,
As if you were dismayed. Be cheerful, sir.
Our revels now are ended. These our actors,
As I foretold you, were all spirits and
Are melted into air, into thin air;   150
And like the baseless fabric of this vision,
The cloud-capped towers, the gorgeous palaces,
The solemn temples, the great globe itself,
Yea, all which it inherit, shall dissolve,
And, like this insubstantial pageant faded,   155
Leave not a rack behind. We are such stuff
As dreams are made on, and our little life
Is rounded with a sleep. Sir, I am vexed.
Bear with my weakness: my old brain is troubled.
Be not disturbed with my infirmity.   160
If you be pleased, retire into my cell
And there repose. A turn or two I'll walk
To still my beating mind.
FERDINAND *and* MIRANDA   We wish your peace.   *Exeunt.*
PROSPERO   Come with a thought. I thank thee, Ariel. Come.
        Enter ARIEL.
ARIEL   Thy thoughts I cleave to. What's thy pleasure?
PROSPERO   Spirit,   165
We must prepare to meet with Caliban.
ARIEL   Ay, my commander. When I presented Ceres
I thought to have told thee of it, but I feared
Lest I might anger thee.
PROSPERO   Say again, where didst thou leave these varlets?   170
ARIEL   I told you, sir, they were red hot with drinking;
So full of valor that they smote the air

144. **works:** affects, afflicts.
146. **movèd sort:** perturbed state.
148. **revels:** entertainment: technically, the dances concluding court masques.
149. **foretold you:** told you before.
151. **baseless fabric:** structure without foundation (or, possibly, purpose).
153. **great globe:** the world, but also recalling the Globe theater.
154. **all . . . inherit:** That is, succeeding generations.
155. **pageant:** A technical term referring to a symbolic scene performed on a stage or to the stage itself; also a theatrical trick (like the "vanity" of line 41).
156. **rack:** cloud, mist.
157. **on:** That is, of.
158. **rounded:** surrounded; concluded.
167. **presented Ceres:** either "played the role of Ceres" or "produced the masque of Ceres."
170. **varlets:** servants; probably also "rogues."

For breathing in their faces, beat the ground
For kissing of their feet; yet always bending
Towards their project. Then I beat my tabor,   175
At which like unbacked colts they pricked their ears,
Advanced their eyelids, lifted up their noses
As they smelt music. So I charmed their ears
That calf-like they my lowing followed through
Toothed briars, sharp furzes, pricking gorse, and thorns,   180
Which entered their frail shins. At last I left them
I'th' filthy-mantled pool beyond your cell,
There dancing up to th' chins, that the foul lake
O'erstunk their feet.
PROSPERO   This was well done, my bird.
Thy shape invisible retain thou still.   185
The trumpery in my house, go bring it hither
For stale to catch these thieves.
ARIEL   I go, I go.   *Exit.*
PROSPERO   A devil, a born devil, on whose nature
Nurture can never stick; on whom my pains,
Humanely taken, all, all lost, quite lost;   190
And, as with age his body uglier grows,
So his mind cankers. I will plague them all,
Even to roaring.
        Enter ARIEL, *laden with glistering apparel, etc.*
        —Come, hang them on this line.
     Enter CALIBAN, STEFANO, *and* TRINCULO, *all wet.*
CALIBAN   Pray you tread softly, that the blind mole may not
Hear a foot fall. We now are near his cell.   195
STEFANO   Monster, your fairy, which you say is a harmless
fairy, has done little better than played the jack with us.
TRINCULO   Monster, I do smell all horse piss, at which my
nose is in great indignation.
STEFANO   So is mine. Do you hear, monster? If I should take   200
a displeasure against you, look you—

---

174. **bending:** That is, moving.
176. **unbacked:** unbroken.
177. **Advanced:** Raised.
178. **As:** As if.
179. **lowing:** mooing.
182. **filthy-mantled:** covered with scum.
184. **O'erstunk:** Smelled more than.
186. **trumpery:** gaudy clothing.
187. **stale:** bait.
192. **cankers:** festers or decays.
193. **line:** Probably a linden or lime tree rather than a clothesline.
197. **jack:** knave.

TRINCULO   Thou wert but a lost monster.

CALIBAN   Good my lord, give me thy favor still.
Be patient, for the prize I'll bring thee to
Shall hoodwink this mischance. Therefore speak softly;   205
All's hushed as midnight yet.

TRINCULO   Ay, but to lose our bottles in the pool!

STEFANO   There is not only disgrace and dishonor in that,
monster, but an infinite loss.

TRINCULO   That's more to me than my wetting. Yet this is   210
your harmless fairy, monster.

STEFANO   I will fetch off my bottle, though I be o'er ears for
my labor.

CALIBAN   Prithee, my king, be quiet. Seest thou here:
This is the mouth o'th' cell. No noise, and enter.   215
Do that good mischief which may make this island
Thine own forever, and I, thy Caliban,
For aye thy foot-licker.

STEFANO   Give me thy hand. I do begin to have bloody thoughts.

TRINCULO   O King Stefano, O peer! O worthy Stefano, look   220
what a wardrobe here is for thee.

CALIBAN   Let it alone, thou fool. It is but trash.

TRINCULO   Oh ho, monster! We know what belongs to a
frippery. O King Stefano!

STEFANO   Put off that gown, Trinculo: by this hand, I'll have   225
that gown.

TRINCULO   Thy grace shall have it.

CALIBAN   The dropsy drown this fool! What do you mean
To dote thus on such luggage? Let't alone
And do the murder first. If he awake,   230
From toe to crown he'll fill our skins with pinches,
Make us strange stuff.

STEFANO   Be you quiet, monster. Mistress line, is not this my
jerkin? Now is the jerkin under the line. Now, jerkin, you
are like to lose your hair and prove a bald jerkin.   235

---

202. **lost:** ruined; banished (as in Stefano's threat at lines 248–49).
205. **hoodwink this mischance:** drive our current misfortune from sight and memory.
218. **For aye:** Forever.
220. **O . . . peer:** An allusion to the old ballad beginning "King Stephen was a worthy peer."
224. **frippery:** secondhand-clothing shop (that is, this is *not* "trash").
228. **dropsy:** a disease characterized by excess fluid in the body; an insatiable thirst.
229. **luggage:** cumbersome baggage.
233. **Mistress line:** Addressed to the tree.
234. **jerkin:** leather jacket; **Now . . . line:** Under the tree, but punning on the sense of having journeyed below the equinoctial or equatorial line.
235. **like:** likely; **lose . . . jerkin:** Sailors on long voyages were said to lose their hair (from scurvy, fever, or other diseases), but Stefano is also playing crudely on the loss of hair from syphilis.

TRINCULO   Do, do! We steal by line and level, an't like your
    grace.
STEFANO   I thank thee for that jest. Here's a garment for't. Wit
    shall not go unrewarded while I am king of this country.
    "Steal by line and level" is an excellent pass of pate. There's   240
    another garment for't.
TRINCULO   Monster, come, put some lime upon your fingers
    and away with the rest.
CALIBAN   I will have none on't. We shall lose our time
    And all be turned to barnacles, or to apes   245
    With foreheads villainous low.
STEFANO   Monster, lay to your fingers. Help to bear this
    away, where my hogshead of wine is, or I'll turn you out of my
    kingdom. Go to, carry this.
TRINCULO   And this.   250
STEFANO   Ay, and this.
            A noise of hunters heard. Enter diverse SPIRITS in
            shape of dogs and hounds, hunting them about,
            PROSPERO and ARIEL setting them on.
PROSPERO   Hey, Mountain, hey!
ARIEL   Silver! There it goes, Silver!
PROSPERO   Fury, Fury! There, Tyrant, there! Hark, hark!
            [CALIBAN, STEFANO, and TRINCULO are chased off by
            SPIRITS.]
            [to ARIEL] Go, charge my goblins that they grind their joints 255
    With dry convulsions, shorten up their sinews
    With agèd cramps, and more pinch-spotted make them
    Than pard or cat o'mountain.
ARIEL   Hark, they roar!
PROSPERO   Let them be hunted soundly. At this hour
    Lies at my mercy all mine enemies.   260
    Shortly shall all my labors end, and thou
    Shalt have the air at freedom. For a little,
    Follow and do me service.   Exeunt.

---

236. **by line and level:** with plumb line and carpenter's level, that is, properly; **an't like:**
    if it please.
240. **pass of pate:** witty stroke (a fencing metaphor: a pass was a thrust and the pate was
    the head, the seat of wit).
242. **lime:** birdlime, to make Caliban's fingers sticky.
243. **away:** make off.
245. **barnacles:** A type of goose, thought to be hatched from barnacles growing on trees
    (though the word was derived from the term for "torturing with pinches," so there
    may be a connection to Prospero's threatened punishments).
246. **villainous:** churlishly; wretchedly.
247. **lay to:** set to work.
251 **SD. diverse:** various.
257. **agèd:** like those of old age.
258. **pard or cat o'mountain:** both refer to the leopard or panther.

5.1

Enter PROSPERO *in his magic robes, and* ARIEL.

PROSPERO   Now does my project gather to a head:
My charms crack not, my spirits obey, and time
Goes upright with his carriage. How's the day?
ARIEL   On the sixth hour; at which time, my lord,
You said our work should cease.
PROSPERO   I did say so   5
When first I raised the tempest. Say, my spirit,
How fares the King and 's followers?
ARIEL   Confined together
In the same fashion as you gave in charge,
Just as you left them; all prisoners, sir,
In the line-grove which weather-fends your cell: 10
They cannot budge till your release. The King,
His brother, and yours abide all three distracted,
And the remainder mourning over them,
Brimful of sorrow and dismay; but chiefly
Him that you termed, sir, the good old Lord Gonzalo: 15
His tears runs down his beard like winter's drops
From eaves of reeds. Your charm so strongly works 'em
That if you now beheld them, your affections
Would become tender.
PROSPERO   Dost thou think so, spirit?
ARIEL   Mine would, sir, were I human.
PROSPERO   And mine shall.   20
Hast thou, which art but air, a touch, a feeling
Of their afflictions, and shall not myself—
One of their kind, that relish all as sharply
Passion as they—be kindlier moved than thou art?
Though with their high wrongs I am struck to th' quick,   25
Yet with my nobler reason 'gainst my fury
Do I take part. The rarer action is

1–2. **project . . . crack:** Prospero is using the language of alchemy to describe the climax of his plan ("project"). The materials, when heated, would "gather to a head"; if the experiment failed, the container would "crack," and if it succeeded, the alchemist would achieve the philosopher's stone (and with it the means of "projection," or transmutation of base metals into gold or silver).
3. **carriage:** burden.
7. **and 's:** and his.
10. **line-grove:** grove of lime or linden trees; **weather-fends:** defends from the weather.
11. **till your release:** until you release them.
17. **eaves of reeds:** thatched roofs; **works:** acts upon; agitates.
21. **touch:** sense.
23–24. **relish . . . they:** feel suffering just as acutely as they do.
24. **kindlier:** more humanely.
25. **quick:** center, most sensitive part.
27. **rarer:** less common; more noble.

In virtue than in vengeance. They being penitent,
The sole drift of my purpose doth extend
Not a frown further. Go, release them, Ariel.   30
My charms I'll break, their senses I'll restore,
And they shall be themselves.
ARIEL   I'll fetch them, sir.   *Exit.*
     [PROSPERO *makes a circle on the stage.*]
PROSPERO   Ye elves of hills, brooks, standing lakes, and groves,
And ye that on the sands with printless foot
Do chase the ebbing Neptune, and do fly him   35
When he comes back; you demi-puppets that
By moonshine do the green sour ringlets make,
Whereof the ewe not bites; and you, whose pastime
Is to make midnight-mushrooms, that rejoice
To hear the solemn curfew; by whose aid—   40
Weak masters though ye be—I have bedimmed
The noontide sun, called forth the mutinous winds,
And twixt the green sea and the azured vault
Set roaring war; to the dread rattling thunder
Have I given fire, and rifted Jove's stout oak   45
With his own bolt; the strong-based promontory
Have I made shake, and by the spurs plucked up
The pine and cedar. Graves at my command
Have waked their sleepers, oped, and let 'em forth
By my so potent art. But this rough magic   50
I here abjure; and when I have required
Some heavenly music—which even now I do—
To work mine end upon their senses that
This airy charm is for, I'll break my staff,
Bury it certain fathoms in the earth,   55
And deeper than did ever plummet sound
I'll drown my book.

33–50. Prospero's speech paraphrases Medea's invocation in Book 7 of Ovid's *Metamorphoses.*
35. **ebbing Neptune**: That is, the waves or tide.
36. **demi-puppets**: small puppets (that is, fairies).
37. **green sour ringlets**: circles made by fairies in the grass.
40. **curfew**: evening bell.
41. **Weak masters**: Agents of limited power.
43. **azured vault**: That is, the sky.
45. **fire**: lightning; **rifted**: split.
46. **promontory**: land jutting into the sea.
47. **spurs**: roots.
51. **required**: requested.
55. **certain**: several.
56. **plummet**: a weight attached to a line, used to measure (sound) the depth of water.

Solemn music.
Here enters ARIEL *before; then* ALONSO *with a frantic*
gesture, attended by GONZALO; SEBASTIAN *and*
ANTONIO *in like manner, attended by* ADRIAN *and*
FRANCISCO. *They all enter the circle which* PROSPERO
had made, and there stand charmed; which PROSPERO
observing, speaks.

A solemn air and the best comforter
To an unsettled fancy cure thy brains,
Now useless, boiled within thy skull. There stand,   60
For you are spell-stopped.
Holy Gonzalo, honorable man,
Mine eyes, e'en sociable to the show of thine,
Fall fellowly drops. [*aside*] The charm dissolves apace
And, as the morning steals upon the night,   65
Melting the darkness, so their rising senses
Begin to chase the ignorant fumes that mantle
Their clearer reason. —O good Gonzalo,
My true preserver and a loyal sir
To him thou follow'st, I will pay thy graces   70
Home both in word and deed. Most cruelly
Didst thou, Alonso, use me and my daughter.
Thy brother was a furtherer in the act:
Thou art pinched for't now, Sebastian. Flesh and blood,
You, brother mine, that entertained ambition,   75
Expelled remorse and nature, whom with Sebastian—
Whose inward pinches therefore are most strong—
Would here have killed your king, I do forgive thee,
Unnatural though thou art. [*aside*] Their understanding
Begins to swell, and the approaching tide   80
Will shortly fill the reasonable shore
That now lies foul and muddy. Not one of them
That yet looks on me or would know me. —Ariel,
Fetch me the hat and rapier in my cell.
                              [ARIEL *exits and returns.*]

57 **SD. frantic:** excited; insane.
58. **air:** musical tune; **and:** That is, which is.
59. **fancy:** imagination.
63. **sociable:** sympathetic.
64. **Fall:** Let fall.
67. **mantle:** cloud.
70–71. **pay . . . Home:** reward your favors fully.
73. **furtherer:** accomplice.
74. **pinched:** punished; suffering.
76. **nature:** human, and brotherly, feelings.
81. **reasonable shore:** That is, the edges of their reason.

I will discase me and myself present   85
As I was sometime Milan. Quickly, spirit!
Thou shalt ere long be free.
          ARIEL *sings and helps to attire him.*
ARIEL   Where the bee sucks, there suck I;
               In a cowslip's bell I lie;
               There I couch when owls do cry;   90
               On the bat's back I do fly
               After summer merrily.
               Merrily, merrily shall I live now,
               Under the blossom that hangs on the bough.
PROSPERO   Why, that's my dainty Ariel! I shall miss   95
Thee, but yet thou shalt have freedom.—So, so, so.
To the King's ship, invisible as thou art;
There shalt thou find the mariners asleep
Under the hatches. The Master and the Boatswain
Being awake, enforce them to this place,   100
And presently, I prithee.
ARIEL   I drink the air before me and return
Or ere your pulse twice beat.   *Exit.*
GONZALO   All torment, trouble, wonder, and amazement
Inhabits here. Some heavenly power guide us   105
Out of this fearful country!
PROSPERO   Behold, sir King,
The wrongèd Duke of Milan, Prospero.
For more assurance that a living prince
Does now speak to thee, I embrace thy body
And to thee and thy company I bid   110
A hearty welcome.
ALONSO   Whe'er thou beest he or no,
Or some enchanted trifle to abuse me—
As late I have been—I not know. Thy pulse
Beats as of flesh and blood; and since I saw thee,
Th'affliction of my mind amends, with which,   115
I fear, a madness held me. This must crave—

85. **discase:** undress.
86. **As . . . Milan:** As when I was Duke of Milan.
90. **couch:** lie down; **when owls do cry:** That is, at night.
92. **After summer:** That is, pursuing it from climate to climate.
96. **So . . . so:** Prospero is either arranging his attire or approving the final look.
100. **Being awake:** Once they are awake; **enforce:** compel, lead.
101. **presently:** immediately.
103. **Or ere:** Before.
104. **amazement:** bewilderment.
111. **Whe'er:** Whether.
112. **trifle:** trick, illusion; **abuse:** deceive; torment.
115. **amends:** improves.
116. **crave:** require.

An if this be at all—a most strange story.
Thy dukedom I resign and do entreat
Thou pardon me my wrongs. But how should Prospero
Be living, and be here?
PROSPERO [*to* GONZALO]   First, noble friend,   120
Let me embrace thine age, whose honor cannot
Be measured or confined.
GONZALO   Whether this be
Or be not, I'll not swear.
PROSPERO   You do yet taste
Some subtleties o'th' isle, that will not let you
Believe things certain. Welcome, my friends all.   125
[*aside to* SEBASTIAN *and* ANTONIO] But you, my brace of
     lords, were I so minded
I here could pluck his highness' frown upon you
And justify you traitors. At this time
I will tell no tales.
SEBASTIAN [*to* ANTONIO]   The devil speaks in him!
PROSPERO   No.
[*to* ANTONIO] For you, most wicked sir, whom to call brother   130
Would even infect my mouth, I do forgive
Thy rankest fault—all of them—and require
My dukedom of thee, which perforce I know
Thou must restore.
ALONSO   If thou beest Prospero,
Give us particulars of thy preservation;   135
How thou hast met us here, whom three hours since
Were wrecked upon this shore, where I have lost—
How sharp the point of this remembrance is—
My dear son Ferdinand.
PROSPERO   I am woe for't, sir.
ALONSO   Irreparable is the loss, and patience   140
Says it is past her cure.
PROSPERO   I rather think
You have not sought her help, of whose soft grace
For the like loss I have her sovereign aid

---

117. **An . . . all:** If this is real.
124. **subtleties:** magical illusions (playing on the additional sense of "elaborate pastries").
126. **brace:** pair (usually applied to animals).
127. **pluck:** pull.
128. **justify:** prove.
132. **rankest:** foulest.
133. **perforce:** necessarily.
139. **woe:** sorry.
142. **soft:** gentle, compassionate.
143. **sovereign:** supreme; potent.

And rest myself content.

ALONSO   You the like loss?

PROSPERO   As great to me as late; and supportable   145
To make the dear loss have I means much weaker
Than you may call to comfort you, for I
Have lost my daughter.

ALONSO   A daughter?
O heavens, that they were living both in Naples,
The King and Queen there! That they were, I wish   150
Myself were mudded in that oozy bed
Where my son lies. When did you lose your daughter?

PROSPERO   In this last tempest. I perceive these lords
At this encounter do so much admire
That they devour their reason and scarce think   155
Their eyes do offices of truth, their words
Are natural breath. But, howsoe'er you have
Been jostled from your senses, know for certain
That I am Prospero, and that very duke
Which was thrust forth of Milan, who most strangely   160
Upon this shore where you were wrecked, was landed
To be the lord on't. No more yet of this,
For 'tis a chronicle of day by day,
Not a relation for a breakfast, nor
Befitting this first meeting. Welcome, sir;   165
This cell's my court. Here have I few attendants
And subjects none abroad. Pray you look in.
My dukedom since you have given me again,
I will requite you with as good a thing;
At least bring forth a wonder to content ye   170
As much as me my dukedom.

                    Here PROSPERO *discovers* FERDINAND *and*
                    MIRANDA *playing at chess.*

MIRANDA   Sweet lord, you play me false.

FERDINAND   No, my dearest love,

---

145. late: recent.
145–46. supportable . . . loss: to make the grievous loss bearable.
150. That they were: In order to make it possible.
151. mudded: buried in the mud.
154. admire: wonder.
156. do . . . truth: perform truthfully.
160. of: from.
163. chronicle: narrative; **day by day:** either requiring several days to tell or involving the details of every day's events.
164. relation: report.
167. abroad: elsewhere.
171 SD. discovers: reveals (probably by pulling back a curtain across a door or recess at the back of the stage).
172. play me false: That is, you are cheating.

I would not for the world.

MIRANDA   Yes, for a score of kingdoms you should wrangle,
And I would call it fair play.

ALONSO   If this prove   175
A vision of the island, one dear son
Shall I twice lose.

SEBASTIAN   A most high miracle!

FERDINAND   Though the seas threaten, they are merciful:
I have cursed them without cause.

        [FERDINAND *kneels.*]

ALONSO   Now all the blessings
Of a glad father compass thee about!   180
Arise, and say how thou cam'st here.

MIRANDA   Oh, wonder!
How many goodly creatures are there here!
How beauteous mankind is! Oh, brave new world
That has such people in't!

PROSPERO   'Tis new to thee.

ALONSO [*to* FERDINAND]   What is this maid with whom thou   185
    wast at play?
Your eld'st acquaintance cannot be three hours.
Is she the goddess that hath severed us
And brought us thus together?

FERDINAND   Sir, she is mortal;
But by immortal Providence she's mine.
I chose her when I could not ask my father   190
For his advice, nor thought I had one. She
Is daughter to this famous Duke of Milan—
Of whom so often I have heard renown
But never saw before—of whom I have
Received a second life; and second father   195
This lady makes him to me.

ALONSO   I am hers.
But oh, how oddly will it sound that I
Must ask my child forgiveness!

PROSPERO   There, sir, stop.
Let us not burden our remembrances with

---

174. **score . . . wrangle:** That is, even if we were playing for twenty ("a score of") king-
    doms, which is less than "the world," you would still contend with me ("wrangle,"
    with a possible implication of cheating).
176. **of the island:** of the kind this island produces.
180. **compass thee about:** surround you.
183. **brave:** excellent, but also beautiful and finely dressed.
186. **eld'st:** longest.
194. **of:** from.

A heaviness that's gone.
GONZALO   I have inly wept,   200
Or should have spoke ere this. Look down, you gods,
And on this couple drop a blessèd crown.
For it is you that have chalked forth the way
Which brought us hither.
ALONSO   I say "Amen," Gonzalo.
GONZALO   Was Milan thrust from Milan that his issue   205
Should become kings of Naples? Oh, rejoice
Beyond a common joy and set it down
With gold on lasting pillars: in one voyage
Did Claribel her husband find at Tunis,
And Ferdinand her brother found a wife   210
Where he himself was lost; Prospero his dukedom
In a poor isle; and all of us ourselves
When no man was his own.
ALONSO [to FERDINAND and MIRANDA]   Give me your hands.
Let grief and sorrow still embrace his heart   215
That doth not wish you joy.
GONZALO   Be it so. Amen.
        Enter ARIEL, *with the* MASTER *and* BOATSWAIN *amazedly*
           following.
Oh, look, sir, look, sir: here is more of us.
I prophesied if a gallows were on land
This fellow could not drown. [to BOATSWAIN] Now, blasphemy,
That swear'st grace o'erboard, not an oath on shore?   220
Hast thou no mouth by land? What is the news?
BOATSWAIN   The best news is that we have safely found
Our king and company; the next, our ship,
Which but three glasses since we gave out split,
Is tight and yare and bravely rigged as when   225
We first put out to sea.
ARIEL [to PROSPERO]   Sir, all this service
Have I done since I went.
PROSPERO [to ARIEL]   My tricksy spirit!

200. heaviness: sadness; inly: inwardly.
203. chalked . . . way: marked the path (as with a piece of chalk).
205. issue: descendants.
213. his own in possession of his senses or identity.
215. still: always.
216 SD. amazedly: with confusion or wonder.
219. blasphemy: That is, blasphemer.
224. glasses: hours; gave out: reported.
225. tight: watertight; yare: ready to sail.
229. tricksy: playful, ingenious.

ALONSO   These are not natural events; they strengthen   230
  From strange to stranger. Say, how came you hither?
BOATSWAIN   If I did think, sir, I were well awake,
  I'd strive to tell you. We were dead of sleep
  And—how we know not—all clapped under hatches,
  Where but even now with strange and several noises   235
  Of roaring, shrieking, howling, jingling chains,
  And more diversity of sounds, all horrible,
  We were awaked; straightway at liberty,
  Where we, in all our trim, freshly beheld
  Our royal, good, and gallant ship, our Master   240
  Cap'ring to eye her. On a trice, so please you,
  Even in a dream were we divided from them
  And were brought moping hither.
ARIEL [*to* PROSPERO]   Was't well done?
PROSPERO [*to* ARIEL]   Bravely, my diligence. Thou shalt be free.
ALONSO   This is as strange a maze as e'er men trod,   245
  And there is in this business more than nature
  Was ever conduct of. Some oracle
  Must rectify our knowledge.
PROSPERO   Sir, my liege,
  Do not infest your mind with beating on
  The strangeness of this business. At picked leisure,   250
  Which shall be shortly, single I'll resolve you—
  Which to you shall seem probable—of every
  These happened accidents. Till when, be cheerful
  And think of each thing well. [*to* ARIEL] Come hither, spirit.
  Set Caliban and his companions free: 255
  Untie the spell.   [*Exit* ARIEL.]
  [*to* ALONSO]   How fares my gracious sir?
  There are yet missing of your company
  Some few odd lads that you remember not.

230. **strengthen:** increase.
233. **of sleep:** That is, asleep.
234. **clapped under hatches:** stowed under the deck.
235. **several:** diverse.
241. **Cap'ring . . . her:** Dancing with joy at the sight of her; **On a trice:** In an instant.
243. **moping:** in a daze.
247. **conduct:** guide.
248. **rectify:** put right.
249. **infest:** trouble; **beating on:** That is, incessantly worrying about.
250. **picked:** chosen.
251. **single:** privately; by my own power; **resolve:** explain to.
252. **every:** all of.
253. **happened accidents:** occurrences.
254. **think . . . well:** look positively on things; meditate on things.
258. **Some . . . lads:** A couple of stray servants.

Enter ARIEL, *driving in* CALIBAN, STEFANO, *and*
TRINCULO *in their stolen apparel.*

STEFANO   Every man shift for all the rest, and let no man take
care for himself; for all is but fortune. *Coraggio,* bully   260
monster, *coraggio!*

TRINCULO   If these be true spies which I wear in my head,
here's a goodly sight!

CALIBAN   O Setebos, these be brave spirits indeed!
How fine my master is! I am afraid   265
He will chastise me.

SEBASTIAN   Ha, ha! What things are these, my lord Antonio?
Will money buy 'em?

ANTONIO   Very like. One of them
Is a plain fish, and no doubt marketable.

PROSPERO   Mark but the badges of these men, my lords;   270
Then say if they be true. This misshapen knave,
His mother was a witch, and one so strong
That could control the moon, make flows and ebbs,
And deal in her command without her power.
These three have robbed me, and this demi-devil—   275
For he's a bastard one—had plotted with them
To take my life. Two of these fellows you
Must know and own; this thing of darkness I
Acknowledge mine.

CALIBAN   I shall be pinched to death.

ALONSO   Is not this Stefano, my drunken butler?   280

SEBASTIAN   He is drunk now. Where had he wine?

ALONSO   And Trinculo is reeling-ripe. Where should they
Find this grand liquor that hath gilded 'em?
How cam'st thou in this pickle?

TRINCULO   I have been in such a pickle since I saw you last that   285
I fear me will never out of my bones: I shall not fear flyblowing.

259. **shift:** look out for.
259–60. **Every . . . himself:** Stefano drunkenly reverses the usual phrases.
260. *Coraggio:* Courage (Italian); **bully:** a term of friendly admiration (here probably
used ironically).
262. **If . . . head:** That is, if my eyes do not deceive me.
268. **like:** likely.
270. **badges:** emblems worn by servants to identify their masters. The insignia on their
clothing would probably be Alonso's.
273. **That could:** That is, that she could.
274. **deal . . . power:** exercise the moon's influence, without her authority or assistance.
276. **bastard:** born out of wedlock; of inferior qualities.
278. **own:** acknowledge, claim.
282. **reeling-ripe:** so drunk that he can hardly walk.
283. **gilded:** made them red-faced.
284. **in this pickle:** in such a sorry state (but Trinculo's reply picks up and continues the
second meaning of "preserved in liquor"—that is, either drunk with wine or soaked
in "horse piss").
286. **flyblowing:** having fly eggs laid on him.

SEBASTIAN   Why, how now, Stefano?

STEFANO   Oh, touch me not! I am not Stefano, but a cramp.

PROSPERO   You'd be king o'the isle, sirrah?

STEFANO   I should have been a sore one then.   290

ALONSO [*indicating* CALIBAN]   This is a strange thing as e'er I
   looked on.

PROSPERO   He is as disproportioned in his manners
   As in his shape. Go, sirrah, to my cell;
   Take with you your companions. As you look   295
   To have my pardon, trim it handsomely.

CALIBAN   Ay, that I will; and I'll be wise hereafter
   And seek for grace. What a thrice-double ass
   Was I to take this drunkard for a god
   And worship this dull fool!

PROSPERO   Go to, away.   300

ALONSO   Hence, and bestow your luggage where you found it.

SEBASTIAN   Or stole it rather.

           [*Exeunt* CALIBAN, STEFANO, *and* TRINCULO.]

PROSPERO   Sir, I invite your highness and your train
   To my poor cell, where you shall take your rest
   For this one night; which—part of it—I'll waste   305
   With such discourse as, I not doubt, shall make it
   Go quick away: the story of my life
   And the particular accidents gone by
   Since I came to this isle. And in the morn
   I'll bring you to your ship, and so to Naples,   310
   Where I have hope to see the nuptial
   Of these our dear-belovèd solemnized,
   And thence retire me to my Milan, where
   Every third thought shall be my grave.

ALONSO   I long
   To hear the story of your life, which must   315
   Take the ear strangely.

PROSPERO   I'll deliver all,
   And promise you calm seas, auspicious gales,
   And sail so expeditious that shall catch
   Your royal fleet far off. —My Ariel, chick,
   That is thy charge. Then to the elements   320

290. **sore:** aching; sorry.
295. **As you look:** If you hope.
296. **trim:** prepare.
305. **waste:** consume.
313. **retire me:** return.
316. **Take:** Strike; **deliver:** explain; set free.
318–19. **sail . . . fleet:** such speed that you will be able to rejoin the rest of the ships in
   your party.

Be free, and fare thou well. —Please you draw near.
                      Exeunt all [except PROSPERO].

                      Epilogue
              Spoken by PROSPERO.
Now my charms are all o'erthrown,
And what strength I have's mine own,
Which is most faint. Now 'tis true
I must be here confined by you,
Or sent to Naples. Let me not,   5
Since I have my dukedom got
And pardoned the deceiver, dwell
In this bare island by your spell,
But release me from my bands
With the help of your good hands.   10
Gentle breath of yours my sails
Must fill or else my project fails,
Which was to please. Now I want
Spirits to enforce, art to enchant;
And my ending is despair,   15
Unless I be relieved by prayer,
Which pierces so that it assaults
Mercy itself and frees all faults.
As you from crimes would pardoned be,
Let your indulgence set me free.   20
                              [*Exit.*]

321. **draw near:** While Prospero may be addressing the audience in preparation for his
     epilogue, he is probably inviting the courtiers into his cell.
9.   **bands:** bonds.
10. **help . . . hands:** That is, by clapping.
11. **Gentle breath:** Approving words, or perhaps whistles (probably in a nautical rather
     than theatrical context: sailors traditionally "whistled after the wind" when stalled
     in calm seas).
13. **want:** lack.
14. **enforce:** command.
17. **pierces:** moves; **assaults:** petitions.
18. **Mercy itself:** That is, God; **frees:** frees from.
20. **indulgence:** favor, but also official release from punishment for sin.

A Note on the Text

No Shakespearean text is simple, but that of *The Tempest* is simpler than most. The play was first entered in the Stationers' Register (record of the governing body for printers and booksellers) on November 8, 1623, and first printed in the First Folio later that year. There is thus only one text with any claim to authority, and it seems to have been produced more carefully than most of the texts in the Folio. We have followed all other modern editors in basing our edition upon this text.

That said, readers should be under no illusion that the words they are reading in this or any other modern edition are exactly those that flowed from Shakespeare's quill pen. As is the case with all of Shakespeare's plays, we do not have a text in Shakespeare's hand; furthermore, as with roughly half of them, we do not have one printed during his lifetime. As always with the works of Shakespeare and his contemporaries, there were a number of intermediaries between the playwright and the printed text, and the process of making the text accessible to modern readers necessarily introduces further modifications (and further distance from Shakespeare's hand).

The text used by the printers of the Folio *Tempest* was evidently prepared by Ralph Crane, a professional scrivener who produced both legal and theatrical manuscripts. Although the copy was therefore almost certainly clean, it also would have incorporated some of Crane's scribal characteristics—which, from surviving copies of his other transcripts, seem to have included a fondness for parentheses and a tendency to insert descriptive stage directions (quite possibly based on what he saw at early productions of the play). The printers who set the Folio text—and there were at least three of them—would have introduced their own habits of spelling and punctuation, and (being both human and unable to consult the late author directly) they would undoubtedly have made mistakes.

In modernizing the text, we have been guided by a goal that is straightforward in theory, if often difficult in practice: We have tried to provide an edition of the play that makes the text as accessible to modern readers as possible without sacrificing the linguistic and rhetorical complexity of the original. We have also tried to

anticipate the needs of a wide range of readers (from those new to
the play to scholars who have edited the text for themselves) and to
be as flexible as possible in matters of staging.

The format and length of this Norton Critical Edition do not
allow us to document, much less discuss, all of the ambiguities and
uncertainties in the text. As mentioned above, some of the stage
directions are probably Crane's rather than Shakespeare's. There
are also confusions in the Folio's distinctions between prose and
verse and, occasionally, in its line divisions (the layout of the songs
is particularly muddled in this play). The spelling and punctuation
have been adapted throughout to conform to current conventions,
but in some places this has involved a decision between several possible meanings in the Folio text—that is, between multiple meanings that Shakespeare may well have wanted to keep in play. And
there are some famous cruxes that require the intervention of editors: Is it Prospero or Miranda who condemns Caliban as an "Abhorrèd slave" (1.2.350)? Does Ferdinand refer to "So rare a wondered
father and a wise" or ". . . a wife" (4.1.123)? Do his female acquain-
tances in 3.1.46 "put it to the foil" or "put it to the soil"? Why is Sycorax described as "blue-eyed" (1.2.269)? And what are the "scamels"
that Caliban promises to fetch for Stefano and Trinculo in 2.2.163
(the *Oxford English Dictionary*'s only citation for the word)? Readers
interested in these details should turn to the textual comments to
the play in the Third Edition of *The Norton Shakespeare* (2016),
where the play text is identical to the one used here, and to the fuller
discussions of such matters in David Lindley's "Textual Analysis" in
his New Cambridge Shakespeare edition of the play (Cambridge:
Cambridge UP, 2013), pp. 237–68, and John Jowett's notes on the
play in Stanley Wells and Gary Taylor, with John Jowett and William
Montgomery, *William Shakespeare: A Textual Companion* (New York:
W. W. Norton, 1997), pp. 612–17.

Textual Notes

The table below lists all significant departures from our copy text
(the First Folio). Our readings appear to the left of the square bracket;
the original reading from the Folio is on the right, with any explanation by the editors in italics. SD is the standard abbreviation for stage
direction, SH for speech heading.

Because this is a modernized edition, we have not listed straightforward changes in punctuation and spelling. We have, however,
tried to include words and phrases when the Folio suggests possibilities of sound or sense that are simplified or edited out in the process
of modernization. This decision is no substitute for examining the

Folio text directly, but it will allow readers to see at a glance which acts of transcription have been especially difficult or interesting. Words added to the text by the editors always appear within square brackets, and they are not collated here. Finally, although some of our readings derive from other editions of the play, a more detailed collation is beyond the scope and purpose of this edition.

The Persons of the Play

The Persons of the Play] Names of the Actors; *at end of text*
PROSPERO] *Sometimes* Prosper
Milan] Millaine *throughout*
ARIEL] Ariell *throughout*
savage] saluage
STEFANO] Stephano *throughout*
The Scene] *at end of text*

1.1

5 cheerly] cheerely
7 SD Ferdinand] Ferdinando
23 Cheerly] cheerely
41 from] for
50 I'm] I'am
62 furze] firrs

1.2

1 art] *capitalized here and throughout*
112 wi'th' King] with King
173 princes] Princesse
200 bowsprit] Bore-spritt
229 Bermudas] Bermoothes
248 made no] made thee no
261 Algiers] Argier
282 she] he
337 vile] vild
381 SD] Burthen dispersedly *at* 380
395 SD] Ariell Song
402 SD] Burthen: ding dong.
430 wert] wer't

2.1

0 SD] and others *after* Francisco.
18 dollar] dollor
60 gloss] glosses

89 Ay] I
158 its] it
273 brother] Brothet

2.2

3 SD] *at head of scene*
45 Moll] Mall
139 o'th'] 'oth
170 SH] *omitted*
173 trencher] trenchering

3.1

2 sets] set
15 busil'est] busie lest
47 peerless] peetlesse

3.2

2 'em] em'
24 debauched] debosh'd
114 scout] cout
115 scout] skowt

3.3

18 SEBASTIAN . . . more] *after SD Solemn . . . depart*
21 SD *Enter . . . depart*] *after 17 SD*
30 islanders] Islands
34 human] humaine
66 plume] plumbe
100 bass] base

4.1

17 rite] right
52 rein] raigne
53 abstemious] abstenious
61 vetches] fetches
75 her] here
83 short-grassed] short gras'd
101 SD] *in right margin next to 73–74*
106 marriage-blessing] marriage, blessing
110 and] *omitted*
146 movèd] mou'd
169 Lest] Least

180 gorse] gosse
193 them on] on them
222 Let it] let's

5.1

20 human] humane
39 midnight-mushrooms] midnight-mushrumps
46 strong-based] strong-bass'd
60 boiled] boile
75 entertained] entertaine
82 lies] ly
111 Whe'er] where
124 not] nor
149 Naples] Nalpes
185 wast] was't
241 her] our
251 shortly, single] shortly single)
259 Coraggio] Corasio
312 dear-belovèd solemnized] deere-belou'd, solemnized
316 strangely] starngely

SOURCES AND CONTEXTS

Magic and Witchcraft

OVID

Prospero's soliloquy in 5.1, where he announces his intention to abjure his "rough magic," has strong echoes of this speech by Medea in the collection of tales titled *Metamorphoses*, by the Roman poet Ovid (43 B.C.E.– 17 C.E.). Since Medea is an enchantress known for her violence and vengefulness, the implicit comparison tends to undermine Prospero's attempt to separate his benign magic from Sycorax's malign sorcery.

[Medea]†

Before the moon should circlewise close both her horns in one
Three nights were yet as then to come. As soon as that she shone
Most full of light, and did behold the earth with fulsome face,
Medea with her hair not trussed so much as in a lace,
But flaring on her shoulders twain, and barefoot, with her gown
Ungirded, got her out of doors and wandered up and down
Alone the dead time of the night. Both man and beast and bird
Were fast asleep; the serpents sly in trailing forward stirred
So softly as you would have thought they still asleep had been.
The moisting air was whist; no leaf ye could have moving seen.
The stars alonely fair and bright did in the welkin shine.
To which she lifting up her hands did thrice herself incline,
And thrice with water of the brook her hair besprinkled she,
And gasping thrice she oped her mouth, and bowing down her knee
Upon the bare, hard ground she said, 'O trusty time of night
Most faithful unto privities, O golden stars whose light
Doth jointly with the moon succeed the beams that blaze by day,
And thou three-headed Hecatè, who knowest best the way
To compass this our great attempt and art our chiefest stay;
Ye charms and witchcrafts, and thou earth, which both with herb
      and weed

---

† From *Ovid's Metamorphoses*, trans. Arthur Golding (London: William Seres, 1567), pp. 83₁–83v.

Of mighty working furnishest the wizards at their need;
Ye airs and winds; ye elves of hills, of brooks, of woods alone,
Of standing lakes, and of the night, approach ye every one,
Through help of whom (the crooked banks much wond'ring at the
    thing)
I have compellèd streams to run clean backward to their spring.
By charms I make the calm seas rough and make the rough seas
    plain,
And cover all the sky with clouds and chase them thence again.
By charms I raise and lay the winds and burst the viper's jaw,
And from the bowels of the earth both stones and trees do draw.
Whole woods and forests I remove; I make the mountains shake,
And even the earth itself to groan and fearfully to quake.
I call up dead men from their graves; and thee, O lightsome moon,
I darken oft, though beaten brass abate thy peril soon;
Our sorcery dims the morning fair and darks the sun at noon.
The flaming breath of fiery bulls ye quenchèd for my sake,
And causèd their unwieldy necks the bended yoke to take.
Among the earth-bred brothers you a mortal war did set,
And brought asleep the dragon fell whose eyes were never shet,
By means whereof deceiving him that had the golden fleece
In charge to keep, you sent it thence by Jason into Greece.
Now have I need of herbs that can by virtue of their juice
To flowering prime of lusty youth old withered age reduce.
I am assured ye will it grant; for not in vain have shone
These twinkling stars, ne yet in vain this chariot all alone
By draught of dragons hither comes.' With that was from the sky
A chariot softly glancèd down, and stayèd hard thereby.

GIOVANNI PICO della MIRANDOLA

From Speech on the Dignity of Man[†]

Pico's *Speech*, written when he was twenty-three years old, is one of
the most impressive pieces of Renaissance humanism, justifying the
human quest for knowledge, struggling with questions of free will and
moral obligation, and attempting to bring together learned traditions
as varied as Neoplatonism and the Cabbala. Although there is no direct
evidence that Shakespeare knew the essay, it was highly esteemed by
English humanists, which has led to suggestions that Prospero may
have been modeled on Pico (1463–1494).

[†] From *The Very Elegant Speech on the Dignity of Man* [1486], trans. Charles Glenn Wal-
lis (Annapolis: The St. John's Book Store, 1940), pp. 3–4, 19–20.

Most venerable fathers, I have read in the records of the Arabians that Abdul the Saracen, on being asked what thing on the world's stage,—so to speak—, he viewed as most greatly worthy of wonder, answered that he viewed nothing more wonderful than man. And Mercury's, "a great wonder, Aesculapius, is man!" agrees with that opinion. On thinking over the reason for these sayings, I was not satisfied by the many assertions made by many men concerning the outstandingness of human nature: that man is the messenger between creatures, familiar with the upper and king of the lower; by the sharp-sightedness of the senses, by the hunting-power of reason, and by the light of intelligence the interpreter of nature: the part in-between the standstill of eternity and the flow of time; as the Persians say, the bond tying the world together, nay, the nuptial bond; and according to David, "a little lower than the angels." These reasons are great but not sufficient,—that is, they are not reasons for a lawful claim to the highest wonder as to a prerogative. Why should we not wonder more at the angels themselves and at the very blessed heavenly choirs?

Finally, I seemed to myself to have understood why man is the animal which is most happy and is therefore worthy of all wonder; and lastly, what the state is which is allotted to man in the succession of things, and which is capable of arousing envy not only in the brutes but also in the stars and even in intelligences beyond the world. The case is wonderful and beyond belief. For this is the reason why man is rightly said and thought to be a great marvel and the animal really worthy of wonder. Now hear what it is, fathers; and with kindly ears and for the sake of your manhood give me your close attention:

* * *

* * * the Best of Workmen decided that that to which nothing of its very own could be given should be, in composite fashion, whatsoever had belonged individually to each and every thing. Therefore He took up man as being, without limitations, a work of mirroring; and, placing him at the midpoint of the world, He spoke to him as follows:

"We have given to thee, Adam, no fixed seat, no form of thy very own, no gift peculiarly thine, that,—as the thirsty drink—, thou mayest feel as thine own, have as thine own, possess as thine own the seat, the form, the gifts which thou thyself shalt desire. A limited nature in other creatures is confined within the laws written down by Us. In conformity with thy free judgment, in whose hands I have placed thee, thou art confined by no bounds: and thou wilt fix the limits of thy nature for thyself. I have placed thee at the center of the world, that from there thou mayest more conveniently look around and see whatsoever is in the world. Neither heavenly nor earthly, neither mortal nor immortal have We made thee. Thou, like a judge appointed for being honorable, art the moulder and maker of thyself; thou mayest knead thyself into whatever shape thou dost prefer. Thou canst grow downward into the lower natures which are brutes. Thou canst again grow upward from thy mind's reason into the higher natures which are divine."

                    *   *   *

I have proposed theorems about magic too, wherein I have signified that there are two magics, the first of which is put together by the act and authorship of the demons, and is a thing monstrous and, as God is true, to be accursed. The second, when well explored, is nothing except the absolute consummation of the philosophy of nature. When the Greeks mention the first they think it by no means worthy of the name of magic and denominate it γοητεία [goeteia]. They call the second by its own peculiar name of μαγεία [mageia], as it were the perfected and highest wisdom. Similarly, as Porphyry says, in the Persian tongue "magus" or "magician" means what "interpreter and husbandman of divine things" means to us. Now there is a great, or rather, fathers, there is the greatest inequality and unlikeness between these arts. Not only the Christian religion but all laws and every good institution punishes, condemns, and curses the first; all wise men, all nations studious of things heavenly and divine, approve and embrace the second. The first is the most fraudulent of the arts; the second is a deeper and holier philosophy; the first, fruitless and in vain; the second, steadfast, faithful, and solid. Whoever has cultivated the first, has always dissimulated it, because it would make for the author's ignominy and disgrace. From the second comes that greatest clarity of the liberal arts and glory of antiquity which has nearly always been sought. * * *

ANONYMOUS

The English philosopher and Franciscan friar Roger Bacon (1214–1292), regarded in the early modern period as a wizard learned in astrology and alchemy, is another suggested source for Prospero. This text is possibly a common source for *The Tempest* and Robert Greene's play *Friar Bacon and Friar Bungay*. See John Henry Jones, ed., *The English Faust Book* (Cambridge: Cambridge UP, 1994), Appendix 4B.

[Friar Bacon's Magical Exploits][†]

[Friar Bacon Performs before the King and Queen]

There presently, to their great amazement, ensued the most melodious music they had ever heard in their lives * * * another kind of music was heard, and presently dancers in antic shapes at a masquerade [were seen] * * * louder music was heard, and whilst that played, a table was placed by an invisible hand, and richly covered with all the dainties that could be thought on; then he bid the King and Queen draw their seats near, and partake of the provisions he had provided for their Highnesses; which they did and all thereupon vanished * * * [and] the place was perfumed with all the sweets of Arabia. * * *

[Bacon's Servant Miles Plays the Tabor and Pipe]

[Bacon] slipped an enchanted pipe into Miles's hand [and] Miles began to play, and [the three thieves began] to dance * * * they followed him dancing, as before, so that he led them through the quagmires. * * *

[Bacon Abjures His Magic]

[Bacon] burnt his books [and] shut himself up in a cell, where he lived two years lamenting for his sins, and dug the grave he was buried in with his own nails * * * at two years' end he died a true penitent. * * *

WILLIAM BIDDULPH

William Biddulph (fl. 1600–12) was one of the earliest chaplains appointed by the Levant Company to minister to the spiritual needs of its outpost in Aleppo, the terminus of the caravans from Persia and Mesopotamia bringing silks and spices. Biddulph spent several years in the Middle East, and this book was compiled from his letters back to England. The extract speaks of an English conjurer raising a storm through his learning, just as Prospero does.

[An English Conjuror on the High Seas][‡]

The Master of the ship, called Andrea, and his brother Stephano (being both owners of the ship) said that surely the English Doctor

---

† From "The Most Famous History of the Learned Friar Bacon" (c. 1590); printed by Thomas Norris, 1627
‡ From The Travels of Certain Englishmen into Africa, Asia, Troy, Bythinia, Thracia, and to the Black Sea (London: Thomas Haveland, 1609), sigs. B2v–B3r.

was a conjuror, for they never saw him without a book in his hand, but still reading until (by his learning) he had raised a storm upon them; and thought it best to make a Jonas out of him, and to cast both him and his books into the sea, which they had done indeed, if God (in mercy towards him) had not prevented them.

REGINALD SCOTT

The Discovery of Witchcraft by Reginald Scott (1538–1599) was a skeptical attack on belief in witchcraft. However, its encyclopedic nature made it a valuable source book for all those with interests in the subject, at that time and subsequently. Here he gives an example of the kind of spell that a magician would utter in order to capture a spirit, in the way that Prospero had captured Ariel. For a broader introduction to the use of texts for controlling spirits, see Barbara A. Mowat, "Prospero's Book," *Shakespeare Quarterly* 52 (2001): 1–33.

[How to Enclose a Spirit]†

O Sitrael, Malantha, Thamaor, Falaur, and Sitrami, written in these circles, appointed to this work, I do conjure and I do exorcise you, by the father, by the son, and by the holy ghost, by him which did cast you out of paradise, and by him which spoke the word and it was done, and by him which shall come to judge the quick and the dead and the world by fire, that all you five infernal masters and princes do come unto me, to accomplish and to fulfil all my desire and request, which I shall command you. * * * Also I conjure you, and every one of you, you infernal kings, by heaven, by the stars, by the ☉ and by the ☽ and by all the planets, by the earth, fire, air, and water, and by the terrestrial paradise, and by all things in them contained, and by your hell, and by all the devils in it, and dwelling about it, and by your virtue and power, and by all whatsoever, and with whatsoever it be, which may constrain and bind you. Therefore by all these foresaid virtues and powers, I do bind you and constrain you into my will and power, that you being thus bound may come unto me in great humility, and to appear in your circles before me visibly, in fair form and shape of mankind kings, and to obey unto me in all things, whatsoever I shall desire, and that you may not depart from me without my licence. And if you do against my precepts, I will promise unto you that you shall descend into the profound deepness of the sea, except that you do obey unto me, in

† From *The Discovery of Witchcraft* (London: W. Brome, 1584), pp. 412–13.

the part of the living form of God, which lives and reigns in the unity of the holy ghost by all world of worlds, Amen.

* * *

I conjure, charge, and command you, and every one of you, Sitrael, Malantha, Thamaor, Falaur, and Sitrami, you infernal kings, to put into this crystal stone one spirit learned and expert in all arts and sciences, by virtue of this name of God Tetragrammaton, and by the cross of our Lord Jesus Christ, and by the blood of the innocent lamb, which redeemed all the world, and by all their virtues and powers I charge you, you noble kings, that the said spirit may teach, show, and declare unto me, and to my friends, at all hours and minutes, both night and day, the truth of all things both bodily and ghostly in this world whatsoever I shall request or desire, declaring also to me my very name. And this I command in your part to do, and to obey thereunto, as unto your own lord and master.

KING JAMES

From Daemonologie[†]

Directed against Scott's skepticism, the much shorter *Daemonologie* by King James VI and I (1566–1625) took witchcraft extremely seriously. Written in the form of a philosophical dialogue, the *Daemonologie* carefully distinguishes between different forms of sorcery and defends the need to persecute witches. Shakespeare very probably drew on this source for *Macbeth*, but it has also been suggested as a source for *The Tempest*: see Jacqueline E. M. Latham, "*The Tempest* and King James's *Daemonologie*," *Shakespeare Survey* 28 (1975): 117–23. King James VI of Scotland when the book was published, he became also King James I of England in 1603 and was present at the first recorded performances of *The Tempest*.

The Preface. To the Reader.

The fearful abounding at this time in this country, of these detestable slaves of the Devil, the witches or enchanters, has moved me (beloved reader) to dispatch in post this following treatise of mine, not in any way (as I protest) to serve for a show of my learning & ingenuity, but only (moved by conscience) to press thereby, so far as I can, to resolve the doubting hearts of many; both that such assaults of Satan are most certainly practised, & that the instruments thereof, merit most severely to be punished, against the damnable opinions of two principally in our

† From *Daemonologie, In Forme of a Dialogie Diuided into three Bookes* (Edinburgh: printed by Robert Waldegrave, 1597), pp. 1–2, 7–9. All notes are by the editors of this Norton Critical Edition.

age, whereof the one called Scott, an Englishman, is not ashamed in public print to deny that there can be such a thing as witchcraft, and so maintains the old error of the Sadducees in denying of spirits. The other called Wierus,[1] of a German physician, sets out a public apology for all these craftsfolk, whereby, procuring for their impunity, he plainly betrays himself to have been one of that profession. And for to make this treatise the more pleasant and facile, I have put it in the form of a dialogue, which I have divided into three books, the first speaking of magic in general and necromancy in special, the second of sorcery and witchcraft, and the third containing a discourse of all these kinds of spirits & spectres that appear & trouble persons, together with a conclusion of the whole work. My intention in this labour is only to prove two things, as I have already said: the one, that such devilish arts have been and are; the other, what exact trial and severe punishment they merit. And therefore reason I, what kind of things are possible to be performed in these arts, & by what natural causes they may be: not that I touch every particular thing of the Devil's power, for that were infinite, but only, to speak scholastically (since this can not be spoken in our language), I reason upon genus, leaving species and differentia to be comprehended therein. As for example, speaking of the power of magicians, in the first book & sixth chapter, I say that they can suddenly cause to be brought unto them all kinds of dainty dishes by their familiar spirit, since as a thief he delights to steal, and as a spirit he can subtly & suddenly enough transport the same. Now under this genus may be comprehended all particulars, depending thereupon, such as the bringing wine out of a wall (as we have heard often to have been practised) and such others; which particulars are sufficiently proved by reasons of the general. And similarly, in the second book of witchcraft in particular, in the fifth chapter, I say and prove by diverse arguments, that witches can, by the power of their Master, cure or cast on diseases. Now by these same reasons that prove their power by the Devil of diseases in general, is as well proved their power in particular: as of weakening the nature of some men, to make them unable for women, and making it abound in others, more than the ordinary course of nature would permit. And such like in all other particular sicknesses. But one thing I will pray thee to observe in all these places, where I reason upon the Devil's power, which is the different ends & scopes, that God as the first cause, and the Devil as his instrument and second cause, shoots at in all these actions of the Devil (as God's hangman). For where the Devil's intention in them is ever to perish either the soul or the body, or both of them, that he is so permitted to deal with, God, by the contrary, draws ever out of that evil glory to himself, either by the wreck[2] of the

---

1. Johann Weyer (1515–1588), Dutch occultist.
2. Destruction.

wicked in his justice, or by the trial of the patient and amendment of the faithful, being wakened up with that rod of correction. Having thus declared unto thee, then, my full intention in this treatise, thou will easily excuse, I doubt not, as well my pretermitting[3] to declare the whole particular rites and secrets of these unlawful arts as also their infinite and wonderful practices, as being neither of them pertinent to my purpose. The reason whereof is given in the hinder end of the first chapter of the third book; and who likes to be curious in these things, he may read, if he will here of their practices, Bodinus's *Daemono-manie*,[4] collected with greater diligence than written with judgement, together with their confessions, that have been at this time appre-hended. If he would know what has been the opinion of the Ancients concerning their power, he shall see it well described by Hyperius & Hemmingius,[5] two late German writers, besides innumerable other neoteric theologues that write largely upon that subject. And if he would know what are the particular rites & curiosities of these black arts (which is both unnecessary and perilous) he will find it in the fourth book of Cornelius Agrippa[6] and in Wierus, whom of I spoke. And so wishing my pains in this treatise (beloved reader) to be effectual in arming all them that reads the same against these above mentioned errors, and recommending my goodwill to thy friendly acceptation, I bid thee heartily farewell.

*　*　*

Book 1, Chapter 2

ARGUMENT What kind of sin the practicers of these unlawful arts commit. The division of these arts. And what are the means that allure any to practise them.

PHILOMATHES But I think it very strange that God should per-mit any of mankind (since they bear his own image) to fall into so gross and filthy a defection.

EPISTEMON Although man in his creation was made to the image of the Creator, yet through his fall having once lost it, it is but restored again in part by grace only to the elect. So all the rest falling away from God, are given over into the hands of the Devil that enemy, to bear his image, and being once so given over, the greatest and the grossest impiety is the pleasantest and most delightful unto them.

---

3. Avoiding.
4. Jean Bodin (1530–1596), French political philosopher.
5. Andrew Hyperius, also known as Gerhard of Yprès (1511–1564), and Nicholas Hem-mingius, also known as Niels Hemmingsen (1513–1600), both Protestant theologians.
6. Cornelius Agrippa (1446–1535), the best-known occultist of this period.

PHI. But may it not suffice him to have indirectly the rule, and procure the perdition of so many souls by alluring them to vices, and to the following of their own appetites, suppose he abuse not so many simple souls, in making them directly acknowledge him for their master?

EPI. No surely, for he uses every man, whom of he has the rule, according to their complexion and knowledge. And so whom he finds most simple, he plainliest discovers himself unto them. For he being the enemy of man's salvation, uses all the means he can to entrap them so far in his snares, as it may be unable to them thereafter (supposing they would) to rid themselves out of the same.

PHI. Then this sin is a sin against the Holy Ghost.

EPI. It is in some, but not in all.

PHI. How that? Are not all these that run directly to the Devil in one category?

EPI. God forbid, for the sin against the Holy Ghost has two branches: the one a falling back from the whole service of God, and a refusal of all his precepts; the other is the doing of the first with knowledge, knowing that they do wrong against their own conscience, and the testimony of the Holy Spirit, having once had a taste of the sweetness of God's mercies. Now in the first of these two, all sorts of necromancers, enchanters or witches are comprehended; but in the last, none but such as errs with this knowledge that I have spoken of.

PHI. Then it appears that there are more sorts than one that are directly professors of his service; and if so be, I pray you tell me how many, and what are they?

EPI. There are principally two sorts, whereunto all the parts of that unhappy art are redacted; whereof the one is called magic or necromancy, the other sorcery or witchcraft.

PHI. What I pray you? and how many are the means whereby the Devil allures persons in any of these snares?

EPI. Even by these three passions that are within our selves: curiosity in great engines; thirst of revenge, for some torts deeply apprehended; or greedy appetite of gear, caused through great poverty. As to the first of these, curiosity, it is only the enticement of magicians or necromancers; and the other two are the allurers of the sorcerers or witches, for that old and crafty serpent, being a spirit, he easily spies our affections, and so conforms himself thereto, to deceive us to our wreck.

                 ❊   ❊   ❊

Politics and Religion

Isaiah XXIX[†]

With its catastrophic tempest, the illusion of food, a slumbering spirit, and the name Ariel, Isaiah XXIX has been suggested as a credible source for *The Tempest*: see Ann Pasternak Slater, "Variations within a Source: From Isaiah XXIX to *The Tempest*," *Shakespeare Survey* 25 (1972): 125–35; and Anthony M. Esolen, "'The isles shall wait for His law': Isaiah and *The Tempest*," *Studies in Philology* 94:2 (1997): 221–47.

1 Woe unto thee, o Ariel, Ariel, thou city that David dwelt in: go on from year to year, and let the lambs be slain.

I will lay siege unto Ariel, so that there shall be heaviness and sorrow in it: and it shall be unto me even an altar of slaughter.

I will besiege thee round about, and will fight against thee through a bulwark, and will rear up ditches against thee.

2 *Thou shalt be brought down, and shalt speak out of the ground, and thy speech shall go low out of the dust:*

Thy voice also shall come up out of the ground, like the voice of a witch, and thy talking shall whisper out of the dust.

Moreover, the noise of the strange enemies shall be like thin dust, and the multitude of tyrants shall be as dry straw that cannot tarry: even suddenly and in haste shall their blast go.

3 *Thou shalt be visited of the Lord of hosts, with thunder, earthquake, and with a great noise, with storm and tempest, and with the flame of a consuming fire.*

4 *And the multitude* of all nations that fight against Ariel, *shall be as a dream seen by night:* even so shall they be that make war against it, and strong holds to overcome it, and that lay any siege unto it.

5 In conclusion, *it shall be even as when an hungry man dreameth that he is eating, and when he awaketh, his soul is empty, or as when a thirsty man dreameth that he is drinking, when he awaketh, he is yet faint, and his soul hath appetite:* even so shall the multitude of all nations be that fight against Mount Zion.

† Translated in the Bishops' Bible (1568). Isaiah was a Jewish prophet in the eighth century B.C.E.

6 Ponder these things once in your minds, and wonder: *Blinded are they themselves, and the blind guides of other, they are drunken, but not with wine: they are unstable, but not through strong drink:*

For the Lord hath covered you with a slumbering spirit, and hath closed your eyes: your prophets also and rulers that should see, them hath he covered. And the vision of all the prophets, is become unto you as the words of a book that is sealed up, which men deliver to one that is learned, saying, Read thou in it: and he sayeth, I cannot, for it is sealed.

And the book is given to him that is not learned, saying, Read thou in it: and he sayeth, I am not learned.

Therefore thus hath the Lord said, For as much as this people, when they be in trouble, do honor me with their mouth, and with their lips, but their heart is far from me, and the fear which they have unto me, proceedeth of a commandment that is taught of men.

7 Therefore I will do marvels among this people, even marvellous things I say and a wonder: for *the wisedome of their wise men shall perish, and the understanding of their witty men shall hide itself.*

8 *Woe unto them that keep secret their thoughts, to hide their counsel from the Lord, and to do their works in darkness, saying, Who seeth us? and who knoweth us?*

9 *Doubtless your destruction is in reputation as the potter's clay: and doth the work say of him that made it, He made not me? And doth an earthen vessel say of him that fashioned it, He had no understanding?*

Is it not hard at hand that Libanus shall be turned into a low field, and that the low field shall be taken as the wood?

10 And in that day shall deaf men hear the words of the book, and *the eyes of the blind shall see even out of the cloud, and out of darkness. The meek spirited also shall be merry in the Lord, and the poor among them that be lowly shall rejoice* in the holy one of Israel:

For he that did violence is brought to nought, and the scornful man is consumed, and they rooted out that made haste early to unrighteousness, Making a man to sin in the world, and that took him in a snare, which reproved them in the open place, *and they that have turned the cause of the righteous to nought.*

Therefore thus sayeth the Lord to the house of Jacob, even thus sayeth he that redeemed Abraham, Jacob shall not now be confounded, nor his face pale. *But when he seeth his children the work of my hands in the midst of him, they shall sanctify my name,* and praise the holy one of Jacob, and fear the God of Israel.

They also that have been of an erroneous spirit, shall come to understanding, and they that have been scornful shall learn doctrine.

SAMUEL PURCHAS

The English settlement of Virginia provided plentiful narratives of plantation and dispossession. Here clergyman and collector Samuel Purchas (1577?–1626) responds angrily to the "treacherous" attack by the Native inhabitants on the English settlement at Jamestown in 1622.

Virginia's Verger†

* * *

This should be, and in most adventurers I hope is the scope of the Virginian plantation, not to make savages and wild degenerate men of Christians, but Christians of those savage, wild, degenerate men, to whom preaching must needs be vain if it begins with public latrociny.[1] And this is sufficient to prevent scruple of the Pope's Bull which (if Basan Bulls roaring were evidence) makes as well against England, this being no less questionable than Virginia, with Paul, Pius, Gregory the Sixth breathing as much fire against the former as Alexander against the latter. But what right can England then challenge to Virginia? I answer that we would be loathe to begin our right at wrong, either to ethnic or Christian; nor need we, having so manifold and just interests. First, as men, we have a natural right to replenish the whole earth; so that if any country be not possessed by other men (which is the case of the Summer Islands, and has been of all countries in their first habitations) every man by law of nature and humanity has right of plantation and may not by other after-comers be dispossessed, without wrong to human nature. And if a country be inhabited in some parts, other parts remaining unpeopled, the same reason gives liberty to other men who want convenient habitations to seat themselves, where (without wrong to others) they may provide for themselves. For these have the same right to these latter parts which the former had to the former, especially where the people are wild and hold no settled possession in any parts. Thus the holy patriarchs removed their habitation and pasturages when those parts of the world were not yet replenished; and thus the whole world has been planted and peopled with former and later colonies; and thus Virginia has room enough for her own (were their numbers a hundred times as many) and for others also who, wanting at home, seek habitations there in vacant places, with perhaps better right

---

† From, *Haklytus Posthumus or Purchas His Pilgrimes* [1625] (Glasgow: James MacLehose and Sons, 1906), XIX: 222–25. All notes are by the editors of this Norton Critical Edition. A verger is an attendant in the Anglican church.
1. Robbery.

than the first who (being like Cain, both murderers and vagabonds in their whatsoever and howsoever own) I can scarcely call inhabitants. To question this right would be to accuse almost all nations, which were rocked (for the most part) in no other cradle; and to disappoint also that Divine Ordinance of replenishing the earth, whose habitations otherwise would be scattered islands in the seas or, like the present Spanish plantations in the Indies, so dispersed and disjoined that one cannot in any distress succour another and therefore are made an easier prey to every invader. Another right is that of merchandise: Non omnia possumus omnes, Nec vero terrae ferre omnes omnia possunt,[2] God in manifold wisdom has diversified every country's commodities, so that all are rich and all poor; not that one should be hungry and another drunken, but that the whole world might be as one body of mankind, each member communicating with others for public good. He has made this immutable decree in the mutability of the winds, commodities, and commodiousness of seas and harbours, variety of bays and rivers, multiplicity of all men's both necessities and superfluities, and their universal desire for novelties. This Solomon and Hiram had right to sail over the ocean and to negotiate with the Ophirians for gems, gold, ivory, and other commodities serviceable for his people's necessities, for pompous magnificence and for the Temple's holies. And if he did not plant colonies there, you must remember that the Jewish Pale was then standing, which prohibited voluntary remote dwellings, where each man was thrice a year to appear before the Lord in Jerusalem. Besides, it is a question whether the country peopled so long before had room for such neighbours.

It is therefore ungodly, and inhuman also, to deny the world to men, or like manger-dogs (neither to eat hay themselves nor to suffer the hungry ox) to prohibit that for others' habitation of which they themselves can make no use; or for merchandise, whereby much benefit accrues to both parts. They who do this, tollunt e vita vitae societatem, to use Tully's phrase, & hominem ex homine tullunt, to borrow St Jerome in another matter.[3] The barbarians themselves by light of nature saw this, and gave our people kind entertainment in mutual cohabitation and commerce; and they having not the law were a law unto themselves, practically acknowledging this law of nature written by him, which is natura naturans,[4] in their hearts; from which if they since have declined, they have lost their own natural and given us another national right, their transgression of the law of nature

---

2. All cannot do all (Virgil, *Eclogues*); Nor indeed can all soils bear all things (Virgil, *Georgics*).
3. Cicero's (Tully) phrase is actually *Quid est aliud tollere ex vita vitae societatem, tollere amicorum conloquia absentium?* (What is this but removing from life the social exchanges of life, to remove the communion of friends in absence?—*Phillipics*). St. Jerome's words convey a similar sentiment.
4. Nature doing what nature does.

which ties men to men in the right of nature's commons, exposing them (like a forfeited bond) to the chastisement of that common law of mankind; and also on our parts to the severity of the law of nations, which ties nation to nation. And if they be not worthy of the name of a nation, being wild and savage, yet as slaves, bordering rebels, excommunicants, and outlaws are liable to the punishments of law, and not to the privileges, so is it with these barbarians, borderers, and outlaws of humanity. Arma tenenti, omnia dat qui justa negat,[5] If the arms be just, as in this case of vindicating unnatural, inhuman wrongs to a loving and profitable nation, entertained voluntarily in time of greatest pretended amity. On this quarrel David conquered all the kingdoms of the Ammonites and left it to his successors in many generations, notwithstanding Moses had otherwise left a special caution for their security, testifying that God had given it the sons of Lot, and prohibiting invasion to Israel. That natural right of cohabitation and commerce we had with others, this of just invasion and conquest, and many others previous to this, we have above others; so that England may both by law of nature and nations challenge Virginia for her own peculiar propriety, and that by all right and rites usual among men, not those mentioned alone but by others also, first discovery, first actual possession, prescription, gift, cession, and livery of seisin, sale for price, that I mention not the natural inheritance of the English there naturally born, and the unnatural outcries of so many unnaturally murdered, for just vengeance of rooting out the authors and actors of such prodigious injustice.

* * *

GABRIEL NAUDÉ

French diplomat and librarian Gabriel Naudé (1600–1653) was another debunker of the occult tradition, arguing that purported acts of magic from the past were illusions generated by those trying to bring about political or religious change, illusions often presented in theatrical form. For more on this tradition, see Peter S. Donaldson, *Machiavelli and Mystery of State* (Cambridge: Cambridge UP, 1989).

[Master Strokes of State][†]

Oh what a despicable thing is man, unless he raises himself above human things; that is, unless he have a strong and fixed eye, and, as

---

5. He who refuses what is just, gives up everything to him who is armed (Lucan, *Pharsalia*).
† From *Political Considerations upon Refin'd Politicks, and the Master-Strokes of State* (1653), trans. William King (London, 1711), pp. 24, 59–60.

if he were placed upon some high tower, looks down upon the world, which appears to him as a theatre, ill regulated, and full of confusion, where some act comedies, and other tragedies, and where he may intervene; "Tanquam Deus aliquis ex Machina", like some divinity from a machine, as often as he pleases or the variety of occasions shall persuade him to do it.

* * * In these master strokes of state, the thunderbolt falls before the noise of it is heard in the skies * * *, prayers are said before the bell is rung for them; the execution precedes the sentence; he receives the blow that thinks he himself is giving it; he suffers who never expected it, and he dies that looked upon himself to be the most secure; all is done in the night and obscurity, amongst storms and confusion * * * .

Geography and Travel

ANONYMOUS

Primaleon of Greece belongs to the Palmerin cycle of Spanish chivalric romances that were extremely popular in Europe in the sixteenth and early seventeenth centuries. Due to a misunderstanding of the kind common in romances, the protagonist Primaleon and an English prince are involved in a dreadful combat at sea when the Knight of the Enclosed Island makes a dramatic appearance, jumping on board their ship and striking the mast with his book, which causes everyone on board to lie down "as if they had been dead," not unlike Ariel's actions on the courtiers' ship. One scholar has noted seventeen significant parallels between the plot of *Primaleon* and that of *The Tempest*: see Gary Schmidgall, "*The Tempest* and *Primaleon*: A New Source," *Shakespeare Quarterly* 37 (1986): 423–39. While Books 1 and 2 were published in English in 1595–1596, Book 3 did not appear until 1619. Schmidgall speculates that there may well have been an earlier (and now lost) edition.

From Primaleon of Greece[†]

[The Knight of the Enclosed Island sends one of his sons, Palantine, to greet the revived Primaleon, and courtesies are exchanged. Asking about the island, Primaleon is told about a terrible giant, whom he insists on going to see and then engaging in combat. The giant is captured and proves susceptible to the charms of the Knight's daughter.]

* * *

'I come', quoth Palantine, 'on my father's behalf, who is Lord of this Island, to tell you that if you seek nothing else, he is content to let you have whatsoever you need, desiring yourself to come on shore while your people have gotten together your provision.' Primaleon thanked him, saying, for his sake, he would go with him. So, calling Torques and five other knights in his company, he went

---

[†] From *The Famous and Renowned History of Primaleon of Greece, Son to the great and mighty Prince Palmerin d'Oliva, Emperor of Constantinople*, translated into English by A[nthony] M[unday] (London: Thomas Snodham, 1619), Book 2, chap. 32, p. 254; chap. 35, p. 279; Book 3, chap. 32, pp. 169–71; chap. 33, pp. 171–72.

on land with Palantine, where they were very much gazed on because they had seldom seen any such knights. The Lord of the Isle courteously welcomed them, and while the ships were providing for victuals, Primaleon and the rest spent the time merrily, conferring on many matters with the Lord's son; of whom he demanded the island's spaciousness, and whether it were throughout inhabited or no, because it seemed so fertile and pleasant. 'Sir', answered Palantine, 'the most inhabitant part of this island, is on the seaside, for the rest is very mountainy, where (no long time since, and yet at this present likewise) hath been seen a people far differing from other, because they are cruel and barbarous, feeding on raw flesh and clothed in wild beasts' skins; beside so ill-favored and deformed as it was a thing right marvellous to behold them, [of] which most usually is seen [he] whom we call Patagon, said to be engendered by a beast in the woods, being the strangest misshapen and counterfeit creature in the world. He hath good understanding, is amorous of women, * * * hath the face of a dog, great ears which hang down upon his shoulders, his teeth sharp and big, standing out of his mouth very much; his feet are like a hart's, and he runneth wondrous lightly.

* * *

Zerphira * * * went boldly to *Patagon*, bidding him go along with her, stroking his head and using him very kindly; which made him forget his former stubbornness and fall at her feet, for he greatly delighted to gaze fair ladies in the face; so taking his chain in her hand, he followed after her as gently as if he had been a spaniel.

* * *

When dinnertime drew near, they were sent for to come into the hall, where they sat down every man in his order, as they did the day before. And after dinner began the Revels, at which time the Emperor called his daughter *Flerida* and *Prince Edward*, and said unto them, 'Seeing we are now here assembled in great joy, I will presently have you espoused together, that my heart may be wholly satisfied and contented, and the feast complete.' At which words the Archbishop rose out of his seat, and suddenly espoused them together, by the means whereof, the joy was so great that all men thought upon nothing else but upon pleasure and delight. And at night, after supper, as every man beheld the sports and pastimes that were made in the hall, suddenly there appeared before them two wild men, as big as giants, with each of them a shield on his arm and a great club in his hand, which began so furious a combat that every man was abashed thereat, especially the ladies, which had so great fear that they had

thought to fly out of the hall if the knights had not stayed them. * * *
Meantime, the wild man and the serpent fought a most fierce combat, which made a great noise and rumor to rise in the hall amongst
the knights that were there and knew not what to think thereof. And
as they all beheld the combat, suddenly the serpent vanished away,
and there was nothing seen but a knight apparelled in a rich cloak,
that went toward the Emperor and, kneeling down before him,
offered to kiss his hand. But the Emperor that presently knew him to
be the Knight of the Enclosed Island, rose up joyfully to receive him
and said, 'You are heartily welcome, I am glad to see you in health.'
'My Lord', said he, 'I am your humble servant, and therefore I was by
great reason bound to do something at so great a feast.' At the sight
of this knight, every man began to be quiet and appeased, all men
being glad of his coming, especially *Maiortes*, for the good that he
and all his friends hoped to receive at his hands, which was to be
wholly delivered out of the long enchantment where he had lived.

The Emperor caused the Knight of the Enclosed Island to be
lodged in the Palace, to honor him the more (for he loved and
esteemed him much) and then went to his chamber, and every man
likewise unto his. *Maiortes* desired *Prince Edward* the next day to
solicit the Knight of the Enclosed Island to disenchant him, which
he did; and having received the book of the Emperor, gave it unto
him, wherewith *Maiortes* left the sword, and presently returned into
the shape of a dog, as he was before. Then the Knight, reading in
[the] book, knew how to disenchant him; and presently *Maiortes*
received the shape of a man again, feeling himself to be in better
disposition than he was before, when he had the Sword, and for that
cause gave to the Knight many thanks for the great good that he had
done unto him.

* * *

GASPAR GIL POLO

There are accounts aplenty of storms in the Atlantic and the Caribbean
that may have furnished Shakespeare with ideas and vocabulary. This
one is a storm in the Mediterranean taken from *La Diana enamorada* by
Gaspar Gil Polo (1530–1584), a continuation of Jorge de Montemayor's
Spanish pastoral romance *Diana*.

[A Mediterranean Storm]†

The shepherdess, thou must know, that after my unfortunate marriage was agreed upon, the King's licence being now come, her old Father Eugerius, who was a widower, his son Polydorus, and his two daughters Alcida and Clenarda, and the hapless Marcelius, who is telling thee his grievous accidents, having committed the charges left us by the King to sufficient and trusty gentlemen, embarked ourselves in the port of Ceuta to go by sea to the noble city of Lisbon, there to celebrate (as I said) the marriage rites in presence of the King. The great content, joy, and pleasure which we all had, made us so blind that in the most dangerous time of the year, we feared not the tempestuous waves which did then naturally swell and rage, nor the furious and boisterous winds which in those months with greater force and violence are commonly wont to blow; but committing our frail bark to fickle fortune, we launched into the deep and dangerous sea, heedless of their continual changes and of innumerable misfortunes incident unto them. For we had not sailed far, when angry Fortune chastised us for our bold attempt, because before night came on, the wary Pilot discovered apparent signs of an imminent and sudden tempest. For the thick and dark clouds began to cover the heavens all over, the waves to roar and murmur, and contrary winds to blow on every side. "Oh what sorrowful and menacing signs", said the troubled and timorous pilot: "Oh luckless ship, what perils assail thee, if God of his great goodness and pity do not succour thee?" He had no sooner spoken these words, when there came a furious and violent blast of wind, that puffed and shook the whole body of the ship, and put it in so great danger, that the rudder was not able to govern it, but that tossed up and down by this mighty fury, it went where the force of the angry waves and winds did drive it. The tempest by little and little with greater noise began to increase, and the raving billows, covered over with a foamy froth, mightily to swell. The skies poured down abundance of rain with throwing out of every part of it fearful lightnings, & threatened the world with horrible thunders. Then might there be heard a hideous noise of sea monsters, lamentable outcries of passengers, and flapping of the sails with great terror. The wind on every side did beat against the ship, and the surges with terrible blows shaking her unsteady sides, rived

---

† From Jorge de Montemayor, *Diana* (with a second part by A. Perez and also a continuation entitled *Enamoured Diana* by Gaspar Gil Polo), trans. Bartholomew Young (London: E. Bollifant; Impensis G.B., 1598), pp. 393–95.

and burst asunder the strong and soundest planchers. Sometimes the proud billow lifted us up to the skies, and by and by threw us down again into deep gulfs. * * * The Pilot being appalled with so cruel Fortune, and his skill confounded by the countenance and terror of the tempest, could now no more govern the tottered rudder. He was also ignorant of the nature and beginning of the winds, and in a moment devised a thousand different things. The mariners likewise aghast with the agony of approaching death, were not able to execute the Master's command, nor (for such lamentations, noise and outcries) could hear the charge & direction of their hoarse and painful Pilot. Some strike sail, others turn the main-yard; some make fast again the broken shrouds; others mend and caulk the riven planks; some ply the pump apace, and some the rudder; and in the end, all put their helping hands to preserve the miserable ship from inevitable loss. * * * In the meanwhile, the forlorn and tossed ship, by the force and violence of the fierce western winds, which by the straits of Gibraltar came blowing as if they were mad, sailed with greater speed than was expedient for our safety, and being battered on every side with the cruel blows of envious fortune by the space of a day and a night * * * ran many leagues in the long Mediterranean sea, wheresoever the force of the waves & winds did carry her. † † † In the end a fierce and mighty tempest came so suddenly upon us, that the ship driven on by the force of a boisterous blast that smit her on the starboard, was in so great danger of turning bottom up, that she had now her forepart hidden under the water: whereupon I undid my rapier from my side (spying the manifest and imminent danger), so that it might not hinder me and, embracing my Alcida, leaped with her into the skiff that was fastened to the ship. * * * The next morning, finding ourselves near to land, we made towards it amain. The two mariners that were very skilfull in swimming, went not alone to the wished shore, but taking us out of the boat carried us safely thither. After we were delivered from the perils of the sea, the mariners drew their skiff to land, and viewing that coast where we arrived, knew that it was the island Formentera. * * *

WALTER RALEGH

A Map of Tunis and Carthage

The quarrel among Gonzalo, Sebastian, and Adrian in 2.1 over the precise relationship between Tunis and Carthage may seem pedantic in the
extreme, but the Hapsburg emperor Charles V had defeated Turkish
forces at Tunis in 1535, a victory hailed for his emulation of Roman
victories over Carthage—themselves described by Walter Ralegh
(1552–1618) in his *History of the World* (1614). See Jerry Brotton, "'This
Tunis, sir, was Carthage': Contesting Colonialism," in Ania Loomba and
Martin Orkin, eds., *Post-Colonial Shakespeares* (London: Routledge,
1998), pp. 23–42.

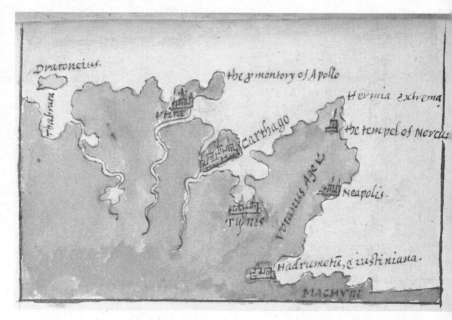

Watercolor map of Tunisia from Sir Walter Ralegh's notebook,
c. 1606–08. British Library Add. MS 57555. Courtesy of British Library
/ Granger. All rights reserved.

RICHARD EDEN

In 1519 the Portuguese captain Ferdinand Magellan crossed the Atlantic in the service of Spain on the first leg of his circumnavigation of the globe. Toward the southern tip of South America he encountered native people who were described by the Italian who accompanied the expedition, Antonio Pigafetta (1480–1534), as "Patagoni." Pigafetta tells of how Magellan captured two of these natives by a trick, imprisoning them in fetters, at which they cried for their devil Setebos to help them. The first published version of Pigafetta was an Italian translation of a French translation of the lost Italian original. That Italian translation was itself translated into English in abbreviated form by Richard Eden (c. 1520–1576) in his *The Decades of the New Worlde*, published in London in 1555, and then posthumously reprinted in an augmented version in 1577, which is where Shakespeare probably came across it.

[A Voyage to the Patagonians][†]

The voyage made by the Spaniards round about the world, is one of the greatest and most marvellous things that have been known to our time.

* * *

In this voyage they saw many strange fishes, & monsters of the sea, beside another strange thing which appeared unto them; for there appeared in their ships certain flames of fire, burning very clear, which they call *Saint Helen*, & *Saint Nicholas*. These appeared as though they had been upon the mast of the ships, in such clearness, that they took away their sight for the space of a quarter of an hour, by reason whereof they so wandered out of their course, and were dispersed in sunder, that they in manner despaired to meet again. But (as God would) the sea and tempest being quieted, they came safely to their determined course. And before I speak any further of the voyage, I have here thought good to say somewhat of these strange fires, which some ignorant folk think to be spirits, or such other fantasies, whereas they are but natural things, proceeding of natural causes, and engendered of certain exhalations. Of these, therefore, the great Philosopher of our time Hieronymus Cardanus, in his second book *De Subtilitate*, writeth in this manner. There are two manner of fires engendered of exhalations, whereof the one is hurtful, the other

† From *The History of Travel in the West and East Indies*, augmented by Richard Willes (London: Richard Jugge, 1577), pp. 429–36.

without hurt. That which is hurtful is fire indeed, engendered of malicious and venomous vapors, which in success of time take fire as apt matters to be kindled. The other kind is not true fire, but like the matter that is in such old putrefied wood, as giveth the shining of fire without the substance or quality thereof. Of the kind of true fire is the fireball or star commonly called *Saint Helen*, which is sometime seen about the masts of ships, being of such fiery nature, that it sometime melteth brazen vessels, and is a token of drowning, forasmuch as this chanceth only in great tempests; for the vapor or exhalation whereof this fire is engendered, cannot be driven together or compact in form of fire, but of a gross vapor, and by a great power of wind, and is therefore a token of imminent peril. As on the contrary part, the like fires called in old time *Castor and Pollux,* and now named *the two lights of Saint Peter and Saint Nicholas*, which for the most part fall on the cables of the ships, leaping from one to another with a certain fluttering noise like birds, are a token of security, and of the tempest overpassed; for they are but vapors cleaving to the cables, which in success of time, the fire passing from one to another, appear in the similitude of a light candle. They are a token of security because they are little, not slow or gross, whereby they might have joined altogether in one and been thereby more malicious, and lasted longer. . . . But let us now return to the voyage.

When they had sailed past the Equinoctial line, they lost the sight of the North Star, and sailed by the southwest, until they came to a land named the land of *Bressil*, which some call *Brasilia*, being 22 degrees and a half toward the South Pole or Pole Antarctic. This land is continuate and one firm land with the cape of Saint Augustine, which is 8 degrees from the Equinoctial. In this land they were refreshed with many good fruits of innumerable kinds, and found here also very good sugar canes, and divers kinds of beasts and other things which I omit for brevity. They entered into this haven on Saint Lucy's bay, where the sun being their zenith (that is, the point of heaven directly over their heads) they felt greater heat that day than when they were under the Equinoctial line. This land of Brasile is very large and great, and bigger than all Spain, Portugal, France, and Italy, and is most abundant in all things. The people of this country pray to no manner of thing, but live by the instinct of nature, and to the age of 120 and 140 years. Both the men and women go naked, and dwell in certain long houses. They are very docile, and soon allured to the Christian faith.

Thirteen days after that they arrived at the said port, they departed from this land and sailed to the 34th degree and a half toward the Pole Antarctic, where they found a great river of fresh water and certain *cannibals*. Of these they saw one out of their ships of stature as big as a giant, having a voice like a bull. Our men pursued them, but they were so swift of foot that they could not overtake them. * * *

After other 15 days were past, there came four other giants without any weapons, but had hid their bows and arrows in certain bushes. The Captain retained two of these, which were youngest and best made. He took them by a deceit, in this manner, that giving them knives, shears, looking-glasses, bells, heads of crystal, & such other trifles, he so filled their hands that they could hold no more; then caused two pair of shackles of iron to be put on their legs, making signs that he would also give them those chains, which they liked very well, because they were made of bright and shining metal. And whereas they could not carry them because their hands were full, the other giants would have carried them, but the Captain would not suffer them. When they felt the shackles fast about their legs, they began to doubt; but the Captain did put them in comfort, and bade them stand still. In fine, when they saw how they were deceived, they roared like bulls, & cried upon their great devil *Setebos* to help them. Being thus taken, they were immediately separated and put in sundry ships. They could never bind the hands of the other two, yet was one of them with much difficulty overthrown by 9 of our men, & his hands bound; but he suddenly loosed himself and fled, as did also the other that came with them. In their fleeing, they shot of their arrows and slew one of our men. They say that when any of them die, there appear 10 or 12 devils, leaping and dancing about the body of the dead, and seem to have their bodies painted with divers colors, and that among other, there is one seen bigger than the residue, who maketh great mirth and rejoicing. This great devil they call *Setebos*, and call the less *Cheleule*. One of these giants which they took declared by signs that he had seen devils with two horns about their heads, with long hair down to their feet, and that they cast forth fire at their throats both before and behind. The Captain named these people *Patagoni*. The most part of them wear the skins of such beasts whereof I have spoken before; and have no houses of continuance, but make certain cottages, which they cover with the said skins and carry them from place to place. They live off raw flesh, and a certain sweet root which they call *Capar*. One of these which they had in their ships did eat at one meal a basket of biscuit, and drunk a bowl of water at a draught.

They remained five months in this port of *Saint Julian*, where certain of the under-captains conspiring the death of the General were hanged and quartered, among whom the Treasurer *Luigo* of *Mendoza* was one. Certain of the other conspirators he left in the said land of *Patagoni*. * * *

They found that in this strait, in the month of October, the night was not past four hours long. They found in this strait, at every three miles, a safe haven and excellent water to drink; wood also, and fish, and great plenty of good herbs. They think that there is not a fairer strait in the world. Here also they saw certain flying fishes. The other giant which remained with them in the ship named bread *Capar*, water *Oli*, red cloth *Cherecai*, red color *Cheiche*, black color *Amel*; and spoke all his words in the throat. On a time, as one made a cross before him and kissed it, showing it unto him, he suddenly cried *Setebos*, and declared by signs that if they made any more crosses *Setebos* would enter into his body and make him burst. But when in fine he saw no hurt come thereof, he took the cross, and embraced and kissed it oftentimes, desiring that he might be a Christian before his death. He was therefore baptised and named Paul.

* * *

CAPT. WYATT

The illegitimate son of Robert Dudley, First Earl of Leicester, Sir Robert Dudley (1574–1649) was an English explorer and cartographer who led an expedition to the West Indies in 1594. This account of a storm on that expedition was written by the ship's captain, of whom nothing else is known, and first published in Hakluyt's *Principal Navigations* (1598–1600). Dudley worked as an engineer and a shipbuilder in Italy, later designing and publishing *Dell'Arcano del Mare* (1645–1646), the first maritime atlas to cover the whole world. For the possible relevance of his early career to *The Tempest*, see Richard Wilson, "Voyage to Tunis: New History and the Old World of *The Tempest*," *English Literary History* 64:2 (1997): 333–57.

[An Atlantic Storm]†

So sailing along by the coast of Virginia we came by the 12th of April, being Friday, so far to the north that we fell with the height of the Bermudas, a climate so far differing from the nature of all others which we had already passed that we might then think ourselves most happy when we were farthest from it. For had I as many tongues as my head has ears, yet might I come too short of the true description of

---

† From "Robert Dudley's Voyage to the West Indies" [1595], in *The Voyage of Robert Dudley to the West Indies*, ed. George F. Warner (London: Hakluyt Society, 1899), pp. 52–56. All notes are by the editors of this Norton Critical Edition. Richard Hakluyt (1553–1616) was an English writer best-known for collecting and publishing *The Principal Navigations, Voyages, Traffiques and Discoveries of the English Nation* (1589–1600).

the extremity of the outrageous weather which this place continually affords without any intermission. Often before we have had dangerous gusts, which vanished as suddenly as they happened; but these were always ordinary and their dangers still extraordinary, their dreadful flashing of lightning, the horrible claps of thunder, the monstruous raging of the swelling seas forced up into the air by the outrageous winds, all together conspiring in a moment our destruction, and breathing out, as it were, in one breath the very last blast of our confusion, so that—this being a general axiom of all seafaring men delivered for a verity, both by our English and the Spanish, French, and Portuguese, that hell is no hell in comparison to this, or that this itself is hell without any comparison—all this together did betoken greater grief to us than can be spoken. But these were but preparations for further dangers.

* * *

And although, Right Honourable,[1] the remembrance of our earlier sorrows will be little less than a present death to our daunted spirits, which we did then endure not without great anguish of soul, neither can I resist without bitterness of passion nor your honour hear without pity. For this was our only comfort that, being mortified and resolved to die, of sinful and earthly creatures we were, by yielding nature her due debt, to be made saints for God, truly believing then to be made partakers of His heavenly happiness and every one giving his last farewell to his best and most dearest friends, desirous to see the last end of this sorrowful stratagem. But at last, when through the fogs that rise out of the seas, the blackness of the sky could not be seen for the darkness of the air, when we expected nothing less than splitting of sails, breaking of shrouds, spending of masts, springing of planks—in a word the dreadful devouring of us all by some sea-swallowing whirlpool we were most miraculously delivered. For this fog being converted into so monstruous a shower of rain that it should seem the very windows of heaven were set open that it might with the more speed work our deliverance, fell with such vehemence that it not only allayed the raging of the fearful seas grown and swollen up into an incredible bigness, but broke the heart of that most bitter storm. Thus, while we were all so mated and amazed that, neither hearing what the master said for the whistling and buzzing of the winds, not knowing for fear what to amend, we were most miraculously by the mighty hand of God, past man's capacity and altogether unlooked for of ourselves, delivered.

1. There is nothing to show who is addressed; probably Sir Robert Cecil, the 1st Earl of Salisbury (1563–1612), who wielded considerable power in England during the transition from Tudor to Stuart rule.

And before it pleased God to inflict upon us this punishment, he foretold us by his warning messenger, a most rare accident, which the mariners called Santelmo or Corposantie,[2] which appear before any tempestuous weather as a sign of a most dangerous storm. And although the opinions of all writers are variable concerning its true essence, I am persuaded there can be no certain truth delivered about it. The Greeks call it Poliduces, the Latins Castor and Pollux; Pliny writes that it is as much seen on land among a great army of men as at sea among mariners; Virgil seems to confirm this in the second book of the Aeneid, saying that it appeared at the head of Julius Ascanius; and Titus Livius affirms that such a thing appeared on the head of Servius Tullius, the sixth King of the Romans. But however it is variably censured in sundry writers, this is certainly agreed upon: that it foretells some great thing to come, and if it appears in two lights, the goodness comes, and if but one, then some eminent danger is at hand to ensue; for, if just one fire is seen, it presages a most cruel, dangerous, and tempestuous storm, hazarding both ship, goods, and lives of all those who happen to be in it. This is not only confirmed by all sorts of nations which are navigators, like the Spaniards, French, Portuguese, Turks, Moors, indeed all kinds of sea-faring men, but we, to our great peril, were made eyewitnesses, which in my opinion was and is more authentic for us than if we received the reports of thousands of others. It is a fearful tale to tell, and a discourse dreadful to the hearer to have delivered as a truth, that in the night a substance of fire resembling the shape of a fiery dragon should fall into our sails and there remain some quarter of an hour, afterwards falling onto the deck and passing from place to place, ready to set everything on fire, since fire most commonly converts all things into the same substance as itself, which is fire, being the true confirmation of that axiom of Aristotle that *omne tale efficit maius tale*.[3] This, I say, might seem dreadful to the hearer, but it was much more dreadful for us, who beheld it with our eyes. This was strange, but the event much more strange, for this fiery dragon, having continued halfway over to the astonishment of us all, vanished without any harm done either to our shipping or to any of our company, except the most strange sequel, as you have already heard in the description of this last storm, and yet not so strange as true.

* * *

2. Corpo Santo and St. Elmo's fire are names given to the balls of electric light seen on the masts and yardarms of a ship in stormy weather.
3. Properly *Quod efficit tale, illud est magistale* (What makes another such is more such itself).

MICHEL DE MONTAIGNE

One of the few undisputed sources for specific passages in *The Tempest* is Michel de Montaigne's essay *Des cannibales* (*Of the Cannibals*), published in French in 1580. Gonzalo's speech, which begins "Had I plantation of this isle" (2.1.138), offers a classic image of a utopian community: "no kind of traffic . . . no name of magistrate . . . riches, poverty, / And use of service, none; . . . No occupation, all men idle . . . ." That exaltation of a golden age quotes directly, as well as paraphrases, John Florio's translation into English of Montaigne's essay. In the essay Montaigne (1533–1592) is in discussion with a Tupi Indian brought to France from Brazil, who is allowed to criticize the injustices of French society.

[The Cannibals of Brazil]†

✠ ✠ ✠ I finde (as farre as I have beene informed) there is nothing in that nation, that is either barbarous or savage, unlesse men call that barbarisme which is not common to them. As indeed, we have no other ayme of truth and reason, than the example and *Idea* of the opinions and customes of the countrie we live in. There is ever perfect religion, perfect policie, perfect and compleat use of all things. They are even savage, as we call those fruits wilde, which nature of her selfe, and of her ordinarie progresse hath produced: whereas indeed, they are those which our selves have altered by our artificiall devices, and diverted from their common order, we should rather term savage. In those are the true and most profitable vertues, and naturall properties most lively and vigorous, which in these we have bastardized, applying them to the pleasure of our corrupted taste. And if notwithstanding, in divers fruits of those countries that were never tilled, we shall finde, that in respect of ours they are most excellent, and as delicate unto our taste; there is no reason, art should gaine the point of honour of our great and puissant mother Nature. We have so much by our inventions surcharged the beauties and riches of her workes, that we have altogether overchoaked her: yet where ever her puritie shineth, she makes our vaine and frivolous enterprises wonderfully ashamed.

---

† From "Of the Caniballes" (1580) in Michel de Montaigne, *The Essayes, or Morall, Politike and Millitarie Discourses*, trans. John Florio (London: V. Sims for E. Blount, 1603), Book 1, chap. 30, pp. 101–02, 104, 106–07, as reprinted in *The Essayes of Michael Lord of Montaigne: The First Booke* (London: Grant Richards, 1908), pp. 257–59, 263, 270–71. All notes are by the editors of this Norton Critical Edition.

Et veniunt hederæ sponte sua melius,
Surgit et in solis formosior arbutus antris,
Et volucres nulla dulcius arte canunt.—Propert. i. *El.* ii. 10.

Ivies spring better of their owne accord,
Unhanted plots much fairer trees afford.
Birds by no art much sweeter notes record.[1]

All our endevour or wit, cannot so much as reach to represent the nest of the least birdlet, it's contexture, beautie, profit and use, no nor the web of a seely[2] spider. *All things* (saith *Plato*) *are produced, either by nature, by fortune, or by art. The greatest and fairest by one or other of the two first, the least and imperfect by the last.* Those nations seeme therefore so barbarous unto me, because they have received very little fashion from humane wit, and are yet neere their originall naturalitie. The lawes of nature doe yet command them, which are but little bastardized by ours, And that with such puritie, as I am sometimes grieved the knowledge of it came no sooner to light, at what time there were men, that better than we could have judged of it. I am sorie, *Lycurgus* and *Plato* had it not: for me seemeth that what in those nations we see by experience, doth not only exceed all the pictures wherewith licentious Poesie hath proudly imbellished the golden age, and all her quaint inventions to faine a happy condition of man, but also the conception and desire of Philosophy. They could not imagine a genuitie[3] so pure and simple, as we see it by experience; nor ever beleeve our societie might be maintained with so little art and humane combination. It is a nation, would I answer *Plato*, that hath no kinde of traffike, no knowledge of Letters, no intelligence of numbers, no name of magistrate, nor of politike superioritie; no use of service, of riches or of povertie; no contracts, no successions, no partitions, no occupation but idle; no respect of kinred, but common, no apparell but naturall, no manuring of lands, no use of wine, corne, or mettle. The very words that import lying, falshood, treason, dissimulations, covetousnes, envie, detraction, and pardon, were never heard of amongst them. How dissonant would hee finde his imaginarie common-wealth from this perfection?

Hos natura modos primùm dedit.

Nature at first uprise,
These manners did devise.[4]

---

1. From the *Elegies* of Sextus Propertius.
2. Silly.
3. Simplicity.
4. From Virgin's *Georgics*.

Furthermore, they live in a country of so exceeding pleasant and temperate situation, that as my testimonies have told me, it is verie rare to see a sicke body amongst them; and they have further assured me, they never saw any man there, either shaking with the palsie, toothlesse, with eies dropping, or crooked and stooping through age. * * *

* * *

[Discusses their cannibalism]

I am not sorie we note the barbarous horror of such an action, but grieved, that prying so narrowly into their faults we are so blinded in ours. I thinke there is more barbarisme in eating men alive, than to feed upon them being dead; to mangle by tortures and torments a body full of lively sense, to roast him in peeces, to make dogges and swine to gnaw and teare him in mammockes[5] (as wee have not only read, but seene very lately, yea and in our owne memorie, not amongst ancient enemies, but our neighbours and fellow-citizens; and which is worse, under pretence of pietie and religion) than to roast and eat him after he is dead. * * *

* * *

[Remembers speaking to three cannibals who had been brought to Rouen]

Afterward some demanded their advise, and would needs know of them what things of note and admirable they had observed amongst us: they answered three things, the last of which I have forgotten, and am very sorie for it, the other two I yet remember. They said, *First, they found it very strange, that so many tall men with long beards, strong and well armed, as it were about the Kings person (it is very likely they meant the Switzers of his guard) would submit themselves to obey a beardless childe, and that we did not rather chuse one amongst them to command the rest. Secondly* (they have a manner of phrase whereby they call men but a moytie one of another.)[6] *They had perceived, there were men amongst us full gorged with all sortes of commodities, and others which hunger-starved, and bare with need and povertie, begged at their gates: and found it strange, these moyties so needy could endure such an injustice, and that they tooke not the others by the throte, or set fire on their houses.* I talked a good while with one of them, but I had so bad an interpreter, and who did so ill apprehend my meaning, and

5. Shreds.
6. They speak of men as halves of each other, that is, in two groups.

who through his foolishnesse was so troubled to conceive my imaginations, that I could draw no great matter from him. Touching that
point, wherein I demanded of him, what good he received by the
superioritie he had amongst his countriemen (for he was a Captaine
and our Marriners called him King) he told me, it was to march for-
most in any charge of warre: further, I asked him, how many men did
follow him, hee shewed me a distance of place, to signifie they were as
many as might be contained in so much ground, which I guessed to
be about 4. or 5. thousand men: moreover I demanded, if when warres
were ended, all his authoritie expired; he answered, that hee had only
this left him, which was, that when he went on progresse, and visited
the villages depending of him, the inhabitants prepared paths and
high-waies athwart the hedges of their woods, for him to passe
through at ease. All that is not verie ill; but what of that? They weare
no kinde of breeches nor hosen.

WILLIAM STRACHEY

Although the account by William Strachey (1572–1621) of the 1609
wreck of the *Sea Venture*, en route to Virginia, and the seemingly
miraculous reappearance in England of its crew over a year later, was
not published until 1625, it has long been accepted that Shakespeare
must have read it in manuscript, so extensive are the verbal and thematic parallels between account and play. See Alden T. Vaughan, "William Strachey's 'True Reportory' and Shakespeare: A Closer Look at
the Evidence," *Shakespeare Quarterly* 59:3 (2008): 245–73.

[Storms and Strife in Bermuda][†]

We were within seven or eight days at the most by Capt. Newport's
reckoning of making Cape Henry upon the coast of Virginia, when
on St James's day, July 24, being Monday (preparing for no less all
the black night before), the clouds gathering thick upon us, and the
winds singing and whistling most unusually, which made us cast off
our pinnace, towed till then astern, a dreadful storm and hideous
began to blow from out of the north-east, which swelling and roaring as it were by fits, some hours with more violence than others, at
length it did beat all light from heaven, which, like a hell of darkness
turned black upon us, so much the fuller of horror, as in such cases
horror and fear are used to overrun the troubled and overmastered

---

† From *A True Repertory of the Wreck and Redemption of Sir Thomas Gates, Knight, upon
and from the Islands of the Bermudas*, in Samuel Purchas, *Haklytus Posthumus or Purchas His Pilgrimes* [1625] (Glasgow: James MacLehose and Sons, 1906), XIX: 5–72. All
notes are by the editors of this Norton Critical Edition.

senses of us all. Our eyes lay so sensible to the terrible cries and murmurs of the winds, and to the distraction of our company since even the most armed and best prepared among us was not a little shaken. * * *

For four and twenty hours the storm in a restless tumult had blown so exceedingly that we could not apprehend in our imaginations any possibility of greater violence, yet we did still find it, not only more terrible but more constant, fury added to fury, and one storm urging a second more outrageous than the former, whether it so wrought upon our fears, or indeed met with new forces. Sometimes strikes in our ship amongst women and passengers, not used to such hurly and discomforts, made us look upon each other with troubled hearts and panting bosoms; our clamours drowned in the winds, and the winds in thunder. Prayers might well be in the heart and lips, but drowned in the outcries of the officers: nothing was heard that could give comfort, nothing seen that might encourage hope. It is impossible for me, had I the voice of Stentor,[1] and the expression of as many tongues as his throat of voices, to express the outcries and miseries, not languishing, but wasting his spirits, and art constant to his principles but not prevailing. Our sails lay wound up without use and if at any time we bore but a hollocks, or half forecourse, to guide her before the sea, six and sometimes eight men were not enough to hold the whipstaff in the steerage and the tiller below in the gunners' room, by which may be imagined the strength of the storm. The sea swelled above the clouds and gave battle unto heaven. It could not be said to rain, the waters like whole rivers did flood the air. And this I still did observe, that whereas upon the land, when a storm has poured itself forth once in drifts of rain, the wind has thereby been beaten down and vanquished, and has not lasted long after, here the glut of water (as if it were meanwhile throttling the wind) was no sooner a little emptied and qualified, than instantly the winds (as having now gotten their mouths free and at liberty) spoke louder and grew more tumultuous and malignant. What shall I say? Winds and seas were as mad as fury and rage could make them. For my own part, I had been in some storms before, on the coast of Barbary and Algiers as well as in the Levant, and one even worse in the Adriatic gulf, in a bottom off Candy, so I may well say: Ego quid sit ater Hadriae novi sinus, & quid albus peccet iapex.[2] Yet all that I had ever suffered gathered together might not hold comparison with this. There was not a moment in which the sudden splitting or instant overturning of the ship was not expected.

---

1. A Greek herald of loud voice, as described by Homer in the *Iliad*.
2. "Ah! well I know / How Hadria glooms, how falsely clear / The west-winds blow" (Horace, *Odes*).

* * *

During all this time, the heavens look'd so black upon us that it was not possible to observe the elevation of the pole: not a star by night nor a sunbeam by day was to be seen. Only upon the Thursday night Sir George Somers, being upon the watch, had an apparition of a little round light, like a faint star, trembling and streaming along with a sparkling blaze, half the height of the main mast, and shooting sometimes from shroud to shroud, tempting to settle as it were upon any of the four shrouds. And for three or four hours together, or rather more, half the night it kept with us, running sometimes along the mainyard to the very end, and then returning. At which, Sir George Sommers called several people about him and showed it them: they observed it with much wonder and carefulness, but all of a sudden, towards the morning watch, they lost sight of it, and knew not which way it went. The superstitious seamen make many constructions of this sea-fire, which nevertheless is usual in storms; the same (it may be) which the Greeks were wont in the Mediterranean to call Castor and Pollux, of which, if one only appeared without the other, they took it for an evil sign of great tempest. The Italians and such, who lie open to the Adriatic and Tyrrene Sea, call it Corpo Santo (a sacred body); the Spaniards call it Saint Elmo and have an authentic and miraculous legend for it. Be it what it will, we laid other foundations of safety or ruin than in the rising or falling of it, could it have served us now miraculously to have taken our height by it, it might have stricken amazement and a reverence in our devotions, according to the due of a miracle. But it did not light us any whit the more to our known way, as we now ran (as do hoodwinked men) at all adventures, sometimes north and north-east, then north and by west, and in an instant again varying two or three points, and sometimes half the compass. East and by south we steered away as much as we could to bear upright, which was no small carefulness nor pain to do, although we much unrigged our ship, threw overboard much luggage, many a trunk and chest (in which I suffered no mean loss) and stave many a butt of beer, hogsheads of oil, cider, wine, and vinegar, and heaved away all our ordinance on the starboard side, and had now purposed to have cut down the main mast, the more to lighten her, for we were much spent, and our men so weary that their strength altogether failed them, with their hearts, having travailed now from Tuesday till Friday morning, day and night, without either sleep or food, for the leakage taking up all the hold, we could neither come by beer nor fresh water, fire we could keep none in the cook-room to dress any meat, and carefulness, grief, and our turn at the pump or bucket were sufficient to hold sleep from our eyes.

* * *

We found it to be the dangerous and dreaded island, or rather islands, of the Bermuda; whereof let me give your Ladyship a brief description before I proceed to my narration. And that the rather, because they be so terrible to all that ever touched on them, and such tempests, thunders, and other fearful objects are seen and heard about them, that they be called commonly, The Devil's Islands, and are feared and avoided of all sea travellers alive, above any other place in the world. Yet it pleased our merciful God to make even this hideous and hated place, both the place of our safetie, and means of our deliverance.

And hereby also, I hope to deliver the world from a foul and general error: it being counted of most, that they can be no habitation for men, but rather given over to devils and wicked spirits; whereas indeed we find them now by experience to be as habitable and commodious as most countries of the same climate and situation; in so much as if the entrance into them were as easy as the place itself is contenting, it had long before this been inhabited, as well as other islands. Thus shall we make it appear that truth is the daughter of time, and that men ought not to deny everything which is not subject to their own sense.

* * *

[There are mutinies and rebellions among the company]

In these dangers and devilish disquiets (whilst the Almighty God wrought for us, and sent us miraculously delivered from the calamities of the sea, all blessings upon the shore, to content and bind us to gratefulness) thus enraged amongst ourselves, to the destruction each of the others, into what a mischief and misery had we been given up, had we not had a Governor with his authority to have suppressed the same?[3] Yet was there a worse practice, faction, and conjuration afoot, deadly and bloody, in which the life of our Governor, with many others were threatened, and could not but miscarry in his fall. But such is ever the will of God (who, in the execution of his judgments, breaks the firebrands upon the head of him who first kindled them) that there were those who conceived that our Governor indeed neither dared, nor had authority to put into execution, or pass the act of justice upon any one, however treacherous or impious. Their own opinions deceived them so much about the unlawfulness of any act which they would execute, as they dared to justify among themselves that if they should be apprehended before the performance, they should happily suffer as martyrs. They therefore persevered not only to draw in as many

3. Sir Thomas Gates.

associates as they could persuade to the abandoning of our governor and the inhabiting of this island. They had now proposed to have made a surprise of the store-house, and to have forced from thence what was therein either of meal, cloth, cables, arms, sails, oars or what else it pleased God that we had recovered from the wreck, and was to serve our general necessity and needs, either for the relief of us while we stayed here, or for the carrying of us from this place again, when our pinnace should have been furnished.

But as all giddy and lawless attempts have always something of imperfection, and that as well by the property of the action, which holds disobedience and rebellion (both full of fear), as through the ignorance of the devisers themselves; so in this (besides those defects) there were some of the association who, not strongly enough fortified in their own conceits, broke from the plot itself, and (before the time was ripe for its execution) discovered the whole order and every agent and actor of it, who nevertheless were not suddenly apprehended, because the confederates were divided and separated in place, some with us, and the chief with Sir George Somers on his island (and indeed all his company). But good watch was placed upon them, every man from then on was commanded to wear his weapon, without which previously we had freely walked from quarter to quarter and conversed among ourselves, and every man was advised to stand upon his guard, his own life not being in safety, whilst his next neighbour was not to be trusted. The sentinels and nightwatchmen doubled, the passages of both the quarters were carefully observed, by which means nothing was further attempted; until a gentleman among them, one Henry Paine, on the thirteenth of March, full of mischief and every hour preparing something or other, stealing swords, adises, axes, hatchets, saws, augers, planes, mallets, etc to make good his own bad end, his watch night coming about, and being called by the captain of the same to be upon the guard, did not only give his said commander evil language, but struck at him, doubled his blows, and when he was not allowed to close with him, went off the guard, scoffing at the double diligence and attendance of the watch, appointed by the governor for much purpose, as he said: upon which, the watch telling him, if the governor should hear of his insolence, it might turn him to much blame and happily be as much as his life was worth. The said Paine replied with a settled and bitter violence, and in such irreverent terms as I should offend the modest ear too much if I expressed it in his own phrase; but the contents were, how the governor had no authority of that quality to justify upon anyone (however mean in the colony) an action of that nature, and therefore let the governor (said he) kiss etc. Which words, being with the omitted additions brought the next day into every common and public discourse, at length they were delivered over to the governor, who, examining well the fact (the transgression so much the more exemplary and odious, as being in a dangerous time, in a confederate, and the success of the same wishtly[4] listened after, with a doubtful conceit, what might be the issue of so notorious a boldness and impudence) calling the said Paine before him, and the whole company, where (being soon convinced both by the witness of the commander and many who were on the watch with him), our governor, who had now the eyes of the whole colony fixed upon him, condemned him to be instantly hanged; and the ladder being ready, after he had made many confessions, he earnestly desired, being a gentleman, that he might be shot to death, and towards the evening he had his desire, the sun and his life setting together.

* * *

Likewise we buried five of our company, Jeffery Briars, Richard Lewis, William Hitchman, and my god-daughter Bermuda Rolfe, and one untimely Edward Samuell, a sailor, being villainously killed by the foresaid Robert Waters (also a sailor) with a shovel, who struck him therewith under the ear, for which he was apprehended and appointed to be hanged the next day (the fact being done in the twilight), but being bound fast to a tree all night, with many ropes and a guard of five or six to attend him, his fellow sailors (watching the advantage of the sentinels sleeping), in despite and disdain that justice should be showed on a sailor, and that one of their crew should be an example to others, not taking into consideration the unmanliness of the murder, nor the horror of the sin, they cut his bands and conveyed him into the woods, where they fed him nightly, and closely. Afterwards, by the mediation of Sir George Somers, upon many conditions, he had his trial respited by our governor.

* * *

SIR HENRY MAINWARING

Sir Henry Mainwaring (1587–1653) was an English lawyer, soldier, author, seaman, and politician. He sailed as a pirate before joining the Royal Navy. His dictionary was the first work in English on seamanship and nautical terms.

4. Intently.

From The Seaman's Dictionary[†]

Blow. Every one knows when the wind blows, but there are some speeches used at sea, which are not generally understood, as the wind *blows home*, or *blows through*; that is, when the wind doth not cease, or grow less till it come past that place: also *blow through* is sometimes used, when they think the wind will be so great that it will blow asunder the sails.

A Butt. By this word taken indefinitely is meant a vessel or cask, as a butt of wine, etc., but in sea language, thus: a *butt* is properly the end of a plank joining to another, on the outward side of the ship under water.

Course is taken for that point of the compass which the ship is to sail upon. . . . *Alter the course*, that is, sail upon another point of the compass; *mistake the course*, that is, not to know how the land lies or which way to go. Also *main course* and *fore course, mizen course* are the sails without the bonnets. Not all ships of great burden have *double courses* to hold more wind and give the ship more way in a fresh gale, but in an easy gale they hinder, as do all things that are weighty overhead.

Fathom. A fathom is six foot; which, though every one know, I set down to give notice that we measure the length of all our ropes by fathoms, and not by any other measure, as we do the compass of the ropes by inches, for we say a cable or hawser of so many fathom long or so many inches about; also we reckon in sounding by fathoms.

Split. When the wind hath blown a sail to pieces, we say the sail is split.

A Tempest. When it overblows so exceedingly that it is not possible to bear any sail, and that it is a wind mixed with rain or hail, they call it a tempest, which they count a degree above a storm.

To Try. Trying is to have no more sail forth but the mainsail, the tack aboard, the bowline set up, the sheet close aft, and the helm tied down close aboard. Some try with their mizen only, but that is when it blows so much that they cannot maintain the mainsail. A ship *a-try* with her mainsail (unless it be an extraordinary grown sea) will make her way two points afore the beam; but with a mizen not so much.

† From *The Seaman's Dictionary* (c. 1623), in *The Life and Works of Sir Henry Mainwaring*, vol. II, edited by G. E. Manwaring and W. G. Perrin for The Navy Records Society, 1922.

CRITICISM

JOHN DRYDEN

[The Character of Caliban][†]

* * * To return once more to Shakespear; no man ever drew so many characters, or generally distinguished 'em better from one another, excepting only Johnson: I will instance but in one, to show the copiousness of his Invention; 'tis that of Caliban, or the Monster in the Tempest. He seems there to have created a person which was not in Nature, a boldness which at first sight would appear intolerable: for he makes him a Species of himself, begotten by an Incubus on a Witch; but this as I have elsewhere prov'd, is not wholly beyond the bounds of credibility, at least the vulgar stile believe it. We have the separated notions of a spirit, and of a Witch; (and Spirits according to Plato, are vested with a subtil body; according to some of his followers, have different Sexes) therefore as from the distinct apprehensions of a Horse, and of a Man, Imagination has form'd a Centaur, so from those of an Incubus and a Sorceress, Shakespear has produc'd his Monster. Whether or no his Generation can be defended, I leave to Philosophy; but of this I am certain, that the Poet has most judiciously furnish'd him with a person, a Language, and a character, which will suit him, both by Fathers and Mothers side: he has all the discontents, and malice of a Witch, and of a Devil; besides a convenient proportion of the deadly sins; Gluttony, Sloth, and Lust, are manifest; the dejectedness of a slave is likewise given him, and the ignorance of one bred up in a Desart Island. His person is monstrous, as he is the product of unnatural Lust; and his language is as hobgoblin as his person: in all things he is distinguish'd from other mortals. * * *

NICHOLAS ROWE

[The Magic of *The Tempest*][‡]

* * *

But certainly the greatness of this author's genius nowhere so much appears as where he gives his imagination an entire loose, and raises his fancy to a flight above mankind and the limits of the visible world. Such are his attempts in *The Tempest, Midsummer Night's Dream, Macbeth* and *Hamlet*. Of these *The Tempest*, however it comes to be

---

† From the Preface to his *Troilus and Cressida, or, Truth found too late* (London, 1679).
‡ From *The Works of Mr. William Shakespear* (London: for Jacob Tonson, 1709), 1: xxiii–xxvi.

placed the first by the former publishers of his works, can never have been the first written by him: it seems to me as perfect in its kind as almost anything we have of his. One may observe that the unities are kept here with an exactness uncommon to the liberties of his writing; though that was what, I suppose, he valued himself least upon, since his excellencies were all of another kind. I am very sensible that he does, in this play, depart too much from that likeness to truth which ought to be observed in these sort of writings; yet he does it so very finely that one is easily drawn in to have more faith for his sake than reason does well allow of. His magic has something in it very solemn and very poetical; and that extravagant character of Caliban is mighty well sustained, shows a wonderful invention in the author, who could strike out such a particular wild image, and is certainly one of the finest and most uncommon grotesques that was ever seen. The observation, which I have been informed three very great men concurred in making upon this part, was extremely just. That Shakespeare had not only found out a new character in his Caliban, but had also devised and adapted a new manner of language for that character. Among the particular beauties of this piece, I think one may be allowed to point out the tale of Prospero in the first act; his speech to Ferdinand in the fourth, upon the making of the masque of Juno and Ceres; and that in the fifth, where he dissolves his charms and resolves to break his magic rod. This play has been altered by Sir William Davenant and Mr Dryden; and though I won't arraign the judgement of those two great men, yet I think I may be allowed to say that there are some things left out by them that might, and even ought, to have been kept in. Mr Dryden was an admirer of our author and, indeed, he owed him a great deal, as those who have read them both may very easily observe. And, I think, in justice to them both, I should not on this occasion omit what Mr Dryden has said of him.

> Shakespeare, *who, taught by none, did first impart*
> To Fletcher *wit, to lab'ring* Johnson *art.*
> *He, monarch-like, gave those his subjects law,*
> *And is that Nature which they paint and draw.*
> Fletcher *reach'd that which on his heights did grow,*
> Whilst Johnson *crept and gather'd all below:*
> *This did his love, and this his mirth digest,*
> *One imitates him most, the other best.*
> *If they have since out-writ all other men,*
> *'Tis with the drops which fell from* Shakespeare's *pen.*
> *The storm which vanish'd on the neighb'ring shore,*
> *Was taught by* Shakespeare's *Tempest first to roar.*
> *That innocence and beauty which did smile*
> In Fletcher, *grew on this enchanted isle.*
> *But* Shakespeare's *magic could not copied be,*

Within that circle none dared walk but he.
I must confess 'twas bold, nor would you now
That liberty to vulgar wits allow,
Which works by magic supernatural things;
But Shakespeare's pow'r is sacred as a king's.
          Prologue to *The Tempest*, as it is altered
          by Mr Dryden.

It is the same magic that raises the fairies in *Midsummer Night's Dream*, the witches in *Macbeth*, and the ghost in *Hamlet*, with thoughts and language so proper to the parts they sustain, and so peculiar to the talent of this writer. But of the two last of these plays I shall occasion to take notice, among the tragedies of Mr Shakespeare. If one undertook to examine the greatest part of these by those rules which are established by Aristotle, and taken from the model of the Grecian stage, it would be no very hard task to find a great many faults; but as Shakespeare lived under a kind of mere light of nature, and had never been made acquainted with the regularity of those written precepts, so it would be hard to judge him by a law he knew nothing of. We are to consider him as a man that liv'd in a state of almost universal licence and ignorance. There was no established judge, but every one took the liberty to write according to the dictates of his own fancy.

* * *

SAMUEL TAYLOR COLERIDGE

From Notes on *The Tempest*[†]

* * *

The Tempest is a specimen of the purely romantic drama, in which the interest is not historical, or dependent upon fidelity of portraiture, or the natural connexion of events,—but is a birth of the imagination, and rests only on the coaptation and the union of the elements granted to, or assumed by, the poet. It is a species of drama which owes no allegiance to time or space, and in which, therefore, errors of chronology and geography—no mortal sins in any species— are venial faults, and count for nothing. It addresses itself entirely to the imaginative faculty; and although the illusion may be assisted by the effect on the senses of the complicated scenery and decorations of modern times, yet this sort of assistance is dangerous. For the principal and only genuine excitement ought to come from within,— from the moved and sympathetic imagination; whereas, where so

† From *The Literary Remains of Samuel Taylor Coleridge*, coll. and ed. Henry Nelson Coleridge (London: W. Pickering, 1836), 2: 92–102. Line numbers to the play have been added. All notes are by the editors of this Norton Critical Edition.

much is addressed to the mere external senses of seeing and hearing, the spiritual vision is apt to languish, and the attraction from without will withdraw the mind from the proper and only legitimate interest which is intended to spring from within.

The romance opens with a busy scene admirably appropriate to the kind of drama, and giving, as it were, the key-note to the whole harmony. It prepares and initiates the excitement required for the entire piece, and yet does not demand any thing from the spectators, which their previous habits had not fitted them to understand. It is the bustle of a tempest, from which the real horrors are abstracted;—therefore it is poetical, though not in strictness natural—(the distinction to which I have so often alluded)—and is purposely restrained from concentering the interest on itself, but used merely as an induction or turning for what is to follow.

In the second scene, Prospero's speeches, till the entrance of Ariel, contain the finest example, I remember, of retrospective narration for the purpose of exciting immediate interest, and putting the audience in possession of all the information necessary for the understanding of the plot. Observe, too, the perfect probability of the moment chosen by Prospero (the very Shakespeare himself, as it were, of the tempest) to open out the truth to his daughter, his own romantic bearing, and how completely anything that might have been disagreeable to us in the magician, is reconciled and shaded in the humanity and natural feelings of the father. In the very first speech of Miranda the simplicity and tenderness of her character are at once laid open;—it would have been lost in direct contact with the agitation of the first scene. The opinion once prevailed, but, happily, is now abandoned, that Fletcher alone wrote for women;—the truth is, that with very few, and those partial, exceptions, the female characters in the plays of Beaumont and Fletcher are, when of the light kind, not decent; when heroic, complete viragos. But in Shakespeare all the elements of womanhood are holy, and there is the sweet, yet dignified feeling of all that *continuates* society, as sense of ancestry and of sex, with a purity unassailable by sophistry, because it rests not in the analytic processes, but in that sane equipoise of the faculties, during which the feelings are representative of all past experience,—not of the individual only, but of all those by whom she has been educated, and their predecessors even up to the first mother that lived. Shakespeare saw that the want of prominence, which Pope notices for sarcasm, was the blessed beauty of the woman's character, and knew that it arose not from any deficiency, but from the more exquisite harmony of all the parts of the moral being constituting one living total of head and heart. He has drawn it, indeed, in all its distinctive energies of faith, patience, constancy, fortitude,—shown in all of them as following the heart, which gives its results by a nice tact and happy intuition, without the intervention of the discursive faculty,—sees all things in and by the light of affections, and errs, if it ever err, in the exaggerations of love alone. In all the Shakespearian women there is essentially the same foundation and principle; the distinct individuality and variety are merely the result of the modification of circumstances, whether in Miranda the maiden, in Imogen the wife, or in Katharine the queen.

But to return. The appearance and characters of the super or ultra-natural servants are finely contrasted. Ariel has in every thing the airy tint which gives the name; and it is worthy of remark that Miranda is never directly brought into comparison with Ariel, lest the natural and human of the one and the supernatural of the other should tend to neutralize each other; Caliban, on the other hand, is all earth, all condensed and gross in feelings and images; he has the dawnings of understanding without reason or the moral sense, and in him, as in some brute animals, this advance to the intellectual faculties, without the moral sense, is marked by the appearance of vice. For it is in the primacy of the moral being only that man is truly human; in his intellectual powers he is certainly approached by the brutes, and, man's whole system duly considered, those powers cannot be considered other than means to an end, that is, to morality.

In this scene, as it proceeds, is displayed the impression made by Ferdinand and Miranda on each other; it is love at first sight;—

> at the first sight
> They have chang'd eyes:— [1.2.439–40]

and it appears to me, that in all cases of real love, it is at one moment that it takes place. That moment may have been prepared by previous esteem, admiration, or even affection,—yet love seems to require a momentary act of volition, by which a tacit bond of devotion is imposed,—a bond not to be thereafter broken without violating what should be sacred in our nature. How finely is the true Shakespearian scene contrasted with Dryden's vulgar alteration of it, in which a mere ludicrous psychological experiment, as it were, is tried—displaying nothing but indelicacy without passion. Prospero's interruption of the courtship has often seemed to me to have no sufficient motive; still his alleged reason—

> lest too light winning
> Make the prize light— [1.2.450–51]

is enough for the ethereal connexions of the romantic imagination, although it would not be so for the historical. The whole courting scene, indeed, in the beginning of the third act, between the lovers is a masterpiece; and the first dawn of disobedience in the mind of Miranda to the command of her father is very finely drawn, so as to seem the working of the Scriptural command, *Thou shalt leave father and mother*, &c. O! with what exquisite purity this scene is conceived and executed! Shakespeare may sometimes be gross, but I boldly say that he is always moral and modest. Alas! in this our day decency of manners is preserved at the expense of morality of heart, and delicacies for vice are allowed, whilst grossness against it is hypocritically, or at least morbidly, condemned.

In this play are admirably sketched the vices generally accompanying a low degree of civilization; and in the first scene of the second act Shakespeare has, as in many other places, shown the tendency in bad men to indulge in scorn and contemptuous expressions, as a mode of getting rid of their own uneasy feelings of inferiority to the good, and also, by making the good ridiculous, of rendering the transition of others to wickedness easy. Shakespeare never puts habitual scorn into the mouths of other than bad men, as here in the instances of Antonio and Sebastian. The scene of the intended assassination of Alonzo and Gonzalo is an exact counterpart of the scene between Macbeth and his lady, only pitched in a lower key throughout, as designed to be frustrated and concealed, and exhibiting the same profound management in the manner of familiarizing a mind, not immediately recipient, to the suggestion of guilt, by associating the proposed crime with something ludicrous or out of place,—something not habitually matter of reverence. By this kind of sophistry the imagination and fancy are first bribed to contemplate the suggested act, and at length to become acquainted with it. Observe how the effect of this scene is heightened by contrast with another counterpart of it in low life,—that between the conspirators Stephano, Caliban, and Trinculo in the second scene of the third act, in which there are the same essential characteristics.

In this play and in this scene of it are also shown the springs of the vulgar in politics,—of that kind of politics which is inwoven with human nature. In his treatment of this subject, wherever it occurs, Shakespeare is quite peculiar. In other writers we find the particular opinions of the individual; in Massinger it is rank republicanism; in Beaumont and Fletcher even *jure divino* principles are carried to excess;—but Shakespeare never promulgates any party tenets. He is always the philosopher and the moralist, but at the same time with a profound veneration for all the established institutions of society, and for those classes which form the permanent elements of the state—especially never introducing a professional character, as such, otherwise than as respectable. If he must have any name, he should be styled a philosophical aristocrat, delighting in those hereditary institutions which have a tendency to bind one age to another, and in that distinction of ranks, of which, although few may be in possession, all enjoy the advantages. Hence, again, you will observe the good nature with which he seems always to make sport with the passions and follies of a mob, as with an irrational animal. He is never angry with it, but hugely content with holding up its absurdities to its face; and sometimes you may trace a tone of almost affectionate superiority, something like that in which a father speaks of the rogueries of a child. See the good-humoured way in which he describes Stephano passing from the most licentious freedom to absolute despotism over Trinculo and Caliban. The truth is, Shakespeare's characters are all *genera*[1] intensely individualized; the results of meditation, of which observation supplied the drapery and the colors necessary to combine them with each other. He had virtually surveyed all the great component powers and impulses of human nature,—had seen that their different combinations and subordinations were in fact the individualizers of men, and showed how their harmony was produced by reciprocal disproportions of excess or deficiency. The language in which these truths are expressed was not drawn from any set fashion, but from the profoundest depths of his moral being, and is therefore for all ages.

LUDWIG TIECK

From Shakespeare's Treatment of the Marvellous[†]

Admiration has often been expressed for Shakespeare's genius, which in so many of his artistic works leaves the common course behind and seeks out new pathways, following the passions now into their most subtle nuances, now to their uttermost bounds, now initiating the spectator into the mysteries of the night, transporting him into the company of witches and ghosts, then again surrounding him with fairies wholly different from those terrible apparitions. Given the boldness with which Shakespeare offends against the customary rules of the drama, we too often overlook the immeasurably greater artistry with which he conceals from our notice such want of regularity: for the touchstone of true genius is to be found in the fact that, for every audacious fiction, every unusual angle of depiction, it is able to predispose the mind of the spectator to the acceptance of illusion; that the poet does not presume on our goodwill but so excites our imagination, even against our wishes, that we forget the rules of aesthetics, together with all the notions

1. Types.
† From "Shakespeare's Treatment of the Marvellous" [1793], trans. Louise Adey, in Jonathan Bate, ed., *The Romantics on Shakespeare* (Harmondsworth: Penguin, 1992), pp. 60–66. Copyright © 1992 Louise Adey. Reprinted by permission of the translator, Louise Adey Huish.

of our enlightened century, and abandon ourselves completely to the lovely delusions of the poet; that after its intoxication the soul willingly yields to fresh enchantments and the playful imagination is not awoken from its dreams by any sudden, unpleasant surprise.

In this highest achievement of dramatic art Shakespeare will perhaps remain forever inimitable—that great alchemy which transformed everything he touched into gold seems to have died with him. For however much his masterpieces are imitated by his contemporaries and by later poets, by the English and the Germans, not one of them has ventured to follow him into that magic circle in which he appears so great and so terrible. Those few who have tried to rival him in this appear in comparison to him like conjurors whom no spirit will obey, despite their mysterious spells, their mystic circles and all their magical apparatus, and who in the end arouse only boredom because they do not possess the artistry to lull to sleep our powers of reason and judgement.

At the time when he lived, Shakespeare, more than any other writer, was the poet of his people; he did not write for the rabble but for his nation, and so, whether he knew the masterpieces of antiquity or not, they were not the tribunal to which he brought his plays, on the contrary, he had learnt what produces an effect on people's minds by studious observation of mankind, and he created his works of art according to his own instinct and the rules which he had derived from experience. This is the reason why most of his plays are so generally effective in performance and when read, and why they must necessarily be effective, for perhaps there is no poet who has calculated the theatrical effect of his works as carefully as Shakespeare, though without treating his audience to hollow *coups de théâtre*, or entertaining them with feeble surprises. He holds their attention rapt to the very end without recourse to the artifices dear to many a calculating poet and without any appeal to curiosity, and he moves them intensely, even to the point of terror, with his bold strokes of genius.

* * *

It is primarily through the characters of Ariel and Caliban that Shakespeare creates this whole marvellous world around us; they are, so to speak, the guardians who never permit our minds to return to the realm of reality; in every serious scene we are reminded by the presence of Ariel of where we are, in every comic scene, by that of Caliban. Prospero's magical contrivances, which occur one after the other without interruption, do not for a single moment permit our eyes to return to the reality which would instantly reduce all the chimeras of the poet to dust and ashes. Even the strange contrast between Ariel and Caliban enhances our faith in the marvellous. The creation of that exotic figure was a most felicitous idea on the part of the poet; in this figure he shows us the strangest mixture of absurdity and abomination; this monster is so remote from humanity and is portrayed with such extreme plausibility and conviction that Caliban's presence alone would persuade us that we had been transported to an utterly strange, as yet unknown world. * * *

FANNY KEMBLE

From Some Notes on *The Tempest*†

* * *

The opening of this play is connected with my earliest recollections. In looking down the 'dark backward and abysm of time' [1.2.50], to the period when I was but six years old, my memory conjures up a vision of a stately drawing-room on the ground-floor of a house, doubtless long since swept from the face of the earth by the encroaching tide of new houses and streets that has submerged every trace of suburban beauty, picturesqueness, or rural privacy in the neighbourhood of London, converting it all by a hideous process of assimilation into more London, till London seems almost more than England can carry * * *

[In the drawing-room a lovely-looking lady] used to tell me the story of the one large picture which adorned the room. Over and over again, at my importunate beseeching, she told it,—sometimes standing before it, while I held her hand, and listened with upturned face, and eyes rounding with big tears of wonder and pity, to a tale which shook my small soul with a sadness and strangeness * * * In the midst of a stormy sea, on which night seemed fast settling down, a helmless, mastless, sailless bark lay weltering giddily, and in it sat a man in the full flower of vigorous manhood. His attitude was one of miserable dejection, and, oh, how I did long to remove the hand with which his eyes were covered, to see what manner of look in them answered to the bitter sorrow which the speechless lips expressed! His other hand rested on the fair curls of a girl-baby of three years old, who clung to his knee, and, with wide, wondering blue eyes and laughing lips, looked up into the half-hidden face of her father.—'And that,' said the sweet voice at my side, 'was the good Duke of Milan, Prospero,—and that was his little child, Miranda.'

---

† From *Notes upon some of Shakespeare's Plays* (London: Richard Bentley & Sons, 1882), pp. 123, 126–28, 131, 132–36, 155–57, 159–61. Line numbers to the play have been added.

There was something about the face and figure of the Prospero that suggested to me those of my father; and this, perhaps, added to the poignancy with which the representation of his distress affected my childish imagination. But the impression made by the picture, the story, and the place where I heard the one and saw the other, is among the most vivid that my memory retains. And never, even now, do I turn the magic page that holds that marvellous history, without again seeing the lovely lady, the picture full of sad dismay, and my own six-year-old self listening to that earliest Shakespearian lore that my mind and heart ever received. I suppose this is partly the secret of my love for this, above all other of the poet's plays:—it was my first possession in the kingdom of unbounded delight which he has since bestowed upon me * * *

The Tempest is, as I have already said, my favourite of Shakespeare's Dramas. The remoteness of the scene from all known localities allows a range to the imagination such as no other of his plays affords * * *

But chiefly I delight in this play, because of the image which it presents to my mind of the glorious supremacy of the righteous human soul over all things by which it is surrounded. Prospero is to me the representative of wise and virtuous manhood, in its true relation to the combined elements of existence—the physical powers of the external world, and the varieties of character with which it comes into voluntary, accidental, or enforced contact.

Of the wonderful chain of being, of which Caliban is the densest and Ariel the most ethereal extreme, Prospero is the middle link. He—the wise and good man—is the ruling power, to whom the whole series is subject.

First, and lowest in the scale, comes the gross and uncouth but powerful savage, who represents both the more ponderous and unwieldy natural elements (as the earth and water), which the wise Magician by his knowledge compels to his service; and the brutal and animal propensities of the nature of man, which he, the type of its noblest development, holds in lordly subjugation.

Next follow the drunken, ribald, foolish retainers of the King of Naples, whose ignorance, knavery, and stupidity represent the coarser attributes of those great unenlightened masses, which in all communities threaten authority by their conjunction with brute force and savage ferocity; and only under the wholesome restraint of a wise discipline can be gradually admonished into the salutary subserviency necessary for their civilization.

Ascending by degrees in the scale, the next group is that of the cunning, cruel, selfish, treacherous worldlings—Princes and Potentates—the peers in outward circumstances of high birth and breeding of the noble Prospero—whose villanous policy (not unaided by his own dereliction of his duties as a governor in the pursuit of his pleasure as a philosopher) triumphs over his fortune, and, through a devilish ability and craft, for a time gets the better of truth and virtue in his person.

From these, who represent the baser intellectual as the former do the baser sensual properties of humanity, we approach by a most harmonious moral transition, through the agency of the skilfully interposed figure of the kindly gentleman, Gonzalo, those charming types of youth and love, Ferdinand and Miranda—the fervent chivalrous devotion of the youth, and the yielding simplicity and sweetness of the girl, are lovely representations of those natural emotions of tender sentiment and passionate desire which, watched and guided and guarded by the affectionate solicitude and paternal prudence of Prospero, are pruned of their lavish luxuriance and supported in their violent weakness by the wise will that teaches forbearance and self-control as the only price at which these exquisite flowers of existence may unfold their blossoms in prosperous beauty, and bear their rightful harvest of happiness as well as pleasure.

Next in this wonderful gamut of being, governed by the sovereign soul of Prospero, come the shining figures of the Masque—beautiful bright apparitions, fitly indicating the air, the fire, and all the more smiling aspects and subtler forces of nature * * *

Last—highest of all—crowning with a fitful flame of lambent brightness this poetical pyramid of existence, flickers and flashes the beautiful Demon, without whose exquisite companionship we never think of the royal Magician with his grave countenance of command—Ariel seems to me to represent the keenest perceiving intellect—apart from all moral consciousness and sense of responsibility. His power and knowledge are in some respects greater than those of his master—he can do what Prospero cannot—he lashes up the Tempest round the Island—he saves the King and his companions from the shipwreck—he defeats the conspiracy of Sebastian and Antonio, and discovers the clumsy plot of the beast Caliban—he wields immediate influence over the elements, and comprehends alike without indignation or sympathy—which are moral results—the sin and suffering of humanity. Therefore, because he is only a spirit of knowledge, he is subject to the spirit of love—and the wild, subtle, keen, beautiful, powerful creature is compelled to serve with mutinous waywardness and unwilling subjection the human soul that pitied and rescued it from its harsher slavery to sin—and which, though controlling it with a wise severity to the fulfilment of its duties, yearns after it with the tearful eyes of tender human love when its wild wings flash away into its newly-recovered realm of lawless liberty * * *

Brought up in all but utter solitude, under no influence but that of her wise and loving father on earth, and her wise and loving

Father in Heaven, Miranda exhibits no more coyness in her acceptance of Ferdinand's overtures than properly belongs to the instinc-
tive modesty of her sex, unenhanced by any of the petty pretty arts
of coquetry and assumed shyness, which are the express result of
artificial female training . . . [She] offers her life to her lover with
the perfect devotion and humility of the true womanly nature:—

> To be your fellow
> You may deny me, but I'll be your servant
> Whether you will or no.
>   [3.1.84–86]

In the purity and simplicity of this 'tender of affection,' Ferdinand
made acquaintance with a species of modesty to which assuredly
none of those ladies of the Court of Naples, 'whom he had eyed with
best regard' [3.1.40], had ever introduced him; and indeed to them
Miranda's proceeding might very probably have appeared highly
unlady-like, as I have heard it pronounced more than once by—
ladies * * *

But Prospero was after all a mere man, and knew no better than
to bring up Miranda to speak the truth, and the fair child had been
so holily trained by him, that her surrender of herself to the man
she loves is so little feminine after the approved feminine fashion,
that it is simply angelic.

That Shakespeare, who indeed knew all things, knew very well
the difference between such a creature as Miranda and a well-
brought-up young lady, is plain enough, when he makes poor Juliet,
after her passionate confession of love made to the stars, and over-
heard by Romeo, apologise to him with quite pathetic mortification
for not having been more 'strange' [*Romeo and Juliet*, 2.2.101]. She
regrets extremely her unqualified expressions of affection,—assures
Romeo that nothing would have induced her to have spoken the
truth, if she had only known he heard her, and even offers * * * to
'frown and be perverse and say him nay' [2.2.96],—and in short has
evidently shocked her own conventional prejudices quite as much
as she fears she has his * * *. But then Juliet was the flower of
Veronese young ladies, and her good mother, and gossiping nurse,
were not likely to have neglected her education to the tune of letting her speak the truth without due preparation. Miranda is to be
excused as a savage—probably Ferdinand thought her excusable.

HENRY JAMES

[Surrendering to *The Tempest*]†

* * * Everything has thus been attributed to the piece before us, and every attribution so made has been in turn brushed away; merely to glance at such a monument to the interest inspired is to recognise a battleground of opposed factions, not a little enveloped in sound and smoke. Of these copious elements, produced for the most part of the best intention, we remain accordingly conscious; so that to approach the general bone of contention, as we can but familiarly name it, for whatever purpose, we have to cross the scene of action at a mortal risk, making the fewest steps of it and trusting to the probable calm at the centre of the storm. There in fact, though there only, we find that serenity; find the subject itself intact and unconscious, seated as unwinking and inscrutable as a divinity in a temple, save for that vague flicker of derision, the only response to our interpretative heat, which adds the last beauty to its face.

* * *

One can speak, in these matters, but from the impression determined by one's own inevitable standpoint; again and again, at any rate, such a masterpiece puts before me the very act of the momentous conjunction taking place for the poet, at a given hour, between his charged inspiration and his clarified experience: or, as I should perhaps better express it, between his human curiosity and his aesthetic passion. Then, if he happens to have been, all his career, with his equipment for it, more or less the victim and the slave of the former, he yields, by way of a change, to the impulse of allowing the latter, for a magnificent moment, the upper hand. The human curiosity, as I call it, is always there—with no more need of making provision for it than use in taking precautions against it; the surrender to the luxury of expertness may therefore go forward on its own conditions. I can offer no better description of *The Tempest* as fresh re-perusal lights it for me than as such a surrender, sublimely enjoyed; and I may frankly say that, under this impression of it, there is no refinement of the artistic consciousness that I do not see my way—or feel it, better, perhaps, since we but grope, at the best, in our darkness—to attribute to the author. It is a way that one follows to the end, because it is a road, I repeat, on which one least misses some glimpse of him face to face. If it be true that the thing was concocted to meet a particular demand, that of the master of

---

† From *The Complete Works of William Shakespeare*, ed. Sidney Lee, vol. 16 (New York: George D. Sproul, 1907), pp. ix–xxxii.

the King's revels, with his prescription of date, form, tone and length, this, so far from interfering with the Poet's perception of a charming opportunity to taste for *himself*, for himself above all, and as he had almost never so tasted, not even in *A Midsummer Night's Dream*, of the quality of his mind and the virtue of his skill, would have exceedingly favoured the happy case. Innumerable one may always suppose these delicate debates and intimate understandings of an artist with himself. 'How much *taste*, in the world, may I conceive that I have?—and what a charming idea to snatch a moment for finding out! What moment could be better than this—a bridal evening before the Court, with extra candles and the handsomest company—if I can but put my hand on the right "scenario"?' We can catch, across the ages, the searching sigh and the look about; we receive the stirred breath of the ripe, amused genius; and, stretching, as I admit I do at least, for a still closer conception of the beautiful crisis, I find it pictured for me in some such presentment as that of a divine musician who, alone in his room, preludes or improvises at close of day. He sits at the harpsichord, by the open window, in the summer dusk; his hands wander over the keys. They stray far, for his motive, but at last he finds and holds it; then he lets himself go, embroidering and refining: it is the thing for the hour and his mood. The neighbours may gather in the garden, the nightingale be hushed on the bough; it is none the less a private occasion, a concert of one, both performer and auditor, who plays for his own ear, his own hand, his own innermost sense, and for the bliss and capacity of his instrument. Such are the only hours at which the artist *may*, by any measure of his own (too many things, at others, make heavily against it); and their challenge to him is irresistible if he has known, all along, too much compromise and too much sacrifice.

The face that beyond any other, however, I seem to see *The Tempest* turn to us is the side on which it so superlatively speaks of that endowment for Expression, expression as a primary force, a consuming, an independent passion, which was the greatest ever laid upon man. It is for Shakespeare's power of constitutive speech quite as if he had swum into our ken with it from another planet, gathering it up there, in its wealth, as something antecedent to the occasion and the need, and if possible quite in excess of them; something that was to make of our poor world a great flat table for receiving the glitter and clink of outpoured treasure. The idea and the motive are more often than not so smothered in it that they scarce know themselves, and the resources of such a style, the provision of images, emblems, energies of every sort, laid up in advance, affects us as the storehouse of a king before a famine or a siege—which not only, by its scale, braves depletion or exhaustion,

but bursts, through mere excess of quantity or presence, out of all
doors and windows. It renders the poverties and obscurities of our
world, as I say, in the dazzling terms of a richer and better. It constitutes, by a miracle, more than half the author's material; so much
more usually does it happen, for the painter or the poet, that life
itself, in its appealing, overwhelming crudity, offers itself as the
paste to be kneaded. Such a personage works in general in the very
elements of experience; whereas we see Shakespeare working pre-
dominantly in the terms of expression, *all* in the terms of the artist's specific vision and genius; with a thicker cloud of images to
attest his approach, at any point than the comparatively meagre
given case ever has to attest its own identity. He points for us as no
one else the relation of style to meaning and of manner to motive; a
matter on which, right and left, we hear such rank ineptitudes
uttered. Unless it be true that these things, on either hand, are
inseparable; unless it be true that the phrase, the cluster and order
of terms, *is* the object and the sense, in as close a compression as
that of body and soul, so that any consideration of them as distinct,
from the moment style is an active, applied force, becomes a gross
stupidity: unless we recognise this reality the author of *The Tempest* has no lesson for us. It is by his expression of it exactly as the
expression stands that the particular thing is created, created as
interesting, as beautiful, as strange, droll or terrible—as related, in
short, to our understanding or our sensibility; in consequence of
which we reduce it to naught when we begin to talk of either of its
presented parts as matters by themselves.

❊ ❊ ❊

So it is then; and it puts into a nutshell the eternal mystery, the
most insoluble that ever was, the complete rupture, for our understanding, between the Poet and the Man. There are moments, I
admit, in this age of sound and fury, of connections, in every sense,
too maddeningly multiplied, when we are willing to let it pass as a
mystery, the most soothing, cooling, consoling too perhaps, that ever
was. But there are others when, speaking for myself, its power to torment us intellectually seems scarcely to be borne; and we know these
moments best when we hear it proclaimed that a comfortable clearness reigns. I have been for instance reading over Mr. Halliwell-
Phillipps, and I find him apparently of the opinion that it is all our
fault if everything in our author's story, and above all in this last
chapter of it, be not of a primitive simplicity. The complexity arises
from our suffering our imagination to meddle with the Man at all;
who is quite sufficiently presented to us on the face of the record. For
critics of this writer's complexion the only facts we are urgently
concerned with are the facts of the Poet, which are abundantly

constituted by the Plays and the Sonnets. The Poet is *there*, and the Man is outside: the Man is for instance in such a perfectly definite circumstance as that he could never miss, after *The Tempest*, the key of his piano, as I have called it, since he could play so freely with the key of his cash-box. The supreme master of expression had made, before fifty, all the money he wanted; therefore what was there more to express? This view is admirable if you can get your mind to consent to it. It must ignore any impulse, in presence of Play or Sonnet (whatever vague stir behind either may momentarily act as provocation) to try for a lunge at the figured arras. In front of the tapestry sits the immitigably respectable person whom our little slateful of gathered and numbered items, heaven knows, does amply account for, since there is nothing in him to explain; while the undetermined figure, on the other hand—undetermined whether in the sense of respectability or of anything else—the figure who supremely interests us, remains as unseen of us as our Ariel, on the enchanted island, remains of the bewildered visitors. Mr. Halliwell-Phillipps' theory, as I understand it—and I refer to it but as an advertisement of a hundred others—is that we too are but bewildered visitors, and that the state of mind of the Duke of Naples and his companions is our proper critical portion.

* * * We stake our hopes thus on indirectness, which may contain possibilities; we take that very truth for our counsel of despair, try to look at it as helpful for the Criticism of the future. That of the past has been too often infantile; one has asked one's self how it *could*, on such lines, get at him. The figured tapestry, the long arras that hides him, is always there, with its immensity of surface and its proportionate underside. May it not then be but a question, for the fulness of time, of the finer weapon, the sharper point, the stronger arm, the more extended lunge?

LYTTON STRACHEY

From Shakespeare's Final Period[†]

* * *

Is it not thus, then, that we should imagine him in the last years of his life? Half enchanted by visions of beauty and loveliness, and half bored to death; on the one side inspired by a soaring fancy to the singing of ethereal songs, and on the other urged by a general disgust to burst occasionally through his torpor into bitter and

---

[†] From *Books and Characters* (London: Chatto & Windus, 1922), pp. 60–64. Line numbers to the play have been added. All notes are by the editors of this Norton Critical Edition.

violent speech? If we are to learn anything of his mind from his last works, it is surely this.

And such is the conclusion which is particularly forced upon us by a consideration of the play which is in many ways most typical of Shakespeare's later work, and the one which critics most consistently point to as containing the very essence of his final benignity—*The Tempest*. There can be no doubt that the peculiar characteristics which distinguish *Cymbeline* and *The Winter's Tale* from the dramas of Shakespeare's prime, are present here in a still greater degree. In *The Tempest*, unreality has reached its apotheosis. Two of the principal characters are frankly not human beings at all; and the whole action passes, through a series of impossible occurrences, in a place which can only by courtesy be said to exist. The Enchanted Island, indeed, peopled, for a timeless moment, by this strange fantastic medley of persons and of things, has been cut adrift for ever from common sense, and floats, buoyed up by a sea, not of waters, but of poetry. Never did Shakespeare's magnificence of diction reach more marvellous heights than in some of the speeches of Prospero, or his lyric art a purer beauty than in the songs of Ariel; nor is it only in these ethereal regions that the triumph of his language asserts itself. It finds as splendid a vent in the curses of Caliban:

> All the infection that the sun sucks up
> From bogs, fens, flats, on Prosper fall, and make him
> By inch-meal a disease!   [2.2.1–3]

and in the similes of Trinculo:

> Yond' same black cloud, yond' huge one, looks like a foul
> bombard that would shed his liquor.   [2.2.20–21]

The *dénouement* itself, brought about by a preposterous piece of machinery, and lost in a whirl of rhetoric, is hardly more than a peg for fine writing.

>   O, it is monstrous, monstrous!
> Methought the billows spoke and told me of it;
> The winds did sing it to me; and the thunder,
> That deep and dreadful organ-pipe, pronounced
> The name of Prosper; it did bass my trespass.
> Therefore my son i' th' ooze is bedded, and
> I'll seek him deeper than e'er plummet sounded,
> And with him there lie mudded.   [3.3.96–103]

And this gorgeous phantasm of a repentance from the mouth of the pale phantom Alonzo is a fitting climax to the whole fantastic play.

A comparison naturally suggests itself, between what was perhaps the last of Shakespeare's completed works, and that early drama

which first gave undoubted proof that his imagination had taken
wings. The points of resemblance between *The Tempest* and *A Midsummer Night's Dream*, their common atmosphere of romance and
magic, the beautiful absurdities of their intrigues, their studied con-
trasts of the grotesque with the delicate, the ethereal with the earthy,
the charm of their lyrics, the *verve* of their vulgar comedy—these, of
course, are obvious enough; but it is the points of difference which
really make the comparison striking. One thing, at any rate, is certain
about the wood near Athens—it is full of life. The persons that haunt
it—though most of them are hardly more than children, and some of
them are fairies, and all of them are too agreeable to be true—are
nevertheless substantial creatures, whose loves and jokes and quarrels
receive our thorough sympathy; and the air they breathe—the lords and
the ladies, no less than the mechanics and the elves—is instinct with
an exquisite good-humour, which makes us as happy as the night is
long. To turn from Theseus and Titania and Bottom to the Enchanted
Island, is to step out of a country lane into a conservatory. The roses
and the dandelions have vanished before preposterous cactuses, and
fascinating orchids too delicate for the open air; and, in the artificial
atmosphere, the gaiety of youth has been replaced by the disillusion-
ment of middle age. Prospero is the central figure of *The Tempest*; and
it has often been wildly asserted that he is a portrait of the author—
an embodiment of that spirit of wise benevolence which is supposed
to have thrown a halo over Shakespeare's later life. But, on closer
inspection, the portrait seems to be as imaginary as the original. To
an irreverent eye, the ex-Duke of Milan would perhaps appear as an
unpleasantly crusty personage, in whom a twelve years' monopoly of
the conversation had developed an inordinate propensity for talking.
These may have been the sentiments of Ariel, safe at the Bermoothes;
but to state them is to risk at least ten years in the knotty entrails of an
oak, and it is sufficient to point out, that if Prospero is wise, he is also
self-opinionated and sour, that his gravity is often another name for
pedantic severity, and that there is no character in the play to whom,
during some part of it, he is not studiously disagreeable. But his Milanese countrymen are not even disagreeable; they are simply dull. 'This
is the silliest stuff that e'er I heard,' remarked Hippolyta of Bottom's
amateur theatricals; and one is tempted to wonder what she would have
said to the dreary puns and interminable conspiracies of Alonzo, and
Gonzalo, and Sebastian, and Antonio, and Adrian, and Francisco, and
other shipwrecked noblemen. At all events, there can be little doubt
that they would not have had the entrée at Athens.

The depth of the gulf between the two plays is, however, best measured by a comparison of Caliban and his masters with Bottom and
his companions. The guileless group of English mechanics, whose
sports are interrupted by the mischief of Puck, offers a strange contrast

to the hideous trio of the 'jester,' the 'drunken butler,' and the 'savage and deformed slave,' whose designs are thwarted by the magic of Ariel. Bottom was the first of Shakespeare's masterpieces in characterisation, Caliban was the last: and what a world of bitterness and horror lies between them! The charming coxcomb it is easy to know and love; but the 'freckled whelp hag-born' moves us mysteriously to pity and to terror, eluding us for ever in fearful allegories, and strange coils of disgusted laughter and phantasmagorical tears. The physical vigour of the presentment is often so remorseless as to shock us. 'I left them,' says Ariel, speaking of Caliban and his crew:

> I' the filthy-mantled pool beyond your cell,
> There dancing up to the chins, that the foul lake
> O'erstunk their feet.   [4.1.182–84]

But at other times the great half-human shape seems to swell, like the 'Pan' of Victor Hugo, into something unimaginably vast.

> You taught me language, and my profit on't
> Is, I know how to curse.   [1.2.362–63]

Is this Caliban addressing Prospero, or Job addressing God? It may be either; but it is not serene, nor benign, nor pastoral, nor 'On the Heights.'[1]

G. WILSON KNIGHT

[Prospero's Lonely Magic][†]

* * *

Now on the island of *The Tempest* Prospero is master of his lonely magic. He has been there for twelve years. Two creatures serve him: Ariel, the 'airy nothing' of poetry; and the snarling Caliban, half-beast, half-man; the embodiment of the hate-theme. These two creatures are yoked in the employ of Prospero, like Plato's two steeds of the soul, the noble and the hideous, twin potentialities of the human spirit. Caliban has been mastered by Prospero and Ariel. Though he revolts against his master still, the issue is not in doubt, and the tunes of Ariel draw out his very soul in longing and desire, just as the power of poetry shows forth the majesty of Timon, whose passion makes of universal hate a noble and aspiring thing. These three are the most vital and outstanding figures in the play:

---

1 The critic Edward Dowden's characterization of Shakespeare's late period.
† From "Myth and Miracle" (1929), in G. Wilson Knight, *The Crown of Life* (London: Methuen, 1947), pp. 25–28. All notes are by the editors of this Norton Critical Edition.

for Shakespeare had only to look inward to find them. But there are other elements that complete the pattern of this self-revelation.

Prospero's enemies are drawn to the magic island of great poetry by means of a tempest raised by Prospero with the help of Ariel. In Alonso, despairing and self-accusing, bereft of his child, we can see traces of the terrible end of *Lear*; in Antonio and Sebastian, the tempter and the tempted, plotting murder for a crown, we can see more than traces of *Macbeth*. But, driven by the tempest-raising power of tragic and passionate poetry within the magic circle of Prospero and Ariel, these hostile and evil things are powerless: they can only stand spell-stopped. They are enveloped in the wondrous laws of enchantment on the island of song and music. Caliban, who has been mastered by it, knows best the language to describe the mystic tunes of Ariel:

> Be not afeard; the isle is full of noises,
> Sounds and sweet airs that give delight and hurt not.
> Sometimes a thousand twangling instruments
> Will hum about mine ears, and sometimes voices,
> That, if I then had waked after long sleep,
> Will make me sleep again; and then, in dreaming,
> The clouds methought would open and show riches
> Ready to drop upon me, that, when I waked,
> I cried to dream again.   (3.2.128–36)

The protagonists of murder and bereavement are exquisitely entrapped in the magic and music of Prospero and his servant Ariel. So, too, were the evil things of life mastered by the poetry of the great tragedies, and transmuted into the vision of the myths. The spirit of the Final Plays also finds its perfected home in this last of the series. Here the child-theme is repeated in Miranda, cast adrift with her father on the tempestuous seas; here the lost son of Alonso is recovered, alive and well, and the very ship that was wrecked is found to be miraculously 'tight and yare and bravely rigg'd' as when it 'first put out to sea' (5.1.225–26). Prospero, like Cerimon over Thaisa, revives, with music, the numbed consciousness of Alonso and his companions; and, as they wake, it is as though mortality were waking into eternity. And this thought makes necessary a statement and a distinction as to the dual possible approaches to the significance of *The Tempest*.

First, we can regard it as the poet's expression of a view of human life. With the knowledge of Shakespeare's poetic symbolism in memory, we will think of the wreck as suggesting the tragic destiny of man, and the marvellous survival of the travellers and crew as another and more perfectly poetic and artistic embodiment of the thought expressed through the medium of anthropomorphic theology in *Cymbeline* that there exists a joy and a revival that makes past misery, in Pericles' phraseology, 'sport.' According to this reading Prospero becomes in a sense the 'God' of the *Tempest*-universe, and we shall find compelling suggestion as to the immortality of man in such lines as Ariel's when Prospero asks him if the victims of the wreck are safe:

> Not a hair perish'd;
> On their sustaining garments not a blemish,
> But fresher than before.   (1.2.217–19)

So, too, thinking of sea-storms and wreckages as Shakespeare's symbols of human tragedy, we shall find new significance in Ariel's lines:

> Nothing of him that doth fade,
> But doth suffer a sea-change
> Into something rich and strange.   (1.2.398–400)

Especially, if we remember that the soul's desire of love in Shakespeare is consistently imaged as a rich something set far across tempestuous seas, we shall receive especial delight in the song:

> Come unto these yellow sands,
>   And then take hands:
> Curtsied when you have, and kiss'd
>   The wild waves whist.   (1.2.374–77)

Commentators divide into two camps and argue long as to the syntax and sense of those last two lines: is 'whist,' or is it not, they say, a nominative absolute? And if not, how can waves be kiss'd? A knowledge of Shakespeare's imagery, however, is needed to see the triumphant mysticism of the dream of love's perfected fruition in eternity stilling the tumultuous waves of time. This is one instance of many where the imaginative interpretation of a poet, and a knowledge of his particular symbolism, short-circuits the travails and tribulations of the grammarian or the commentator who in search for facts neglects the primary facts of all poetry—its suggestion, its colour, its richness of mental association, its appeal, not to the intellect, but the imagination.

The second approach is this, which I have already indicated. *The Tempest* is a record, crystallized with consummate art into a short play, * * * of the spiritual progress from 1599 or 1600 to the year 1611, or whenever, exactly, *The Tempest* was written. According to this reading Prospero is not God, but Shakespeare—or rather the controlling judgement of Shakespeare, since Ariel and Caliban are also representations of dual minor potentialities of his soul. From this approach three incidents in the play reveal unique interest. First, the dialogue between Prospero and Ariel in 1.2. where Ariel is tired and cries for the promised freedom, and is told that there is one last work to be done—which is in exact agreement with my reading of the faltering art of *Cymbeline*; second, Prospero's well-known farewell to his art, where commentators have seldom failed to admit what Professor Saintsbury calls a 'designed personal allegory,' and where I would notice that Prospero clearly regards his art as pre-eminently a tempest-raising magic, and next refers to the opening of graves at his command, thereby illustrating again the sequence from tragedy to myth which I have described; and third, Prospero's other dialogue with Ariel in 5.1 where Ariel pities the enemies of his master and draws from Prospero the words:

> Hast thou, which art but air, a touch, a feeling
> Of their afflictions, and shall not myself,
> One of their kind, that relish all as sharply,
> Passion as they—be kindlier moved than thou art? (5.1.21–24)

In poetic creation 'all is forgiven, and it would be strange not to forgive'[1]; but the partial and fleeting flame of the poet's intuition may light at last the total consciousness with the brilliance of a cosmic apprehension. This speech suggests the transit from the intermittent love of poetic composition to the perduring love of the mystic.

Now these two methods of approach considered separately and in sequence are not so significant as they become when we realize that they are simultaneously possible and, indeed, necessary. Together they are complementary to *The Tempest*'s unique reality. For it will next be seen that these two aspects when considered together give us a peculiar knowledge of this act of the poet's soul in the round: so that the usual flat view of it which reads it as an impersonal fairy story—corresponding to my reading of it as an objective vision of life—becomes a three-dimensional understanding when we remember the implicit personal allegory. Only by submitting our faculties to both methods can we properly understand the play to the full. *The Tempest* is at the same time a record of Shakespeare's spiritual progress and a statement of the vision to which that progress has brought him. It is apparent as a dynamic and living act of the soul, containing within itself the record of its birth: it is continually re-writing itself before our eyes. Shakespeare has in this play so become master of the whole of his own mystic universe that that universe, at last perfectly projected in one short play into the forms and shapes of objective human existence, shows us, in the wreck of

---

1. From the *Note-book of Anton Chekhov* (1921).

The Tempest, a complete view of that existence, no longer as it normally appears to man, but as it takes reflected pattern in the still depths of the timeless soul of poetry. And, since it reveals its vision not as a statement of absolute truth independently of the author, but related inwardly to the succession of experiences that condition and nurture its own reality, it becomes, in a unique sense beyond other works of art, an absolute. There is thus now no barrier between the inward and the outward, expression and imitation. God, it has been said, is the mode in which the subject-object distinction is transcended. Art aspires to the perfected fusion of expression with imitation. *The Tempest* is thus at the same time the most perfect work of art and the most crystal act of mystic vision in our literature.

A Chart of Shakespeare's Dramatic Universe[†]

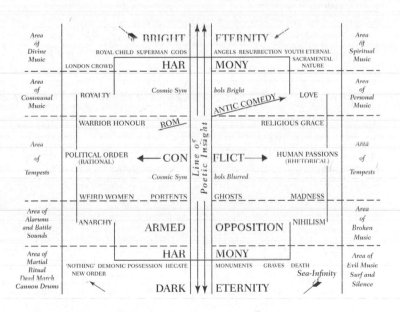

† From G. Wilson Knight, *The Shakespearean Tempest, with a Chart of Shakespeare's Dramatic Universe* (Oxford: Oxford University Press, 1932)

OCTAVE MANNONI

[Prospero and Caliban]†

The dependence relationship requires at least two members, and where a colonial situation exists, if one of them is the native of the colony, the other is likely to be the colonizer, or rather the colonial, for he it is who offers us the more interesting subject of study. The real colonizer is almost of necessity a man of strong character, a creator rather than an accepter of relationships, at least at the outset. It is only later that he becomes a colonial. The typical colonial, on the other hand, finds the relationship ready made; he takes it up, adapts himself to it, and very often exploits it. And in any case, whether he accepts it passively or seizes upon it greedily, the relationship changes him more than he it. It is precisely this transformation which sets a stamp on him, which makes him a colonial. And it is this which we must now study if we are to find out the exact psychological nature of the relations which form between the European colonial and the dependent native—if we are to understand how and why these relations change with time and what effect they have on the two members.

The reader will see that in trying to discover how it is that a European, to all appearances indistinguishable from other Europeans, can become, sometimes in a very short space of time, a typical colonial and very different from his former self, I have reached a conclusion which is at first sight paradoxical—namely, that the personality of the colonial is made up, not of characteristics acquired during and through experience of the colonies, but of traits, very often in the nature of a complex, already in existence in a latent and repressed form in the European's psyche, traits which the colonial experience has simply brought to the surface and made manifest. Social life in Europe exerts a certain pressure on the individual, and that pressure keeps the personality in a given shape; once it is removed, however, the outlines of the personality change and swell, thus revealing the existence of internal pressures which had up to then passed unnoticed.

Of course that is simply a metaphor; what I want to bring out is that what happens to a European when he becomes a colonial is the result of unconscious complexes, and these I propose to analyse. The shape assumed by a deep-sea fish when it is brought up to the

---

† From *Prospero and Caliban: The Psychology of Colonization*, trans. Pamela Powesland (Ann Arbor: U of Michigan P, 1990), pp. 97–102, 105–09. Reprinted by permission of the University of Michigan Press. First published as *Psychologie de la Colonisation* (Paris: Editions du Seuil, 1950). Line numbers to the play have been added. Notes are by the author unless otherwise specified.

surface is due to differences in pressure, certainly, but it is also due to its own internal anatomical structure. Logically, what my theory amounts to is this, that a person free from complexes—if such a person can be imagined—would not undergo change as a result of experience of the colonies. He would not in the first place feel the urge to go to the colonies, but even should he find himself there by chance, he would not taste those emotional satisfactions which, whether consciously or unconsciously, so powerfully attract the pre-destined colonial.

These complexes are formed, necessarily, in infancy; their later history varies according to whether they are resolved, repressed, or satisfied in the course of a closer and closer contact with reality as the age of adulthood is reached. The best description of them is to be found in the works of some of the great writers who projected them on to imaginary characters placed in situations which, though imaginary, are typically colonial. The material they drew directly from their own unconscious desires. This is proof enough that the complexes exist even before the colonial situation is experienced.

It is easy, for instance, to establish that Defoe had no other model for Robinson Crusoe but himself. Of the 'real Robinsons' known at the time none had been able to withstand the solitude. Selkirk, the best known, had entirely lost the power of speech. The man who was taken off Mauritius was mad, and John Segar died on seeing white men again. It is just because it is a fable that the story of Crusoe, which came straight from the author's unconscious, makes such an appeal to our own. Defoe himself, in a letter to Bishop Hoadley in 1725, said that the tale of Robinson was an allegory of his own life. He only realized it (as Flaubert did his identification with Madame Bovary) later on. We know that he wrote the novel in two parts. The second part (travels on the Continent) he wrote to order for his publisher, and he wrote it laboriously and with diffi-culty. But the first part—the one which interests us—he wrote straight off by force of inspiration, at the dictate of his own uncon-scious. * * *

The story of the friendship of Robinson and Friday no doubt accounts for many colonial callings. However, it is not this unsur-prising aspect of the novel to which I want to draw attention, but the fact that it reveals the colonial vocation *in esse*, as it exists in the unconscious before there is any question of influence or emulation and as it must necessarily have existed in the unconscious of Defoe. He was not to respond to the call; nevertheless in 1702 he was responsible for a strange proposal for an expedition against Spain's American colonies, and he officially offered to lead it. It was only in his later years, when he was nearly sixty, that he satisfied a long-felt desire—we shall see which—by writing his novel about Crusoe.

Shakespeare's *The Tempest*—he, too, wrote it in his old age—presents a situation which is, psychoanalytically, almost identical with that of Crusoe. We can be sure that Shakespeare had no other model but himself for his creation of Prospero.

It is characteristic of this type of story—the remark applies equally, for instance, to the *Odyssey*, *Sinbad the Sailor* and *Gulliver's Travels*—that the hero has to face either the perils or the miseries of exile; they are either punishments or, as it were, scarecrows, the two ideas being easily linked in that of prohibition. The reason for them is usually a wrongdoing, deliberate or otherwise, and it constitutes disobedience of the gods, the customs, or more generally the father. Prospero had neglected the duties of his office and had been betrayed by his brother in complicity with a king—psychoanalytically a king is a father-image. Even the real travellers, Baudelaire, Trelawny and many others, obediently conform to the unconscious schema.[1] The story-book travellers encounter parental prohibitions in the form of monsters: Cyclops, the Roc bird, the cannibals. They are full of regrets—'Ah, how much better it would have been . . . !' and so on. When they get back they have nothing but misfortunes to relate: 'So we worked at the oar' says Robinson, 'and the wind driving us towards the shore, we hastened our destruction with our own hands. . . .' Nevertheless their adventures rouse envy in their stay-at-home readers, especially if they are young.

Prospero is the least evolved of all these literary figures, according to the criteria of psychoanalysis, for he is endowed with magical power, and so is not required to display those virile and adult qualities to which Ulysses and Crusoe owe their salvation. Crusoe is psychologically the least archaic, as is shown by his faith in technical skill—he is a veritable Jack-of-all-trades. He is in line with the current of ideas flowing from Locke to the Encyclopaedists; Prospero, on the other hand, is reminiscent rather of Bacon, who thought in terms of experiment but dreamed of magic; nor is he the only character in the play to repudiate technique, for there is Gonzalo, too, the Utopist. Between them, therefore, these characters appear to cover the whole of the subject we are studying. Chronology is of no importance, and so we shall begin with an analysis of Crusoe and see what we can learn from it.

First, it is very significant that he is much less unhappy when he is absolutely alone than when he is afraid he may not be. I must dwell on this paradox, for our familiarity with it dulls our surprise at it; man is afraid because he is alone and his fear is the fear of other

---

1. A particularly interesting traveller to study is R. L. Stevenson. In his story Ariel and Caliban are called Jekyll and Hyde. In the remote Pacific he found courage to grapple with the image which had driven him that far, and began writing the *Weir of Hermiston*. He died before victory was won, leaving his chef-d'oeuvre incomplete.

men. Fear of solitude is fear of intrusion upon that solitude. (It is the same in *The Tempest*: Prospero's solitude is finally broken in upon.) Contemporary critics even pointed out this 'contradiction' in Robinson Crusoe. But perhaps it was not a contradiction, after all.

At all events, every sign of another living thing, a goat, a footprint, anything put fear into the heart of Crusoe—even his parrot, which was nonetheless a first configuration of the companion he both dreaded and desired in an ambivalent complex of feelings. * * * In fact, Daniel Defoe's story recounts *the long and difficult cure of a misanthropic neurosis*. His hero, who is at first at odds with his environment, gradually recovers psychological health in solitude. He comes to accept the presence of creatures upon whom he tries to project the image—at once terrifying and reassuring—of *another*. Then he has a friend, 'dumb' at first, like his parrot. Later he has the courage to fight against the 'others' in the form of hostile cannibals. Finally he has to deal with a terribly bad lot who are, however, more akin to himself, and he manages to subdue them by his authority. He even assumes the title of governor of the island. His cure is assured; he is even reconciled with the father-image, and, by the same token, with God (God is also mentioned in the *Serious Reflections*). So, then, Crusoe can return, like Ulysses, *'plein d'usage et raison'*[2]—and money, too, gained chiefly through slave-trading.

Let us leave Defoe's case for a moment to consider that of his reader and discover why he finds Defoe's book so interesting. His interest itself is enough to show that there is in the child some trait which is partly misanthropic, or at any rate anti-social, a trait which, for lack of a better term, I would call 'the lure of a world without men'. It may be repressed to a greater or less extent, but it will remain, nonetheless, in the unconscious.

It is the existence of this trait which makes the idea of the desert island so attractive, whereas in reality there is little to be said for it, as the real Robinsons discovered. The desert islands of the imagination are, it is true, peopled with imaginary beings, but that is after all their *raison d'être*. Some of the semi-human creatures the unconscious creates, such as Caliban or the Lilliputians, reveal their creator's desire to denigrate the whole of mankind. Others are a compound of the bad creatures on whom the child projects his own desire to be naughty and the parents who forbid him to be naughty— for the father who tells his child that the wicked bogey-man will get him if he does not behave, himself becomes a bogey-man in the eyes of the child. And all external dangers, such as the wolf and the policeman, are felt to be his allies, especially as they are specifically referred to by the parents. We have already seen how often this

---

2. "Seasoned in the ways of men"; from a poem by Joachim du Bellay. [*Editors*]

fusion occurs in the dreams of Malagasy children where the 'naughty' (i.e. guilty) child is pursued by the wicked Senegalese soldier who is at the same time his father, both being represented by the bull.

It is a fact, however, that in spite of prohibitions, or perhaps because of them, the child longs to escape. Some time after he is four years of age he makes surreptitious attempts to venture out alone. Sometimes he 'loses' himself or he makes a tour of a block of houses and returns to his starting-point, as if he wanted to verify some topographical intuition or prove that the world is round. Sometimes he longs to be invisible, and hides himself; when his mother calls him anxiously he does not reply. She calls these escapades silly, but perhaps they are something more than mere games. Or again the child may long to go and hide far away from everybody, and so he goes to the bottom of the garden to play at being Robinson; the fact that several children may take part in this game makes no difference—it is still a flight from mankind, and intrusion must be guarded against.

The real attraction of solitude, however, is that if the world is emptied of human beings as they really are, it can be filled with the creatures of our own imagination: Calypso, Ariel, Friday. But if we are to achieve a complete and adult personality it is essential that we should make the images of the unconscious tally, more or less, with real people; flight into solitude shows that we have failed to do so. In *The Tempest*, when Miranda cries:

> . . . O brave new world,
> That has such people in't   [5.1.183–84]

we realize, with an emotion which reveals the importance of the fact, that she has accomplished in one step that adjustment of the archetypes to reality which her neurotic father had so surely missed. His scornful reply, ' 'Tis new to thee', proves that he is not yet cured. Where there is a preference for Ariel or Friday to real persons, it is clear that there has been a failure in adaptation, resulting usually from a grave lack of sociability combined with a pathological urge to dominate. These characteristics, which are traceable in the unconscious of Prospero–Shakespeare and Crusoe–Defoe, are very probably present in all children too, but they may develop in one of many ways.

* * *

The colonial situation is even more clearly portrayed in *The Tempest*[3] than in *Robinson Crusoe*, which is the more remarkable in

---

3. On the analytical interpretation of the text of Shakespeare's play, see Abenheimer: 'Shakespeare's Tempest', in the *Psychoanalytic Review* of October 1946.

that Shakespeare certainly thought less about it than did Defoe.
Shakespeare's theme is the drama of the renunciation of power and
domination, which are symbolized by magic, a borrowed power
which must be rendered up. Man must learn to accept himself as
he is and to accept others as they are, even if they happen to be
called Caliban. This is the only wise course, but the path towards
wisdom is long and infinitely painful for Prospero.

There is no doubting the nature of Prospero's magical power, for
at his side we find his obedient daughter—and magic is the child's
image of paternal omnipotence. Whenever his absolute authority is
threatened, and however slight the threat, Prospero—our aspirant
to wisdom—always becomes impatient and almost neurotically
touchy. The essence of the problem is revealed at the outset; Prospero lays down his magic garment and prepares to tell Miranda the
story of his life. In other words, he tries to treat Miranda as an
equal; but he fails. He begins with 'Obey and be attentive,' and the
recital is punctuated with other orders of the same kind, all absurd
and quite unwarranted; later in the play he even goes so far as to
threaten Miranda with his hatred. It is the same with Ariel; Prospero has promised him his liberty, but fails to give it to him. He
constantly reminds Ariel that he freed him from the knotty entrails
of a cloven pine in which the terrible mother, Sycorax, had confined
him. This again means that Prospero has the absolute authority of
the father. Caliban is the unruly and incorrigible son who is dis-
owned. Prospero says he was 'got by the devil himself'. At the same
time he is the useful slave who is ruthlessly exploited. But Caliban
does not complain of being exploited; he complains rather of being
betrayed, in Künkel's sense of the word; he says, explicitly,

> . . . When thou camest first,
> Thou strok'dst me, and mad'st much of me; wouldst give me
> Water with berries in't; and teach me how
> To name the bigger light, and how the less,
> That burn by day and night: and then I lov'd thee, [1.2.332–36]

but now

> . . . you sty me
> In this hard rock, whiles you do keep from me
> The rest o' the island.   [1.2.342–44]

Caliban has fallen prey to the resentment which succeeds the
breakdown of dependence. Prospero seeks to justify himself: did
Caliban not attempt to violate the honour of his child? After such
an offence, what hope is there? There is no logic in this argument.
Prospero could have removed Caliban to a safe distance or he could
have continued to civilize and correct him. But the argument: you

tried to violate Miranda, *therefore* you shall chop wood, belongs to a nonrational mode of thinking. In spite of the various forms this attitude may take (it includes, for instance, working for the father-in-law, a common practice in patriarchal communities), it is primarily a justification of hatred on grounds of sexual guilt, and it is at the root of colonial racialism.

I was given a clue to the explanation of this racialism while questioning a European colonial, who expressed the belief that the black race had become inferior to the white through excessive masturbation! The man himself was troubled by parental prohibitions in this respect. The 'inferior being' always serves as scapegoat; our own evil intentions can be projected on to him. This applies especially to incestuous intentions; Miranda is the only woman on the island, and Prospero and Caliban the only men. It is easy to see why it is always his daughter or his sister or his neighbour's wife (never his own) whom a man imagines to have been violated by a negro; he wants to rid himself of guilt by putting the blame for his bad thoughts on someone else. Caliban, in this hopeless situation, begins plotting against Prospero—not to win his freedom, for he could not support freedom, but to have a new master whose 'foot-licker' he can become. He is delighted at the prospect. It would be hard to find a better example of the dependence complex in its pure state. In the play the complex must be a projection, for where else could it have come from? The dependence of colonial natives is a matter of plain fact. The ensuing encounter between the European's unconscious and a reality only too well prepared to receive its projections is in practice full of dangers. Colonials live in a less real social world, and this diminished reality is less able to wake the dreamer. . . .

Among the castaways in *The Tempest* there is one rather strangely-drawn character: Gonzalo. The list of *dramatis personae* describes him as an 'honest old counsellor'. He once rendered Prospero great service, and Prospero treats him with immense respect. He is, however, simply a variant of Polonius, a garrulous old dotard, but more of a caricature. *The Tempest* repeats, in order to resolve it, the Hamlet situation: brother ousted by brother, guilty father (here the King of Naples), hatred of the mother, brooding instead of action—the latter a regression due to loss of real power. And in both cases, alongside the father, there is the uncle or some other father-image: a doddering and impotent old man. Gonzalo, the Utopist, dreams of turning the island into a Land of Cockaigne:

> All things in common nature should produce
> Without sweat or endeavour . . .   [2.1.154–55]

no toil, no government, no institutions. His attitude is in fact identical with Prospero's and shows the same infantile regression—but he lacks the omnipotence of the father, that is to say magic, the power which is the cause of all difficulties and must be rejected. How reluctantly Prospero gives up his daughter to Ferdinand! And he cannot restore Ariel to liberty without asking him to perform yet one more task. He forgives his enemies, but only after he has avenged himself on them and thoroughly humiliated them. In Milan, where he will be duke in name only, he says, 'Every third thought shall be my grave' [5.1.314]. In the Epilogue Prospero declares

> Now my charms are all o'erthrown,
> And what strength I have's mine own;
> Which is most faint.   [Epilogue 1–3]

In this, his will, he gives back everything he acquired by magic—all, that is, that he lost by betrayal, including his birthright. Surely the man who wrote this play must have harboured in his unconscious a strange and potent desire to possess power over men, if only by prestige, and this desire must in its way have been as powerful and as difficult to overcome as that of Defoe.

In any case it was from the unconscious that the two islands of these tales emerged. The parallels between the two works assure us that we are in the presence of archetypes: Ariel, Friday, Caliban, the cannibals. And as in these works of art these archetypes governed the imagination, so in real life they govern behaviour. The typical colonial is compelled to live out Prospero's drama, for Prospero is in his unconscious as he was in Shakespeare's; only the former lacks the writer's capacity for sublimation. The colonial's personality is wholly unaffected by that of the native of the colony to which he goes; it does not adapt itself, but develops solely in accordance with its own inner structure. It is inevitable, therefore, that misunderstandings should arise, for there can be no harmony between monads.

It is always worth while considering the opinions of the colonialists, for they are necessarily very revealing, and in this case they confirm my views. What they say in effect is: there is no misunderstanding to clear up; it would not be worth the trouble, anyway; the Malagasy personality is whatever you like to make of it—for in fact it does not exist; ours alone counts. In other words, they do not acknowledge the Malagasy personality. Nothing outside themselves affects them. After all, what sorts of personalities have Miranda, Ariel, and Friday? None at all, so long as they remain submissive. Caliban, it is true, asserts himself by opposing, but he is mere bestiality.

What the colonial in common with Prospero lacks, is awareness of the world of Others, a world in which Others have to be respected. This is the world from which the colonial has fled because he cannot accept men as they are. Rejection of that world is combined with an urge to dominate, an urge which is infantile in origin and which social adaptation has failed to discipline. The reason the colonial himself gives for his flight—whether he says it was the desire to travel, or the desire to escape from the cradle or from the 'ancient parapets', or whether he says that he simply wanted a freer life—is of no consequence, for whatever the variant offered, the real reason is still what I have called very loosely the colonial vocation. It is always a question of compromising with the desire for a world without men. As for the man who chooses a colonial career by chance and without specific vocation, there is nevertheless every possibility that he too has a 'Prospero complex', more fully repressed, but still ready to emerge to view in favourable conditions.

In his *Traité de sociologie*, p. 394, Mr Gaston Bouthoul says:

> 'Of all the elements which go to make up a society, its mentality is the most difficult to destroy. A man may be uprooted from his surroundings and taken to the antipodes or shut up in a cell, but the society to which he belongs will continue to live in him, in his beliefs and in the entire content of his mental life and the knowledge he takes with him. If such a man has the strength, or if he meets some of his fellows, he may build in some distant spot a society almost identical with the one he left behind. This was the case with many of the colonies.'

It is true that an *adult* man carries with him wherever he goes all that he is, and experience is powerless to add or subtract anything of any importance. What a man is, however, is not all manifest; he contains latent possibilities. In other circumstances—at the Antipodes, for instance—there is an inevitable shifting of the boundary between the latent and the manifest personalities. Thus, although it is the same material a man takes with him into the new environment, it assumes a new shape there, partly as a result of the difference in social pressure but also, and more particularly, as a result of the inner pressures of the man's own personality.

GEORGE LAMMING

A Monster, a Child, a Slave†

The Tempest is a drama which grows and matures from the seeds of exile and paradox. Through a process of poetic schematisation, it

† From *The Pleasures of Exile* (London: Michael Joseph Ltd., 1960; rpt. Ann Arbor: U of Michigan P, 1992), pp. 95–117. Copyright © 1960 by George Lamming. Amended by the author for the first Norton Critical Edition. Reprinted by permission of the publisher, University of Michigan Press. Line numbers to the play have been added. Notes are by the author.

contains and crystallises all the conflicts which have gone before. It
is the poet's last will and testament; but the details of the legacy read
like an epitaph: an apology for any false dividends which Art—
meaning all method and experience of transformation—may have
brought home.

> Now my charms are all o'erthrown,
> And what strength I have's mine own,
> Which is most faint: now, 'tis true,
> I must be here confin'd by you,
> Or sent to Naples. Let me not,
> Since I have my dukedom got,
> And pardon'd the deceiver, dwell
> In this bare island by your spell;
> But release me from my bands
> With the help of your good hands:
> Gentle breath of yours my sails
> Must fill, or else my project fails,
> Which was to please. Now I want
> Spirits to enforce, Art to enchant;
> And my ending is despair,
> Unless I be reliev'd by prayer,
> Which pierces so, that it assaults
> Mercy itself, and frees all faults.
> As you from crimes would pardon'd be,
> Let your indulgence set me free.   [Epilogue, 1–20]

It is the Epilogue which reminds us that the Voyage is not over.
Indeed, we are right back where we started:

ACT I. Scene 1

(On a ship at sea a tempestuous noise of thunder and lightning
heard)

Will the magic of prayer help Prospero and his crew safely towards
Milan where the marriage of Miranda and Ferdinand may remind
them that Innocence and Age are two sides of the same coin; that
there are no degrees of forgiveness; that compassion will not exclude
any? Will Prospero, no longer interested in temporal success, enter
his grave without admitting that his every third thought remains
alive? For where, we wonder, is our excluded Caliban? And what
fearful truth will Caliban discover now the world he prized has
abandoned him to the solitude of his original home: the Island
which no act of foreign appropriation ever could deprive him of.

It is not only aesthetic necessity, but the *facts* of lived experience
which demanded that the territory of the drama had to be an island.
For there is no landscape more suitable for considering the question

of the sea, no geography more appropriate to the study of exile. And it is that ruthless, though necessary wreck, which warns us that we are all deeply involved in the politics of intrigue. The tides have turned treacherous. Thunder is talking a language which everyone understands; and in this moment of peril we are reminded by the loyal that there are very important people on board: a King and his heir, the King's brother, a Duke who has important connections not far away. There is panic among the great; and the old counsellor, Gonzalo—loyal even to his mistakes, Gonzalo the perfect embodiment of servitude, thinks not of himself but of his master's safety:

> GONZALO: Nay, good, be patient.
> BOATS: When the sea is. Hence! What cares these roarers for the name of King? To cabin: silence! trouble us not.
> GONZALO: Good, yet remember whom thou hast aboard.
> [1.1.14–17]

It is an expression of the perfect colonial concern: what will happen if the edifice of one man's presence crumbles? But these sailors have always sojourned with danger. Their harbour is no more than a postponement of peril. The sea is their kingdom, and they don't give a damn about the King who is essentially a land-crab. That's how they think; and confidence demands that they should say so:

> BOATS: None that I more love than myself. You are a counsellor; if you can command these elements to silence, and work the peace of the presence, we will not hand a rope more; use your authority: if you cannot, give thanks you have lived so long, and make yourself ready in your cabin for the mischance of the hour, if it so hap. Cheerly, good hearts! Out of our way, I say. [1.1.18–24]

It is a fine piece of straight talking and is in direct contrast to the forgivable stammering which comes from dear, old Gonzalo. We shall draw attention to another contrast when we encounter Ariel and Caliban in a similar situation of servant and master. But this wreck strikes terror in every heart; for it was Nature combined with Art which brought it about. Men seem to think that it is their last chance to call a spade a spade; and there is a good deal of bad language as the ship surrenders its sails to the total embrace of the sea. But the sea in conspiracy with the Art which also created these characters has returned them to safety.

According to plan they will reach shore; for it's on land and among the living that the awkwardness of the past must be resolved. Yet there must have been an interval of absolute hell: the purgatorial journey from origins to some landmark which reminds that you are always in transit. Ariel, in a spirit of pure and diabolical delight, gives a first-hand account of their suffering:

ARIEL: Not a soul
But felt a fever of the mad, and play'd
Some tricks of desperation. All but mariners
Plung'd in the foaming brine, and quit the vessel,
Then all afire with me: the King's son, Ferdinand,
With hair up-staring,—then like reeds, not hair,—
Was the first man that leap'd; cried, 'Hell is empty,
And all the devils are here.' [1.2.208–15]

To which Prospero replies: 'Why, that's my spirit!'

A most appropriate parallel in contemporary history is the unforgettable transport of slaves from Africa to the Caribbean . . .

> 'On ship the slaves were packed in the hold on galleries one
> above the other. Each was given only four or five feet in length
> and two or three feet in height, so that they could neither lie at
> full length nor sit upright . . . In this position they lived for the
> voyage, coming up once a day for exercise and to allow the sail
> ors "to clean the pails." But when the cargo was rebellious or the
> weather bad, then they stayed below for weeks at a time. The
> close proximity of so many naked human beings, their bruised
> and festering flesh, the foetid air, the prevailing dysentery, the
> accumulation of filth, turned these holds into a hell. During the
> storms the hatches were battened down, and in the close and
> loathsome darkness they were hurled from one side to another
> by the heaving vessel, held in position by the chains on their
> bleeding flesh. No place on earth, observed one writer of the
> time, concentrated so much misery as the hold of a slave ship.'[1]

That purgatory of the Middle Passage lasted six thousand miles;
and like Prospero commending his 'brave spirit,' there was the captain of the slave ship with so clear a conscience that one of them, in
the intervals of waiting to enrich British capitalism with the profits
of another valuable cargo, enriched British religion by composing
the hymn:

'How sweet the name of Jesus sounds!'

But these 'savage and deformed slaves' arrived; and like the character who or which fits this description in *The Tempest*, they worked,
and were rebellious and often went wild with the spirit of freedom,
and were imprisoned, and yet, like Caliban, they survived as though
there were some divinity which made them unique in their capacity
to last.

We are back, then, to the Island, once the birthright of Caliban,
and now the Kingdom of a Duke who lives in exile.

---

1. From C. L. R. James, *The Black Jacobins* [1938] (New York. Vintage Books, 1963), p. 8.

If we consider the politics of the Island, the size of its population as well as its relation to the world beyond its shores, we are left with a remarkable example of a State which is absolutely run by one man. Absolute is the only word for a power which does not even require an army. Prospero has no need of bureaucrats. Caliban is his slave, which means, among other things, his physical survival:

> But, as 'tis,
> We cannot miss him: he does make our fire,
> Fetch in our wood, and serves in offices
> That profit us. What, ho! slave! Caliban!
> Thou earth, thou! speak. [1.2.310–14]

We are trying to suggest the way in which Prospero saw himself in relation to the immediate neighbourhood around him. It is in his relation to Caliban, as a physical fact of life, that we are allowed to guess some of Prospero's needs. He needs this slave. Moreover, he must be cautious in his dealings with him, for Caliban contains the seed of revolt.

After the slaves were encamped in Haiti, torture became a common method of persuading them to work. In some cases, they were roasted; others were buried alive up to the neck, their heads smeared with sugar that the flies might devour them; they were fastened to nests of wasps, made to eat their excrement, drink their urine, and lick the saliva of other slaves. A great pastime too, was to fill them with gunpowder and strike a match somewhere near the hole of the arse. There is a similar sadism in Prospero whenever he is moved to threaten Caliban for his rebellion:

> PROSPERO: For this, be sure, tonight thou shalt have cramps,
> Side-stitches that shall pen thy breath up; urchins
> Shall, for that vast of night that they may work,
> All exercise on thee; thou shalt be pinch'd
> As thick as honeycomb, each pinch more stinging
> Than bees that made 'em. [1.2.325–30]

But Prospero dare not dynamite Caliban; for there is one slave only, one pair of hands that labour. To murder Caliban would be an act of pure suicide. But Caliban is more than his source of food as we shall see. Caliban haunts him in a way that is almost too deep and too intimate to communicate.

But we must return to the politics of the island, to Ariel's function in this drama of intrigue. For Ariel, like Caliban, serves Prospero; but Ariel is not a slave. Ariel has been emancipated to the status of a privileged servant. In other words: a lackey. Ariel is Prospero's source of information; the archetypal spy, the embodiment—when and if made flesh—of the perfect and unspeakable secret police. It is Ariel who tunes in on every conversation which the degradation of his duty demands that he report back to Prospero. Of course, he knows what's going on from the very beginning. Ariel is on the inside. He knows and serves his master's intention, and his methods are free from any scruples:

> ARIEL: All hail, great master! grave sir, hail! I come
> To answer thy best pleasure; be 't to fly,
> To swim, to dive into the fire, to ride
> On the curl'd clouds, to thy strong bidding task
> Ariel and all his quality. [1.2.189–93]

But it is a dangerous partnership, and Prospero never hesitates to remind him of his servitude. Like some malevolent old bitch with a bad conscience, Prospero's habit is to make you aware of his power to give. He is an expert at throwing the past in your face. And Ariel is no exception:

> PROSPERO: Dost thou forget
> From what torment I did free thee?
> ARIEL: No.
> PROSPERO: Thou dost, and think'st it much to tread the ooze
> Of the salt deep,
> To run upon the sharp wind of the north,
> To do me business in the veins o' th' earth
> When it is bak'd with frost.
> ARIEL: I do not, sir.
> PROSPERO: Thou liest, malignant thing! Hast thou forgot
> The foul witch Sycorax, who with age and envy
> Was grown into a hoop? hast thou forgot her?
> ARIEL: No, sir.

> * * *

> PROSPERO: Thou best know'st
> What torment I did find thee in; thy groans
> Did make wolves howl, and penetrate the breasts
> Of ever-angry bears: it was a torment
> To lay upon the damn'd, which Sycorax
> Could not again undo: it was mine Art,
> When I arriv'd and heard thee, that made gape
> The pine, and let thee out.
> ARIEL: I thank thee, master. [1.2.250–59, 286–93]

It is at this point that we can offer the contrast between Ariel and Caliban in a similar encounter with Prospero. Caliban is a victim of mental torture. It weakens him; and sometimes it seems that his confidence is lost. But the spirit of freedom never deserts him.

When he makes his first appearance in the play, it is at the order of Prospero.

> PROSPERO: Thou poisonous slave, got by the devil himself
> Upon thy wicked dam, come forth!
>
> *Enter* CALIBAN
>
> CALIBAN: As wicked dew as e'er my mother brush'd
> With raven's feather from unwholesome fen
> Drop on you both! a south-west blow on ye
> And blister you all o'er!
> PROSPERO: For this, be sure, tonight thou shalt have cramps,
> Side-stitches that shall pen thy breath up; urchins
> Shall, for that vast of night that they may work,
> All exercise on thee; thou shalt be pinch'd
> As thick as honeycomb, each pinch more stinging
> Than bees that made 'em.
> CALIBAN: I must eat my dinner.
> This island's mine, by Sycorax my mother,
> Which thou tak'st from me. When thou cam'st first,
> Thou strok'st me, and made much of me; wouldst give me
> Water with berries in't; and teach me how
> To name the bigger light, and how the less,
> That burn by day and night: and then I lov'd thee,
> And show'd thee all the qualities o' th' isle,
> The fresh springs, brine-pits, barren place and fertile
> Curs'd be I that did so! All the charms
> Of Sycorax, toads, beetles, bats, light on you!
> For I am all the subjects that you have,
> Which first was mine own King: and there you sty me
> In this hard rock, whiles you do keep from me
> The rest o' th' island. [1.2.319–44]

Caliban has not lost his sense of original rootedness, and for this reason Prospero must deal with him harshly. The rock imprisonment is, in our time, a form of the emergency regulation which can forbid a son of the soil to travel outside a certain orbit; marked out and even made legal by a foreign visitor. But Caliban keeps answering back, and it is his refusal to be silent which now bullies Prospero into the crucial charge:

> PROSPERO: Thou most lying slave,
> Whom stripes may move, not kindness! I have us'd thee,
> Filth as thou art, with human care; and lodg'd thee
> In mine own cell, till thou didst seek to violate
> The honour of my child.
> CALIBAN: O ho, O ho! would't had been done!

> Thou didst prevent me; I had peopled else
> This isle with Calibans. [1.2.344–50]

What an extraordinary way for a slave to speak to his master and in the daughter's presence. But there is a limit to accepting lies and it was the Lie contained in the charge which the man in Caliban could not allow. 'I wish it were so.' But he does not wish it for the mere experiment of mounting a piece of white flesh. He goes further and imagines that the consequence of such intercourse would be a fabulous increase of the population.

> I had peopled else
> This isle with Calibans.

Is there a political intention at work? Does he mean that he would have numbers on his side; that he could organise resistance against this obscene, and selfish monster. But why, we wonder, does Caliban think that the population would be Calibans? Why would they not be Mirandas? Does he mean that they should carry the father's name? But these children would be bastards and should be honoured no less with their mother's name. Or were there other possibilities?

Did Caliban really try to rape her? This is a case where the body, in its consequences, is our only guide. Only the body could establish the truth; for if Miranda were made pregnant, we would know that someone had penetrated her. We might also know whether or no it was Caliban's child; for it is most unlikely that Prospero and his daughter could produce a brown skin baby. Could Prospero really have endured the presence and meaning of a brown skin grandchild. It would not be Miranda's own doing. It would not be the result of their enterprise. It would be Miranda's and Caliban's child. It would be *theirs*: the result and expression of some fusion both physical and other than physical: a fusion which, within himself, Prospero needs and dreads!

Prospero is a Duke who has been deprived of his kingdom. Through the logical treachery of his brother, Antonio, and the conspiracy of the neighbouring King of Naples, Alonso, Prospero was thrown out of his kingdom. Miranda, his heir, was then no more than three years old. Father and child were hurried on a bark, taken out to sea and then dumped on

> A rotten carcass of a butt, not rigg'd
> Nor tackle, sail, nor mast. [1.2.146–47]

But all this happened twelve years before the wreck which brings some visitors on to the island, and Miranda, now grown into a virtuous beauty, is hearing about these events for the first time. She is at the ripe and provocative age of fifteen, a virgin and, like her father, curious about the facts of life. She had witnessed or had some vision of the wreck which has just taken place; and it is an appeal on behalf of those, presumably dying at sea, which leads to her father's recapitulation of the times before they were expelled from Milan. She tries to explain what of the wreck she has seen; and her vision of their suffering is also the measure of the pain she feels on their behalf.

> MIRANDA: O, I have suffered
> With those I saw suffer! A brave vessel
> (Who had, no doubt, some noble creature in her)
> Dashed all to pieces. O, the cry did knock
> Against my very heart!
> PROSPERO: Be collected:
> No more amazement: tell your piteous heart
> There's no harm done. [1.2.5–15]

It is this contrast of attitude towards a common disaster which introduces the noble and compassionate nature of Miranda on the one hand, and the supernatural power of her father on the other. Equally noble in their origins, Father and Child are different only in the degrees of their knowledge. What comes between them is the distance which separates Age that apprehends, from Innocence which can only see. Prospero, who is also her first and only teacher, now gives Miranda a lesson in their domestic history. She learns that the wrecked crew will land safely on this island; and she learns, stage by fastidious stage, the circumstance and purpose of the happy misfortune. And so her curiosity, an essential logic of the drama, forces Prospero to give a hurried lesson in domestic history. He begins, as is his custom with all people, by drawing her attention to her limitations:

> PROSPERO: I have done nothing but in care of thee,
> Of thee, my dear one; thee, my daughter, who
> Art ignorant of what thou art; nought knowing
> Of whence I am, nor that I am more better
> Than Prospero, master of a full poor cell,
> And thy no greater father. [1.2.16–21]

Now the search for time lost has begun. He traces the orbit of memory in which she will travel back to find some image of her infancy. And the first landmark, the first anchor which comes to mind, is a memory of her maids. She can remember three or four. Prospero assures her there were many more. He coaxes her to dig up some more evidence of that lost infancy; but she can't get much further.

PROSPERO: What seest thou else
In the dark backward and abysm of time?
If thou rememberest aught ere thou cam'st here,
How thou cam'st here thou mayst.
MIRANDA: But that I do not. [1.2.49–52]

What impresses us here is the fact that she has, it seems, absolutely no recollection of her mother. Nor does she raise the question until Prospero's ambiguous way of explaining relations forces
her to ask:

MIRANDA: Sir, are you not my father?

To which he gives a reply characteristic of his method of rendering information:

PROSPERO: Thy mother was a piece of virtue, and
She said thou wast my daughter; and thy father
Was Duke of Milan; and his only heir
And princess, no worse issued. [1.2.56–59]

It is the first and, if I am not mistaken, the very last reference we
have to Miranda's mother who was, presumably, Prospero's wife. Is
she alive? Or did she die in the treacherous *coup d'état* which led to
Prospero's exile? But Prospero does not mention her again; for he is
busy giving his daughter a summary account of events which led to
his brother's conspiracy with the King of Naples, who, with his son,
Ferdinand, is among the survivors destined for this Island. So is the
old counsellor Gonzalo who was given the job of designing Prospero's
downfall. The whole gang are alive and well, but ignorant of what's
in store for them.

Resurrected from the water, innocent and guilty, they offer a striking parallel with the Haitian Ceremony of Souls. Prospero is the
bitter reality which they cannot avoid; and Miranda is no more than
an initiate who is being briefed at lightning speed about the necessary
facts. These are carefully chosen, for the techniques of propaganda
are not unknown to Prospero; and he emerges swiftly, but surely, as
the outraged martyr: the embodiment of an original nobility, a cri-
terion of virtue which bears witness to the disgrace of his degenerate adversaries.

This is the only light in which Miranda can see him; for she has
no experience of the world beyond this island, no instruments for
making a comparative judgment. Caliban is the only other man she
has seen; but his whole relation to the condition meant by Man is
gravely in doubt. Her father's account of history—which is no more
than a schematic arrangement of necessary and self-protective

emphasis—fills her with an admiration which she can only express through regret. She regrets that she should have been so much trouble to him.

> MIRANDA: Your tale, sir, would cure deafness. [1.2.106]

Her case is perhaps not unrelated to what, in our time, is called brain-washing. Virtue, nobility, chastity and beauty, degeneracy, bestiality, lust, and physical deformity are the antitheses which she has thoroughly absorbed and which will, in the course of time, be exemplified by those she meets. Caliban, her first experience of a stranger, is already the black temple of every tendency that characterises the beast, and he serves as a reminder to any noble spirit which may be tempted to overreach the laws of its nature. It is against this moral background of opposites that Miranda learns how it came about that her father could have lost his dukedom.

> PROSPERO: I pray thee, mark me.
> I, thus neglecting worldly ends, all dedicated
> To closeness and the bettering of my mind
> With that which, but by being so retir'd,
> O'er-priz'd all popular rate, in my false brother
> Awak'd an evil nature; and my trust,
> Like a good parent, did beget of him
> A falsehood in its contrary, as great
> As my trust was; which had indeed no limit,
> A confidence sans bound. . . .
>   Me, poor man, my library
> Was dukedom large enough: of temporal royalties
> He thinks me now incapable; confederates,
> So dry he was for sway, wi' th' King of Naples
> To give him annual tribute, do him homage,
> Subject his coronet to his crown, and bend
> The dukedom, yet unbow'd,—alas, poor Milan!—
> To most ignoble stooping.
> MIRANDA: O the heavens!
> PROSPERO: Mark his condition, and th' event; then tell me
> If this might be a brother.
> MIRANDA: I should sin
> To think but nobly of my grandmother:
> Good wombs have borne bad sons. [1.2.88–97, 109–20]

And when she asks the pertinent question:

> MIRANDA: Wherefore did they not
> That hour destroy us? [1.2.138–39]

he congratulates her on the acuity of her attention, and proceeds to explain that his survival was due entirely to the love his people—meaning the common herd of men and women—bore him.

His absence could probably be explained in much the same way that the political exile of African chiefs could be given 'some rational interpretation.' The present Asantehene, Otumfuo Sir Osei Agyeman Prempeh II, K.B.E., suffered a similar fate when he was banished by a British Administration to the Seychelles. . . . It was some years before he was returned. So also did King Jaja of Nigeria, who, for some odd reason, was removed to Barbados, the island of the author's birth. The latter episode enriched the almost absent folk music with a tune about Jaja.

Prospero is not only a ruler, but a philosopher as well; and we can assume that this combination: the Philosopher-King—the hereditary right to rule people and the spiritual need to organise reality— is directly related to that creative will to conquer the absolute: a will which finds its most perfect vessel in the infinitely expanding powers of transformation that characterise the timeless frontiers of the Poetic Vision. This is the total atmosphere of expectation in which Miranda lives. Her father will arrange her future; and all will be well provided the references of truth are not disturbed by some fearful contingency. Sooner or later the wrecked crew will come safely to shore; ignorance will be dispelled by Prospero's light. Like the miraculous discovery of one's empty purse, the guilty will find their conscience. The magic of birth will sail Miranda, young, beautiful and a virgin, into the arms of a King's only son. Her eye will show her at one glance who is her heart's desire. The rest is forgiveness and preparation for a marriage whose future must remain promising and absent as paradise.

> Was Milan thrust from Milan, that his issue
> Should become Kings of Naples? O, rejoice
> Beyond a common joy! [5.1.205–07]

Caliban cannot be revealed in any relation to himself; for he has no self which is not a reaction to circumstances imposed upon his life. He is not seen as a possibility of spirit which might fertilise and extend the resources of any human vision. Caliban is the very climate in which men encounter the nature of ambiguities, and in which, according to his desire, each man attempts a resolution by trying to slay the past. Caliban's history—for he has a most turbulent history—belongs entirely to the future. It is the wind which reminds us that trouble has gone into hiding. In all his encounters with his neighbours—whether they be Kings or drunken clowns— Caliban is never accorded the power *to see*. He is always the measure of the condition which his physical appearance has already defined. Caliban is the excluded, that which is eternally below possibility, and always beyond reach. He is seen as an occasion, a state of existence which can be appropriated and exploited for the purposes of another's own development. Caliban is a reminder of lost virtue or the evil vigour of the Beast that is always there: a magnetic temptation, and an eternal warning against the contagion of his daemon ancestry.

The difficulty is to take from Caliban without suffering the pollution innate in his nature. To yield to Caliban's natural generosity is to risk the deluge: for his assets—such as they are—are dangerous, since they are encrusted, buried deep in the dark. It is not by accident that his skin is black; for black, too, is the colour of his loss; the absence of any soul. If he shows an aptitude for music, it is because the perfection of harmonies can strike some chord in his nervous system.

> CALIBAN: Be not afeard; the isle is full of noises,
> Sounds and sweet airs, that give delight, and hurt not.
> Sometimes a thousand twangling instruments
> Will hum about mine ears; and sometimes voices,
> That, if I then had wak'd after long sleep,
> Will make me sleep again: and then, in dreaming,
> The clouds methought would open, and show riches
> Ready to drop upon me: that, when I wak'd,
> I cried to dream again. [3.2.128–36]

Caliban is in his way a kind of Universal. Like the earth he is always there, generous in gifts, inevitable, yet superfluous and dumb. And like the earth which draws attention to age and therefore to the past, he cannot be devoured. Caliban is, therefore, the occasion to which every situation, within the context of the Tempest, must be related. No Caliban no Prospero! No Prospero no Miranda! No Miranda no Marriage! And no Marriage no Tempest! He confronts Prospero as a possibility; a challenge; and a defeat.

> This thing of darkness
> I acknowledge mine. [5.1.278–79]

He confronts the drunken butler Stephano, and the jester Trinculo, as a commercial speculation, a promising investment:

> STEPHANO: If I can recover him, and
> keep him tame, I will not take too much for him; he shall pay
> for him that hath him and that soundly. [2.2.71–73]

But it is the difference in these intentions which suggest the difference between Prospero and Trinculo; it is a difference which has

to do with birth and the inescapable law of heredity. Caliban's inca
pacity to see that Trinculo and Stephano are crooks, his readiness
to accord them the worship he had once given Prospero, are proof
of his condition. And it is this condition which Prospero, in the role
of philosopher, would like to experiment with. The problem of
learning is now firmly stated. Education, meaning the possession of
the Word—which was in the beginning or not at all—is the tool
which Prospero has tried on the irredeemable nature of his savage
and deformed slave. We are brought to the heart of the matter by
the cantankerous assertion, spoken by Miranda, but obviously the
thought and vocabulary of her father.

> MIRANDA: Abhorred slave,
> Which any print of goodness wilt not take,
> Being capable of all ill! I pitied thee,
> Took pains to make thee speak, taught thee each hour
> One thing or other: when thou didst not, savage,
> Know thine own meaning, but wouldst gabble like
> A thing most brutish, I endow'd thy purposes
> With words that made them known. But thy vile race,
> Though thou didst learn, had that in't which good natures
> Could not abide to be with; therefore wast thou
> Deservedly confin'd into this rock,
> Who hadst deserv'd more than a prison. [1.2.350–61]

There is no escape from the prison of Prospero's gift. This example of deformity was a challenge to Prospero's need to achieve the
impossible. Only the application of the Word to the darkness of
Caliban's world could harness the beast which resides within this
cannibal. This is the first important achievement of the colonising
process. This gift of Language is the deepest and most delicate
bond of involvement. It has a certain finality. Caliban will never be
the same again. Nor, for that matter, will Prospero.

Prospero has given Caliban Language; and with it an unstated
history of consequences, an unknown history of future intentions.
This gift of Language meant not English, in particular, but speech
and concept as a way, a method, a necessary avenue towards areas
of the self which could not be reached in any other way. It is this
way, entirely Prospero's enterprise, which makes Caliban aware of
possibilities. Therefore, all of Caliban's future—for future is the
very name for possibilities—must derive from Prospero's experiment which is also his risk.

Provided there is no extraordinary departure which explodes all of
Prospero's premises, then Caliban and his future now belong to
Prospero. Caliban is Prospero's risk in the sense that Adam's aware-
ness of a difference was a risk which God took with Man. Prospero

believes—his belief in his own powers demands it—that Caliban can learn so much and no more. Caliban can go so far and no farther. Prospero lives in the absolute certainty that Language which is his gift to Caliban is the very prison in which Caliban's achievements will be realised and restricted. Caliban can never reach perfection, not even the perfection implicit in Miranda's privileged ignorance.

For Language itself, by Caliban's whole relation to it, will not allow his expansion beyond a certain point. This kind of realisation, this kind of expansion, is possible only to those who reside in that state of being which is the very source and ultimate of the language that bears them always forward. The difference between Caliban and the sinner is this. A sinner remains a child of God, and redemption is not so much an order as a natural duty. Grace is the sinner's birthright. But Caliban is not a child of anything except Nature. To be a child of Nature, in this sense, is to be situated in Nature, to be identified with Nature, to be eternally without the seed of a dialectic which makes possible some *emergence* from Nature.

Such is Caliban, superfluous as the weight of the earth until Prospero arrives with the aid of the Word which might help him to clarify the chaos which shows its true colours all over his skin. But he can never be regarded as an heir of that Language, since his use of Language is no more than his way of serving Prospero; and Prospero's instruction in this Language is only his way of measuring the distance which separates him from Caliban. If it were possible for Caliban to realise Language as his perfect inheritance, and if, in spite of this new power, Prospero could still appropriate and imprison him at will; then Prospero would have achieved the triplicity which he is pursuing: 'The Power and Fortune of a King, the knowledge and illumination of a priest, and the learning and the universality of a philosopher.' The seeds of this triplicity are within Prospero; but there is one disqualification which hounds him slowly to despair. Prospero is getting old, and the powers he would claim are associated in his mind with youth. Caliban at twenty-four is certainly young. But he has no *sight*. He is without that necessary light which is the very origin of Language, the light which guides Prospero, and which, at the same time, Prospero is trying to surpass.

Caliban may become Man; but he is entirely outside the orbit of Human. It is not Prospero who keeps him there; nor is it his own fault that he is there. It is some original Law which exists even beyond Prospero's seeing. It is this Law which has ordained the state of existence we call Caliban. If Caliban turns cannibal, it is not because human flesh may appear a necessary substitute for food which is absent. It is rather because he is incapable of differentiating between one kind of reality and another. His hunger is too large—not his greed but his hunger—too large to be harnessed by any process of selection. He cannot distinguish between Man, the object, and Human, the form and ideal which auras that object. He could not recognise the difference of quality between Prospero and Trinculo or between Stephano and Ferdinand. Language may help him to describe the physical attributes which nobility calls beautiful; but language will not help him to distinguish between separate personalities. Word and concept may be part of his vocabulary; but they are no part of his way of seeing.

Caliban is not allowed to distinguish, for the eyes that register personality must belong to, must derive from a consciousness which could be regarded as person. And Caliban is a condition.

Hence the charge of rape. Caliban would think no more of raping Miranda than he might of eating her if she were alone, and he was hungry or feeling too idle to go swimming.

This is precisely Miranda's view of Caliban also; for her father and only teacher throughout her life is Prospero. It would not be difficult for Miranda to accuse Caliban also of having actually raped her; for she probably dreams about him, and does not trust his heredity when she is asleep. If she dreamt that Caliban had raped her, she would not be able to tell whether it had happened or not; for Caliban, as the descendant of a Devil, may have inherited that traditional power which allowed Devils to put their female victims asleep while they had their pleasure. It is through Miranda, the product of Prospero's teaching, that we may glimpse the origin and perpetuation of myth coming slowly but surely into its right as fact, history, absolute truth.

Throughout the play we are impressed by the affinities, the likeness of circumstance between Miranda and Caliban. Like many an African slave child, Miranda has no recollection of her mother. The actual Caliban of The Tempest has the advantage—regrettable as he makes it sound—of having known the meaning and power of his mother Sycorax.

But Miranda has a deeper affinity than this likeness of circumstance. She was no more than an infant when she and her father met Caliban on the island. Prospero says she was scarcely three. Caliban would have been about twelve. As time passed, and Prospero grew more and more occupied with his Book, Caliban and the child, Miranda, must have grown closer by the necessary contact of servant and mistress. Before the emergency regulation which imprisoned him in a rock, Caliban must have taken this child for walks about the island. He probably had to carry her on his back, the way we have seen African servants showing their affection to European children. Between the age of three and five Miranda must have spent a lot of time playing with Caliban, the way European children, during their parents' absence, monopolise the African servant's rest hour.

Miranda and Prospero may be equal in their assumed superiority
of origins over Caliban. But Caliban and the Duke's daughter have a
bond that is not easily broken. They are alike in their ignorance; and
there are parallels in their response to strangers from the world
beyond these shores. The moment Miranda sets eyes on Ferdinand—
handsome, noble and a prince—she suffers a genuine attack of
lovesickness.

> MIRANDA: I might call him
> A thing divine; for nothing natural
> I ever saw so noble. [1.2.416–18]

And Ferdinand, who is her equal in vigour and her other half in
chastity, lets her know exactly his intentions.

> FERDINAND: O, if a virgin,
> And your affection not gone forth, I'll make you
> The Queen of Naples. [1.2.446–48]

Ferdinand does not yet know that his father is alive; hence his
promise to Miranda that she will be queen. It is at this point that
Prospero intervenes to supply us again with the kind of stuff he is
made of: an imperialist by circumstance, a sadist by disease; and,
above all, an old man in whom envy and revenge are equally matched.
Immediately after Ferdinand's offer of marriage, Prospero says:

> PROSPERO: Soft, sir! one word more.
> (*Aside*) They are both in either's pow'rs: but this swift business
> I must uneasy make, lest too light winning
> Make the prize light. (*To Ferdinand*) One word more; I charge
>   thee
> That thou attend me: thou dost here usurp
> The name thou ow'st not; and hast put thyself
> Upon this island as a spy, to win it
> From me, the lord on't. [1.2.448–55]

It is possible that Prospero envies and admires the passion which
is an essential part of the couple's youth. It is likely that he had never
experienced any such feeling towards his wife. His imperialism is
like an illness, not only in his personal relationships, but in his relation to the external and foreign world. This island belongs to Caliban
whom he found there; yet some privilege allows Prospero to assert—
and with an authority that is divine—that he is lord of the island.

Sadism is characteristic of this type. He approves of the union of
Ferdinand and his daughter. Indeed, it is a part of his overall
arrangement; but youth and innocence must be punished before
they can partake of the pleasures and paradox of love. He accuses
Ferdinand of being a spy when he knows that the shipwrecked boy

is occupied with sorrow for the imagined death of his father. He tells Miranda that she must not rush these things; and again that loathsome habit of cutting people down to size is revealed:

> PROSPERO: Thou think'st there is no more such shapes as he,
> Having seen but him and Caliban: foolish wench!
> To th' most of men this is a Caliban,
> And they to him are angels. [1.2.477–80]

His accusation of espionage is also intended to test Ferdinand's nobility. Enraged, the boy draws his sword, and is immediately charmed into immobility by Prospero's magic. Even Miranda, who has not long heard what an excellent specimen of nobility and wisdom her father is, even she is shaken by the appearance of the monster in Prospero. Torn between her love for the young prince and her tribal allegiance to Prospero, she tries to cheer Ferdinand up:

> Be of comfort;
> My father's of a better nature, sir,
> Than he appears by speech: this is unwonted
> Which now came from him. [1.2.494–97]

An opinion which we know to be in direct contradiction with the facts; for the obscenity of Prospero's rage knows no bounds in his dealings with Ariel and Caliban: the two agents of labour and public relations without whom he would be helpless. It is this innocence and credulity in Miranda which—were it not for a difference in their degrees of being—would have made her and Caliban almost identical.

For Caliban also has this tendency to take people at their face value. Whereas Prospero's fear springs from a need to maintain his power—for to lose his power is to lose face—and it is only through power that the world knows him; Caliban is the epitome of a pure and uncalculated naïveté. Having been deprived of his freedom, it seems that Caliban has nothing to lose but his goodwill; and one meaning we can extract from this is that the suspension of a man's freedom can have the effect of returning him to the fundamental sources of integrity. Temporary imprisonment is the greatest service an imperialist can do to a nationalist leader. It is in the solitude of the cell that he gets a chance, free from the indulgence of his followers, to think things out. When he is freed—as we shall see with Caliban—he returns to the streets with a formidable power born of suffering and reflection. But it is this original tendency to welcome which gets Caliban into trouble. We recall what he tells Prospero:

> CALIBAN: This island's mine, by Sycorax my mother
> Which thou tak'st from me. [1.2.331–32]

And later, in his state of utter displacement brought about by Prospero's betrayal of love, Caliban makes the same mistake again. Trinculo is a jester, a man who lives at the mercy of a successful joke. Stephano is a butler and an irresponsible and adventurous drunk. In their original home, they bear much the same relation to royalty that Caliban here bears to Prospero. They are scum. It is to these innocent bandits that Caliban turns for help. He is plotting revolution with them; but they have absolutely no idea what it means for Caliban that he should get Prospero out of the way. To them, it is no more than cutting another throat. To Caliban it is an enterprise of colossal importance. Yet it is to these men that Caliban will surrender his secrets:

> CALIBAN: I prithee, let me bring thee where crabs grow;
> And I with my long nails will dig thee pig-nuts;
> Show thee a jay's nest, and instruct thee how
> To snare the nimble marmoset; I'll bring thee
> To clustering filberts, and sometimes I'll get thee
> Young scamels from the rock. Wilt thou go with me?
> [2.2.158–63]

In some real, though extraordinary way, Caliban and Miranda are seen side by side: opposite and contiguous at the same time. They share an ignorance that is also the source of some vision. It is, as it were, a kind of creative blindness.

In different circumstances, they could be together in a way that Miranda and her father could not. For Prospero is alone. He hates and fears and needs Caliban. The role of father demands that he should pay Miranda some attention, equip her with a few basic prejudices; but he is not really interested in her as a person. The education he bestows is in the nature of a formality. Miranda herself has told him that he was always postponing to tell her certain things.

It has taken him twelve years to tell the child one or two things which any decent parent of his intelligence would have passed on long ago. When she asked him: Are you not my father? he talks about the chastity of her mother; and we realise—with some knowledge of this type—that he is taking refuge in the lesson of chastity in order to evade or obscure any talk about the woman who is supposed to be his wife. Who, we are left to wonder, was really Miranda's mother? And what would she have had to say about this marvellous monster of a husband who refuses us information?

An interesting contrast is seen in his dealing with Caliban on the same subject. For some reason or other, the memory of Sycorax, Caliban's mother, arouses him to rage that is almost insane. For all that he is a Duke and noble, Prospero can't conquer that obscene habit of throwing the past, turning your origins into a weapon of slander. In Caliban's case it takes the form of his mother being a so-and-so.

We ask ourselves why a Duke should debase himself to speak in such a way. The tone suggests an intimacy of involvement and concern which encourages speculation. But we could not speak with authority on the possibilities of this defect until we had heard from Sycorax and Miranda's mother. They are both dead; and so our knowledge must be postponed until some arrangement comparable to the Haitian Ceremony of Souls returns them to tell us what we should and ought to know.

We begin to distrust this Duke. Why should we believe, in the light of all that has happened now, that the people of Milan really loved him. For it's a difficult love: the love of a dispossessed crowd for a rich and absent idol. Prospero contributed in no uncertain terms to his brother's treachery. If he wanted to retain the honour and privilege of Duke, then he should have been prepared to undertake the responsibilities. If the Book dominated his deepest interest; then he should have told the people that in the interest of learning which would be to their benefit, he would have to abdicate. It was the only decent thing to do.

Antonio can be forgiven for usurping the rights and privileges that were not his. Prospero sees this as another occasion of ingratitude. When he hears of Caliban's conspiracy to overthrow him, he is again plunged into rage. For this is seen as ingratitude of a most bestial nature. Caliban whom he had given Language conspiring with men not much better than himself to sabotage the divine hierarchy of which he is the most privileged on earth!

> PROSPERO: He is as disproportion'd in his manners
> As in his shape. Go, sirrah, to my cell;
> Take with you your companions; as you look
> To have my pardon, trim it handsomely. [5.1.293–96]

One wonders whether it is ingratitude that bothers Prospero. Could it not be a shattering kind of self-knowledge, the knowledge that he really deserves such ingratitude? Prospero's gifts are no part of his concern for those who receive. Could it be that Prospero didn't really care any more about the people of Milan than he cared about his wife? Is it that age and the pressure of a simple honesty had forced him to see his total indifference to his neighbour as a perfect example of human degradation? For the real sin is not hatred, which implies an involvement, but the calculated and habitual annihilation of the person whose presence you can ignore but never exclude. What can he feel when he recalls the statement which tells us what Caliban truly felt?

CALIBAN: When thou cam'st first,
Thou strok'dst me, and made much of me; wouldst give me
Water with berries in't; and teach me how
To name the bigger light, and how the less,
That burn by day and night: and then I loved thee.
    [1.2.332–36]

Will the Lie upon which Prospero's confident authority was built
be discovered? For tomorrow they will take to sea, rehearsing again
the distance and purgatory which have always separated them from
their forgotten slave.

We can assume that they are gone. Dawn has rigged their sails;
the clouds have dispersed; and the sun is loud as wedding bells. But
no one bade them farewell.

Tonight, in his deformity and his solitude, Caliban, like Ishmael,
is left alone.

STEPHEN ORGEL

Prospero's Wife†

This essay is not a reading of *The Tempest*. It is a consideration of
five related moments and issues. I have called it *Prospero's Wife*
because some of it centres on her, but as a figure conspicuous by
her absence from the play, I take her as a figure of my larger subject: the absent, the unspoken, that seems to me the most powerful
and problematic presence in *The Tempest*. In its outlines, the play
seems a story of privatives: withdrawal, usurpation, banishment,
becoming lost, shipwreck. As an antithesis, a principle of control,
preservation, re-creation, the play offers only magic, embodied in a
single figure, the extraordinary power of Prospero.

FAMILY HISTORY

Prospero's wife is alluded to only once in the play, in Prospero's
reply to Miranda's question, 'Sir, are you not my father?'

    Thy mother was a piece of virtue, and
    She said thou wast my daughter; and thy father
    Was Duke of Milan; and his only heir
    And princess: no worse issued.
                              (1.2.56–59)[1]

---

† From *Representations* 8 (1985): 1–13. Amended by the author for the first Norton Critical Edition. © The Regents of the University of California. Reprinted by permission of
  University of California Press. All notes are by the author.
1. In this instance, I have restored the folio punctuation of line 59.

Prospero's wife is identified as Miranda's mother, in a context implying that although she was virtuous, women as a class are not, and that were it not for her word, Miranda's legitimacy would be in doubt. The legitimacy of Prospero's heir, that is, derives from her mother's word. But that word is all that is required of her in the play; once he is assured of it, Prospero turns his attention to himself and his succession, and he characterises Miranda in a clause that grows increasingly ambivalent: 'his only heir / And princess: no worse issued.'

Except for this moment, Prospero's wife is absent from his memory. She is wholly absent from her daughter's memory: Miranda can recall several women who attended her in childhood, but no mother. The attitudes implied toward wives and mothers here are confirmed shortly afterward when Prospero, recounting his brother Antonio's crimes, demands that Miranda 'tell me / If this might be a brother', and Miranda takes the question to be a charge of adultery against Prospero's mother:

> I should sin
> To think but nobly of my grandmother:
> Good wombs have borne bad sons.
> (1.2.118–20)

She immediately translates Prospero's attack on his brother into an attack on his mother (and the best she can produce in her grandmother's defence is a 'not proved'); and whether or not she has correctly divined her father's intentions, Prospero makes no objection.

The absent presence of the wife and mother in the play constitutes a space that is filled by Prospero's creation of surrogates and a ghostly family: the witch Sycorax and her monster child Caliban (himself, as becomes apparent, a surrogate for the other wicked child; the usurping younger brother), the good child/wife Miranda, the obedient Ariel, the violently libidinised adolescent Ferdinand. The space is filled, too, by a whole structure of wifely allusion and reference: widow Dido, model at once of heroic fidelity to a murdered husband and the destructive potential of erotic passion; the witch Medea, murderess and filicide; three exemplary goddesses, the bereft Ceres, nurturing Juno, and licentious Venus; and Alonso's daughter Claribel, unwillingly married off to the ruler of the modern Carthage and thereby lost to her father forever.

Described in this way, the play has an obvious psychoanalytic shape. I have learned a great deal from Freudian treatments of it, most recently from essays by David Sundelson, Coppélia Kahn, and Joel Fineman in the volume called *Representing Shakespeare*.[2] It is

2. Murray M. Schwartz and Coppélia Kahn (eds.), *Representing Shakespeare* (Baltimore, 1980).

almost irresistible to look at the play as a case history—*whose* case history is a rather more problematic question and one that criticism has not, on the whole, dealt with satisfactorily: not, obviously, that of the characters. I want to pause first over what it means to consider the play as a case history.

In older psychoanalytic paradigms (say Ernest Jones's), the critic is the analyst, Shakespeare the patient, the plays his fantasies. The trouble with this paradigm is that it misrepresents the analytic situation in a fundamental way. The interpretation of analytical material is done in conjunction with, and in large measure by, the patient, not the analyst; what the analyst does is to *enable* the patient, to free the patient to interpret. An analysis done without the patient, like Freud's of Leonardo, will be revealing only about the analyst. A more recent paradigm, in which the audience's response is the principal analytic material, seems to me based on even more fundamental misconceptions, first because it treats an audience as an entity, a unit, and moreover a constant one; and more problematically, because it conceives of the play as an objective event, so that the critical question becomes, 'This is what happened: how do we respond to it?'

To take the psychoanalytic paradigm seriously, however, and treat the plays as case histories, is surely to treat them *not* as objective events but as collaborative fantasies and to acknowledge thereby that we, as analysts, are implicated in the fantasy. It is not only the patients who create the shape of their histories, and when Bruno Bettelheim observes that Freud's case histories 'read as well as the best novels',[3] he is probably telling more of the truth than he intends. Moreover, the crucial recent advances in our understanding of Freud and psychoanalysis have been precisely critical acts of close and inventive reading—there are, in this respect, no limits to the collaboration. But if we accept this as our paradigm and think of ourselves as Freud's or Shakespeare's collaborators, we must also acknowledge that our reading of the case will be revealing, again, chiefly about ourselves. This is why every generation, and perhaps every reading, produces a different analysis of its Shakespearean texts. In the same way, recent psychoanalytic theory has replaced Freud's central Oedipal myth with a drama in which the loss of the seducing mother is the crucial infant trauma. As men, we used to want assurance that we could successfully compete with or replace or supersede our fathers; now we want to know that our lost mothers will return. Both of these no doubt involve real perceptions, but they also undeniably serve particular cultural needs.

3. Bruno Bettelheim, *The New Yorker*, 1 March 1982, p. 53.

Shakespeare plays, like case histories, derive from the observation of human behaviour, and both plays and case histories are
imaginative constructs. Whether or not either is taken to be an
objective report of behaviour has more to do with the reader than
the reporter, but it has to be said that Shakespearean critics have
more often than not treated the plays as objective accounts. Without
such an assumption, a book with the title *The Girlhood of Shakespeare's Heroines* would be incomprehensible. We feel very far from
this famous and popular Victorian work now, but we still worry
about consistency and motivation in Shakespearean texts, and much
of the commentary in an edition like the Arden Shakespeare is
designed to explain why the characters say what they say—that is, to
reconcile what they say with what, on the basis of their previous
behaviour, we feel they ought to be saying. The critic who worries
about this kind of consistency in a Shakespeare text is thinking of it
as an objective report.

But all readings of Shakespeare, from the earliest seventeenth-
century adaptations through eighteenth century attempts to produce 'authentic' or 'accurate' texts to the liberal fantasy of the old
Variorum Shakespeare, have been aware of deep ambiguities and
ambivalences in the texts. The eighteenth century described these
as Shakespeare's errors and generally revised them through plausible emendation or outright rewriting. The argument was that Shakespeare wrote in haste and would have written more perfect plays
had he taken time to revise; the corollary to this was, of course, that
what we want are the perfect plays Shakespeare did not write rather
than the imperfect ones that he did. A little later the errors became
not Shakespeare's but those of the printing house, the scribe, the
memory of the reporter or the defective hearing of the transcriber;
but the assumption has always been that it is possible to produce a
'perfect' text: that beyond or behind the ambiguous, puzzling, incon-
sistent text is a clear and consistent one.

Plays, moreover, are not only—and one might argue, not primarily—
texts. They are performances, too, originally designed to be read only
in order to be acted out, and the gap between the text and its performance has always been, and remains, a radical one. There always has
been an imagination intervening between the texts and their audiences, initially the imagination of producer, director, or actor (roles
that Shakespeare played himself), and since that time the imagination
of editors and commentators as well. These are texts that have always
had to be realised. Initially unstable, they have remained so despite
all attempts to fix them. All attempts to produce an authentic, correct, that is, stable text have resulted only in an extraordinary variety of versions. Their differences can be described as minor only if

one believes that the real play is a Platonic idea, never realised but
only approached and approximately represented by its text.

This is our myth: the myth of a stable, accurate, authentic, legitimate text, a text that we can think of as Shakespeare's legitimate
heir. It is, in its way, a family myth, and it operates with peculiar
force in our readings of *The Tempest*, a play that has been, for the
last hundred and fifty years, taken as a representation of Shakespeare himself bidding farewell to his art, as Shakespeare's legacy.

THE MISSING WIFE

She is missing as a character, but Prospero, several times explicitly,
presents himself as incorporating the wife, acting as both father and
mother to Miranda, and, in one extraordinary passage, describes the
voyage to the island as a birth fantasy:

> When I have decked the sea with drops full salt,
> Under my burden groaned, which raised in me
> An undergoing stomach, to bear up
> Against what should ensue.
>
> (1.2.155–58)

To come to the island is to start life over again—both his own and
Miranda's—with himself as sole parent, but also with himself as
favourite child: he has been banished by his wicked, usurping, possibly illegitimate younger brother Antonio. This too has the shape
of a Freudian fantasy: the younger child is indeed the usurper in
the family, and the kingdom he usurps is the mother. On the island,
Prospero undoes the usurpation, recreating kingdom and family
with himself in sole command.

But not quite, because the island is not his alone—or if it is, then
he has repeopled it with all parts of his fantasy, the distressing as
well as the gratifying. When he arrives he finds Caliban, child of
the witch Sycorax, herself a victim of banishment. The island provided a new life for her too, as it did literally for her son, with whom
she was pregnant when she arrived. Sycorax died some time before
Prospero came to the island; Prospero never saw her, and everything he knows about her he has learned from Ariel. Nevertheless,
she is insistently present in his memory—far more present than his
own wife—and she embodies to an extreme degree all the negative
assumptions about women that he and Miranda have exchanged.

It is important, therefore, that Caliban derives his claim to the
island from his mother: 'This island's mine, by Sycorax my mother'
(1.2.331). This has interesting implications to which I shall return,
but here I want to point out that he need not make the claim this
way. He could derive it from mere prior possession: he was there first.

This, after all, would have been the sole basis of Sycorax's claim to the island, but it is an argument that Caliban never makes. And in deriving his authority from his mother, he delivers himself into Prospero's hands: Prospero declares him a bastard, 'got by the devil himself / Upon thy wicked dam' (1.2.319–20), thereby both disallowing any claim from inheritance and justifying his loathing for Caliban.

But is it true that Caliban is Sycorax's bastard by Satan? How does Prospero know this? Not from Sycorax: Prospero never saw her. Not from Caliban: Sycorax died before she could even teach her son to speak. Everything Prospero knows about the witch he knows from Ariel—her appearance, the story of her banishment, the fact that her pregnancy saved her from execution. Did Sycorax also tell Ariel that her baby was the illegitimate son of the devil? Or is this Prospero's contribution to the story, an especially creative piece of invective and an extreme instance of his characteristic assumptions about women? Nothing in the text will answer this question for us; and it is worth pausing to observe first that Caliban's claim seems to have been designed so that Prospero can disallow it, and second that we have no way of distinguishing the facts about Caliban and Sycorax from Prospero's invective about them.

Can Prospero imagine no good mothers, then? The play, after all, moves toward a wedding, and the most palpable example we see of the magician's powers is a betrothal masque. The masque is presided over by two exemplary mothers, Ceres and Juno; and the libidinous Venus with her destructive son Cupid has been banished from the scene. But the performance is also preceded by the most awful warnings against sexuality, male sexuality this time: all the libido is presumed to be Ferdinand's while Miranda remains Prospero's innocent child. Ferdinand's reassuring reply, as David Sundelson persuasively argues,[4] includes submerged fantasies of rape and more than a hint that when the lust of the wedding night cools, so will his marital devotion:

> the murkiest den,
> The most opportune place, the strong'st suggestion
> Our worser genius can, shall never melt
> Mine honor into lust, to take away
> The edge of that day's celebration . . .
>
> (4.1.25–29)

This is the other side of the assumption that all women at heart are whores: all men at heart are rapists—Caliban, Ferdinand, and of course that means Prospero too.

4. David Sundelson, 'So Rare a Wonder'd Father: Prospero's *Tempest*', in *Representing Shakespeare*, p. 48.

THE MARRIAGE CONTRACT

The play moves toward marriage, certainly, and yet the relations it postulates between men and women are ignorant at best, characteristically tense, and potentially tragic. There is a familiar Shakespearean paradigm here: relationships between men and women interest Shakespeare intensely, but not, on the whole, as husbands and wives. The wooing process tends to be what it is here: not so much a prelude to marriage and a family as a process of self-definition—an increasingly unsatisfactory process, if we look at the progression of plays from *As You Like It, Much Ado about Nothing, Twelfth Night* through *All's Well that Ends Well, Measure for Measure, Troilus and Cressida* to *Antony and Cleopatra* and *Cymbeline*. If we want to argue that marriage is actually the point of the comic wooing process for Shakespeare, then we surely ought to be looking at how he depicts marriages; and here Petruchio and Kate, Capulet and Lady Capulet, Claudius and Gertrude, Othello and Desdemona, Macbeth and Lady Macbeth, Cymbeline and his queen, Leontes and Hermione will not persuade us that comedies ending in marriages have ended happily—or if they have, it is only because they have ended there, stopped at the wedding day.

What happens after marriage? Families in Shakespeare tend not to consist of husbands and wives and their offspring but of a parent and a child, usually in a chiastic relationship—father and daughter, mother and son. When there are two children, they tend to be presented as alternatives or rivals: the twins of *The Comedy of Errors*, Sebastian and Viola, infinitely substitutable for each other; or the good son–bad son complex of Orlando and Oliver, Edgar and Edmund. We know that Shakespeare himself had a son and two daughters, but that family configuration never appears in the plays. Lear's three daughters are quite exceptional in Shakespeare, and even they are dichotomised into bad and good. We may also recall Titus Andronicus's four sons and a daughter and Tamora's three sons, hardly instances to demonstrate Shakespeare's convictions about the comforts of family life.

The family paradigm that emerges from Shakespeare's imagination is a distinctly unstable one. Here is what we know of Shakespeare's own family: he had three brothers and three sisters who survived beyond infancy, and his parents lived into old age. At eighteen he married a woman of twenty-four by whom he had a daughter within six months, and a twin son and daughter a year and a half later. Within six more years he had moved permanently to London, and for the next twenty years—all but the last three years of his life—he lived apart from his wife and family. Nor should we stop here: we do not in the least know that Susanna, Hamnet, and Judith were his only children. He lived in a society without contraceptives, and unless we want to believe that he was either exclusively homosexual or celibate, we must assume a high degree of probability that there were other children. That they are not mentioned in his will may mean that they did not survive, but it also might mean that he made separate, non-testamentary provision for them. Certainly the plays reveal a strong interest in the subject of illegitimacy.

Until quite late in his career, he seems to have expressed his strongest familial feelings not toward children or wives but toward parents and siblings. His father dies in 1601, the year of *Hamlet*, his mother in 1608, the year of *Coriolanus*. And if we are thinking about usurping bastard younger brothers, it cannot be coincidental that the younger brother who followed him into the acting profession was named Edmund. There are no dramatic correlatives comparable to these for the death of his son Hamnet in 1596. If we take the plays to express what Shakespeare thought about himself (an assumption that strikes me as by no means axiomatic) then we will say that he was apparently free to think of himself as a father—to his two surviving daughters—only after the death of both his parents: 1608 is the date of *Pericles* as well as *Coriolanus*.

One final biographical observation: Shakespearean heroines marry very young, in their teens. Miranda is fifteen. We are always told that Juliet's marriage at fourteen is not unusual in the period, but in fact it is unusual in all but upper-class families. In Shakespeare's own family, his wife married at twenty-four and his daughters at twenty-four and thirty-one. It was Shakespeare himself who married at eighteen. The women of Shakespeare's plays, of course, are adolescent boys. Perhaps we should see as much of Shakespeare in Miranda and Ariel as in Prospero.

POWER AND AUTHORITY

The psychoanalytic and biographical questions raised by *The Tempest* are irresistible, but they can supply at best partial clues to its nature. I have described the plays as collaborative fantasies, and it is not only critics and readers who are involved in the collaboration. It is performers and audiences, too, and I take these terms in their largest senses, to apply not merely to stage productions but also to the theatrical dimension of the society that contains and is mirrored by the theatre. Cultural concerns, political and social issues, speak through *The Tempest*—sometimes explicitly, as in the open-ended discussion of political economy between Gonzalo, Antonio, and Sebastian in Act II. But in a broader sense, family structures and sexual relations become political structures in the play, and these are relevant to the political structures of Jacobean England.

What is the nature of Prospero's authority and the source of his power? Why is he Duke of Milan and the legitimate ruler of the island? Power, as Prospero presents it in the play, is not inherited but self-created: it is magic, or 'art', an extension of mental power and self-knowledge, and the authority that legitimises it derives from heaven—*Fortune* and *Destiny* are the terms used in the play. It is Caliban who derives his claim to the island from inheritance, from his mother.

In the England of 1610, both these positions represent available, and indeed normative, ways of conceiving of royal authority. James I's authority derived, he said, both from his mother and from God. But deriving one's legitimacy from Mary Queen of Scots was ambiguous at best, and James always felt exceedingly insecure about it. Elizabeth had had similar problems with the sources of her authority, and they centred precisely on the question of her legitimacy. To those who believed that her father's divorce from Katherine of Aragon was invalid (that is, to Roman Catholics), Elizabeth had no hereditary claim; and she had, moreover, been declared legally illegitimate after the execution of her mother for adultery and incest. Henry VIII maintained Elizabeth's bastardy to the end; her claim to the throne derived exclusively from her designation in the line of succession, next after Edward and Mary, in her father's will. This ambiguous legacy was the sole source of her authority. Prospero at last acknowledging the bastard Caliban as his own is also expressing the double edge of kingship throughout Shakespeare's lifetime (the ambivalence will not surprise us if we consider the way kings are represented in the history plays). Historically speaking, Caliban's claim to the island is a good one.

Royal power, the play seems to say, is good when it is self-created, bad when it is usurped or inherited from an evil mother. But of course the least problematic case of royal descent is one that is not represented in these paradigms at all; it is one that derives not from the mother but in the male line from the father: the case of Ferdinand and Alonso, in which the wife and mother is totally absent. If we are thinking about the *derivation* of royal authority, then, the absence of a father from Prospero's memory is a great deal more significant than the disappearance of a wife. Some have dealt with this in a psychoanalytic framework, whereby Antonio becomes a stand-in for the father, the real usurper of the mother's kingdom.[5] Here again, however, the realities of contemporary kingship seem

5. Coppélia Kahn makes this point, following a suggestion of Harry Berger, Jr, in 'The Providential Tempest and the Shakespearean Family', in *Representing Shakespeare*, p. 238. For an alternative view, see the exceptionally interesting discussion by Joel Fineman, 'Fratricide and Cuckoldry: Shakespeare's Doubles', in *Representing Shakespeare*, p. 104.

more enlightening, if not inescapable. James in fact had a double claim to the English throne, and the one through his father, the Earl of Darnley, was in the strictly lineal respects somewhat stronger than that of his mother. Both Darnley and Mary were direct descendants of Henry VII, but under Henry VIII's will, which established the line of succession, descendants who were not English-born were specifically excluded. Darnley was born in England, Mary was not. Indeed, Darnley's mother went from Scotland to have her baby in England precisely in order to preserve the claim to the throne.

King James rarely mentioned this side of his heritage, for perfectly understandable reasons. His father was even more disreputable than his mother; and given what was at least the public perception of both their characters, it was all too easy to speculate about whether Darnley was even in fact his father.[6] For James, as for Elizabeth, the derivation of authority through paternity was extremely problematic. Practically, James's claim to the English throne depended on Elizabeth's naming him her heir (we recall Miranda's legitimacy depending on her mother's word), and James correctly saw this as a continuation of the protracted negotiations between Elizabeth and his mother. His legitimacy, in both senses, thus derived from two mothers, the chaste Elizabeth and the sensual Mary, whom popular imagery represented respectively as a virgin goddess ('a piece of virtue') and a lustful and diabolical witch. James's sense of his own place in the kingdom is that of Prospero, rigidly paternalistic but incorporating the maternal as well: the king describes himself in *Basilicon Doron* as 'a loving nourish father' providing the commonwealth with 'their own nourishmilk'.[7] The very etymology of the word *authority* confirms the metaphor: *augeo*, increase, nourish, cause to grow. At moments in his public utterances, James sounds like a gloss on Prospero: 'I am the husband, and the whole island is my lawful wife; I am the head, and it is my body.'[8] Here the incorporation of the wife has become literal and explicit. James conceives himself as the head of a single-parent family. In the world of *The Tempest*, there are no two-parent families. All the dangers of promiscuity and bastardy are resolved in such a conception—unless, of course, the parent is a woman.

My point here is not that Shakespeare is representing King James as Prospero or Caliban or both, but that these figures embody the

---

6. The charge that he was David Rizzio's child was current in England in the 1580s, spread by rebellious Scottish Presbyterian ministers. James expressed fears that it would injure his chance of succeeding to the English throne, and he never felt entirely free of it.

7. C. H. McIlwain, *Political Works of James I* (Cambridge, MA, 1918), p. 24.

8. From the 1603 speech to parliament; McIlwain, *Political Works*, p. 272.

predominant modes of conceiving of royal authority in the period. They are Elizabeth's and James's modes, too.

THE RENUNCIATION OF MAGIC

Prospero's magic power is exemplified, on the whole, as power over children: his daughter Miranda, the bad child Caliban, the obedient but impatient Ariel, the adolescent Ferdinand, the wicked younger brother Antonio, and indeed, the shipwreck victims as a whole, who are treated like a group of bad children. Many critics talk about Prospero as a Renaissance scientist and see alchemical metaphors in the grand design of the play. No doubt there is something in this; but what the play's action presents is not experiments and empiric studies but a fantasy about controlling other people's minds. Does the magic work? We are given a good deal of evidence of it: the masque, the banquet, the harpies, the tempest itself. But the great scheme is not to produce illusions and good weather: it is to bring about reconciliation, and here we would have to say that it works only indifferently well. 'They being penitent', says Prospero to Ariel, 'The sole drift of my purpose doth extend / Not a frown further' (5.1.28–30). The assertion opens with a conditional clause whose conditions are not met: Alonso is penitent, but the chief villain, the usurping younger brother Antonio, remains obdurate. Nothing, not all Prospero's magic, can redeem Antonio from his essential badness. Since Shakespeare was free to have Antonio repent if that is what he had in mind—half a line would have done for critics craving a reconciliation—we ought to take seriously the possibility that repentance is not what he had in mind. Perhaps, too, penitence is not what Prospero's magic is designed to elicit from his brother.

Why is Prospero's power conceived as magic? Why, in returning to Milan, does he renounce it? Most commentators say that he gives up his magic when he no longer needs it. This is an obvious answer, but it strikes me as too easy, a comfortable assumption cognate with the view that the play concludes with reconciliation, repentance, and restored harmony. To say that Prospero no longer needs his magic is to beg all the most important questions. What does it mean to say that he needs it? Did he ever need it, and if so, why? And does he in fact give it up?

Did he ever need magic? Prospero's devotion to his secret studies is what caused all the trouble in the first place—this is not an interpretation of mine; it is how Prospero presents the matter. If he has now learned to be a good ruler through the exercise of his art, that is also what taught him to be a bad one. So the question of his need for magic goes to the heart of how we interpret and judge his character: is the magic a strength or a weakness? To say that he no longer needs it is to say that his character changes in some way for the better; that by renouncing his special powers he becomes fully human. This is an important claim. Let us test it by looking at Prospero's renunciation.

What does it mean for Prospero to give up his power? Letting Miranda marry and leaving the island are the obvious answers, but they can hardly be right. Miranda's marriage is *brought about* by the magic; it is part of Prospero's plan. It pleases Miranda, certainly, but it is designed by Prospero as a way of satisfying himself. Claribel's marriage to the King of Tunis looks less sinister in this light. daughters' marriages, in royal families at least, are designed primarily to please their fathers. And leaving the island, reassuming the dukedom, is part of the plan, too. Both of these are presented as acts of renunciation, but they are in fact what the exercise of Prospero's magic is intended to effect, and they represent his triumph.

Prospero renounces his art in the great monologue at the beginning of Act V, 'Ye elves of hills, brooks, standing lakes and groves', and for all its valedictory quality, it is the most powerful assertion of his magic that the play gives us. It is also a powerful literary allusion, a close translation of a speech of Medea in Ovid,[9] and it makes at least one claim for Prospero that is made nowhere else in the play, that he can raise the dead. For Shakespeare to present this as a *renunciation* speech is upping Prospero's ante, to say the least.

In giving up his magic, Prospero speaks as Medea. He has incorporated Ovid's witch, prototype of the wicked mother Sycorax, in the most literal way—verbatim, so to speak—and his 'most potent art' is now revealed as translation and impersonation. In this context, the distinction between black magic and white magic, Sycorax and Prospero, has disappeared. Two hundred lines later, Caliban too is revealed as an aspect of Prospero: 'This thing of darkness I acknowledge mine.'

But Caliban is an aspect of Antonio, the evil child, the usurping brother. Where is the *real* villain in relation to Prospero now? Initially Antonio had been characterised, like Caliban and Sycorax, as embodying everything that is antithetical to Prospero; but in recounting his history to Miranda, Prospero also presents himself as deeply implicated in the usurpation, with Antonio even seeming at times to be acting as Prospero's agent: 'The government I cast upon my brother'; '[I] to him put the manage of my state'; 'my trust . . . did beget of him / A falsehood', and so forth. If Prospero is accepting the blame for what happened, there is a degree to which he is also taking the credit. Antonio's is another of the play's identities that Prospero has incorporated into his own; and in that case, what is there to forgive?

9. *Metamorphoses*, 7.197–209, apparently at least partly refracted through Golding's English version.

Let us look, then, at Prospero forgiving his brother in Act V. The pardon is enunciated—'You, brother mine, that entertain ambition . . . I do forgive thee' (ll. 75–78)[1]—and qualified at once ('unnatural though thou art'), reconsidered as more crimes are remembered, some to be held in reserve ('at this time I will tell no tales' [ll. 128–29]), all but withdrawn ('most wicked sir, whom to call brother / Would even infect my mouth' [ll. 130–31]), and only then confirmed through forcing Antonio to relinquish the dukedom, an act that is presented as something he does unwillingly. The point is not only that Antonio does not repent here but also that he is not allowed to repent. Even his renunciation of the crown is Prospero's act: 'I do . . . require / My dukedom of thee, which perforce, I know, / Thou must restore' (ll. 131–34). In Prospero's drama, there is no room for Antonio to act of his own free will.

The crime that Prospero holds in reserve for later use against his brother is the attempted assassination of Alonso. Here is what happened: Prospero sends Ariel to put all the shipwreck victims to sleep except Antonio and Sebastian. Antonio then persuades Sebastian to murder Alonso—his brother—and thereby become king of Naples. Sebastian agrees, on the condition that Antonio kill Gonzalo. At the moment of the murders, Ariel reappears and wakes Gonzalo:

> My master through his art foresees the danger
> That you his friend are in; and sends me forth—
> For else his project dies—to keep them living.
>   (2.1.290–92)

This situation has been created by Prospero, and the conspiracy is certainly part of his project—this is why Sebastian and Antonio are not put to sleep. If Antonio is not forced by Prospero to propose the murder, he is certainly acting as Prospero expects him to do and as Ariel says Prospero 'through his art foresees' that he will. What is clearly taking place is Prospero restaging his usurpation and maintaining his control over it this time. Gonzalo is waked rather than Alonso so that the old courtier can replay his role in aborting the assassination.

So at the play's end, Prospero still has usurpation and attempted murder to hold against his brother, things that still disqualify Antonio from his place in the family. Obviously there is more to Prospero's plans than reconciliation and harmony—even, I would think, in the forthcoming happy marriage of Ferdinand and Miranda. If we look at that marriage as a political act (the participants are, after all, the children of monarchs) we will observe that in order to prevent the

---

1. Kermode and most editors read 'entertained', but I have restored the folio reading, which seems to me unexceptionable.

succession of his brother, Prospero is marrying his daughter to the
son of his enemy. This has the effect of excluding Antonio from any
future claim on the ducal throne, but it also effectively disposes of the
realm as a political entity: If Miranda is the heir to the dukedom,
Milan through the marriage becomes part of the kingdom of Naples,
not the other way round. Prospero recoups his throne from his brother
only to deliver it over, upon his death, to the King of Naples once
again. The usurping Antonio stands condemned, but the effects of
the usurpation, the link with Alonso and the reduction of Milan to a
Neapolitan fiefdom are, through Miranda's wedding, confirmed and
legitimised. Prospero has not regained his lost dukedom; he has
usurped his brother's. In this context, Prospero's puzzling assertion
that 'every third thought shall be my grave' can be seen as a final assertion of authority and control: he has now arranged matters so that his
death will remove Antonio's last link with the ducal power. His grave is
the ultimate triumph over his brother. If we look at the marriage in
this way, giving away Miranda is a means of preserving his authority,
not of relinquishing it.

A BIBLIOGRAPHICAL CODA

The significant absence of crucial wives from the play is curiously
emphasised by a famous textual crux. In Act IV Ferdinand, overwhelmed by the beauty of the masque being presented by Prospero,
interrupts the performance to say,

> Let me live here ever.
> So rare a wondered father and a wise
> Makes this place Paradise.
> (ll. 122–24)

Critics since the eighteenth century have expressed a nagging
worry about Ferdinand's celebrating his betrothal by including
Prospero but not Miranda in his paradise. In fact, what Ferdinand
said, as Jeanne Addison Roberts demonstrated only in 1978, reads
in the earliest copies of the folio, 'So rare a wondered father and a
wife', but the crossbar of the f broke early in the print run, turning
it to a long s and thereby eliminating Miranda from Ferdinand's
thoughts of wonder.[2] The odd thing about this is that Rowe and
Malone in their eighteenth-century editions emended wise to wife
on logical grounds, the Cambridge Shakespeare of 1863 lists wife
as a variant reading of the folio, and Furnivall's 1895 photographic
facsimile was made from a copy that reads wife, and the reading is
preserved in Furnivall's parallel text. Nevertheless, after 1895 the

---

2. '"Wife" or "Wise"—The Tempest 1. 1786', University of Virginia Studies in Bibliography,
   31 (1978).

wife became invisible: bibliographers lost the variant, and textual critics consistently denied its existence until Roberts pointed it out. Even Charlton Hinman with his collating machines claimed that there were no variants whatever in this entire forme of the folio. And yet when Jeanne Roberts examined the Folger Library's copies of the book, including those that Hinman had collated, she found that two of them have the reading *wife*, and two more clearly show the crossbar of the *f* in the process of breaking. We find only what we are looking for or are willing to see. Obviously in 1978, this was a reading whose time had come. And whose time, at the beginning of the twenty-first century, may already be past. Peter Blayney, observing that the physical construction of a piece of type surely precludes the crossbar of an *f* breaking and migrating, examined the "wife" copies under a high-powered microscope. What Jeanne Roberts was seeing, he believes, was probably the effects of ink on a piece of lint, caught, for the time it took to print off a few copies, between the *s* and *e* of "wise," after which it was dislodged and made its leisurely way out of the text.[3] Once again, we find what we are looking for and are willing to see. Typography, it now appears, will not rescue Shakespeare from patriarchy and male chauvinism after all. Prospero's wife—and Ferdinand's—remain invisible.

COPPÉLIA KAHN

Caliban at the Stadium: Shakespeare and the Making of Americans[†]

> The audience itself is Caliban!
> Monstrous and murmuring beneath the stars,
> It sees slim Beauty pass, and Poetry,
> And hears the thrilling voice of Song.
>   So crouched,
> Profoundly moved yet inarticulate. . . .
> (Florence Ripley Mastin, "Caliban at the Stadium")

In the spring of 1916, a flyer circulated by Doubleday and Company announced the publication, well in advance of its first performance on May 24, of a drama entitled *Caliban by the Yellow Sands*. Its two productions, in Lewisohn Stadium in New York City and a year later in Harvard Stadium in Cambridge, involved a total of nearly 7000

---

3. Introduction to the 2nd ed. of *The First Folio of Shakespeare*, ed. Charlton Hinman (New York: W. W. Norton, 1996), p. xxxi.

† From *The Massachusetts Review* 41:2 (2000): 256–84. Reprinted by permission of *The Massachusetts Review*. Notes are by the author unless otherwise specified.

performers, and about 344,000 people attended them.[1] By performing, watching, and hearing this adaptation of *The Tempest*, ever more
diverse and divided segments of American society were meant to
become a single unified "imagined community." This curious project
bears out in many ways Michael Bristol's claim that "Interpretation
of Shakespeare and interpretation of American political culture
are mutually determining practices" (1990: 3). *Caliban* can only be
understood in terms of agendas born from the social conflicts America was experiencing at the start of the 20th century well into the
1920's—agendas fraught with ideological contradictions that *Caliban* struggles to resolve.[2] No single act of bardolatry ever had more
riding on it.

The text was written and produced by Percy MacKaye, described
in a 1916 *New York Evening Globe* article as "the foremost man of
letters in this country today" (qtd. Grover, 1932: 183). Son of Steele
MacKaye, a luminary of American theatre as actor, playwright, and
producer, Percy MacKaye wrote numerous volumes of poetry and
essays, but his favored medium was theatre. In a biographical statement reprinted from his 25th Harvard reunion yearbook in 1922,
MacKaye notes proudly, "Together father and son have contributed
to the American drama an average of one dramatic work a year for

1. Estimates of the number of performers range from 1500 to 2500 for the New York performance, but remain at 5000 for the one at Harvard Stadium. Estimates of audience
   size for each production vary also. For New York, they run from 135,000 (MacKaye,
   1922; Shattuck, 1987: 306) to 200,000 (MacKaye, 1932: 107; Green, 1989: 59). The
   capacity of Lewisohn Stadium was augmented to about 20,000 for the pageant, and
   there were ten performances, but no newspapers report that the stadium was consistently full. For Harvard Stadium, which had a capacity of 18,000, newspaper accounts
   mention audiences of 10,000 and 12,000 at a single performance; the production ran
   for twelve nights. MacKaye claims a total of 250,000 spectators (1932: 107). Based on
   these figures, the two productions together might have drawn a total audience of
   344,000 at most.
2. Several mainly descriptive accounts of the pageant exist, by Franck (1964), Gordon
   (1976), Shattuck (1987), and Green (1989). Others place *Caliban* in diverse dramatic
   traditions; that of the Renaissance masque (Brock and Welsh, 1972) and the American
   pageant movement (Prevots, 1990). Cohn (1976) parallels the drama with Ernest
   Renan's version of *The Tempest*, while Vaughan and Vaughan (1991) interpret Mac-
   Kaye's Caliban as "the untutored 'other,' [viewed] from the perspective of Anglo-Saxon
   superiority" (114) but don't develop that approach. Bloom (1992) argues that the drama
   "affirms prevailing hierarchies" (55). Potter (1996) emphasizes MacKaye's attempt to
   "reconcile the polarities of aristocratic and democratic ideals in the drama" (71). She
   raises but does not pursue the question of whether the drama amounts to "an affirmation of the superiority of English tradition" (76).
      The most astute and sophisticated treatment of *Caliban* is by Cartelli (1998). Like
   Potter, he focusses on "contradictions between the democratic claims advanced on
   behalf of the masque and the largely anti-democratic bias of its themes and organization" (74). In line with his aim of exploring how American culture in a "residually
   postcolonial phase" renegotiates Shakespeare, he views *Caliban* as "an internal or
   domestic colonizing venture that seeks to enlist the consent and participation of the
   masses in their enforced acculturation" (75). While he too deals with the immigration
   controversy and the Americanization movement in relation to the pageant, he does not
   attempt to identify "the masses" specifically, as I do, in terms of a racialized nativism
   and its Anglo-Saxonist agenda. I am grateful to Cartelli for generously sharing a draft
   with me, when we discovered that we were both working on *Caliban*.

fifty years" (MacKaye, 1922). His Broadway plays were critical suc-
cesses and box office failures, but his tireless efforts as champion of
"community drama" and major writer-producer of historical pageants
kept him in the limelight from about 1914 well into the thirties.[3]
MacKaye had an intense lifelong romance with Shakespeare that
culminated in a dramatic tetralogy he published in 1950 at the age of
seventy-five, *The Mystery of Hamlet, King of Denmark, Or What We
Will.* A prolonged fantasy on Shakespeare's play that turns it into the
love-story of King Hamlet and Gertrude, this massive work was, the
author explains, "compelled . . . by powers within and beyond this
material scene," "a sacred task" imposed upon him (MacKaye, 1950:
655).

That messianic note, that urge to fuse his artistic personality with
Shakespeare's, also marks MacKaye's creation and promotion of *Caliban*, which is dedicated to "Master . W . S" [*sic*] as "onlie begetter."
The drama could be described as a fantasia on themes from *The
Tempest*—a fantasia nurtured by the collective Shakespeare-worship
that found vigorous expression in 1916, the three hundredth anniversary of Shakespeare's death. In the spring of 1914, the Drama League
of America, an organization of clubwomen, college professors, and
theatre aficionados across America that aimed to encourage "good
theatre," began to plan a nationwide commemoration of the 300th
anniversary of Shakespeare's death for 1916. They envisioned many
local celebrations culminating in "some large municipal festival in
which the whole city can have a part" (*New York Times*, March 19,
1916). New York presented itself as the site of that festival. Its mayor
appointed an Honorary Committee of financial magnates such as
Jacob and Mortimer Schiff and J.P. Morgan, civic leaders such as the
socialite and philanthropist Mrs. August Belmont, the prominent
rabbi Dr. Stephen S. Wise, and Lillian D. Wald, founder of the Henry
Street Settlement. They were joined by a spectrum of artists and
intellectuals including Nicholas Murray Butler, president of Columbia University, Walter Damrosch, conductor of the New York Philhar-
monic, the painter Charles Dana Gibson, the poets Edwin Markham
and Louis Untermeyer. Percy MacKaye, already well known as the
creator of a pageant for the city of St. Louis seen by about 400,000
people, was appointed to create another.

In *Caliban*, MacKaye sets out to make Shakespeare the genius—
in every sense—of America, the poet who speaks to all Americans. It
is the seeming cultural dissonance between Shakespeare as the pre-
eminent poet of England, and Shakespeare as the poet of American

---

3. For an account of MacKaye's career up to 1922, see MacKaye, 1922; for an account up
   to 1932 with useful citations of reviews and newspaper articles, see Grover, 1932; for a
   critical review of his entire career, see Glassberg, 1990: 168–70.

national identity that I want to explore today.[4] Of course, England and America share a certain history, a cultural legacy, and most significantly, a common language. But the connections between English as a language and American as a nationality have, over time, formed a complex circuitry.[5] I want to show how, at this cultural moment, Shakespeare became the switchpoint between them, and thus to make *Caliban* legible as more than mere bardolatry.

To begin with, the choice of New York City as the venue of a national Shakespeare celebration made the perennial issue of national identity more pointed, because New York was the notorious port of entry for millions of immigrants. Furthermore, by 1916 the war in Europe was almost two years old. The imminent possibility of America's entry into it cast the loyalty of anyone born on foreign soil—even those who had become American citizens—in doubt. Thus the long-standing question of what transformed an immigrant into an American became more urgent than ever before, and intensified an ideological ambivalence at the core of the concept of Americanness.

To understand the philosophical and social issues underlying this ambivalence—and how Shakespeare came to be MacKaye's solution for them—we must go back to the beginnings of the American republic. The founding fathers envisioned the basis of nationhood and citizenship as a set of universal principles rather than as any particular national, linguistic, religious or ethnic heritage. As Philip Gleason notes, "To be or become an American . . . all [a person] had to do was commit himself to the political ideology centered on the abstract ideals of liberty, equality, and republicanism" (Gleason, 1980: 32). In 1790, roughly 8 out of 10 white Americans were of British derivation (Gleason, 1980: 32). Thus, when in *The Federalist Papers* John Jay defined Americans as "one united people—a people descended from the same ancestors, speaking the same English, professing the same religion, attached to the same principles of government, very similar in their manners and customs," he saw no conflict between asserting both the universal validity of those principles and

4. For a groundbreaking examination of "the formation of an implicit cultural policy in and through the practice of Shakespeare scholarship" in America, see Bristol, 1990. I am much indebted to his framing of the historical and theoretical questions prior to any study of the institutionalization of Shakespeare in America. As an inquiry into that process in the public sphere, as opposed to scholarship in the academy, this essay is intended to complement Bristol's valuable work. For studies of the creation of Shakespeare's authority in Anglo-American culture, see Taylor, 1989; of his prominence in a contemporary global setting, Bristol, 1996.
5. For a fascinating study of Shakespeare's place in American culture from the nineteenth into the early twentieth century, see Lawrence Levine's richly documented chapter "William Shakespeare in America" (Levine, 1988). I first learned of the existence of *Caliban* from his mention of it. I am also indebted to Jessie Givner, whose remarks on the pageant in an unpublished paper got my attention.

the specific ethnicity of the colonists as the basis for the new nation (Fairfield, 1981: 6).

Such a conflict, however, was latent. It can be found in a frequently quoted passage from Crèvecoeur's *Letters of an American Farmer*, published in 1782 but written in the decade before the Revolution. "What then is an American?" Crèvecoeur asks, and answers,

> He is either a European, or the descendant of an European . . . who leaving behind him all his ancient prejudices and manners, receives new ones from the new mode of life he has embraced, the new government he obeys, and the new rank he holds. . . . Here individuals are melted into a new race of man. . . . (Crèvecoeur, 1904: 54–5)

Crèvecoeur's metaphor of metallurgic transformation (which became a cliché more than a century later) works in one direction only: those who arrive in the new nation "leave behind" the mores and mindset of their European origins, which disappear in the melting process of Americanization. In fact the word "immigrant" itself reflects this definition. Crèvecoeur and others had referred to "emigrants," identifying newcomers with the country from which they came, but in 1789 "immigrant" cropped up as a new word defining newcomers from the perspective of the society to which they sought entrance, and to which they were expected to adapt themselves (Higham, 1975: 5–6).[6]

An American identity based on abstract ideals allows all people, regardless of different national origins or specific ethnicities, equal access to the basic human rights implicit in those ideals. But at the same time, the would-be American must, in Crèvecoeur's formulation, *give up* the prejudices and manners of his current "mode of life" for an American one: he must surrender his cultural specificity, his difference, in order to blend into a homogeneous "new race." Thus his culture and American culture don't meet on equal terms: the latter takes precedence over the former. As Alan Trachtenberg observes, this liberal formulation of American identity requires "a fundamental separation of political and cultural identities" (Trachtenberg, n.d.: 9).[7]

However universal the principles immigrants were prepared to accept, in practice they also had to meet the specific demands of the

6. The first usage of "immigrant" given by the OED is Belknap, *Hist. New Hampsh.* III.Pref.6; the second, from Kendall, *Trav.* II.lv.252 is dated 1809 and reads: "*Immigrant* is perhaps the only new word, of which the circumstances of the U.S. has in any degree demanded the addition to the English language."

7. I owe special thanks to Alan Trachtenberg for sharing his work on American identity with me. For a far-reaching critique of Americanization as assimilation to the norm of "the contemporary representative 'average' American of British stock," see MacKaye's contemporary, the social philosopher Horace Kallen. Arguing that "The most eagerly American of the immigrant groups are also the most autonomous and self conscious in spirit and culture," Kallen outlines a four-phase process of "dissimilation" culminating when "ethnic and national differences change in status from disadvantages to distinctions" (Kallen, 1915: 219).

dominant, English-speaking culture: they had to learn English. Of the approximately 450,000 immigrants who arrived on these shores over the course of the 18th century, more than half did speak English; they were Irish, most of them Protestant. Only during the second phase of immigration, beginning in the 1820's and lasting until the establishment of quotas in 1924, did the newcomers' nationalities diversify so as to bring out fully the latent conflict between universalist principles on the one hand and specific ethnic identities on the other to which I have alluded. For as the sheer numbers of immigrants swelled, their ethnic composition also changed markedly; while immigrants from Germany and Ireland decreased by half, those from Russia, Poland, Austria, Hungary and Italy doubled (Cayton, *et al.*, 1993: 936). By 1900, the annual total of immigrants numbered 300,000 for the first time; it doubled three years later, and in 1907, hit the all-time high of one million. From 1907 to the beginning of World War I, about 650,000 immigrants per year arrived at Ellis Island (Higham, 1969: 159). As America went to war in 1917, one of every three Americans was either foreign-born or the child of a foreign-born parent (Cayton, *et al.*, 1993: 936).

Not simply the high proportion of foreign-born in the general population, but the specific ethnic origins of the more recently arrived immigrants, and the fact that English was not their mother tongue, renewed the long-established fears and hatreds called nativism. Nativists insisted on making a distinction between people like themselves—former immigrants, but now citizens who called themselves "natives"—and newly arrived prospective citizens called foreigners. During the 19th century, nativists defined the foreigners they deemed unassimilable to American values and the American way of life variously as Catholics, political radicals, Germans.[8] Between 1906 and 1914, however, their categories of exclusion had acquired a new edge: nativists began to speak of "old" and "new" immigrants. In their view, "old" immigrants from northern and western Europe belonged to the same racial stock that had founded America, and thus had readily become part of it. The new ones from southern and eastern Europe, however, were unassimilable. In the words of Madison Grant's influential anti-immigration treatise of 1916, *The Passing of the Great Race*, they were "the weak, the broken, and the mentally crippled of all races drawn from the lowest stratum of the Mediterranean basin and the Balkans, together with hordes of the wretched, submerged populations of the Polish Ghettos" (Grant, 1916, rpt. 1923: 89).

8. I am indebted to the work of John Higham for much of the following discussion of immigration and controversies over Americanization. See his *Strangers in the Land: Patterns of American Nativism 1860–1925* (1963) and *Send These to Me: Jews and Other Immigrants in Urban America* (1975).

Nativism had become racialized. Drawing on a pseudo-scientific classification developed in physical anthropology, advocates such as Grant argued that the inferior "Alpine" and "Mediterranean" races now swarming into America were genetically equipped to thrive in the sweatshops and slums where they congregated, while the superior "Nordic" peoples who had settled America, being gifted only for conquest and exploration, were slated for extinction.[9] "These immigrants," Grant warned, "adopt the language of the native American [English], they wear his clothes, they steal his name and they are beginning to take his women; all too soon, they will exterminate him" (Grant, 1916, rpt. 1923: 91).[1] Thus in place of the benign melting process imagined by Crèvecoeur, whereby learning a new language would have been a normal part of "melting" into a "new race of man," Grant viewed the immigrants' mastery of English as part of a duplicitous masquerade whereby they aimed to extinguish "Anglo-Saxon" racial stock.

In the 1890's, Grant, founder and chair of the New York Zoological Society, and other patrician intellectuals from the Northeast such as Henry Cabot Lodge, senator from Massachusetts, and Francis A. Walker, president of MIT, racialized the ethnic bias implicit in the founders' universalist principles by preaching a belief in the superiority of "Anglo-Saxon" culture. The concept originates with Richard Verstegen, who in 1605 argued that the English were descended not from Brut and the Trojans, but from the Saxons, a Germanic people that had filtered into Albion, and that their Germanic traits made them superior to other races. Interest in this theory burgeoned in the political controversies surrounding the English Civil War. Parliamentarians defended "the immemorial liberties of the English people" as based on a supposedly native, "Anglo-Saxon" love of liberty contrasted to the "Norman yoke" of feudal law introduced in 1066 that eventuated in the absolutism of Charles II.[2] Thus, out of a certain ethnic pride

---

9. In his *The Races of Europe* (1899), William Z. Ripley developed the three categories of Nordic, Alpine, and Mediterranean on which Grant and others drew. Higham observes that the infusion of "science" into the immigration controversy gave "clarity, definition, and some intellectual substance to fears and anxieties that were much more broadly based" (Higham, 1975: 47).

1. Grant isn't the only writer in this period to link rampant reproduction with linguistic estrangement in describing the new immigrants. Samuel P. Orth's *Our Foreigners* (1920) offers one of many examples: "Alien in language, custom, in ethnic affinities and political concepts, in personal standards," these immigrants create a "Congeries of foreign quarters, whose alarming fecundity fills the streets with progeny, and whose polyglot chatter . . . turns even many a demure New England town into a veritable babel" (163), noting that "this racial seepage is confined almost wholly to the Italian and the Slav" (210).

2. In *Desire for Origins: New Language, Old English, and Teaching the Tradition* (1990), Allen Frantzen argues that "The values and beliefs of Anglo-Saxon language, literature and history were always—and only—asserted in the presence of an opposing set of values and beliefs" and "always undertaken by those who were engaged in pursuit of self definition" (xv, 20). He is speaking of the pursuit of Anglo-Saxon scholarship, but

based on a theory of national origins, they characterized their commitment to republicanism and the rule of law as "Anglo-Saxon"—but in the sense of, as Philip Gleason phrases it, "their native genius, the form of social life and organization ... for which they were particularly well suited," rather than that of an immutable, inexorable genetic strain (Gleason, 1980: 41).[3]

Yet at the same time, the belief in America as a land of opportunity and asylum for everyone, and an abiding confidence in assimilation as a normal, gradual, spontaneous process, persisted. In seemingly clear opposition to the nativists, a spectrum of reformers cherished a vision of America as inherently pluralistic. Pageants such as *Caliban* were deeply implicated in reforms advocated by the Progressive Party, whose 1912 platform was the first ever to denounce "indifference and neglect" toward immigrants and to propose federal action "to promote their assimilation, education, and advancement" (Higham, 1963: 238). Such concerns about immigrants were, in turn, bound up with a focus on urban reform. Rapid urbanization had brought tenements, poverty, crime, corruption, and a deracinated, impersonal mode of life. Immigrants from peasant backgrounds and untutored in democracy poured into cities, clustered in slums, and were easily manipulated by urban political bosses. Progressive-minded educators, social workers, settlement house workers, playground directors, and advocates of the Social Gospel—a Protestant reform movement—turned their attention to immigrants in the city (Hofstadter, 1961: 173–84; Higham, 1963: 116–23).[4]

Pageantry flourished during the reform era, especially from 1900 to 1920, and rapidly became an American institution, indeed, a profession. The American Pageant Association, founded in 1913,

his terms pertain to my interpretation of *Caliban* as a response to immigration. For a coherent account of how the myth of Anglo-Saxon England as a golden age of good government merged with "the classic Whig view" of English political history, and travelled across the Atlantic to influence the writers of the Constitution, see Horsman (1981: 9–24). Notably, Thomas Jefferson cherished "the vision of heroic, freedom-loving Anglo-Saxon England" that he gleaned from seventeenth-century parliamentary propagandists and from the radical Real Whigs of the 1690's. Jefferson wrote an Anglo-Saxon grammar and included the language in his curriculum for the University of Virginia in the hope that students would "imbibe with the language free principles of government" (Horsman, 1981: 18–19).

3. By the year of the tercentenary, Shakespeare too had been associated with the Anglo-Saxon heritage by two professors of English. Charles Mills Gayley of the University of California at Berkeley contributed a poem to *A Book of Homage to Shakespeare*, the British Academy's tercentenary tribute, that encapsulates his full-length study of Shakespeare's affinity with the Anglo-Saxon ideals brought to America by the colonists (Gollancz, 1916). Frederic Morgan Padelford, professor of English at the University of Washington, published an essay in *South Atlantic Quarterly* asserting that Shakespeare's art follows the same Germanic or Teutonic "racial artistic creed" as that which produced Gothic cathedrals, calling the poet "a true child of the north" in whom "the spirit of a race" is reincarnate (Padelford, 1916: 225, 240).

4. See Cartelli's discussion of Jane Addams's interpretation of *King Lear*, inspired by the Pullman Strike of 1894, as "Shakespeare's unequivocally progressive critique of feudal family relations" (1998: 48).

published monthly bulletins on the technical aspects of the form. Summer courses on pageantry were taught at Harvard, Yale, Columbia and other universities, and "pageant-masters" trained to write, direct and produce the dramas were certified. Appealing to the widest possible public and performed largely by ordinary citizens, these outdoor spectacles dramatized local history. They cohered with the aims of reformers because they were imagined as "instrument[s] of communal transformation" that could actually break down social and cultural barriers to create a solidarity transcending conflicting class and ethnic interests. By providing images of a supposedly shared past and narratives that knit that past to the present moment, pageants were intended to foster a spirit of community, and thus to overcome the fragmented, polyglot character of modern—especially urban—life. David Glassberg, the leading historian of American pageantry, comments,

> At a time when Americans' lives were increasingly shaped by their contacts with ever more distant organizations . . . historical pageants projected the town as a manageable arena for reconstructing the intimacies of community while fostering loyalty to nation, for asserting the essential continuity of local tradition in the midst of sweeping social and economic change. (Glassberg, 1990: 156)

In *Caliban*, Percy MacKaye hoped to make not "the town" but rather New York itself "a manageable arena" for the creation of that community. Between about 1910 and 1916, he had already been campaigning for "community drama" by lecturing around the country and publishing his lectures.[5] He laid out three requisites for this drama. It would be absolutely independent from the commercial theatre through some form of endowment; under the direction of experts in theatrical art, it would meet the highest artistic standards; and it would at the same time serve the people's desire "to seek expression through a drama of and by the people, not merely *for* the people" (MacKaye, 1916: xviii).[6] In the large urban setting of St. Louis in 1914, according to his lights he had realized that

---

5. He had also created or collaborated in several ventures in community drama: in 1909, a pageant in Gloucester, Massachusetts involving 1500 performers, and a masque advocating wildlife preserves, performed outdoors in Cornish, New Hampshire, a summer colony of artists; in 1913, an allegorical masque for the woman suffrage pageant procession in Washington, D.C.

6. For explications of these principles, see his essay "The Drama of Democracy" (MacKaye, 1909: 89–120); his address "The Civic Theater" (MacKaye, 1910); the Appendix to *St. Louis: A Civic Masque* (MacKaye, 1914: 86–7); and "Preface" to *Caliban by the Yellow Sands* (MacKaye, 1916: xiii–xxviii). [MacKaye's Preface is reproduced below, pp. 330–38—*Editors*.]

"regeneration of community life" which, he believed, pageants could effect (MacKaye, 1915: 41).[7]

In reality, however, the institution of pageantry exhibited certain ideological tensions evident within Progressive-minded reform. Pageant-promoters such as MacKaye, like many reformers, claimed to foster a vision of America based on democracy and community. But they were actually members of a genteel elite that tended to identify its Anglo-Protestant heritage with the nation's.[8] "A social and ideological gulf" yawned between their conception of immigrants as passive and malleable under the uplifting influence of an anglicized American culture, and the complex accommodations and resistances of immigrant life (Higham, 1963: 118, 119). Looking to medieval and Renaissance Europe for a tradition of artistically rich civic celebration that would redeem the drab regimens of industrial America, reformers and pageant-makers alike thought of what the newcomers could contribute to American society as "immigrant gifts," folk costumes and folk dances, ballads and games (Higham, 1963: 122–3).[9] Moreover, the progressive-minded sense of embracing community that pageant-makers strove to foster through spectacles involving hundreds or thousands of people actually involved top-down organization and tight discipline. The stylistic marker of pageantry, idealized abstraction, homogenized diverse ethnic groups, effacing their particular interests and identities. On the whole, "the art of pageantry . . . involved creating the illusion of the public appearing to speak for itself, in the process defining the terms" in which it could speak (Glassberg, 1990: 199).

---

7. The St. Louis pageant was credited with spurring the passage of a revised city charter one month after the performance, but Glassberg argues that the new charter actually limited working-class representation on the city council. Noting that a segregated housing ordinance passed two years later, he concludes, "Although pageant planners claimed that their giant municipal celebration suppressed internal divisions citywide, its virtual exclusion of black St. Louis effectively sharpened the differences between black and white residents" (1990: 197). Compare MacKaye's assertion that "in a single community meeting . . . a poor immigrant shopkeeper, a millionaire, a labor leader, a professor of fine arts, brought thus together for the first time, enthusiastically supported one another's proposals" (1914: 87).
8. MacKaye links himself strongly to an Anglo-Saxon tradition. At the start of an autobiography written for the yearbook of his twenty-fifth-year Harvard reunion, and later reprinted (with a bibliography of his works as *A Sketch of His Life*), he describes himself as a direct descendant of Governor William Bradford and Roger Williams (MacKaye, 1922). Elsewhere he states that he studied Anglo-Saxon at Harvard, and when living in Europe after his marriage, went to Leipzig, "to get the Germanic idea of English literature" (*Boston Transcript*, October 8, 1927). In 1932, he calls Shakespeare the "folk-poet not only of America's origins in old England, but of all modern Anglo-Saxon civilization" (1932: 117).
9. Higham distinguishes, however, between such reformers and "democratic humanists," especially in the settlement house movement, who "want[ed] to work with the people of the slums as well as for them" and who "planted the seeds of a public welfare program directed specifically at immigrant needs," among them Lillian D. Wald, Peter Roberts, and Frances Kellor (Higham, 1963: 119, 120, 238–241).

Caliban is subtitled "A Community Masque," and it aimed to create precisely the sort of community that Progressive-minded reformers envisioned. According to an editorial in the *New York Tribune* that endorsed the masque,

> . . . endless variety of population forms the chief obstacle to that fellow-understanding which is the true basis of community spirit. The avowed hope of those who have toiled hardest for the spectacle is that something more than a theatrical success will be achieved. A uniting of the entire city, a rebirth of local pride and civic spirit, is the ambitious goal fore-seen. . . .
> (*New York Tribune*, 5/26/16)

"Endless variety of population" was, of course, a polite euphemism for the masses of immigrants pouring into New York in 1916. Even a prominent Progressive urban reformer such as Frederic L. Howe, the first U.S. commissioner of immigration, worried about how to absorb foreigners into the mainstream of national life. "Thirteen million foreign-born in our midst and eighteen million more who are [their] immediate descendants," he declared, made it hard to "keep the well-springs of American citizenship, American civilization, and American culture to their proper standards" (MacKaye, 1915: viii).[1] That same year Percy MacKaye was invited to devise a "civic ritual" for newly naturalized citizens that might address the problem Howe described. MacKaye's ritual anticipates the strategies he uses a year later in *Caliban*.

In his preface, he imagines "our new citizens" gathering at "the altar of our English-speaking tradition of liberty . . . [for] the welcoming of all world-cultures to create an American excellence" (MacKaye, 1915: 14–15). MacKaye then refers the reader to a table of immigration statistics in the Appendix that classifies the foreign-born on an ascending scale of language competence and education, as those that are illiterate in any language; that can't speak English; that are attending school; that have been naturalized (and who can therefore read and write English). Implicitly, literacy in English appears as the key to Americanization.

The ritual begins with a procession of "national group leaders" carrying symbols of the "arts and crafts" of their homelands. After readings from Jefferson, Washington, and Lincoln, each group presents the flag of its native land as a token of "love, labor, and loyalty to the flag of our children's Fatherland" (MacKaye, 1915: 67–8).

---

1. Howe's statement comes from his preface to MacKaye's *The Immigrants* (1915), an opera commissioned by the Boston Opera House with music by Frederick Converse. This "lyric drama" (heavily indebted to the *verismo* of Puccini) depicts Italian immigrants oppressed in their native land, inveigled into immigration and finally driven to violent crime by an unscrupulous Irish steamship agent.

Thus "world-cultures" are "melted into" America. Each nationality is typified by the "folk costumes" its members wear, and by performing a "folk dance, native ballad, athletic game, rondel, choral, or any appropriate distinctive art or craft" (MacKaye, 1915: 67)—signifiers of native origin, also common in pageants, that convey an antiquarian, pre-industrial idea of European nations.

Note that MacKaye describes the American tradition of liberty as "English-speaking." Here we must recall the Anglo-Saxonists' sense of English culture and language as a signifier of racial superiority. In the wake of the severe economic depression of 1893–7, the newly-founded Immigration Restriction League, working closely with Henry Cabot Lodge and drawing on grassroots support from the Pacific Coast states and the South (which had long shared the folkways of white superiority) and from labor unions, had devoted itself to limiting and controlling immigration under the guise of a literacy requirement (Higham, 1975: 164–5). The League touted a literacy test aimed specifically at keeping out newcomers from southern and eastern Europe—whom it characterized as illiterate paupers, criminals and madmen who endangered "American character" and "American citizenship" (Higham, 1969: 103). In 1895 Senator Lodge introduced in the senate a bill drawn up by the League, requiring that men and women over the age of fourteen be prevented from entering as immigrants if unable to read and write in some language; his co-sponsor in the House presented the test as a way to keep out the "new," largely illiterate southern Europeans. The bill lost but, reintroduced four more times, it finally passed in 1917, a year after *Caliban* made its debut.

In *Caliban*, MacKaye goes one step farther than the literacy test, which only required foreigners to read and write in any language, by symbolically staging embrace of "the English-speaking tradition," represented by Shakespeare. As we will see, however, he does so by making Shakespeare encompass the historical diversity of theatrical art through the ages: from Egyptian ritual right up to Ibsen, somehow Shakespeare, "not of an age but for all time," contains world drama. Through these conflicting figurations of Shakespeare as English and Shakespeare as comprehending all cultures and nations, MacKaye thus re-plays the controversy between the Anglo-Saxonists and the pluralists. Fittingly enough, the stadium in which he re-plays it had been erected only the year before, the munificent gift of Adolf Lewisohn, a wealthy German-Jewish immigrant become philanthropist.

The central dramatic action of *Caliban* is the education of its titular hero as an appreciative devotee of Shakespeare. Robert Edmond Jones's stage design mirrors the quasi-Platonic design of this action, which takes place on three "planes." The "middle stage" where the characters of *The Tempest* interact is dominated by a gigantic two-headed idol, "half tiger, half toad," representing Setebos. The idol looms over Caliban's cave, located under the middle stage adjacent to the "ground circle" or third plane. In Shakespeare, Setebos is merely the unseen god Caliban's deceased mother had worshipped; here, he is the creature's father, a physical presence onstage, and the evocation of all that is barbarian and inimical to western civilization. His priests are "War, Lust, and Death," who command masses of followers in several spectacular episodes of "primeval pageantry and dance" or chaotic struggle that serve to enlarge the threat Caliban represents.

The "second plane" of the action takes place on the "Inner Stage," a curtained recess raised two feet above the middle stage: in this recess the scenes from Shakespeare that will raise Caliban from his bestial state are performed. Finally, the "third plane" takes place on the "ground circle," otherwise the actual playing field of the stadium, analogous to the orchestra of the Greek theater. It represents the yellow sands, the realm of historical time and also the realm of drama where cooperation and creativity, in MacKaye's vision, "take hands." Here, in three non-speaking spectacles called "Interludes," each involving hundreds of amateur performers, MacKaye chronicles the history of world drama.

The masque begins at a point prior to Shakespeare's play, when Caliban still reigns on the island and Prospero is just arriving. More blatantly than *The Tempest*, the dramatic action emphasizes Caliban's primitive, unbridled sexuality, partly through the character and partly through an allegorical over-plot involving Setebos. As in *The Tempest*, Caliban desires both Miranda and Prospero's powers, represented by the wand that Caliban calls a "playstick," so that he can multiply himself. Like the Caliban in Browning's poem, he plays at making his own creatures from mud, and readily thinks of Miranda as a mate: "So shall us twain / Caliban all this world!," he cries (MacKaye, 1916: 19). No fewer than three times, Miranda is threatened with rape, each attempt provoking a stupendous spectacle.

In the second rape episode, the powers of Setebos imitate a Roman orgy, seizing Miranda to serve Caligula's lust. This time prevention comes in the form of "a colossal CROSS [*sic*], burning with white fire," accompanied by the spirits of Ariel chanting Latin verses praising the cross, the Passion, and the Trinity, while on the inner stage St. Agnes appears in an early Christian shrine, holding a lamb.[2] This configuration of rape forestalled by the power of Christ finds a

---

2. Prospero had already made his initial entrance seated on "a glowing, winged throne . . . in one hand, a scroll; in the other a miraculous staff" (MacKaye, 1916: 23–4). Cartelli notes that the entrance "doubly echoes Christ's harrowing of hell and Moses's destruction of the idols at the base of Mt. Sinai," thus laying the foundation for "The allegorical triumph of the Christian dispensation" in the second rape episode (1998: 68, 69).

possible source, or at least an analogue, in D.W. Griffith's *The Birth of a Nation*, released the previous year in 1915. The pathbreaking film "builds to its sustained climax from two attempted rapes of white women by black men," assaults that produce the famous "rides to the rescue" by the Ku Klux Klan. These rides anticipate the spectacular rescues of Miranda, first by Prospero and then symbolically by the intervention of a Christian God.[3] Michael Rogin argues convincingly that the negroes who threaten to impede America's birth into nationhood in the film are the counterparts of those southern and eastern European immigrants who, nativists believed, were inimical to Americanness (Rogin, 1985: 154–5).

Only when Caliban "shall rise / To lordly reason" (26), declares Prospero, can Miranda be "free," that is, safe from rape. But the real point of his education isn't so much to assure Miranda's purity as to interpellate Caliban, the cultural—and racial—Other, into Anglo-American culture. That is accomplished by making him a spectator of Shakespeare rather than the playwright's rival. Modelling the audience watching him, Caliban views scenes from Shakespeare performed on the "inner stage" raised above and recessed from the main stage, scenes selected and arranged so as to suggest the chronology of world history from Egypt (*Antony and Cleopatra*) to Greece and Rome (*Troilus and Cressida, Julius Caesar*) and finally Elizabethan England (*As You Like It, The Merry Wives of Windsor,* and *Henry V*)—as though Shakespeare had encompassed western civilization with what Bristol calls the "extraordinary transumptive power" attributed to him (Bristol, 1990: 125). Caliban watches and listens, sometimes stirred to lust and rebellion, sometimes awestruck at the beauty and nobility of the characters paraded before him. In the crisis preceding his final transformation, moved by the passion of King Henry's "Once more unto the breach," Caliban marshals the powers of Setebos and with "flashing fireworks and bombs," takes Miranda, Prospero and Ariel captive, boasting "Who now is master-artist? Who wieldeth now the world?" (140).

But Caliban is stymied: he can't use Prospero's power without the master-artist's consent, and Miranda's "chastity of soul," like that of the Lady in *Comus*, charms her against rape. The would-be master artist is at last persuaded to content himself with watching Prospero's visions rather than trying to create his own by the biggest spectacle of all: "A Pageant of the great Theatres of the world—from the ancient Theatre of Dionysus to the Comédie Francaise" (143).

3. Conversely, Glassberg comments, "In many ways, D.W. Griffith's *Birth of a Nation* resembled a pageant, with its abstract symbolism, allegorical finale, and tableaux vivants of famous historical scenes" (1990: 155). The community drama movement and the Drama League both aimed to wean the American public away from what it considered low-level forms of entertainment, among them the movies.

Trooping forth through the mouths of colossal masks of Comedy and Tragedy come groups representing these theatres, the performers being drawn from among the immigrants themselves: "members of the Italian colony" (as MacKaye quaintly termed them), the German University League, the Alliance Française, the English Folk Dance Society, etc. Like the "national groups" of MacKaye's citizenship ritual, and carrying the same kinds of banners and insignia as they carried, these immigrants, while celebrating Shakespeare's universalized preeminence, enact their assimilation into American society as Shakespeare's audience.[4] At the same time, MacKaye makes Shakespearean drama the culmination of all theatrical art from its inception in Greece to its current manifestation in Ibsen—literally "not of an age but for all time," apparently transcending any associations with the Anglo-Saxon tradition.

It is noteworthy that African-Americans were not represented among the groups enacting their claim to Americanness by paying homage to Shakespeare. Literally American and not foreign, but nonetheless historically excluded from "the English-speaking tradition of liberty," they were "generally absent" from pageants, and if present, depicted in stock terms as comic buffoons (Glassberg, 1990: 132).[5] In a section of the *Caliban* program listing city-wide observances of the tercentenary, however, there is a heading titled "Colored Organizations." The first entry reads, "For the first time in the history of the negro race, a company of negro actors gave 'Othello' during the week April 17th." In fact, the Astor Place Company of Colored Tragedians had performed *Othello* in 1884 at the Brooklyn Atheneum, and between 1900 and 1916, "a black Shakespearean repertoire was kept alive in different parts of the country by a variety of performing groups" (Hill, 1984: 45, 82).[6]

4. Glassberg notes that while pageant-masters invoked "the democratic and cooperative spirit of the playground in their work, welcoming all into the embrace of the community pageant," at the same time they "recommended that the casting and rehearsal of each pageant episode be placed under the direction of a different group, whose members already knew one another" (133, 113). This practice had the effect of "accentuating, rather than submerging, local social distinctions" (114). I would add that it also had the effect of setting immigrants off from each other and from "Americans." The reviewer for *The Chicago Sunday Herald* itemizes the groups thus: "Community group after community group passed in review—the Pan-hellenic League, the East Side Settlements, the Greenwich Villagers, the Bronx district, the schools, the representatives of all races, classes and conditions in the great city" (MacKaye, 1917: 56).
5. Though the 1910 St. Louis census listed 44,000 Black inhabitants, more than any other group of recent immigrants, no Blacks were appointed to pageant committees or assigned roles in the 1914 St. Louis pageant. So few Blacks attended performances that no questions about segregated seating arose (Glassberg, 1990: 179–80).
6. The unnamed company listed in the *Caliban* program was in fact a group of "Shakespearean students and college graduates" without much stage experience, directed by Edward Sterling Wright, a trained lecturer and "song recitalist" who also played the title role. The production was staged by A.C. Winn, a white director and stage manager for the Lafayette Theatre (also the home of a professional black company, the Lafayette Players). Rehearsed for only two weeks, the production also travelled to Boston and was reviewed favorably in both cities (Hill, 1984: 92–7).

At the conclusion of this gigantic spectacle, from amongst the mass of performers representing the great actors and playwrights of "world" theater, Thespis to Edwin Booth, Aeschylus to Ibsen, Shakespeare gradually emerges. He and Prospero exchange gazes: then Prospero places his cloak on Shakespeare's shoulders and exits. Thus they enact the autobiographical interpretation of Prospero as surrogate for the playwright (initiated by Thomas Campbell in 1838) that is implicit in the power of MacKaye's Prospero to summon up scenes from Shakespeare's plays. Caliban, then, is literally subjected not to Shakespeare's spokesman but to the poet himself. Crouching (as he is described in the epigraph to this essay, a poem printed in the *New York Times* during *Caliban's* run) at Shakespeare's feet, he pleads "More visions," but the poet intones, "Our revels now are ended," lines from Prospero's speech being echoed by the large choir and orchestra housed above the stage. MacKaye's ending, then, expressly denies Caliban his aspiration to artistic visions of his own, his desire to wield a "playstick" like Prospero's.[7] What frees Caliban from his brute nature is, rather, passively watching Shakespeare's visions, becoming his audience.

But I have omitted mention of a third structural element in the masque that belies MacKaye's representation of Shakespeare as the poet of a disinterested universalism. Threaded through the core drama of Caliban's transformation to Shakespearean devotee are three spectacular "Interludes" depicting the dramatic art of antiquity, of medieval Europe, and finally, of Elizabethan England. The third Interlude, the biggest production number of the three, involved 400 participants rather than 150 as the others did. It staged "an Elizabethan May Day festival on the outskirts of an English town," which included: first, a Contest between Spring and Winter; second, a Processional Dance through the Village; third, Revels and Amusements, including a Punch and Judy show and the Noah's Ark episode from a mystery cycle; fourth, a May Pole Procession of Jack o'Greens, plough boys, sowers, reapers, oxen-drawn wagons, milkmaids, blacksmiths, wheelwrights, carpenters, butchers, shoemakers; fifth, the election of a May Queen and May Pole Dance; sixth, a Hobby Horse and Padstow May Song; seventh, Morris Dancers; eighth and finally, Country Dances and a Recessional. In short, it was a virtual inventory of the folk customs that supposedly typified the deeply communal nature of life in Shakespeare's England.

At this point, the masque coheres all too well with the Anglo-Saxon vision of America into which many reformers expected immigrants to blend. The folk dancing that figures so prominently

---

7. Nor does a concluding speech given to Caliban in the official program, in which he identifies himself with the audience as "fellow dreamers in the dark," suggest that he might be able to realize the visions he has gleaned from Shakespeare; see Green, 1989: 67.

in this May Day Festival was introduced to schools and playgrounds during the reform era by "genteel intellectuals concerned with public recreation" who viewed Elizabethan pastimes as a part of America's cultural heritage that had been suppressed by the Puritans (Glassberg, 1980: 354). They adapted dances from other ethnic traditions into "Maypole Festivals," using the English form as a way to assimilate immigrant customs into an Anglo-American norm (Glassberg, 1980: 359). While retaining its association with "merry old England," maypole dancing was promoted as "a wholesome Anglo-American play tradition for native-born and immigrant children alike" (Glassberg, 1990: 56, 58–9).[8] Not only MacKaye but many newspaper reports noted that his masque "enlist[ed] the services of people from every section of the city, geographically and socially" (*New York Times,* qtd. MacKaye, 1917: 55). Those who actually danced around MacKaye's Maypole, then, may have been Polish or Sicilian, Russian or Portuguese, but they were dancing an English dance. Despite its democratic context and teleology, *Caliban* functioned like a court masque in that it mirrored to the audience an ideal vision of itself, a vision culminating in the final dance.[9] Here immigrant energy fused with Anglo-Saxon form, however ethnically diverse the dancers, thus validating the subtitle "community masque."

Did the masque realize MacKaye's progressive-minded goal: "to help unite all classes and all beliefs in a great cooperative movement for civic expression through dramatic art" (MacKaye, 1916: xx)? If one can believe the press, it provided at least the fleeting impression of a diverse population drawn together by Shakespeare. *The New York Times* declared it attracted "A Representative Audience," from "every part of the city . . . the lower east side to Riverside Drive," and called it "more nearly a community affair, perhaps, than any dramatic performance that has ever been held here" (May 25, 1916). Listing the professional actors, musicians and college students who participated along with "factory-workers, business men, boy scouts, and students of public and private schools,"

8. Glassberg notes that in contrast to the 1864 Tercentenary, in 1916 Shakespeare was insistently connected with the Elizabethan era through folk dances: the cover of the New York Public Library manual for Shakespeare celebrations in the schools was adorned with a Maypole dance, New York settlement houses collaborated on an "Old English Fair," and 10,000 girls from the girls' branch of the Public School Athletic League performed Elizabethan folk dances in Central Park (Glassberg, 1980: 362).
9. MacKaye distinguished between the pageant, which he viewed as dramatizing local history through "a pictorial sequence of groups (usually designed to be faithfully historic in character), unrelated . . . to any inhering plot of drama, or to any organic structure of poetry," and the masque, which he described as "A poem: a symbolic folk-poem—designed to be spoken, acted, danced and sung" (MacKaye, 1932: 105, 106).

another journal remarked, "Such a spectacle has definite value in knitting together the population of a city" (*The Literary Digest*, June 10, 1916). Its more than 1500 performers were sufficiently inspired to vote that the performances be continued for an additional week. Representing the thirty professional actors who joined them, Howard Kyle, who played Prospero, stated "We all believe in one city, in the community idea, in the spirit of fellowship" (*New York Times*, May 30, 1916).

At a number of points, however, discrepancies between the "English-speaking tradition" represented by the spoken word, Shakespeare's and MacKaye's, and pageantry as drama by and for the entire "community," compromise MacKaye's agenda. These discrepancies, ultimately, are symptomatic of the deeper contradiction of this historical moment—between the vision of a culturally diverse America in which immigrants can find a place without surrendering ethnic difference, and that of an Anglo-Saxon America that requires them to adopt English tradition as the foundation of American culture. To begin with, the very magnitude of the production, its site, and its audience kept people from hearing the actors. Some thousands of auditors sat as far away as "the distance of two city blocks," from which, one reviewer claimed, "about ten words out of a hundred could, with a certain amount of effort, be grasped" (*Musical America*, June 3, 1916). *The New York Globe*'s review of the opening night called the masque "a gallant attempt to stimulate the civic spirit and a gallant failure":

> Perhaps some of the people in the boxes could understand it all. But the amphitheatre was full of people utterly unable to make out what on earth it was all about. No doubt a thorough study of the printed version would enable every spectator to grasp the significance of the thing. But in an audience of 10,000 how many are to be found so conscientious?
> (*New York Globe*, May 25, 1916)

Audibility was won at the expense of "incessant stentorian declamation," especially in "the otherwise forceful impersonation" of Caliban, the biggest role, which "grew extremely monotonous in its sustained roars, groans and nondescript gurgles" (*Musical America*, June 3, 1916). The very scenes from Shakespeare that moved and molded Caliban, ironically enough, "remain[ed] inaudible or suffer[ed] severely from the strain of being yelled," despite the special sounding boards installed (at the St. Louis pageant, the audience had been provided with cardboard "ears" to help catch the sound). The opening night performance lasted till five minutes after midnight, even though people began to leave at ten; thereafter an hour's worth was cut to advantage. The goal of uniting diverse segments of a multitudinous city in a single "community" mandated a huge production, performed by a huge cast for a huge audience. However, the comment that the masque produced "a great deal of democracy," but "not much Shakespeare" (*The Literary Digest,* June 10, 1916) points to an impasse between MacKaye's means for achieving his Progressivist goal of creating community through drama and the specifically Anglo-Saxonist means he wants to use for achieving it: Shakespeare's English.

Theatrically speaking, ideological contradiction was played out in a vexed relation between language and spectacle. In his preface to *Caliban,* MacKaye claims, "If no word of the masque be heard by the audience, the plot, action and symbolism will still remain understandable . . . Synchronous with every speech occur, in production, effects of pantomime, lighting, music, and movement with due proportion and emphasis." He explicitly takes issue with the noted English designer Edward Gordon Craig, a proponent of state-subsidized outdoor theatre and practitioner of "the new stagecraft."[1] The new people's theatre Craig envisions is one of "Sound, Light, and Motion" without speech; in contrast, MacKaye envisions "a structure in which the English language, spoken by actors, is an essential dramatic value" (MacKaye, 1916: xxii, xxv). Reviewers were unanimous, however, in according success to *Caliban* as "a spectacle which depended for its beauty on the marvelous lighting effects," while many of them criticized MacKaye for an "obstinate refusal to realize the preponderating importance of the eye" required by pageantry (*Musical Audience,* July; *New York Globe,* 25 May). In visual style, the masque was up to the minute or even *avant-garde.* Joseph Urban, the Viennese (fittingly, he had recently become an American citizen) stage designer and practitioner of the new stagecraft, constructed two large towers flanking the stage in order to transmit the unheard-of 1200 amperes that enabled him "to play and paint with . . . light" (*New York Times,* May 21):

> Now vague and sinister purples focused themselves on a point of the inner stage; now a magical mixture of green and

1. "The new stagecraft" is defined by Cary Mazer as "A collective redefinition of theatre art occurring across Europe" that engaged a range of aesthetic idioms and new technologies, lighting notable among them. It flourished in the Russian Ballet, the Moscow Art Theatre, the Theatre des Arts in Paris, and the Deutsches Theater of Vienna; before World War I, it had made its mark on the English stage. In general, it marked a break with the internally-consistent imagined "reality" of the Victorian stage set; instead, the new stagecraft sought "evocation and suggestion over direct statement" through effects rather than historical realism, and experimented with new theatrical spaces, such as outdoor amphitheatres and circuses (Mazer, 1981: 85–94).

yellow set off in a circumference of night. And then, of a sudden, the outer blackness vanished in an exultant noonday glamor of silver sheen and the whole field glittered; then a voluptuous orange, then pink, then green, then yellow, then red.

(*Musical America*, June 3)

Reviewers single out the three interludes performed on the oval playing field, covered with yellow canvas to represent "the yellow sands," for "The exquisite lighting, the handling of masses of color in the mob scenes, the concerted, rhythmic movements of the dancers and athletes" (*New York Globe*, May 25). They were accompanied by music for orchestra and choir that was deemed "pleasing, grateful to the ear, well performed and distinctly audible" (*Musical Advance*, July). Robert Edmond Jones's simple, stylized costumes show the influence of Diaghilev's designs for the Ballets Russes, and helped create "the potency of pure color on a large scale" (*Theatre Arts Magazine*, February 1917) that evidently made the interludes the highlight of the whole production.

To involve the whole "community" of New York in the masque entailed a huge spectacle and a mass audience, but a large portion of that audience, it seems, didn't actually hear even the excerpts from Shakespeare, that genius of "the English-speaking tradition," which were performed at the farthest remove from them, on the inner stage. Rather, as Charles Shattuck suggests, what they may have heard was "the sound of poetry . . . 'Shakespeare,' archaic and inaccessible"—what Shakespeare had become, Lawrence Levine argues, to the vast majority of Americans (Shattuck, 1987: 307; Levine, 1988: 11–81). Nonetheless, they could not have been oblivious to the idea, conveyed through wordless spectacle on the stadium field, that many cultural traditions were being subsumed under the aegis of an English poet. Perhaps they also sensed an analogy with the idea that many nationalities might also be subsumed under an American nationality.

MacKaye had worked hard in advance, however, to make the action of the masque perfectly clear to those who had never heard of Shakespeare. A flyer that accompanied the published script explained that action, in the simple language and form of a catechism:

What is Percy MacKaye's masque about?
    About Caliban, by the Yellow Sands. . . .
What is Caliban like?
    He is something like you and me—sometimes good, sometimes bad. . . .

What is the magic of Prospero?
The same as that of Shakespeare.

Whether or not a spectator had the benefit of this drill, she or he could hardly have escaped, in the tercentennial year of Shakespeare in New York, some encounter with Shakespeare. The *Caliban* program lists hundreds of activities of which the masque was the intended capstone: high school Shakespeare performances; songs, games, recitations and "quotations" in elementary schools and community centers; in clubs, debates, lectures, and even a "Shakespeare Suffrage Soirée"; in Central Park, a Shakespeare May Festival with 10,000 schoolgirls dancing on the "greenswards" and the planting of an English oak from Stratford-upon-Avon in the Shakespeare Garden.[2]

Like Caliban, both the performers and the audience assembled in those vast stadiums on starry summer evenings were supposed to sublimate any urges toward mastery of their own into a reverence for Shakespeare's supreme mastery—and thereby enter into the Anglo-American community that MacKaye's masque hopes to create. MacKaye's central role as *auteur*, however, belies that community. He not only wrote the script for *Caliban*, he also produced and directed the production, supervising a cadre of professionals who organized and coached its hundreds of amateur performers. A stream of articles in New York newspapers, beginning in March, 1916 and running through the final performances in June, testifies to MacKaye's total artistic control over a spectacle that he saw as a drama not "for the people" but rather "by the people," and tirelessly promoted (MacKaye, 1916: xviii). So far as I can discover, though, there was no community input into either script or production.

Furthermore, MacKaye wrests his celebration of Shakespeare from *The Tempest* at the cost of an egregiously reductive reading of the play. His grotesque, fur-covered Caliban owes more to F. R. Benson's 1891 ape-like "missing link" interpretation of the role than to the "sensitive and potentially noble" one of Beerbohm Tree in 1904, which had been acclaimed as both innovative and moving (Orgel, 1987: 73, 26). MacKaye goes much further than Benson, though, to demonize the character as the ally of "War, Lust, and Death." Thus he deprives the drama of precisely those dialogical dimensions that make Shakespeare endlessly interpretable and help to account for his long-lasting, widespread appeal: the interplay of multiple points of view, the presence of dialogue within

2. Naima Prevots lists twenty Shakespeare pageants commemorating the tercentenary, from Wellesley, Massachusetts to Paducah, Kentucky; Denton, Texas to Grand Forks, North Dakota (1990: 193ff.). I would add another: *Old English Pageant: A London May-Day in Elizabethan England*, performed in Columbia, South Carolina.

the text that gives rise to dialogues *with* the text. In *Caliban*, despite the flyer's description of the title character as "sometimes good, sometimes bad," Caliban—except for his capacity to appreciate Shakespeare—is childishly impulsive and destructive.

The past decade of debate over the canon and Shakespeare's place in it has made us rightly self-conscious about the ideological uses to which he can be put. Drawing from Renaissance England a model of the embracing community that Progressive reformers sought in America, a model inflected with the idea of Anglo-Saxon racial superiority, MacKaye calls upon Shakespeare to resolve the cultural dissonances for which immigrants were being held respon sible. At this specific moment, the American playwright and the Progressive-minded civic elite he served tried to make *The Tempest* an instrument of "the English-speaking tradition"—with limited success, it would seem. An inquiry into how immigrants read and performed Shakespeare for themselves is beyond the scope of this study, but even a brief example might suggest a counter-hegemonic perspective. It is possible to compare MacKaye's appropriation of Shakespeare to those of the Yiddish theatre flourishing in Manhattan from the 1890's into the 1920's. *Romeo and Juliet*, for example, was set not in Verona but in the old country, the Capulets and the Montagues transformed to rationalist *Mithnagdim* and pietist *Hasidim*, while Friar Lawrence became a Reform rabbi. In 1892, Jacob Gordin's *The Jewish King Lear* dramatized filial ingratitude in terms of the generational conflicts endemic to immigrant experience. Nor did *Hamlet* escape similar treatment. According to a revealing anecdote, at its first performance the enthusiastic audience called for the author, and were told that he was an Englishman and hence not immediately available (Howe, 1976: 160–96). In this context, that Shakespeare is English merely means that he lives on the other side of the Atlantic and can't take a bow. Those in the Yiddish theatre who translated, adapted, borrowed from and acted in Shakespeare's plays had, we can assume, a more sophisticated and informed sense of the poet's historical importance. But most people in their audiences didn't; they applauded Shakespeare not as the icon of the English-speaking tradition, but because he had been appropriated to express their dilemmas and desires as newcomers to America.[3] When Shakespeare's plays don't speak English, are they still part of the

3. Irving Howe, to whom I am indebted for this discussion of Shakespeare in the Yiddish theatre, distinguishes between popular art or *Shund*, drawing on the Bible and Jewish history for melodrama and romance, and translations of Shakespeare, Schiller or Goethe "reflecting an innocent respect for the idea of culture." But Shakespeare was frequently deployed in the service of *Shund*: in the works of Morris Horowitz, for example, "A simple tailor jealous of his wife would make a speech taken from *Othello*" (Howe, 1976: 466, 465). See also Sandrow (1996).

English-speaking tradition? Is Shakespeare still an "American" poet when a Lithuanian or Italian Caliban takes the "playstick" from Shakespeare's hand?

Works Cited

Bloom, James. *Left Letters: The Culture Wars of Mike Gold and Joseph Freeman.* New York: Columbia University Press, 1992.
Bristol, Michael. *Shakespeare's America, America's Shakespeare.* London: Routledge, 1990.
———. *Big Time Shakespeare.* London: Routledge, 1996.
Brock, D. Heyward and James M. Welsh, "Percy MacKaye: Community Drama and the Masque Tradition," *Comparative Drama* 6, 1 (Spring, 1972): 68–84.
Caliban: Shakespeare Tercentenary Celebration (Program for *Caliban by the Yellow Sands*). New York: 1916.
Cartelli, Thomas. *Repositioning Shakespeare: National Formations, Postcolonial Appropriations.* London: Routledge, 1999.
Cayton, Mary Cupiec, Elliott J. Gorn, Peter W. Williams, eds. *Encyclopedia of American Social History.* New York: Scribner's, 1993.
Cohn, Ruby. *Modern Shakespeare Offshoots.* Princeton: Princeton University Press, 1976.
Crèvecoeur, J. Hector St. John. *Letters from an American Farmer.* New York: Fox, Duffield, 1904.
Fairfield, Roy P., ed. *The Federalist Papers.* Baltimore, MD: Johns Hopkins University Press, 1981.
Franck, Jane P. "*Caliban* at Lewisohn Stadium, 1916," in *Shakespeare Encomium.* Ed. Anne Paolucci. New York: The City College Papers I, 1964.
Frantzen, Allen. *Desire for Origins: New Language, Old English, and Teaching the Tradition.* New Brunswick, NJ: Rutgers University Press, 1990.
Gayley, Charles Mills. "Heart of the Race," in Israel Gollancz, ed. *A Book of Homage to Shakespeare.* Oxford: Oxford University Press, 1916.
Glassberg, David. *American Historical Pageantry: The Uses of Tradition in the Early Twentieth Century.* Chapel Hill: University of North Carolina Press, 1990.
———. "Restoring 'Forgotten Childhood': American Play and the Progressive Era's Elizabethan Past," *American Quarterly* 32, 4 (Fall, 1980): 351–68.
Gleason, Philip. "American Identity and Americanization," in *Harvard Encyclopedia of American Ethnic Groups.* Ed. Stephan Thernstrom. Cambridge, MA: Harvard University Press, 1980: 31–58.
Gordon, Mel. "Percy MacKaye's Masque of *Caliban* (1916)," *Tulane Drama Review* 20 (1976): 93–107.
Green, William. "'Caliban on these yellow sands': Percy MacKaye's Adaptation of *The Tempest*," *Maske und Kothurn* 35, 1 (1989): 59–69.
Grover, Edwin Osgood, ed. *Annals of an Era: Percy MacKaye and the MacKaye Family 1829–1932.* Washington, D.C.: The Pioneer Press, 1932.
Higham, John. *Send These to Me: Jews and Other Immigrants in Urban America.* New York: Atheneum, 1975.
———. *Strangers in the Land: Patterns of American Nativism 1860–1925*, rpt. 1955. New York: Atheneum, 1963.
Hill, Errol. *Shakespeare in Sable: A History of Black Shakespearean Actors.* Amherst, MA: University of Massachusetts Press, 1984.
Hofstadter, Richard. *The Age of Reform from Bryan to F.D.R.* New York: Knopf, 1961.
Horsman, Reginald. *Race and Manifest Destiny: The Origins of American Racial Anglo-Saxonism.* Cambridge: Harvard University Press, 1981.

Howe, Irving. *World of Our Fathers*. New York and London: Harcourt, Brace, Jovanovich, 1976.

Levine, Lawrence. *Highbrow, Lowbrow: The Emergence of Cultural Hierarchies in America*. Cambridge, MA: Harvard University Press, 1988.

MacKaye, Percy. *The Playhouse and the Play*. New York: Macmillan, 1909.

———. *The Civic Theater: Suggestions Regarding Its Scope and Organization*. Washington, D.C., 1910.

———. *St. Louis: A Civic Masque*. Garden City, NY: Doubleday, Page, 1914.

———. *Caliban by the Yellow Sands*. Garden City, NY: Doubleday, 1916.

———. *The Immigrants: A Lyric Drama*. New York: B.W. Huebsch, 1915.

———. *The New Citizenship: A Civic Ritual Devised for Places of Public Meeting in America*. New York: Macmillan, 1915.

———. *Community Drama, Its Motive and Method of Neighborliness: An Interpretation*. Cambridge, MA: The Riverside Press, 1917.

———. *A Sketch of His Life* (rpt. from *Twenty-Fifth Annual Report of the Class of 1897*). Cambridge, MA: Harvard University Press, 1922.

———. *Wakefield: A Folk Masque of America*. Washington, D.C.: United States George Washington Bicentennial Commission, 1932.

Mastin, Florence Ripley. "Caliban at the Stadium," *New York Times*, May 31, 1916.

Mazer, Cary. *Shakespeare Re-Fashioned: Elizabethan Plays on Edwardian Stages*. Ann Arbor, MI: UMI Research Press, 1981.

Orth, Samuel P. *Our Foreigners*. The Chronicles of America Series, vol. 35. New Haven: Yale University Press, 1920.

Padelford, Frederic Morgan. "The Gothic Spirit in Shakespeare," *South Atlantic Quarterly* 15, 3 (July, 1916): 223–240.

Potter, Vilma Raskin. "Percy MacKaye's Caliban for a Democracy," *Journal of American Culture* 19, 4 (Winter, 1996).

Prevots, Naima. *American Pageantry: A Movement for Art and Democracy*. Ann Arbor: UMI Research Press, 1990.

Ripley, William Z. *The Races of Europe*. New York: D. Appleton and Co., 1899.

Rogin, Michael. *Blackface, White Noise: Jewish Immigrants in the Hollywood Melting Pot*. Berkeley and Los Angeles: University of California Press, 1996.

Ross, Edward A. *The Old World in the New*. New York, 1914.

Sandrow, Nahma. *Vagabond Stars: A World History of Yiddish Theatre*. Urbana, IL: University of Illinois Press, 1996.

Shattuck, Charles. *Shakespeare and the American Stage*. Washington, D.C.: Folger Shakespeare Library, 1987.

Taylor, Gary. *Reinventing Shakespeare: A Cultural History from the Restoration to the Present*. London: Oxford University Press, 1989.

Trachtenberg, Alan. "Being and Becoming an American." Unpublished paper, n.d.

Vaughan, Alden and Virginia Vaughan. *Shakespeare's Caliban*. Cambridge: Cambridge University Press, 1991.

JULIA REINHARD LUPTON

Creature Caliban[†]

What is a creature? Derived from the future-active participle of the Latin verb *creare* ("to create"), *creature* indicates a made or fashioned thing but with the sense of continued or potential process, action, or emergence built into the future thrust of its active verbal form. Its tense forever imperfect, *creatura* resembles those parallel constructions *natura* and *figura*, in which the determinations conferred by nativity and facticity are nonetheless opened to the possibility of further metamorphosis by the forward drive of the suffix *-ura* ("that which is about to occur").[1] The *creatura* is a thing always in the process of undergoing creation; the creature is actively passive or, better, *passionate*, perpetually becoming created, subject to transformation at the behest of the arbitrary commands of an Other. The creature presents above all a theological conceptualization of natural phenomena. In Judaism and Christianity (and indeed it is only via the Latin of late antiquity that the word enters the modern languages), *creature* marks the radical separation of creation and Creator.[2] This separation can in turn articulate any number of cuts or divisions: between world and God; between all living things and those that are inert, inanimate, or elemental; between human beings and the "other creatures" over which they have been given rule; or, in more figurative uses, between anyone or anything that is produced or controlled by an agent, author, master, or tyrant.[3] In modern usage *creature* borders on the monstrous and unnatural, increasingly applied to those created things that warp the proper canons of creation. It can even come to characterize the difference between male and female or between majority and

---

† From *Shakespeare Quarterly* 51 (2000): 1–23. © 2000 Folger Shakespeare Library. Reprinted with permission of Johns Hopkins University Press. All notes are by the author.

1. See Erich Auerbach on *figura*: "this peculiar formation expresses something living and dynamic, incomplete and playful. . . . the notion of the new manifestation, the changing aspect, of the permanent runs through the whole history of the word" (*Scenes from the Drama of European Literature* [Minneapolis: U of Minnesota P, 1984], 11–76, esp. 12).
2. *Creatura* does not appear in the *Oxford Latin Dictionary*. In Charlton T. Lewis and Charles Short, *A Latin Dictionary* (New York: Oxford UP, 1980), the following entry traces the first uses of the word to the patristic period: "*creatura, ae,* f. [creo], only concr., a creature, thing created (late Lat.); Tertullian, Apologeticum 30; Prudentius, Ham. [?] 508: omnes creaturae tuae, Vulg. Tob. 8,7.—II. The creation: Deus caelorum et Dominus totius creaturae, Vulg. Jud. 9,17: Dei, id. Apoc. 3,14 al."
3. In *The Tempest* Prospero activates this sense when he tells Miranda that Antonio "new created / The creatures that were mine" (1.2.81–82). Quotations of *The Tempest* follow Stephen Orgel's 1987 edition of the play for the Oxford Shakespeare. See *The Oxford English Dictionary*, 2d ed., J. A. Simpson and E.S.C Weiner, eds. (Oxford: Clarendon Press, 1989), s.v. *creature*, 1b, 2a, and 4 (fig.); cf. Romans 1:25.

minority: as a term of endearment *creature* is generally used of women and children, and *creatura* itself might be said to break into formed and formless segments, with *creat-* indicating the ordered composition of humanity and the *-ura* signaling its risky capacities for increase and change, foison and fusion. At various points in the theological imagination of the West, creatureliness has served to localize a moment of passionate passivity, of an abjected, thinglike (non)being, a being of subjected becoming, that precipitates out of the divine Logos as its material remnant.

The word *creature* appears in one of *The Tempest*'s most famous passages:

> O wonder!
> How many goodly creatures are there here!
> How beauteous mankind is! O brave new world
> That has such people in't!
>
> (5.1.181–84)

Miranda's exclamation begins under the sign of wonder, her signature affect, by including the approaching Italians within the expansive world of creatures: "How many goodly creatures are there here!" She then narrows the global copia of the creaturely to its exemplary consummation in humanity: "How beauteous mankind is!" Her apostrophe ends by containing the multitude of creatures within the unity of a "brave new world," referring at once to the cosmos in its totality, ever renewed and maintained by God's ongoing creative will, and to the particular world of Italian citizens, new to her, which she will soon rejoin.

Caliban, I argue here, takes shape beneath the arc of wonder that moves throughout the play between "creatures" and "mankind," between animate beings in general and their realization in the form of humanity. Is he man or fish? creature or person? This indeterminacy at the heart of Caliban also sets him adrift between the cosmos in its vast totality—the brave new world of primal Creation—and the particular worlds defined by culture and nation: Bermuda, Algiers, Milan, Naples. Although in *The Tempest* the word *creature* appears nowhere in conjunction with Caliban himself, his character is everywhere hedged in and held up by the politico-theological category of the creaturely. As a solitary Adam on an island to which he is native but not natural, Caliban first stood apart from the rest of creation as his "own king" (1.2.342). Now enslaved to a Master-Maker, he finds himself locked within the swarming ranks of scamels, filberts, and the nimble marmoset, a natural wonder in a world of wonders. As such, he becomes an emblem of what Giorgio Agamben has called "bare life," pure vitality denuded of its symbolic significance and political capacity and then sequestered within the domain of civilization as its disavowed core.[4]

In the discourse of the creaturely, the image of cosmos—the totality that subsumes the singularity of the Creature in the register of a limited or general Creation—is never distant. The arc of wonder leaps from the sublime variety of creatures to the synthetic unity conferred by a world, cosmos, or order. Hence Miranda's "wonder" at such "goodly creatures" finds rest in the empyrean clarity of the "brave new world" they surely represent. A similar reflex has characterized critical responses to Caliban, which tend to naturalize his strangeness either within the macrocosmic synthesis of a general humanity (as either its exemplum or its exception) or—following the strain of much recent criticism—within the smaller worlds defined by race, nation, or culture. The political theology of the Creature avoids the traps presented by humanist/universalizing readings on the one hand and culturalist/particularizing readings of the play on the other.[5] As part of Creation, Caliban shares the universe of Adam, thwarting attempts by both characters and readers to exclude him from the common lot of humanity. At the same time, his creaturely monstrosity foils any normative reading of this humanity which would raise Caliban into an exemplar of basic drives. The play includes him within the cosmos of Adam but only as its chaotic exception.

If the creature Caliban both invites and resists universalizing readings, the same is true for the drive to particularize him. As a monstrous exception to the human norm, Caliban's creatureliness propels him into the conceptual space occupied by ideas of national and racial difference, eliciting a long line of culturalist readings of his oppression. Yet Caliban's exceptionality, both deeply singular and highly indeterminate, also prevents him from becoming the

---

4. *"The originary relation of law to life is not application but Abandonment.* The matchless potential of the *nomos, its originary 'force of law,'* is that it holds life in its ban by abandoning it" (Giorgio Agamben, *Homo Sacer: Sovereign Power and Bare Life,* trans. Daniel Heller-Roazen [Stanford, CA: Stanford UP, 1998], 29). Agamben's prime example of humanity reduced to mere life is the inmate of the concentration camp.

5. For a sensitive and eloquent rendering of the universalist approach, see Harry Berger Jr.'s assessment of Caliban: "he *stands for* the world; a handy and compact symbol of human nature, not as we know it, but as we might have found it at the beginning of time" ("Miraculous Harp: A Reading of Shakespeare's *Tempest*" (1969), *Shakespeare Studies* 5 (1970): 253–83, esp. 260. Psychoanalysis comprises the most vital current strain of the universalist approach, as Meredith Anne Skura's psychoanalytic critique of culturalist readings demonstrates; see "Discourse and the Individual: The Case of Colonialism in *The Tempest,*" *Shakespeare Quarterly* 40 (1989): 42–74. Skura's essay explicitly thematizes the polarization between universalizing and particularizing interpretations. The culturalist view is perhaps best represented in Stephen Greenblatt, *Learning to Curse: Essays in Early Modern Culture* (New York: Routledge, 1990); Paul Brown, "'This thing of darkness I acknowledge mine': *The Tempest* and the discourse of colonialism" in *Political Shakespeare: New essays in cultural materialism,* Jonathan Dollimore and Alan Sinfield, eds. (London: Manchester UP, 1985), 48–71; and Peter Hulme, *Colonial Encounters: Europe and the native Caribbean, 1492–1797* (London: Methuen, 1986).

articulate representative of a single race or culture, be it Atlantic or
Mediterranean. He subsists within an unredeemed Creation not yet
divided into nations, forming the forgotten ground of a heteroge-
neous universalism irreducible to either the economies of a normative humanity or the semiotic coherence of individual cultures. At
once monstrous and human, brutely slavish and poignantly subjective, the creature Caliban takes shape at the negative intersection
between (general) Humanity and (specific) Culture. As such, Caliban's creatureliness *precedes* secular humanism, since the universe
of creatures is measured neither by the totality of humanity nor the
authenticity of a culture but rather by the infinity of life forms that
burgeon around the human as its limit points. Caliban's creatureliness may also *exceed* the increasingly troubled solutions of secular
humanism in its historicist variants, pointing to a new universalism
defined by a cosmopolitical community of differences rather than by
an exclusive set of national markers. Such a reclaimed universalism
just might offer an antidote to the impasses of culturalism, whose
investment in identities conferred by national belonging uncannily
links the progressive goals of liberal antiracism to the reactionary
impulses of ethnic cleansing.[6]

Approaching the Creature

The German-Jewish philosopher Franz Rosenzweig initiated
twentieth-century discussion of Creation as a category of critical
reflection rather than as scientific or religious controversy. His
magnum opus, *The Star of Redemption* (1921), locates Creation as
one point in a triad completed by Revelation and Redemption. Creation, Rosenzweig insists, is an ongoing process: "For the world, its
required relationship to the creator was . . . not its having been created once and for all, but its continuing to manifest itself as creature."[7] The creature, writes Rosenzweig, is the subject of a special
consciousness: "being created would mean for it manifesting itself
as creature. This is creature-consciousness, the consciousness not
of having once been created but of being everlastingly creature."[8]

6. Etienne Balibar analyzes the paradox of the current situation, in which the idea of
   cultural identity, the mainstay of traditional antiracism, has become the banner for
   new forms of racism: "Anthropological culturalism, which is entirely orientated
   towards the recognition of the diversity and equality of cultures . . . had provided the
   humanist and cosmopolitan anti-racism of the postwar period with most of its arguments" ("Is There a Neo-Racism?" in *Race, Nation, Class: Ambiguous Identities*, Etienne Balibar and Immanuel Wallerstein, eds., trans. Chris Turner [London: Verso,
   1991], 17–28, esp. 21–22). Precisely the same arguments, he points out, are used to
   defend ethnic cleansing and the rhetoric of anti-immigration, mounted in the name of
   the purity of cultures.
7 Franz Rosenzweig, *The Star of Redemption*, trans. William W. Hallo (New York: Holt,
   Rinehart and Winston, 1971), 120.
8. Rosenzweig, 120.

Everlastingly creature: in this phrase Rosenzweig unfolds the philosophical consequences of the *-ura*, finding in it the expression of a
continuously subjected subjectivity in relation to a Creator who
remains sublimely other from it.

In *The Origin of the German Tragic Drama* (1927), Walter Benjamin read Rosenzweig's existential analysis of the Creature as a
political category embedded in the absolutisms of Reformation and
Counter-Reformation Europe.[9] Benjamin identifies the creaturely
with the peculiarly baroque perception of human finitude, everywhere infused with the sense of both the *necessity* and the *evacuation*
of theological frameworks:

> the baroque . . . had . . . a clear vision of the misery of man-
> kind in its creaturely estate. If melancholy emerges from the
> depths of the creaturely realm to which the speculative thought
> of the age felt itself bound by the bonds of the church itself,
> then this explained its omnipotence. In fact it is the most gen-
> uinely creaturely of the contemplative impulses, and it has
> always been noticed that its power need be no less in the gaze
> of a dog than in the attitude of a pensive genius.[1]

Following Rosenzweig, Benjamin identifies the creaturely with a
peculiar form of consciousness, impelled by idealism yet forever
earthbound by the weight of corporeality, at once sullen angel and
pensive dog. From one point of view the Creature is *too much body*,
collecting in its leaden limbs the earthenness and passionate intensity of mere life uninspired by form. From another the Creature
suffers from *too much soul*, taking flight as "speculation," as reason
soaring beyond its own self-regulating parameters toward a second-
order materiality of signifiers unfixed to signifieds. In Benjamin's
analysis, melancholy identifies the psychosomatic foundations of
this creaturely consciousness, its violent yoking of an excessive,
even symptomatic mental production to the dejected gravity of an
unredeemed body. Benjamin encounters this creaturely melancholy
in "the gaze of a dog" precisely because the Creature, caught
between mud and mind, dust and dream, measures the difference
between the human and the inhuman while refusing to take up
residence in either category.

In Benjamin's discourse—and here he builds explicitly on the work
of the conservative jurist Carl Schmitt—the Creature represents the
flip side of the political theology of absolute sovereignty developed in
the late-sixteenth and early-seventeenth centuries. In Schmitt's

9. See Walter Benjamin, *The Origin of the German Tragic Drama*, trans. John Osborne
   (London: New Left Books, 1977).
1. Benjamin, 146.

analysis the king is like God in the creative-destructive potential of
his decisive word, his juris-diction.[2] By extension, his subjects are his
creatures, the objects of his continual sovereign activity, which is a
power that comes to the forefront during states of emergency, when
the normal functioning of positive law is lifted in favor of the king's
executive decisions. In English *emergency* is defined by the state of
emerging, a condition in which forms are no longer fixed, when
new—potentially dangerous, revolutionary, or counterrevolutionary—
forms of political life can arise.[3] In German, the *Ausnahmezustand*—
literally, "state of exception"—is ruled by the idea of exception. The
Ausnahmezustand is that condition in which what is outside the
law—the exception to the rule—comes to define the very essence of
the law through the cut of the sovereign's de-cision. In the state of
emergency the sovereign stands outside a legal order that includes
him as the necessity of its own suspension.

In Benjamin's resolutely materialist analysis of political theology,
the sovereign, unlike God, is himself a creature: "however highly he
is enthroned over subject and state, his status is confined to the world
of creation; he is the lord of creatures, but he remains a creature."[4]
The Creature is finally both sovereign and subject, mind and matter,
tyrant and martyr, but he suffers the two modalities in a wildly dis-
junct form that refuses to resolve into a reciprocal or homogeneous
economy. The creature is never simply sovereign over himself, in a
condition of stable autonomy in which the terms would balance each
other in a just distribution: his self-rule is tyrannous, and he suffers
that rule as mere creature. His reason takes flight as speculation; his
law is that of the state of emergency, not the state of nature; and his
body forever speaks in the hagiographies of dismemberment, torture,
deformity, and symptom.

The Genesis of Caliban

Almost all the geographical indicators of *The Tempest* mark Caliban as an Old World figure, born from an Algerian mother and an

2. See Carl Schmitt, *Political Theology: Four Chapters on the Concept of Sovereignty*,
trans. George Schwab (Cambridge, MA: MIT Press, 1985), 31–32 and 46–47.
3. *Emergency* derives from the Latin preposition *ō* , "out of," and *mergere*, "to dip," with
the sense of "To rise by virtue of buoyancy, *from* or *out of* a liquid" (*OED*, s.v. *emerge*,
v. 1). Its fluid associations are resonant with liquefactional theories of creation and
creatures as "emergent" from a primal slime or soup. *Emergency* initially appeared in
English as a substantive of this process and a simple variant of *emergence*: "The rising
of a submerged body above the surface of water" (1646; *OED* 1). But around the same
time, the word appears to accrue its modern sense of historic urgency, as "The arising,
sudden or unexpected occurrence (of a state of things, an event, etc.)" (1665; *OED* 3);
"A juncture that arises or 'turns up'; *esp.* a state of things unexpectedly arising, and
urgently demanding immediate action" (1663; *OED* 4)
4. Benjamin, 85.

unnamed father on an unnamed island between Tunis and Naples, perhaps somewhere off the coast of Sicily.[5] In this mapping Caliban might appear to be a sorry cousin of Othello, a young man of North African descent and Punic features who finds himself the unwilling inhabitant of a Mediterranean island newly under Italian control. In this reading "Cannibal" rhymes with "Hannibal," deriving Caliban from a long line of Semitic ancestors, from Sidonian Dido to Algerian Sycorax. Yet the language of Old World Moorishness rolls off the tempest-tested gabardine of Caliban, who insistently emerges in the world of the play and its criticism as more a New World than an Old World figure. Part of this effect surely arises from the sheer force and power of the play's creative re-appropriations by anticolonial writers beginning in the nineteenth century as well as the renaissance of historicism in our own moment.[6] It is not only an accident of the play's reception, however, that leads to this critical disabling of Caliban's Mediterranean genealogy. I would argue that it is also a function of the biblical typing that silhouettes Caliban as creature, exiled to an island of Edenic nature (caught in the register of mere life, of purely animate being) and forever exiled from it, insofar as his melancholic capacity for both depressive pain and poetic speculation separates him from the natural world he emblematizes.

Caliban thus enters the play under the sign of the creature:

> This island's mine by Sycorax my mother,
> Which thou tak'st from me. When thou cam'st first,
> Thou strok'st me and made much of me; wouldst give me
> Water with berries in't, and teach me how

---

5. Although New World readings of Caliban have become commonplace in current criticism, the Old World markers are the more insistent and self-evident in the play and indeed have yielded some of the most promising strains in recent interpretation; see, for example, Kim F. Hall, *Things of Darkness: Economies of Race and Gender in Early Modern England* (Ithaca, NY: Cornell UP, 1995). Ralph Hexter's analysis of the "Sidonian Dido" would also usefully illumine the Semitic (Punic and Arab) shadings of the play's Mediterranean world; see "Sidonian Dido" in *Innovations of Antiquity*, Ralph Hexter and Daniel Selden, eds. (New York: Routledge, 1992), 332–84. For a summary of the possible geographical coordinates of Caliban, see Alden T. Vaughan and Virginia Mason Vaughan, *Shakespeare's Caliban: A Cultural History* (Cambridge: Cambridge UP, 1991), 23–55. I suggest a Sicilian locale because of the literary kinship between Caliban and Polyphemos, that island's Homeric inhabitant, as well as the later history of contestation and communication between Muslim and Christian forces in that region. Sicily was conquered by the Arabs between 827 and 902 but was reclaimed by Christian invaders later in the tenth century. Sicily's Norman rulers exercised some tolerance toward the island's Muslim population. A major geographical work, *The Book of Roger*, was written by a Muslim geographer in Sicily under the patronage of the Norman king Roger II in 1154. See Bernard Lewis, *The Muslim Discovery of Europe* (New York: W. W. Norton, 1982), 18, 20, 22, and 147.
6. On the history of anti- and postcolonial readings of *The Tempest*, see Trevor Griffith, "'This Island's Mine': Caliban and Colonialism," *Yearbook of English Studies*, 13 (1983): 159–80.

To name the bigger light and how the less,
That burn by day and night; and then I loved thee,
And showed thee all the qualities o'th' isle,
The fresh springs, brine pits, barren place and fertile—
Cursed be that I did so! All the charms
Of Sycorax, toads, beetles, bats light on you!
For I am all the subjects that you have,
Which first was mine own king, and here you sty me
In this hard rock, whiles you do keep from me
The rest o'th' island.

(1.2.331–44)

As the proof text of Caliban's language lesson, Stephen Orgel cites Genesis 1:16: "God then made two great lights: the greater light to rule the day, and the less light to rule the night."[7] The allusion places Caliban in the order not of history but of creation, the pristine landscape of the world's birthday. In learning to name "the bigger light and . . . the less," Caliban becomes a type of Adam, naming the elements of God's creation in a childlike, naively concrete language.[8] Caliban and Adam's shared connection to the earth marks their creaturely status: these primal men are made from dust, fashioned by a divine potter-sculptor, forever emerging (*creat-ura*, "about-to-be-created") from the base matter of the elements into the more fixed forms of animate life. "Thou earth, thou" (1.2.314), "A thing most brutish" (1.2.356), "this thing of darkness" (5.1.278): throughout the play, Caliban appears as a *thing* made of *earth*, a characteristic that marks the elemental quality of the Adamic creature. Caliban's earthen core recalls the first fashioning of conscious life out of an inert yet infinitely malleable substance, as if the very plasticity of mud prompted the idea of conscious life in the Creator. In this scenario, as in so many creation myths involving an originary pottery, the Golem precedes and informs the Human; the manikin is father to the man.[9]

In his history of the island, Caliban, like Adam, names the objects of creation, yet, unlike his antitype, he must be taught this language

---

7. Orgel, ed., 119n. My own quotations of Genesis and references to the Pentateuch follow the *Soncino Chumash: The Five Books of Moses with Haphtaroth* (Hebrew and English with English commentary), ed. Dr. A. Cohen (London: Soncino Press, 1983); subsequent citations will appear parenthetically in the text.

8. The name *Adam* is etymologically linked to the Hebrew word *'ădâmâh*, "country, earth, ground, husband [-man], . . . land"; see James Strong, ed., *Strong's New Exhaustive Concordance of the Bible* (Iowa Falls: World Bible Publishers, 1980), Hebrew and Chaldee Dictionary, items 119–28, esp. item 127.

9. For classical *midrashin* on the Golem, an animate clay figure who is the subject of various Kabbalistic legends, see Hayim Nahman Bialik and Yehoshna Hana Ravnitzky, *The Book of Legends / Sefer Ha-Aggadah*, trans. William G. Braude (New York: Schocken Books, 1992), 15.

rather than discovering it within himself.[1] Whereas Adam's naming project places him at the head of creation, Caliban's language lesson places him *within* creation, as one creature among others, a creature who bears no obvious resemblance to his Creator. Caliban is Mere Creature, a creature separate (like Adam) from the Creator but (unlike Adam) not reflected back to the Creator as His image. The uncertainty throughout the play as to Caliban's shape—"a man or a fish?—dead or alive?" (2.2.24)—reflects this fundamental lack of reflection, this inchoate muddiness at the heart of Caliban's oddly faceless and featureless being, caught at the perpetually flooded border between metamorphic mud and mere life, without the solidifying breath of an instilled form.[2] Naming, language, serves to bring some order to this emergent world, this state of emerg-ency; and it is perhaps in search of such clarity that Caliban is taught to name not "every living creature" (Genesis 1:29), as Adam does, but rather the "bigger light and . . . the less," placing the swarming dominions of bird and beast beneath his rational gaze.

Yet sun and moon, purveyors of light and models of Logos, also install within the scene of education the possibility of inveterate rivalry. Rashi, one of the great medieval Rabbinic commentators on the Bible, adduced the following midrash from the passage: "They were created of equal size, but that of the moon was diminished because she complained and said, 'It is impossible for two kings to make use of one crown.'"[3] Abhorring equality, the moon suffers diminishment at the hands of her Maker. Sun and moon, Prospero and Caliban, Creator and Creature, king and subject: the image of the two lights inserts an unequal couple within the apparent innocence of the recollected lesson, an incipient movement toward rivalry and protest that structures the entire speech. The moon's lessened light glimmers in Caliban's closing reminder that Prospero's sovereignty depends on its reflection back to him in the form of his subject's unwilling recognition: "For I am all the subjects that you have, / Which first was mine own king" (1.2.341–42). In the place of divine similitude, the special stamp of Adam, Caliban is left with the baser mimesis born from rivalry and the quest for recognition. The language lesson lessens the "mooncalf" Caliban

1. See Genesis 2:19–20.
2. For the play's systematic association of Caliban with muddy "bogs, fens, [and] flats" (2.2.2), see John Gillies, "Shakespeare's Virginian Masque," *ELH* (1986): 673–707, esp. 684–85.
3. Rashi, *Chumash with Targum Onkelos, Haphtaroth and Rashi's Commentary*, ed. A. M. Silberman, 5 vols. (Jerusalem: Feldheim Publishers, 1934), 1:16. For a narrative amplification of Rashi, see Louis Ginzberg, *The Legends of the Jews*, trans. Henrietta Szold, 5 vols. (Baltimore: Johns Hopkins UP, 1998), 1:23–24. For a contemporary analysis of Rashi's parable, see Avivah Gottlieb Zornberg, *Genesis: The Beginning of Desire* (Philadelphia: Jewish Publication Society, 1995), 13–14.

(2.2.126), indicating his demotion within Prospero's sovereign remapping of the island.

Symptoms Taken for Wonder

Caliban is thus left with resentment, the creaturely passion that flares up from the hinge of the hierarchical coupling between sun and moon. It is, of course, a passion previously tapped and tested by Shakespeare: resentment describes the chip on the ugly shoulder of Richard III, the incalculable debt of Shylock, and the motiveless malignancy of Iago. And close behind each of these figures is Lucifer, clothed in the secular garments of the stage Vice and Machiavel. Lucifer, the Morning Star, reflectively intensifies Rashi's eclipsed moon in his hatred of subordination and in his sudden fall from originary brightness to darkness visible. In his earlier plays Shakespeare had consistently fashioned Luciferian resentment as an emblem of market modernity, predicting Nietzsche's analysis of *ressentiment*, in which culture itself in its higher forms reworks an essentially economic relation: "the feeling of guilt, of personal obligation, had its origin, as we saw, in the oldest and most primitive personal relationship, that between buyer and seller, creditor and debtor."[4] In Shakespearean drama resentment is a mark of villainy under the law, the sign of a soulless legalism, a kind of second-order secularized Judaism that separates the modern ethos of markets, contracts, and Realpolitik from the (nostalgically reconstructed) civility of dying feudal institutions of life and love. To restore grace, in its theological and aesthetic registers, to the legalized, economized world of a dispersed and generalized resentment is a dream that animates any number of Shakespeare's plays, from *The Merchant of Venice* to *The Winter's Tale*.

The Tempest changes tack by locating resentment not within but prior to the law, as the passion of a prehistoric world that takes shape at the shores of the economic as such. In *The Tempest* resentment belongs to the protosocial world of the creature, a (living) thing but not yet an object of exchange, subsisting at the threshold of commerce and conversion. The creature does not respond to the exigencies of exchange so much as it functions as a first quantity of subjected, "created" value that sets the possibility of exchange into motion. In *The Tempest* power requires a moment of enforced inequality in order to mobilize. The name of this originary expropriation is slavery, which maintains a creaturely preserve of bare life within a system of sovereignty and covenant, the latter represented

4. Friedrich Nietzsche, *On the Genealogy of Morals*, trans. Walter Kaufmann and R. J. Hollingdale (New York: Random House, 1967), 70.

in the play by Prospero's contractual relation to Ariel. Prospero defends the necessity of maintaining Caliban within the *oikos*, the household, of the master: "He does make our fire, / Fetch in our wood, and serves in offices / That profit us" (1.2.311–13). This reduction of Caliban to his labor places the creature at the heart of an economy governed by the necessities of life. At the same time, Prospero's enslavement of Caliban, founded on the very purity of that reduction, implies the possibility of an economy of exchange, of "offices / That profit us."

Caliban's counternarrative recounts this originary expropriation: he who was once "mine own king" is now "all the subjects that you have." His own self-rule, his prior self-possession, can be conceived only in the terms of sovereignty that he experiences under Prospero, in which the latter's kingship depends on the former's exacted recognition. The institution of sovereignty through the enforced establishment of difference creates the conditions for resentment, a passion that looks forward to the possibility of usurpation and backward to the positing of a self-kingship that would be free from (and yet remains fundamentally modeled on) the dialectic of recognition within a hierarchical couple. Resentment brings Caliban to speech at the level of the symptom, a psychosomatic phenomenon that articulates and inflames the creaturely edges of his being. The pinches and cramps that Prospero visits upon Caliban need have no magical or physical source at all; they may simply manifest the passion born of enforced service, the stinging nettles of resentment as it flowers on the body of the creature inhabiting the edge of symbolization. The aches and pains caused by Prospero's commands are the bodily registration and primitive equivalent of Hamlet's "slings and arrows of outrageous fortune": they are a passionate inscription on the body of Caliban of his master's rule, the moon's continued hatred of the sun. "Thou shalt have cramps, / Side-stitches that shall pen thy breath up" (1.2.325–26): the phenomenology of the cramp that pens up breath with its suturing side-stitches describes the suffocating, claustrophobic response, the oppressive sense of internal constraint, that occurs in reaction to Prospero's archaic, noncontractual rule over Caliban. Caliban's pains also materialize in the form of the symptom, the protosymbolic dimension of a constraint that as yet bears no epochal force because neither master nor slave is partner to an agreement. Shylock's resentment emblematizes morality under the law—he is the arch-accountant of slights and grudges—and thus takes shape as bonds, contracts, and scriptural commentary. Caliban's resentment is fundamentally preliterate: he can speak but not read; he suffers not under the law but rather outside the law. Lacking access to legal types of accounting, the Creature keeps track of servitude in the only writing available to him: the cramped script, the tatooing side-stitches of the symptom.

Caliban's bodily suffering of resentment comes to speech in two more articulate forms of discourse: as curse and as counternarrative. The punctual, invective quality of the curse as well as its nagging, repetitive strain and its capacity for vivid if profoundly localized expression place it one step away from the symptom, as an act of minimal verbalization of the hieroglyphs of pain, a first gesture toward an act of imaginative creation around the insistent *nihil* of bodily distress. Caliban's counternarrative represents a more coherently symbolized articulation of bodily resentment into rational speech; in counternarrative the abrupt, pointed, explosive trajectory of the curse unfolds in the fuller form of story and history. Yet counternarrative also remains a limited form of political discourse in the play. Part of the pathos of Caliban's position vis-à-vis Trinculo and Stephano is his inability to communicate his counternarrative to them:

CALIBAN . . . Wilt thou be pleased to hearken once again to the suit I made to thee?

STEPHANO Marry, will I. Kneel and repeat it. I will stand, and so shall Trinculo.
Enter Ariel, invisible.

CALIBAN As I told thee before, I am subject to a tyrant, a sorcerer that by his cunning hath cheated me of the island.

ARIEL Thou liest.

CALIBAN (*to Trinculo*) Thou liest, thou jesting monkey, thou! I would my valiant master would destroy thee! I do not lie.

(3.2.35–44)

In a pattern repeated throughout the scene, Caliban attempts to relate his counternarrative, only to be interrupted by the sound of the invisible Ariel mimicking the skeptical voice of Trinculo. The result is inarticulate fist-fighting rather than the creation of a new political community around a shared narrative and set of values. If the symptom instantiates Caliban's bodily transcription of Prospero's law, the voice of Ariel represents the phantasmatic dematerialization of that same law, its ghostly dissemination into every cove and corner of the island, its effective disabling of any counterhegemonic movement.

Symptom, curse, and counternarrative: these are the oppositional forms that the passion of resentment takes in Caliban's discourse. Although they cover a full range of articulate speech and open up the possibility of the creature's own creativity, they share the structure of reaction-formation and do not lead Caliban into successful conspiracy, let alone toward a genuine political program or philosophy. Yet there is a more positive dimension to Caliban's speech: the passion of wonder that characterizes the creature's response to Creation. Caliban (not unlike Miranda) is a *wonder who wonders*, a creature capable of an affective response to the world around him.[5] The key passage here is Caliban's fullest poetic response to the island:

> Be not afeard, the isle is full of noises,
> Sounds, and sweet airs, that give delight and hurt not.
> Sometimes a thousand twangling instruments
> Will hum about mine ears; and sometimes voices,
> That if I then had waked after long sleep,
> Will make me sleep again, and then in dreaming
> The clouds methought would open and show riches
> Ready to drop upon me, that when I waked
> I cried to dream again.
>
> (3.2.128–36)

Caliban imagines a rain that would be the fructifying antidote to the violence of Prospero's storm.[6] In its positive evocation of place, Caliban's wonder also corrects the negative animus behind the passion of resentment. The passage thus opposes Caliban both to Prospero and to a version or aspect of Caliban himself, and it does so through crafting a response to the island's physical attributes. The passion of wonder affectively relates the Creature to the rest of Creation, finding a home for him there through the re-creative resources of poetic language. An emergent historical dimension structures Caliban's poetry of wonder, since the register of dream introduces an element of linguistic mediation and temporal recollection into the ekphrastic presencing that tends to characterize the poetry of place. When Caliban declares "when I waked, / I cried to dream again," he represents the island's beauty as a fundamentally lost dimension of his relation to it, a relation interrupted by Prospero's expropriative entry onto the scene but also made available to language by that same emergency. Wonder, that is, occurs across the divide articulated by resentment; it does not precede it as its lost

---

5. Critics have often commented on Caliban's special relation to the beauty of the island. Cf. Berger, 259; and Gillies, 702.
6. If "hurricane" is indeed the unspoken New World coinage behind the play's opening storm, as Peter Hulme has suggested (108), its transcription of "Huracan," Mayan god of storms, opens onto a world in which rain took both creative and destructive forms, and played a major role in the successive creation and decreation of the orders of the world. See the Mayan epic *Popol Vuh: The Mayan Book of the Dawn of Life*, trans. Dennis Tedlock (New York: Simon and Schuster, 1996). A fascinating project would involve comparing concepts of creation in *The Tempest* and the *Popol Vuh*.

ground but rather succeeds it as its refraction and aftermath, an imaginative arch thrown across the tempest's destructive breach.

Caliban's poetry thus indicates, in a more elaborated, world-making form, the creative potentials of the Creature himself: the *creat-ura* is a created thing who is himself on the verge of creating. This creativity is still, however, only an incipient one (the emergence or potential marked by the *-ura*), located at the origins of civilization, at the border of the real and the symbolic. The lovely yet random sound of a "thousand twangling instruments" evokes the classical motif of the Aeolian harp, in which the wind blows through chimes or strings in order to make a natural music; in this it is the primitive antetype of the "miraculous harp" of Amphion (2.1.82), whose more reasoned music had raised the walls of Thebes. The two harps echo each other but in different keys: whereas Amphion's harp is tuned to the political sphere, the Aeolian harp remains within the natural world it passively indexes. So, too, Caliban's *poetry of place* is not yet a *politics of the polis*. If Aristotle defines man as the *zoon politikon*, the Creature lives at the fold of this formula, between the zoo and the polis, at home in the taxonomy of neither. Here Caliban's wonder differs from that of Miranda, who marvels—first at Ferdinand, then at the other Italians—in response to the possibility of intersubjective relations, whether in the form of marital union or of integration in a larger community. It is an established determinant of her character that she is a *human* creature, and her wonder links her to the brave new world of both a universal and a particular humanity reconstituted in the wake of Prospero's tempest. Caliban's humanity, on the other hand, remains a question rather than a given in the play. This question is raised by the limited vector of Caliban's wonder: he is a mere creature who wonders at creation—without a reflex toward the Creator and also without recourse to a subjective or sexual relation. However full the island is to him, he remains alone on it. The island's plenitude masks its fundamental emptiness for him, its lack of a subjective partner for him within its natural abundance. Caliban's loneliness is a further sign of his imprisonment, of his exile *from* the island *on* the island, but it may also represent the possibility of another type of subjectivization, another model of humanity resident in the motif of the creature, that exists somewhere just beyond the conceptual limits of the play.

Man or Fish?

In the epochs of Christian history, the Creature lies before or outside the law. In *The Merchant of Venice* and *Othello* the dominant types of ethnic alterity are identified with the epoch *sub lege*, under the

law, their contracts marked by the Judeo-Islamic signature of circumcision.[7] The floating world of *The Tempest* reaches back to the
epoch of the Flood, *ante legem*, in which unredeemed Creation suffers a sea change on the road to law and grace. Like the Flood, the
tempest creates a state of emergency in which primitive instincts
emerge in a clarified form, leading to the reassertion of positive law
and the reinclusion of the sovereign within its normative order.[8] Caliban's island is postlapsarian, faulted by sin and potential monstrosity and not yet brought into the higher significations of Revelation
and Redemption.[9] The Creature, existing before the law yet in desperate need of its discipline, offered a fitting emblem for the new
peoples discovered across the Atlantic, since the *figura* of the *creatura* includes within its swampy matrix the possibility for both noble
savagery and incorrigible drives, for prelapsarian innocence and
postlapsarian lawlessness.[1]

Prospero's storm threatens Creation much as God's flood does,
and the rainbow announcing the marriage masque evokes among
other motifs the contract of reconciliation sent by God when the
Flood ended. As Northrop Frye noted long ago, "The masque has
about it the freshness of Noah's new world, after the tempest had
receded and the rainbow promised that seedtime and harvest should
not cease."[2] The rainbow, harmonious mixture of sun and rain in the
aftermath of a violent storm, announces "A contract of true love"
(4.1.84), the union between Ferdinand and Miranda taking on a

---

7. See Lupton, "*Othello* Circumcised: Shakespeare and the Pauline Discourse of
   Nations," *Representations* 57 (1997): 73–89; and Lupton, "*Ethnos* and Circumcision in
   the Pauline Tradition: A Psychoanalytic Exegesis" in *The Psychoanalysis of Race*, Christopher Lane, ed. (New York: Columbia UP, 1998), 193–210.
8. This is the emphasis given the story of the Flood in the Renaissance's greatest treatment of it, Michelangelo's Sistine Chapel fresco, in which salvation on the ark unfolds
   far in the background, and the state of emergency brought about by natural disaster
   dominates the foreground. As Howard Hibbard remarks, "We see brother attacking
   brother in order to survive, and elsewhere we see examples of what Michelangelo
   thought of primitive life and instincts—an interest that was common in Florence
   around 1500. Mothers and children, fathers and sons, husbands and wives are shown
   in extremis, saving and clutching, fighting and pushing. Yet one woman calmly saves
   her belongings amidst the rout. Noah, the chosen man, is seated up in his ark in the far
   distance: what we witness is the effect of God's wrath" (*Michelangelo* [London: Allen
   Lane, 1975], 132). On the history of Noah iconography, including Michelangelo's
   humanist treatment of the theme, see Don Cameron Allen, *The Legend of Noah:
   Renaissance Rationalism in Art, Science, and Letters* (Urbana: U of Illinois P, 1949).
9. The rabbis imagined the world before the Flood as an Eden spoiled by its own plenty:
   "The wantonness of this generation was in a measure due to the ideal conditions under
   which mankind lived before the flood. They knew neither toil nor care, and as a consequence of their extraordinary prosperity they grew insolent" (Ginzberg, I:152).
1. For example, the *Requerimiento*, the document recited by the Spaniards before each
   battle with the Indians, begins with a statement of common humanity: "the Lord our
   God, living and eternal, created the heaven and the earth, and one man and one
   woman, of whom you and we, and all the men of the world, were and are descendants,
   as well as those who come after us" (quoted here from *The Spanish Tradition in America*, ed. and trans. Charles Gibson [Columbia: U of South Carolina P, 1968], 58–60,
   esp. 58).
2. *The Tempest*, ed. Northrop Frye (Baltimore: Penguin Books, 1970), 15–26, esp. 18.

cosmic significance in the masque's celebration of "Earth's *increase*" (l. 110, emphasis added), its promise of plenty etymologically linked to creation.

In Genesis, God uses the rainbow to sign a contract, a marriage *ketubah*, not only with all humanity but with all creatures: "And the bow shall be in the cloud; and I will look upon it, that I may remember the everlasting covenant between God and *every living creature of all flesh* that is upon the earth" (Genesis 9:16, emphasis added). Accompanying this broader promise are the Noachide commandments, a set of seven laws addressed to all humanity that locate mankind within the order of living creation.[3] In this they differ significantly from the Ten Commandments, at once greater in number, more comprehensive in scope, yet more limited in their address, pertaining initially only to the nation of Israel.[4] Re-signing the work of Creation itself (of which the Ark, with its encyclopedic collection of animals, is a kind of summa), God's rainbow covenant with all creatures provides an enduring and comprehensive basis for Jewish, Christian, and Islamic universalisms.

Yet even within the biblical text itself, as well as in the traditions it has spawned, God's covenant with a universe of creatures almost immediately gives way to the first division of the world into the primeval branches of the nations, or *ethne*. From Noah's three sons, Shem, Japheth, and Cham, stem the subsequent genealogies of mankind, the so called Table of Nations, a roll of generations marked for the first time by national difference: "These are the families of the sons of Noah, after their generations, in their nations [*hagoyim*]; and of these were the nations divided in the earth after the flood" (Genesis 10:32).[5]

---

3. See Genesis 9:1–7. The Noachide commandments reiterate the commandment "Be fruitful and multiply"; give humanity sovereignty over all living things (who had taken over the world in the aftermath of the Flood); extend this sovereignty to the right to eat meat; forbid, however, eating meat from any living animal or consuming the blood of any animal; prohibit murder (including perhaps suicide); and institute capital punishment. Unlike the Decalogue, the Noachide Laws concern humanity's relation to other creatures, both the rights and responsibilities that accrue to human beings as sovereigns of the earth within the context of renewed creation. In the Noachide setting, the prohibition against murder might be seen as regulating man's relation to other men *qua* creatures. See commentary to Genesis 9:1–7 in the *Soncino Chumash* and the *JPS Torah Commentary*, ed. Nahum S. Sarna, 5 vols. (Philadelphia: Jewish Publication Society, 1989), 1:60–62.

4. See Exodus 20:1–14 and Deuteronomy 6:1–18.

5. The Hebrew *goyim* is translated as *ethne* in Greek and *gentes* in Latin. The original Hebrew word does not have pejorative connotations (unlike its modern Yiddish equivalent), but in the plural it does tend to be used of "other nations"—nations other than Israel. In the Christian tradition (e.g., Paul) *ethne* generally refers to the nations of the world united in Christ. The Table of Nations introduces the word *goyim* into the discourse of the Bible; as the *JPS Torah Commentary* notes, "Hitherto, all such accounts in Genesis have related to individuals. Now we are given a genealogy of nations" (1:67). This newly divided world is "of one language and one speech" (Genesis 11:1), but Babel will be built and destroyed shortly after. On the relation between the Table of Nations and the story of Babel that follows it (with reference to the passages' conflicted legacy of universalism), see Robert Alter, *Genesis: Translation and Commentary* (New York: W. W. Norton, 1996), 42–45.

Moreover, this Table is divided into three unequal parts: the progeny of Cham, whose sins may have included intercourse with his wife on the ark, was cursed by his father with slavery: "Cursed be Canaan [son of Cham]; A servant of servants shall he be unto his brethren" (Genesis 9:25).[6] In all three monotheisms Cham's curse provided an etiology of blackness as well as a proof text for slavery based on descent; taken together, the two uses of the story would provide a powerful rationale for race-based slavery.[7] If the arc of the rainbow embraces the Creature as the constitutive element of an everlasting covenant, the institution of slavery identifies the Creature as mere life, as pure labor deprived of rights within a system of national division. The Flood thus represents a watery dividing line between the shifting shores of universalism and particularism as they have been variously imagined, reconfigured, and reduced in the ethnopolitical legacies of monotheism.

From the broadest of universalisms—a covenant with all creatures—to the narrowest of particularisms—the establishment of slavery based on descent—via a sexual crime: this mapping of the Flood and the successive waves of its exegesis also describes the history of Caliban on his island. "[F]irst mine own king" and now decried as a "savage and deformed slave" of "vile race" by his masters, Caliban passes from freedom to bondage as the result of a sexual crime, the attempted rape of Miranda. Shakespeare had explored some of this typological territory earlier. Several critics have linked Othello to Cham via his "monstrous" sexuality, reading him as a positive instantiation of Cham's slavish blackness. As I have argued elsewhere, however, Othello is as much the typological negation and redemption as the inveterate repetition of Cham.[8] For example, Othello and Desdemona arrive in Cyprus, across the "enchafèd flood" (2.1.17) of a tempest-riled sea, *in separate ships,* a decision that, in delaying the consummation of their marriage, may also in the play's typological register prevent Othello from repeating Cham's blackening crime of intercourse on the ark. From this perspective Othello's sexual restraint reverses and redeems Cham's promiscuity, marking his probationary entrance into the universe of Christian brotherhood and its promise of freedom.

Whether understood as the typological redemption of Cham's curse or as its incorrigible replay, the Cham-like face of Othello

6. In Ginzberg's synthetic redaction of the midrashic tradition, the curse of blackness is tied to Cham's intercourse on the ark, while the enslavement of his progeny occurs as a consequence of viewing his father naked (1:166–67).

7. On the role of Cham's curse in the Judaic, Christian, and Islamic rationalizations of African slavery, see Robin Blackburn, *The Making of New World Slavery: From the Baroque to the Modern, 1492–1800* (London: Verso, 1997), 64–76.

8. For Othello as the typological overturning of Cham, see Lupton, "*Othello* Circumcised," 77.

binds his fate with that of Africa and its peoples, and hence with the history of the postdiluvian world.[9] Unlike Othello, Caliban appears to like sex in the rain; at the very least, his attempt on Miranda's honor occurred in the environs of a cave, linked since the *Aeneid* with tempestuous passions of a Sidonian savor.[1] Yet, whereas Othello's links to Cham place him within the order of law and history, Caliban resides just outside the rainbow world of ethnic groups, as primal cause rather than historic symptom or typological redemption of the continental divides brought about by Cham's transgressions. As creature, Caliban straddles the universalist and particularist faces of the Flood, at once included in God's contract with the infinitude of life (but as the measure of difference between the human and the inhuman) and deposited at the scandalous origin of national differentiation (but without clear identification with any racial stem or continent). In the epochal mapping of the play, the creature Caliban exists somewhere over the rainbow, on the far side of the law, an emblem of mere life who treads water in a flooded Eden, fallen from grace and not yet healed by covenant.

Caliban's enslavement, like that of Cham's progeny, is the consequence of a sexual act; in Prospero's account Caliban sought "to violate the honour of Miranda" (1.2.347–48). Caliban's response is ambiguous, neither a denial nor a confession, since his terms for understanding sexuality are at odds with those of Prospero:

> O ho, O ho! Would't had been done!
> Thou didst prevent me—I had peopled else
> This isle with Calibans.
>
> (1.2.348–50)

For Prospero and Miranda this response reinforces their view of his unregenerate nature, his status as Mere Creature, outside the borders of the human community. His desire to reproduce links him to the animals, to whom God grants the blessing of increase: "And God blessed them, saying, 'Be fruitful, and multiply'" (Genesis 1:22). Yet Caliban's morphological proximity to the human makes his advances on Miranda all the more heinous, placing him below even the bestial, in the category of the monstrous. According to Prospero, Caliban is

---

9. For identifications of Othello with the negative and monstrous legacy of Cham, see for example, Karen Newman, "'And wash the Ethiop white': femininity and the monstrous in *Othello*" in *Shakespeare Reproduced: The Text in History and Ideology*, Jean E. Howard and Marion F. O'Connor, eds. (New York: Methuen, 1987), 143–62, esp. 147; and Arthur Little, "'An essence that's not seen': The Primal Scene of Racism in *Othello*," SQ 44 (1993): 304–24, esp. 306–8.

1. On *The Tempest*'s extensive borrowing from the *Aeneid*, see, for example, Donna B. Hamilton, *Virgil and The Tempest: The Politics of Imitation* (Columbus: Ohio State UP, 1990).

A devil, a born devil, on whose nature
Nurture can never stick; on whom my pains,
Humanely taken, all, all lost, quite lost;
And as with age his body uglier grows,
So his mind cankers.

(4.1.188–92)

Caliban's physical deformity mirrors his moral limitations, which, in Prospero's analysis, are inborn and native to him. In this respect he resembles not so much the "swarms of living creatures" (Genesis 1:20) who are characterized by their buzzing multiplicity, their dizzying embodiment of pure increase, as the sublime singularity of Leviathan.[2] Leviathan, the rabbis suggested, was first created as part of a couple ("the great sea-monsters," in the plural, of Genesis 1:21); the female was later slain in order to prevent their disastrous reproduction.[3] From this perspective, Caliban's enforced celibacy is designed to prevent him as singular Leviathan from begetting a whole swarm of monsters.

Yet Caliban's desire to have "peopled . . . / This isle with Calibans" also evokes the Adamic dimensions of a more recuperative typological reading. After all, Caliban's turn to Miranda is not unlike Adam's desire for a mate. Having named "every living creature"—having brought into discourse the fullness of Creation—Adam nonetheless finds himself alone, the very copia of other creatures pointing to his own isolation.[4] So, too, Caliban, unique in his ability to apprehend the island's beauties, is not only *at one* with the island, a part of Creation, but also, like Adam, *alone* on the island, apart from Creation. To "people" the island with Calibans is to find himself in another, to realize his potential humanity by entering into the sexual couple of man and woman. It is significant here that Caliban does not speak of mere "increase" (with its etymological link to *creature*) but rather of *peopling*, rhetorically linking himself to the human kindness from which Prospero and Miranda would exclude him.

Genesis likewise distinguishes creaturely increase from human coupling. Although the phrase "Be fruitful and multiply" occurs in connection with both animals and humans, the rabbis noted that God simply "blessed" the animals with this dictum; whereas he directly addressed Adam and Eve in the form of a command: "God blessed them *and God said unto them*, 'Be fruitful and multiply'" (Genesis 1:28). This apparently minor variation emphasizes the fact of God's linguistic utterance, a scene of heteronomous command that forever reorients and displaces the sexual act it mandates by

---

2. On the swarming quality of mere creatures, see Zornberg, 7–14.
3. See Rashi, 1:5.
4. See Genesis 2:19.

removing it from the realm of the merely creaturely. What is in effect *descriptive* in the animal context (though it is an inaugural or creative description) becomes *legislative* in the human context, a demand from the Other that forever separates human being from biological *jouissance*.[5]

Caliban's urge toward Miranda links him to Adam's blessing and identifies him with Adam's sin. In both cases the turn toward woman is a move not only toward fuller humanity but also toward humanity defined as creatureliness, as marked by material urges and base passions. Woman represents the creatureliness of man; in her capacity for increase she separates out the *-ura* of the *creat-ura*, its capacity for generation and metamorphosis. In Genesis the urge toward woman marks the beginning of the fall into a secondary creatureliness defined by its growing distance from the Creator: Genesis moves from the order of mere creatures (swarming beasts and single monsters) to the human creature created in God's image, to the epoch of fallen creatures who frantically increase and multiply between Eden and Flood. In the typological imagination such a fall in turn implies the hope of redemption, and this chance distinguishes Adam from Leviathan, the human creature from the monstrous one, the rule from its exception.

Read in this light, Caliban's desire to "people . . . / This Isle with Calibans" aligns rather than separates Caliban and Adam, inviting Shakespeare's creature into the fold of "people" as such, into a common humanity marked by both passion and possibility. The arc of such a reading animates Caliban's final lines in the play, "I'll be wise hereafter, / And seek for grace" (5.1.297–98); it also echoes in Prospero's grudging recognition of Caliban, "This thing of darkness I / Acknowledge mine" (5.1.278–79), in which Prospero accepts both commonality with and responsibility for his creature. Yet, like Shylock's conversion, Caliban's passage from a position *ante legem* to a position *sub gratia* feels rushed, forced, and dramatically unprepared for; in both plays the typological reading remains somehow incomplete and imperfect, bearing the continued mark of the *-ura*. In both cases it is a *forced* conversion, in which entrance into the totality of humankind (conceived in Pauline terms as the potential unity of all nations, or *ethne*, in Christ) occurs at the cost of a felt singularity.

The universalism implied by such a conversion, that is, fails to account for the particularism implied by Caliban's desire to have

---

5. So, too, in Genesis only humanity is specifically created as "male and female"; sexual difference appears to be a dimension of *human* being that separates man and woman from other creatures. The *JPS Torah Commentary* notes: "No such sexual differentiation is noted in regard to animals. Human sexuality is of a wholly different order from that of the beast" (1:13).

"*peopled* / This isle with Calibans." "People" implies not only people as such—humanity taken as a whole—but also *a* people, an *ethnos, gens,* or nation of Calibans that would take its place among other *ethne.* Caliban, born on one side of the rainbow (before the law and before the ethnic divisions instituted by Noah's sons), desires through his Cham-like actions to cross over to the other side of the rainbow: to a world of covenant and contract but also to a world of peoples, in which his language and *bios,* or in Miranda's phrase his "vile race," would take on a historical identity. It is perhaps in this space of an imagined particularism that the order of the circumcised, called up in the play through the various markers of Semitism (Algiers, Tunis, Carthage), might finally take root. In the speculative space of an island peopled by Calibans—a national homeland called Calibania—the potential kinship between Othello and Caliban might finally gain some dramatic currency, some mimetic viability. This particularism is the end-point of Stephen Greenblatt's analysis, where it takes the name of "culture."[6]

It is precisely the particularism of culture, set against a universalism presumed bankrupt, that neohistoricist readers of Shakespeare have attempted to salvage, whether in the guise of Othello's blackness, Shylock's Judaism, or Caliban's indigenous claims. In the process, however, the religious foundations of the plays' conceptions of these positions are necessarily occluded, reduced, or secularized. Yet, just as Caliban never crosses over into grace but merely sues for it, so, too, Caliban desires to found a people of Calibans but remains radically singular. As with Frankenstein's monster, no female Leviathan joins him at the end of the play, and no brave new world springs from their loins. Shakespeare is interested in Caliban precisely insofar as he embodies the antediluvian moment before *ethnos,* insofar as he does not and cannot cross over into the post-Noachide Table of Nations. If, in Miranda's vocabulary, Caliban is of "vile race," his moral and physical deformities marking him for slavery, in conception and composition he remains one of a kind, a lonely monster rather than the representative of a nation or a race, a strange exception born in a state of emerg-ency. But it is here, in this singularity, at once Adamic and monstrous, that another universalism might accrue, one that would acknowledge the creature's difference without resolving that difference into an identity, whether subsumed in the macrocosmic totality of "humanity" or the local habitation of "culture."

Conceiving of Caliban as creature, Shakespeare manages to isolate within the idea of the human, forever divided between

6. Citing Vico, Greenblatt writes: "Each language reflects and substantiates the specific character of the culture out of which it springs" (32).

universalist and particularist strains, an elemental category of bare sentience which refuses to resolve into the homogenizing ideal of the one pole or the identitarian tendency of the other. That is, in response to the forced choice between universalism and particularism, the Creature takes shape as their negative intersection. As an Adamic figure, the Creature resides in a concertedly prenational, universal scheme; by definition, the Creature belongs to Creation, not to Nation. Thus the Creature would appear to belong in the general field of universal humanity. At the same time, however, he/it is not equal to Adam. The creature Caliban partakes of Adam's earthen-ness but is deprived of the *imago dei*. The creature Caliban shares Adam's sexual passion but, like Leviathan, never finds a mate. The creature Caliban takes up the burden of Adam's labor, the curse of the fall, but as slave, as pure labor separated from human freedom, who does not partake in Sabbath rest. In the chronologic of Cre-ation, we could say that Caliban lives in a perpetual five-day week, created on the fifth day along with the "great sea monsters" (Genesis 1:21) but living fundamentally unpartnered by the human-defining help-meet created on the sixth day, and finding his burden never alleviated by the suspension of labor instituted on the seventh. This fifth-day Creature cannot become a model or paradigm for the humanity of other creatures; he does not represent the genetic origin or primal design of either a universal or a particular stem. He is for-ever undergoing creation, forever *creatura creaturans*; he falls within the field of general humanity but only as the exception to its rule. This exceptionality in turn exiles him to the particularism of *ethnos*, yet the lack of a sexual relation, of a means of peopling—his both originary and enforced singularity—denies the Creature permanent residence there as well.

The world of Creatures constitutes an infinity rather than a totality since it is made up of a series of singularities that do not congeal into a single set. It is here, in this singularity, at once Adamic and monstrous, that another universalism, a universalism after culturalism, might accrue, one that would acknowledge the creature's difference without resolving that difference into the identity of an *ethnos*. By preserving Caliban as creature, Shake-speare manages to isolate within the category of the human, with its potential for both universalist and particularist determinations, a permanent state of emergency, of exemplarity in crisis. The crea-ture thus isolates a profane moment within the idealism of theology and defines in its very primitivism a possible face of modernity, understood not as the negation but as the remainder of a theologi-cal vision. If we want to find a new universalism in the play (as I believe, urgently, we must), we will do so not by simply reasserting that "Caliban is human" but rather by saying that "all humans are creatures," that all humans constitute an exception to their own humanity, whether understood in general or particular terms.

If we were to look to the visual tradition for a comparable engagement with the discourse of the creaturely—perhaps in search of dramaturgic cues that might help us to stage Caliban as Creature in the theater—we would do well to situate Shakespeare's Caliban in the dialectical space between the two great Renaissance artists of Creation, Hieronymus Bosch and Michelangelo Buonarroti. The Flemish painter's zoological imagination continuously turns on the exceptionality of the Creature, be it human or inhuman, black or white, hybrid or pure, plant or animal; his is a liquid world in which ponds, streams, and fountains teem with the swarming marginalia of mere life, with animated gargoyles set free to wander the pages of natural history. Bosch's God is the God of creatures, in love and hate with the obscene and wonderful variety of desiring, fornicating, breeding, and crossbreeding life. Michelangelo, on the other hand, endlessly seeks the exemplary—the statue behind the painting, the idea behind the statue, the logos behind the idea—while keeping each template of significance in luminous touch with the next, like God's finger on Adam's. The Sistine Chapel ceiling, which sets forth the history of the world from Creation to Flood, strives to equate the creativity of God with the *disegno* of the artist, mediated by the great human types of the classical tradition. Such an enterprise takes place on a stage largely devoid of flora and fauna, of creatures in their extrahuman dimension. The separation of light from dark (the primal act of drawing) and the creation of sun and moon (conditions for visibility) stand in for God's creation of the world before humanity, as if Michelangelo had strategically avoided representing nature in its promiscuous plenty in order to focus on the beauty and promise of the human form.

One can imagine Caliban struggling to pass from Bosch's world to Michelangelo's, striving to abandon the Flemish painter's botanical bestiary of mystical symbols for the clarity and dignity of the Italian's anti-landscape. At the same time, in trying to make that crossing, perhaps he stumbles on and, in the process, articulates the necessity of each field to the other, but only as its excluded term. As Ernesto Laclau has argued in his attempt to reclaim universalism within a post-foundationalist paradigm,

> Totality is impossible, and, at the same time, is required by the particular as that which is absent, as a constitutive lack which constantly forces the particular to be more than itself, to assume a universal role that can only be precarious and unsutured. It is because of this that we can have democratic politics:

a succession of finite and particular identities which attempt to assume universal tasks surpassing them; but that, as a result, are never able to entirely conceal the distance between task and identity, and can always be substituted by alternative groups.[7]

Or, in the terms developed here, the very intensity of Caliban's incarnation of the creaturely position, itself a kind of particularism-before-all-particularisms, a nondifferential specificity awash in a primal universe, allows him to begin to represent a universal function of political liberation into full humanity for the Trinculos, Stephanos, and Ariels who struggle alongside yet apart from him. That universe toward which he strives, however, remains intrinsically empty, the placeholder that enables but also renders unstable the flux of a democracy always to come.

The universe of liberated humanity is always just beyond the horizon—the horizon of Caliban's world but also of Shakespeare's. The full elaboration of its economy would require recourse to later moments in the articulation of typology and its heritage, not only in the works of Rosenzweig and Benjamin but also in the fundamental rethinking of Rosenzweig's paradigms by Emanuel Levinas. (While Shakespeare did not, of course, read Rosenzweig or Benjamin or Levinas, they surely read him.) Caliban's final suit for grace reveals the playwright still caught in the stranglehold of humanism's forced choice. Yet Shakespeare's play is part of the conversation about universals and particulars that grips us still. His decisive crystallization of a certain material moment within the theology of the Creature might help us find a postsecular solution to the predicament of modern humanity, trapped in the increasingly catastrophic choice between the false universalism of global capitalism on the one hand and the crippling particularisms of apartheid, separatism, and segregation on the other.

JOHN GILLIES

The Figure of the New World in *The Tempest*[†]

> The projected creations of primitive men resemble the personifications constructed by creative writers, for the latter externalise in the form of separate individuals the opposing instinctual impulses struggling within them.[1]

---

7. Ernesto Laclau, *Emancipation(s)* (London: Verso, 1996), 15–16.
† From *The Tempest and Its Travels*, ed. Peter Hulme and William H. Sherman (London: Reaktion Books, 2000), pp. 180–200. Reprinted by permission of the publisher. All notes are by the author.
1. Sigmund Freud, 'Totem and Taboo', in *The Pelican Freud Library*, vol. 13, trans. James Strachey (London, 1955), p. 121, n. 3.

The question of precisely how *The Tempest* touches on the New World is nowhere more pressing or more elusive than in this exchange between Miranda and Prospero:

> MIRANDA   O wonder!
> How many goodly creatures are there here!
> How beauteous mankind is! O brave new world
> That has such people in't!
> PROSPERO   'Tis new to thee.   (5.1.181–84)

A 'close reading' will help to a certain extent. Raised in isolation from European society, Miranda looks on human beings as a species for the first time, recognizing in them a 'world' of beauty, goodliness and utopian possibility. With no direct experience of 'human' (as distinct from native) depravity, she misses what Prospero sees: creatures whose potential is perpetually cancelled by their history.

It is a moot point which of these visions is privileged, that of 'wonder' (an emotion which Renaissance artists associated not merely with children but with poetry as prophecy), or that of 'irony' (the 'knowing' response to history purchased at the price of being perpetually consumed by it). What we are left with is a stand-off: each vision defining, haunting, provoking, yet disallowing the other. For a play in which prophecy has been the controlling mode, the moment is especially disturbing. How far back does Prospero's irony reach? How much of his own prophetic, masque-like design is called into question? Potentially, all of it. In the play's most puzzling moment, we have already seen Prospero effectively abdicate his rôle of *vates*—or prophetic maker of visions of chastisement and renewal—when abruptly terminating his masterpiece, the betrothal masque of Act IV. Logically, then, the power of irony is all but complete. And it would be complete in an aesthetic sense too, but for the fact that we experience the play from start to finish not in reverse, such that the irony is too belated and understated to cancel the effect of the previous four acts.

There is, however, something about the metaphoric structure of Miranda's 'brave new world' which goes uncomprehended and unchecked by Prospero's apparently all-embracing irony. This is that Miranda's phrase is displaced from its own historical and tropological roots, from precisely what a contemporary audience must have recognized as its primary referential horizon: the New World as historico-geographic trope. In addition to the words themselves, the very construction of this moment (a species of 'first encounter' scenario) inscribes it within New World discourse. Whereas in voyage literature from Columbus to Hariot, the encounter is between Europeans and New World natives, in Shakepeare it is an exclusively European affair. There are other differences. Where in voyage literature, the natives wonderingly see the Europeans as gods, in Shakespeare Miranda looks on the Europeans as 'mankind'. Where in the voyage literature, the Europeans wonder at the natives for their Edenic quality, their 'otherness', or in some way for bearing the mystery of the New World (its promise, wealth or horror); in Shakespeare, the Europeans view Miranda essentially as one of themselves.

This is not to say that the figure of the native is excluded from *The Tempest*, nor indeed from other versions of 'first encounter' in the play. In spite of the fact that 'the scene' of the play is described above the cast-list as 'an uninhabited island', images of the native are everywhere. Shortly after this moment, Caliban too gazes on the same group of Europeans, with the words, 'O Setebos, these be brave spirits indeed' (5.1.264); thus echoing his earlier wonder at Stephano as 'a brave god' (2.2.108) and, as it were, reciprocating Gonzalo's earlier wonder at the 'strange shapes' (3.3.20 SD) who proffer a 'banquet' to the famished European castaways. But if 'natives' wonderingly encounter Europeans in fictional moments that shadow the 'encounters' of the voyage literature, such moments are effectively divorced from the theme of renewal and from any 'prophetic' or rhetorically privileged order of 'wonder'. The exultant cry, "Ban, 'Ban Ca-Caliban / has a new master—get a new man' (2.2.174–75), with which Caliban follows Stephano, must, we know, end in the same disappointment as Caliban's earlier infatuation with Prospero.

In the very moment of being cited, therefore, the trope of the New World is subtly re-engineered. To employ an Aristotelian distinction, Shakespeare splits the *pathos* (or feeling) of the 'first encounter' scenario from its *ethos* (or meaning) which is accordingly recast. The *pathos* (wonder) is further 'sublimed' (to use an alchemical term) by its linkage to the theme of renewal and the prophetic or masque-like idiom in terms of which that theme is enacted. We may think of it as the idiom of Miranda—the name represents a gerundive form of the Latin *miror/mirari*, thus 'fit to be wondered at'. But the *ethos* of that wonder is altered in the sense that the native has been removed from its content, and is thus no longer part of its meaning. In Julia Kristeva's terms, he has been 'abjected', plucked from the heart of the mystery of renewal and left in a realm of the monstrous or farcical.[2] The historico-geographic trope of the New World becomes a purely fictional trope, but one that is intimately parasitic on its original, one in which the original energies undergo a sea-change into 'something rich and strange', but not something without historic and geographic meaning. It is this deep act of occultation at the

2. Julia Kristeva, *Powers of Horror: An Essay on Abjection*, trans. Leon S. Roudiez (New York, 1982).

metaphoric core of Miranda's 'brave new world' that escapes Prospero's irony. I am suggesting that the real relationship between Shakespeare's 'brave new world' and the historical New World is veiled in a way that requires an 'archaeological' reading rather than a 'close' reading to unpack (that is, to comprehend with a species of historicising irony beyond the ken of Prospero's irony). This in turn must begin with the 'invention' of the New World as a trope, a verbal and conceptual object.

As various accounts of it have now argued, the New World was a deeply unstable figure by the early seventeenth century. In his study of the evolution of the New World as concept, the Mexican historian Edmundo O'Gorman finds it harbouring two essentially contrary orders of value and meaning.[3] The first derives from the earliest usages of the term by Peter Martyr and Amerigo Vespucci. In Peter Martyr's redaction of Vespucci's *mundus novus* as *novus orbis*, the new geographic entity was posited as a 'world' in the ancient sense of being humanly inhabited.[4] While both *mundus* and *orbis* carried the same literal sense of habitation, the eventual preference for the term *orbis* further stressed the uniqueness of the new entity by its association with the ancient title for 'the world' proper, the *orbis terrarum* (or inhabited earth). As such, 'New World' strongly implied an *orbis alterius,* that species of entirely separate human and animal creation posited in ancient philosophy and outlawed by the Christian doctrine of the unity of creation.[5] For such reasons, the term 'new' was left deliberately vague. The New World might have been 'new' in a genuinely ontological sense, but then again it might have been 'new' merely in the contingent sense of only recently having come to European notice.

The second value which O'Gorman finds in the idea of the New World dates from the invention of the name 'America' by Martin Waldseemüller in the *Cosmographiae Introductio* (1507), where the New World is defined as a 'fourth part' of the world on the assumption of its comprising a 'continent' (America) in addition to the three continents of the ancient world.[6] This represented a novel (indeed contradictory) use of the term 'continent' (*terra continens*) because America was an island rather than a large land-mass abutting other

3. Edmundo O'Gorman, *The Invention of America: An Inquiry into the Historical Nature of the New World and the Meaning of Its History* (Bloomington, 1961).
4. *Ibid.,* p. 84.
5. *Ibid.,* p. 86. In *New Worlds, Ancient Texts: The Power of Tradition and the Shock of Discovery* (Cambridge, MA, 1992), Anthony Grafton points out that whereas 'Columbus used his texts to make the new familiar, to locate it,' Vespucci 'did the reverse. He emphasized that . . . familiar terms could not apply. He framed his whole account . . . as something new' (p. 84).
6. O'Gorman, *The Invention of America,* pp. 122–3.

large land-masses. Why then did America continue to be called a 'continent? By virtue, O'Gorman argues, of the deep elemental and ontological connection thereby implied between the two 'worlds'.[7] As one of four continents (as distinct from two worlds), America's unsettling novelty was brought under control. It was not an entirely 'other' geological and biological creation, just an unexplored part of the old one. Far from dropping out of currency, however, the term 'New World' persisted, though at the price of a semantic occultation. The New World now began to take on an historical and teleological dimension in the sense of fulfilling or completing the lost potentialities of the Old World—a sense anticipated by Columbus in a letter written during his third voyage when, drawing on the prophetic language of St John and Isaiah, he speaks of himself as a divine messenger chosen to make 'a new voyage to the new heaven and world, which up till then had remained hidden'.[8] While this second value of the term 'New World' might be modified in respect of various colonial projects at different places and times, its burden was to stress its ontological continuity, rather than its alterity.

In the long view of history, the second valency would eventually drive out the first. In the northern European experience, however, for all of the sixteenth century and much of the seventeenth, the two values would remain in tension. In world maps of the early to mid seventeenth century, the tension is harmonious.[9] America characteristically comprises a second 'world' in the sense of occupying the left half of the map and balancing the three continents of the Old World on the right. But it is also visually personified as a 'continent' in the iconographic border of the map, where it is joined by the personifications of Europe, Africa and Asia (the usual scheme is for the four continents to be arranged at the four corners of the sheet). The 'otherness' of America is further blunted by the frequent inclusion of the four Elements and/or the four Seasons in the iconographic programme, the implication of which is that the four continents and two worlds are linked by a fundamental 'natural' rubric. In voyage literature and colonial discourse (and their literary offshoots), however, the tension between the two values is more unstable, more dynamic, and more agonized. Earlier discourse tends to emphasize and even idealise the 'otherness' of the New World, whereas later discourse tends to elide and, finally, bury it. As this process (a process bearing uncanny similarities to the deep occultation within Miranda's 'brave new world') is best appreciated in a long historical

7. *Ibid.*, p. 140.
8. *Ibid.*, p. 100.
9. See my analysis of such maps in *Shakespeare and the Geography of Difference* (Cambridge, 1994), pp. 156–88.

view, I would like to illustrate it by reference to two studies of the iconographic shift within the New World trope.

E. McClung Fleming shows how the standard sixteenth-century European image of the Indian queen becomes (specifically in the context of North America, and in the course of the seventeenth and eighteenth centuries) an Indian princess, and finally (in the eighteenth century) a Greek goddess.[1] In the first stage of this evolution, America is an Indian queen: an heroic and gorgeous female nude, often with a feather headdress, jewellery, weapons (club or bow and arrow), and exotic and/or monstrous beasts (parrot, armadillo or alligator). In some versions of the iconography she is depicted in association with images of wealth (gold or silver), and in some she is depicted beside a severed head (suggestive of cannibalism). If the preponderance of savage (and generally Caribbean) attributes suggest her 'otherness', her attraction for Europeans is explicitly signalled by her wealth (in Anverian and London pageantry, she obligingly offers such wealth to the reigning monarch). Less explicitly, her interest for Europeans is suggested by her sexual allure. Of the psychic content of such iconography (as ambivalent compound of horror and desire), McClung Fleming has little to say. He is equally reticent when explaining the shifts to the second and third stages, beyond venturing the thought that some attributes were more pertinent than others to differing historical circumstances and geographic locations. Thus, the Indian queen's Southern American attributes—club, parrot, doubloons and silver-mine—were dispensed with because of their irrelevance to North America. When the queen becomes a princess, resigning her splendid independence to become a 'ward of the state' (a daughter or step-daughter to Britain) this is merely a recognition of contemporary colonial reality. McClung Fleming is likewise incurious about the loss of sexual frisson involved in the domesticating change from queen to princess.

What deeper pressures might lie behind such transformations? While not about personification as such, another study of New World iconography is enlightening in this regard. In her analysis of iconographic formations within the visual programme of the De Bry family's *Great Voyages* (a thirteen-volume compendium of major European discovery narratives, published serially between 1590 and 1634), Bernadette Bucher offers a kind of structuralist–psychoanalytic account.[2] For Bucher, the graphic image of the

---

1. E. McClung Fleming, 'The American Image as Indian Princess', *Winterthur Portfolio*, 2 (1965), pp. 65–81; 'From Indian Princess to Greek Goddess: The American Image, 1783–1815', *Winterthur Portfolio*, 3 (1967), pp. 37–66. See also Clare Le Corbeiller, 'Miss America and Her Sisters: Personifications of the Four Parts of the World', *Metropolitan Museum of Art Bulletin*, 19 (April 1961), pp. 209–23.
2. Bernadette Bucher, *Icon and Conquest: A Structural Analysis of the Illustrations of de Bry's Great Voyages* (Chicago, 1981).

Indian throughout this compilation evolves according to an informal but entirely consistent 'mythology' with its roots in the Protestant unconscious. While such images derive in the first instance
from eyewitness drawings (such as the work of Jacques Le Moyne de
Morgues in Florida and John White in Virginia), they develop
according to a logic which is independent of those sources. Thus, at
a certain stage in the series, we find images of Indian women with
sagging breasts. At later stages, we discover Indians (male and
female) with other types of physical deformity—ranging to outright
monstrosity. Where do these doctorings of the visual record originate? For Bucher, there are roughly two levels of explanation. In the
process of copying the original drawings into copperplate engravings, much characterizing information (colour, visual freshness and
idiosyncrasy, emotional toning) was lost. Accordingly, a complex
and nuanced visual record became flattened into a monochromatic
formula based on a simplified version of the Renaissance classical
nude. In this form, the Indians are classicized and idealized (their
bodies invariably young and graceful) in line with the myth of New
World infancy. While such images are in sympathy with the more
lyrical (and in general earlier) encounter narratives, they clash
markedly with narratives of a more aggressively colonial character.
Physical deformities such as sagging breasts originate in illustrations of these later narratives as ways of suggesting the depravity of
the Indians—as, for example, in a series of engravings of Indian
women preparing cannibal feasts illustrating the narrative of Hans
Staden's capture by the Tupinambas of Brazil. What is interesting
about such alterations for Bucher, however, is that they are systematic rather than opportunistic: that they appear in connection with
a range of different narratives as distinct from randomly varying
according to the requirements of individual narratives. Moreover
the system is increasingly word- rather than picture-driven; which is
to say that an original (and relatively small) stock of ethnographic
images is increasingly plundered, fractured and recombined in the
context of increasingly remote narrative and discursive pressures:

> Old materials going back fifty years and more are thus sepa-
> rated from their original settings and turn up again in new
> arrangements. We are, then, confronted with a sort of Tower
> of Babel of the Amerindian peoples. Physical types, articles of
> ornamentation, and hairstyles, all borrowed from different
> cultures appear together quite incongruously in a single plate.[3]

The babelesque image of the Indian is driven by a kind of unconscious taboo mechanism whereby the Indian, originally imagined as

3. *Ibid.*, p. 18.

a potential partner in relationships of exchange, alliance and marriage, is rejected via a mythological transformation affirming 'mutual incompatibility between the two peoples and a taboo of miscegenation and intercultural marriage.'[4] Several aspects of this conclusion are of particular interest for our purposes. In the first place, the progressive deformation of the pristine Amerindian female body opens up a rift within the ambivalence (horror and desire) figured by America as cannibal queen. Second, where the Amerindians are originally taken to be endemic to the New World (they are what make it a 'world' in the human sense, and their conversion by the European and potential partnership with him, justifies the Protestant colonization by contrast with the forcible seizure—or 'rape'—of the Spanish), they end by being extirpated from it. But the Protestant vision of the New World nevertheless remains that of a 'world', rather than a geographic blank indifferent to whether it is unpopulated or populated, or to the character of any population it may have.

Quite apart from the interest of their explanations, Bucher and McClung Fleming significantly bear out O'Gorman's elucidation of the bipolarity in the New World as representative object. All three posit a process whereby the New World is first apprehended as both *alter-* and *mundus-orbis* (a compound of 'lands and peoples'), and next apprehended as ontologically *idem* (same), though in the sense of a teleological extension (old-new). This second stage itself evolves through two stages. The teleological vision of renewal begins by including 'lands and peoples', but ends by excluding 'peoples'.[5] In the end only these are *alter*, but by this stage the land is supplied with new peoples (Europeans), and together they comprise another species of new world which can be less problematically viewed as an offshoot of the old one.

This process is exemplified over the long term in the Jacobean discourse of Virginia. Between 1610 (the probable year of composition of *The Tempest*) and 1623 (the date of its publication in the First Folio), 'Virginia' can be seen to undergo a figurative evolution anticipating that traced by McClung Fleming. Moreover, this evolution appears to have been pushed by the same order of unconscious mythologization—roughly the same psychic tectonics—as that detected by Bucher.

The historical 'moment' of *The Tempest* (c. 1610) coincides closely with a burst of sermons and pamphlets sponsored by the Virginia Company, promoting the colony as an object of messianic national

---

4. *Ibid.*, p. 102.
5. My reference is to Richard F. Thomas, *Lands and Peoples in Roman Poetry: The Ethnographical Tradition* (Cambridge, 1982). Conceiving a 'land' independently of its 'peoples' represented a complete departure from the authority of the ancient tradition charted by Thomas.

destiny and spiritual renewal.[6] In one of the most elaborate of these, the Reverend William Crashaw's sermon on 21 February 1609—before 'The right honorable the Lord Lawarre' on his departure as governor (in the *Sea-Venture*, whose shipwreck is echoed in *The Tempest*)—the goal of the colony is identified as 'the plantation of a church of English Christians there, and consequently the conversion of the heathen from the divel to God.'[7] This messianic destiny, insists Crashaw, arises from England's own providential conversion in the distant past by the 'Apostles and their disciples' (following on the civilizing of Britain by the Romans). It is for such reasons that, even though Crashaw flags the possibility of contextualizing Virginia in the genocidal discourse of the Old Testament Canaan, he prefers to do so in the messianic idiom of the Acts of the Apostles. Hence, instead of arguing that the Indians be justly extirpated as the Canaanites were by the Israelites, he argues that they should be converted in line with the covenant of Grace that Christ made with Peter. The sermon ends with a kind of messianic apostrophe to Virginia:

> And thou Virginea, whom though mine eies see not, my heart shall love; how hath God honoured thee! Thou hast thy name from the worthiest Queene that ever the world had: thou hast thy matter from the greatest King on earth: and thou shalt now have thy forme from one of the moste glorious nations under the sunne . . . But this is but a little portion of thy honour: for thy God is coming towards thee, and in the meane time sends to thee, and salutes thee with the best blessing Heaven hath, the blessed Gospell. Looke up therefore, and lift up thy head, for thy redemption draweth nie.

Appended to the sermon is a kind of Blakean dialogue between God and the nations, a scripturally inspired prophetic masque entitled 'A New Yeere's Gift to Virginea' (which I here reproduce in full):

> *God to Europe:* The Kingdome of God shall bee taken from you and given to a Nation that shall bring foorth the fruits thereof.
> *God to England:* But I have praied for thee that thy faith faile not: therefore when thou art converted, strengthen thy brethren. (Luk, 22.32)
> *England to God:* Lord heere I am: Send me. (Essay, 6.7)
> *God to Virginea:* He that walketh in darknesse, and hath no light, let him trust in the name of the Lord, and stay upon his God. (Essay, 50.10)

---

6. An account of these is given in Louis B. Wright, *Religion and Empire: The Alliance between Piety and Commerce in English Expansion*, 1558–1625 (Chapel Hill, NC, 1943), chap. 4.
7. Short Title Catalogue 6029, University Microfilms reel 727.

> *Virginea to God:* God be mercifull to us, and blesse us, and cause
> the light of thy countenance shine upon us: let thy waies
> be knowen upon earth, and thy saving health among all
> Nations. (Psal.67.1.2)
> *England to Virginea:* Behold I bring you glad tidings: Unto you
> is borne a Saviour, even Christ the Lord. (Luk.1)
> *Virginea to England:* How beautifull are the feet of them that
> bring glad tidings, and publish salvation! (Es.52.7)
> *England to Virginea:* Come children, hearken unto me: I will
> teach you the feare of the Lord. (Psal.34.11)
> *Virginea to England:* Blessed bee hee that cometh to us in the
> name of the Lord. (Psal.118)

What is particularly striking about both of these passages is the
depth at which the separate identities of land and people are elided
within the figure of 'Virginea'. This personification is of neither land
nor people, but a neophyte 'nation' conscious of itself as newly
emerging from darkness into light. As a national personification
'Virginea' corresponds to McClung Fleming's Indian princess rather
than his Indian queen, having exchanged her barbarous independence for tutelage in Christianity from a patriarchal 'England'.
However ominous 'England's' promise to the 'children' of Virginea
(the Indians) to teach them 'the feare of the Lord', the Indians are
not only included within the vision of renewal but constitute its origin and justification.

In Samuel Purchas's *Virginias Verger* of 1623, however, 'Virginia' is
very differently imagined.[8] While ostensibly just another 'discourse
shewing the benefits which may grow to this Kingdome from American English Plantations', Purchas's tract reconstitutes the English
title to Virginia independently of any ongoing tie with the Indians
(patently in response to the Indian uprising of 18 April 1622). While
an ongoing duty to proselytize is acknowledged (where that is feasi-
ble), the stress here is on Virginia as a vacant land rather than a
compound of land and people. Considering that 'every man by Law
of Nature and Humanitie hath right of Plantation' from God's command to the children of Noah to 'replenish the whole earth', the
English are allowed to replenish the greater part of Virginia which is
not occupied by the Indians, and to hold those parts which they have
already purchased.[9] In view of the uprising, moreover, they are
allowed a right of 'forfeiture'. At exactly this point in the argument,
Virginia is personified anew:

8. 'Virginias Verger: Or a Discourse shewing the benefits which may grow to this Kingdome from American English Plantations and specially those of Virginia and Summer
Ilands' (1625), in *Hakluytus Posthumus or Purchas His Pilgrimes*, 20 vols. (Glasgow,
1905), XIX, pp. 218–67.
9. *Ibid.*, p. 222.

. . . howsoever since they have beene perfidious . . . this per-
fidiousnesse of theirs hath further warranted the English Title.
Temperance and Justice had before kissed each other, and
seemed to blesse the cohabitations of English and Indians in
Virginia. But when Virginia was violently ravished by her owne
ruder Natives, yea her Virgin cheekes dyed with the bloud of
three Colonies . . . Temperance could not temper her selfe, yea
the stupid Earth seemes distempered with such bloudy potions
and cries that shee is ready to spue out her Inhabitants.[1]

While Purchas still wants to 'espouse Virginia to one husband, pre
senting her as a chast Virgin to Christ', the quasi-nuptial imagery
which had once functioned within a millennial discourse of conversion now becomes a coy invitation to repopulate:

But looke upon Virginia; view her lovely lookes (howsoever like
a modest Virgin she is now vailed with wild Coverts and shadie
Woods, expecting rather ravishment then Mariage from her
Native Savages) . . . and in all these you shall see, that she is
worth the wooing and loves of the best Husband.[2]

As a personification of the land only, we cannot tell exactly what this
Virginia would look like in terms of a graphic image, except that she
would not have any Indian attributes. We notice that her relationship
to the colonizer has also changed. She is no longer ward or neophyte
or convertee, but a prospective spouse—not so much of Crashaw's
'England' but of whichever English choose to settle. The sexual
allure of the Indian queen has returned but with an entirely new
logic: this Virginia is to be sexually possessed through legal espousal.

Where does *The Tempest* stand in relation to the New World
trope, and the symbolic shift we have found within different stages
and instances of it: 'invention' (O'Gorman), formal personification (McClung Fleming), informal visual iconography (Bucher),
and finally the Jacobean Virginia discourse? I suggest that the resonance is powerful and many-layered.

The earlier valency of the trope is ironically cited—'historicized'
we might almost say—at various points of the play. Thus, in Act I,
scene ii, Gonzalo imagines himself governing a 'plantation' of New
World natives according to the ancient formula of the 'golden age'
that had been routinely invoked in first encounter discourses. Two
specifically literary spin-offs of such discourse are registered here.
The phraseology of Gonzalo's primitivist fantasy is that of a passage in Florio's English translation (1603) of Montaigne's 'Of the

1. *Ibid.*, p. 229.
2. *Ibid.*, pp. 231, 242.

Caniballes' (1578/80). Its situation—a counsellor to a European prince suddenly conceiving the possibility of using the celebrated communism of the New World Indians as the basis for a radical critique of European institutions—is that of More's *Utopia* (1516). As Arthur J. Slavin has argued, the radical thought experiments of More and Montaigne are predicated on an 'American principle': the perception that ideal prehistoric forms of political organization posited in ancient poetry, philosophy and Natural Law thinking (and completely at odds with the contemporary or historical European political order) actually existed in the New World, and were therefore pertinent to political thought in a way that they had never been before.[3] Aside from the fact of its very existence, the quality that More and Montaigne most respond to in the New World is its radical alterity. Only in the glass of this *orbis alterius*—a space and a population unmortgaged to European history—is a 'utopian' critique of European society imaginable. Cited in *The Tempest,* however, the utopian mode becomes old-hat and just plain wrong-headed—their founding proposition (that the New World really is different) seemingly disproved by common sense and subsequent contact.

Successively later New World scenarios are also echoed in the play. In the 'several strange shapes' who prepare a banquet for the European castaways, we appear to have a variation on a slightly later type of encounter discourse. While these islanders are still able to call European society into radical question (as befits their utopian pedigree), their powers of question are limited. This is because, while 'different' from the Europeans—monstrous, speechless and yet of more gentle 'manners'—their difference is measured on an implicitly European scale of values, in terms of which they are judged to be inferior on the first two counts and superior on the third. What has happened here, then, is that the image of the native has shifted from being radically 'other' to being merely 'different' within a broad assumption of parity—putting the native in the position of European neophyte. Caliban's apprenticeships to Miranda, Prospero and Stephano echo yet later versions of this positionality. Miranda's efforts to teach Caliban language and Prospero's efforts to foster him as a kind of ward, seem to echo the Indian policy propounded by Virginia Company sermons contemporary with the play's composition. In this succession of 'moments', the position of the Indian shifts from being that of a radical 'other' capable of a wholesale interrogation of European social norms, to that of an apprentice European (a neophyte at the altar of civilization), to that of the apostate neophyte (Caliban).

3. Arthur J. Slavin, 'The American Principle from More to Locke', in Fredi Chiappelli, ed., *First Images of America* (Berkeley, 1976), pp. 139–64.

The radical opposition of Miranda and Caliban, however, represents something beyond the citations of earlier moments within the New World discourse, and beyond the Virginia discourse of 1610. What it figures is something like the final state of the New World trope in which the dream of a 'brave new world' is defined against rather than with or through the Indian. Neither 'historicizing' citation nor contemporary colonial ideology, it is more like a 'mythological' activity in Bucher's sense, the willed transformation of an existing repertory of meanings. The opposition has a peculiar character: on the one hand so 'natural' as to defeat question, but on the other hand provoking question by means of its very over-insistence. What I am suggesting is that Caliban's 'abjectness' and Miranda's 'sublimity' need not be taken at face value. The symbolism is open to a decoding, a reading such as that to which Bucher subjects De Bry. In place of Bucher's structuralist paradigm however, I prefer to make use of Julia Kristeva's theory of 'abjection' and 'sublimation'. Like Freud, Kristeva thinks of the 'personifications of creative writers' in terms of a 'primitive' projection outwards of internal emotional content (where 'primitive' has the sense of the psychologically archaic and occult).[4] Again, like Freud, she takes such projection to be motivated by an intolerable emotional ambivalence. Kristeva, however, understands 'projection' in far more radical terms than Freud. For her, the founding division between self and other has the character of a projection. The external world is only knowable once the self has been split off from engulfment within its own abjection: 'in the symptom, the abject permeates me, I become abject. Through sublimation, I keep it under control. The abject is edged with the sublime.'[5] It is then on the basis of the emotional economy made possible by this constant dialectic of affirmation and denial that the world becomes knowable—and acceptable. (An object which is too emotionally ambivalent is not acceptable to the subject and thus not properly knowable.) Roughly this, I suggest, was behind the metamorphosis of the New World object in the course of the sixteenth and seventeenth centuries. In the sheer shock of its original novelty, the New World was figured as ontologically 'other' and emotionally ambivalent in ways too disturbing to endure. The inherent instability led to a transformation whereby ontological otherness was refigured as ontological affiliation, and the ambivalent became split into figures of desire (the land, the dream of renewal, Miranda) and figures of abjection (the dispossessed savage, Caliban). Kristeva is suggestive for another reason:

4. Kristeva cites the same passage I cited at the beginning of this essay (see *Powers of Horror*, pp. 60–61).
5. Kristeva, *Powers of Horror*, p. 11.

namely that while the self represses the dialectic of sublimation and abjection by which its world comes into existence as an already cathected object, it is also condemned in some shadowy sense to remember.[6] What I should now like to suggest is that the sheer energy invested in stating the opposition between Caliban and Miranda, is in some sense haunted by a remembering—a faint but definite suggestion that the two figures share a common imaginative element, a common root.

Let us begin with how the opposition is declared within the play. Miranda is 'sublime' (a 'goddess' to Ferdinand, a 'nonpareil' to Caliban), beautiful, associated with a thematic of temperance, nurture, education, renewal, and finally with a masque in which nuptial imagery harmonizes with agricultural imagery, fertility with temperance, and Spring with Harvest. By contrast, Caliban is abject, physically and morally monstrous, intemperate, ignorant, futile, lustful and violent. Where Miranda's symbolism culminates in the masque of Ceres, Caliban's culminates in the 'filthy-mantled pool' (4.1.182) by Prospero's cell. The very symmetry of these oppositions, however, bespeaks a shadowy alliance, a primordial togetherness. Thus each is more 'natural' than the visiting Europeans (Caliban in a 'wild' sense and Miranda in a 'pristine' sense). Both inhabit the emotional element of 'wonder' (as wonderers and as objects of wonder to Europeans), both are structurally speaking children, both are wards of Prospero within his project of education and renewal. Their paths have crossed twice: first when Miranda teaches Caliban 'language' with the intention of conscripting him within the project of moral renewal; second when Caliban attempts to violate Miranda and is driven from her presence.

What, we might ask, is the burden of this earlier alliance up to the moment of its rupture? It points to a relationship of filiation of the order envisioned by Crashaw in 1609, a species of potential partnership such as that represented in the earlier volumes of the *Great Voyages*. Even in these terms however, the affiliation is highly ambiguous and correspondingly unstable. The project of teaching Caliban 'language' potentially inducts him into the civilized order itself, and from there into a potential marital partnership with Miranda. Even though already figured as conspicuously ineligible, his status as ward gives him a kind of parity with Miranda, and indeed with Ferdinand, the successful marital partner with whom Caliban is clearly juxtaposed (each is figured as a 'natural man', each is situated within a redemptive ordeal, each is shown bearing wood, each is figured as inherently

6. 'The abject from which he does not cease separating is for him, in short, a land of oblivion that is constantly remembered. Once upon blotted-out time, the abject must have been a magnetized pole of covetousness' (Kristeva, *Powers of Horror*, p. 8).

lustful). Yet if the potential nuptial relationship between Caliban and Miranda in some senses suggests that of contemporary Virginian discourse, there is also a striking difference: the sexual polarity is reversed. Whereas in Crashaw (and the historical marriage of Pocahontas with John Rolfe) the native is female and the European male, here the European is female and the native male.

Miranda, however, is not just any European. As an embodiment of wonder and exemplar of renewal she is heavily suggestive of New World symbolism—and not least for feminizing and sexualizing these themes. If her lack of savage 'otherness' is discounted, Miranda's first encounter with Ferdinand can read like a bowdlerized version of Theodore Galle's engraving of Vespucci encountering a naked female 'America': there is the same sense of mutual wonder, the same sexual polarity, the sexual magnetism (though without the sexual threat), the sense of mutual 'discovery', the sense of radical difference and mutual destiny, and the sea-shore setting.[7] There may indeed be a direct New World echo in this encounter. If it is true, as Frank Kermode suggests, that the 'curious burthen of Ariel's first song (*bowgh wawgh* in F) may derive from James Rosier's account of a ceremonial Virginian dance', then it would appear that this particular echo has undergone the order of alienating 'sea change' I have suggested in the case of Miranda's 'brave new world'.[8] The ceremonial dance of the Other is translated into a European courtly ceremony (hand-taking and curtsying). To adapt the description of 'altogether Estrangefull, and *Indian* Like' torchbearers in Chapman's *Memorable Masque* (1613), Ferdinand and Miranda are wonderfully 'Estrangefull' here, but hardly '*Indian* Like'. Again, if the imagined *mise-en-scène* rather suggests Inigo Jones's 'Sceane of an Indian shore and a sea' from *The Temple of Love* (1634), there is no equivalent for 'Indamora', Davenant's Indian queen. Masque indeed is highly suggestive here. Prospero stages the encounter literally as a 'discovery' within the idiom of spectacle ('the fringèd curtains of thine eyes advance'; 1.2.407) and frames it within a masque-like symbolism of death, transformation and rebirth. In its prophetic register, the theme of New World discovery was more generically at home in masque than the popular theatre.[9] Thus, Crashaw had inveighed bitterly against the stage representation of

---

7. Galle's engraving (c. 1600) is taken from a drawing by Jan van der Straet (c. 1575).
8. Frank Kermode, ed., *The Tempest, The Arden Shakespeare* (London, 1962), p. xxxiii. Kermode quotes the relevant passage from *Purchas His Pilgrimage* (1613): 'One among them, the eldest as he is iudged, riseth right up, the others sitting still: and looking about, suddenly cries with a loud voice, *Baugh, Waugh* . . . the man altogether answering the same, fall a stamping round about the fire . . . with sundrie outcries.'
9. For a useful account of New World masques in England, see Virginia Mason Vaughan, '"Salvages and Men of Ind". English Theatrical Representations of American Indians, 1590–1690', in R. Doggett, ed., *New World of Wonders: European Images of the Americas, 1492–1700* (Washington, D.C., 1992), pp. 114–23.

'Virginea' in his sermon, before fancifully staging her encounter with England as a masque.

While her discursive intertext is hazier than Caliban's, Miranda resonates far more strongly with the evolving discourse of the Virginia plantation than with earlier stages of New World discourse. Various aspects of her rôle point in this direction. The imagery of temperance and fruitfulness associated with Miranda suggests a similar imagery in the Virginia discourse.[1] Nuptial symbolism is common to both. Miranda's attempt to educate Caliban corresponds with Crashaw's idea of educating the Indians. Most important perhaps is the patriarchal and 'Natural Law' character of her own 'training', for which, in Prospero's account, geographic isolation is a positive advantage (1.2.171–4). More so than a conventional education in 'the liberal arts', this education takes the 'nature' of the pupil as its primary focus. What appears to be at work here is a Protestant philosophy of Natural Law whereby education is envisaged as a process of emphasizing the innate inscription of Natural Law in the heart, at the expense of a conventional socialization.[2] Thus, Miranda is educated in ignorance of identity, rank or privilege; heavily against the grain of a conventional aristocratic socialization. She responds to people for their 'natural' or moral qualities alone: Caliban himself she has cared for simply on the assumption of an answerably 'natural' receptiveness to the 'print of goodness' (1.2.351)—and with no hint of the socialized contempt which is the reflex response of the visiting Europeans. Ferdinand's ordeal on the island also has a Natural Law character, its added harshness explained by its function as a 're-education'. Authorizing all these educational projects is the patriarchal figure of Prospero.[3] The same complex of Natural Law ideas makes sense of the masque of Ceres, with its vision of an earthly paradise in which nature is simultaneously perfected by nurture but is also strenuously unfallen. (Ceres, mother of Proserpine, is gratified to hear that Venus and Cupid have not been allowed to re-enact the rape of her daughter—and hence the classical version of the Christian Fall.) It also seems behind the dream of renewal (nature is renewable if its primitive virtue is 'educable').

Natural Law thinking may explain the curious mix of failure and success in Caliban's education. Significantly, Caliban's overall failure

1. See my 'Shakespeare's Virginian Masque', *ELH*, 53 (1986), pp. 673–707.
2. For an illuminating account of Natural Law in the period, see R. S. White, *Natural Law in English Renaissance Literature* (Cambridge, 1996).
3. Patriarchal symbolism is very important to the Virginia discourse. Crashaw and others imagine the 'planting' of a godly commonwealth in the wilderness as equivalent to the feats of the Biblical patriarchs. An image of bearded and robed patriarchs tending plants adorns the title page of *A True Declaration of the Estate of the Colonie in Virginia* (London, 1610), a direct source of the play. Prospero's harshness in some way suggests Sir Thomas Dale's regime of 'laws moral and martiall' in Virginia.

seems to hinge not on an absence of intellectual ability but on the absence of any counterpart of 'Natural Law' in his nature ('thy vile race— / Though thou didst learn—had that in't which good natures / Could not abide to be with'; 1.2.357–59). It is no accident that it should be Miranda who pronounces the rationale of Caliban's slavery, nor that this rationale should be modishly Aristotelian (Caliban is a 'slave by nature').[4] The idea that the native is beyond Natural Law would of course directly contradict the root assumption of the utopian writing characteristic of an earlier stage of New World discourse: that the New World peoples were actually closer to Natural Law than the Europeans were. But if Shakespeare contradicts Montaigne here, he also contradicts the thrust of the contemporary Virginia discourse, based as it was on the assumption that the savages were reclaimable.[5] Denial of any Natural Law status to the Indian is fully in line with the transformation within the New World trope that we have been positing. By covertly Europeanizing this status in Miranda, indeed, Shakespeare manages to have his cake and eat it. The 're-education' of Ferdinand and his fellow visitors to the island suggests that the utopian function of the New World (as a 'natural' touchstone of civilization) is retained in spite of the reassignment of Natural Law status from the native to Miranda. The importance of Natural Law to Miranda's character—specifically the peculiar quality of her 'innocence'—is perhaps best illustrated by comparing her to her counterparts in Dryden's adaptation of *The Tempest* in 1670. Here Miranda's rôle is multiplied by three in order to furnish multiple opportunities for erotic titillation. Effectively, the Natural Law theorem of educated innocence has been translated into the Restoration syllogism of Wycherley's 'country wife'.[6] 'Natural Law' becomes the law of nature, or the commonplace sex drive. In the absence of a climate receptive to Natural Law belief, Miranda's higher innocence collapses into the merest pretext. Prospero's 'Temperance' league becomes a bit of a joke.

While Miranda's imaginative being corresponds to the most fully evolved stage of New World tropology—its most sublime and

4. An important source of Natural Law thinking in the period, Aristotle also provided the principal authorization for slavery in the New World. See Lewis Hanke, *All Mankind Is One: A Study of the Disputation between Bartolomé de las Casas and Juan Ginés de Sepúlveda in 1550 on the Intellectual and Religious Capacity of the American Indians* (DeKalb, IN, 1974).

5. In Robert Johnson's *The New Life of Virginea* (1612), the project of civilizing the Indians is conceived in terms of returning them to an aboriginal state of virtue from which they have degenerated since the dispersal of peoples after Babel. The combination of history and nature puts the Indians on a par with the primitive Britons.

6. R. S. White makes the point that the traditional Thomist idea of natural law (that human beings were naturally virtuous) and the Puritan assumption that natural virtue was radically accessible (in spite of the Fall) were made obsolete by Hobbes, who saw no reason for believing that virtue was innate to human nature (White, *Natural Law*, 'Epilogue', pp. 243–51).

'prophetic' possibility—Caliban's seems rooted in a much older imagery. Like the 'tower of Babel of Amerindian types' that Bucher finds in De Bry, Caliban has no coherent ethnographic model. The sole principle of coherence lies in his abjectness. It is this that accounts for the dominance of the older Caribbean and Patagonian elements over the newer Virginian. The Caribbean element shows up in his name, an anagram of 'canibal'. But we may well ask why, as 'cannibalism' is not part of his character or action. His mother's god, Setebos, derives from Antonio Pigafetta's narrative of Magellan's encounter with the Indians of Tierra del Fuego—for centuries, the most primitive and forlorn of Indian types (a type particularly influential in the De Bry iconography). Where Virginian elements do emerge, they seem either alienated from Caliban (as in Ariel's 'bowgh wawgh') or retrojected through the older imagery. Thus, the ironic conversion tableau in which Caliban 'kisses' Stephano's bottle—as though it were a font of 'language' (2.2.77)—would appear to echo a passage from Hariot's *Report*:

> Many times and in every towne where I came . . . I made declaration of the concepts of the Bible . . . And although I tolde them the booke materially and of it selfe was not of any such vertue, as I thought they did conceive, but onely the doctrine therein conteined: yet woulde many be glad to touche it, to embrace it, to kisse it, to holde it to their breastes and heades, and stroke over all their body with it, to shew their hungrie desire of that knowledge which was spoken of.[7]

Behind the strange Machiavellian ambivalence of this passage (so much more naked in Stephano), however, lies an older conversion scenario from Magellan's encounter with the Patagonians. In Richard Eden's translation it is subtitled 'The gyantes language . . . the gyant is baptised':

> The other gyante which remayned with them in the shyp . . . spoke al his wordes in the throte. On a tyme, as one made a crosse before him and kyssed it, shewynge it vnto him, he suddeynely cryed *Setebos*, and declared by signes that if they made any more crosses, *Setebos* wold enter into his body and make him brust. But when in fine he sawe no hurte coome thereof, he tooke the crosse and imbrased and kyssed it oftentymes, desyringe that he myght be a Chrystian before his death. He was then baptysed and named Paule.[8]

7. 'Hariot's Brief and True Report of the New Found Land of Virginia', in A. L. Rowse, ed., *Voyages to the Virginia Colonies by Richard Hakluyt* (London, 1986), pp. 107–36.
8. Richard Eden, *A Vyage rounde about the worlde* (1526), in Edward Arber, ed., *The First Three English Books on America* (New York, 1971), p. 252.

Shakespeare, we know, took the name Setebos from this account. Whether he used Harriot as well, he appears to have drawn the same moral: the savage is capable only of a debauched and Papist form of Christianity, even when it is preached by Protestants. Conversion thus becomes a farce on one side and 'policy' on the other.

One Virginian detail, however, stands out in Caliban's iconography. In the course of his exultant celebration of 'freedom', Caliban cries out: 'No more dams I'll make for fish' (2.2.170). Of this line, Sir Sidney Lee remarks that 'Shakespeare's very precise mention of Caliban's labours as a fisherman is the most literal of all transcriptions in the play from records of Virginian native life', and significant moreover as 'a vivid and penetrating illustration of a peculiar English experience in Virginia'.[9] Lee points out that Elizabethan and Jacobean colonists had expressed 'amazement at the mechanical skill which the natives brought to the construction of their fish-dams'; also that 'the secret of construction was well kept . . . and European visitors to their embarrassment, never learned it'.[1] More than embarrassment was at stake: Lane, Smith and Strachey all remarked on the colonists' dependence on the dams for food. Dam failure meant starvation, and 'was a chief cause of the disastrous termination of the sixteenth century efforts to found an English colony in Virginia'. The significance of this for Lee is that 'Caliban's threat . . . consequently exposed Prospero to a very real and a familiar peril.'[2] While this is true, the real significance is surely greater—namely that the logic of the idea is never registered in the play. The reasons are obvious. If taken seriously, the notion that Caliban possesses a technology unmastered by Prospero must have deconstructed the hierarchy of skill, power, value and right which is presupposed in Prospero's subjection of Caliban. It would, moreover, have made nonsense of Caliban's symbolic association with evil-smelling fens and filthy mantled ponds, which (particularly in the context of the imagery of artful land-drainage in the masque of Ceres) epitomize nature in its wild and potentially malevolent state (the fens supply Sycorax with her 'wicked dew'). For such reasons the idea is not developed. It is elided with Caliban's refusal to 'fetch in firing at requiring' in the very next line, and buried beneath numerous suggestions of Caliban as hunter-gatherer; one who snares 'the nimble marmoset', who gathers 'berries', 'crabs', 'pig-nuts', 'jay's eggs' and 'clustering filberts'. Finally, it vanishes into the common European impression that Caliban is himself a fish: he

9. *Elizabethan and Other Essays by Sir Sidney Lee*, ed. Frederick S. Boas (Freeport, NY, 1968), p. 297.
1. *Ibid.*, p. 298.
2. *Ibid.*, p. 299.

smells like a fish, looks like a fish and might be sold as a fish. The way in which the text suppresses what it also adverts—the Virginian discourse of Indian dams—is akin to a repression.

'History', writes Michel de Certeau in a reading of Freud strikingly complementary to Julia Kristeva's, 'is "cannibalistic", and memory becomes the closed arena of conflict between two contradictory operations: forgetting, which is not something passive . . . but an action directed against the past; and the mnemic trace, the return of what was forgotten . . . an action by a past that is now forced to disguise itself.'[3]

While generically a romance rather than a history, *The Tempest* (in de Certeau's metaphor) 'bites' the subject which it represents.[4] What is bitten or cannibalized? The earlier ethnographic repertory, the 'beautiful' Amerindian body which Montaigne projects from that repertory, any possibility of representing the Amerindian without projection or 'prejudice' (which is to say outside of the available language).[5] What need is fed by this 'biting'? The inner compulsion of the New World trope to divest itself of the savage 'Other', precisely the dissimulation which escapes Prospero's ironic surveillance. If all this is to suggest that the play is a strategic 'forgetting' or (worse) propaganda in the service of early European colonialism, it is also to suggest something more.[6] There is, as Peter Hulme reminds us, a 'difference' between Prospero's play and Shakespeare's: namely that '*The Tempest* stages Prospero's staging of his play'.[7] To the extent that this is so, we have an uncanny sense of the repressed content of Prospero's play returning to 're-bite' (to de-form, undo, haunt) that which represses it.

Suggestions of this are legion. Prospero is linked to Sycorax by a subterrene set of correspondences: each a sorcerer, each an enslaver of Ariel, each an echo of Medea, each in some sense a parent of

3. Michel de Certeau, 'Psychoanalysis and Its History', in his *Heterologies: Discourse on the Other* (Manchester, 1986), pp. 3–16.
4. De Certeau, 'Psychoanalysis and Its History', p. 3.
5. See de Certeau's suggestive essay 'Montaigne's "Of Cannibals": The Savage "I"', in *Heterologies*, pp. 67–79. On the absence of objective reportage, Grafton observes that whereas 'from the standpoint of the modern historian of the Great Encounter . . . pure accounts—straight transcripts of Columbian logs and Indian speeches—would be far more valuable than the mediated knowledge their texts offer . . . no such texts could in fact have been produced in the early modern world (if indeed they could be produced now)' (*New Worlds, Ancient Texts*, p. 147).
6. For complex and nuanced accounts of 'forgetting' in *The Tempest*, see Jonathan Baldo, 'Exporting Oblivion in *The Tempest*', *Modern Language Quarterly*, 56/2 (June 1995); pp. 111–44; Mary Fuller, 'Forgetting the *Aeneid*', *American Literary History*, 4 (1992), pp. 517–37.
7. Peter Hulme, *Colonial Encounters: Europe and the Native Caribbean, 1492–1797* (London, 1986), p. 118.

Caliban. Prospero's gnomic acknowledgement of Caliban ('this thing of darkness I / Acknowledge mine'; 5.1.278–79) hints at deeper wells of complicity, of remorse—both personal and historical—than we can ever say (De Certeau's 're-bite', *re-mordre*, puns directly on 'remorse', *remords*).[8] Miranda too seems haunted, her notional sublimity jarring with her invocation of the Aristotelian argument for 'natural' slavery. For his part, Caliban's very abjectness calls forth poetry, beauty, pathos—and a devastating sense of 'natural' justice. The sheer overdetermination of Caliban's monstrosity leads to the continuing enigma of his appearance. Behind the enigma lurks something deeper: the physical appearance which is the master sign of Caliban's existence is actually a relational term whereby Caliban appeals over the heads of his fellow characters to audiences past and present, First World and Third.

The most telling of all disjunctions between Prospero's play and Shakespeare's, however, is provided by Prospero himself. Famously, the symbolic centre of the play enshrines an enigma: the 'strange hollow and confused noise' (4.1.138 SD) to which the masque of Ceres 'heavily' dissolves. If the masque of Ceres represents the crowning moment of the theme of renewal—the high point of its prophetic mode—then the failure to consummate it represents something deeper, unplumbable, a deliberate *aporia*. The moment is unpackable to certain levels. There is Prospero's own explanation: 'I had forgot the foul conspiracy / Of the beast Caliban and his confederates / Against my life. The minute of their plot / Is almost come' (4.1.139–42). But a scheduling error is hardly sufficient. Then there is a formalistic explanation to the effect that the masque has to be truncated to allow the play to continue as a play. Yet this explanation fails to take account of the fact that masque has been the dominant mode of the play in any case up to this moment, and it ignores the deliberate inversiveness of the moment—the way in which Prospero's 'beating mind' and 'distempered' visage represent a resurgence of the chaotic imagery of tempestuousness and disordered passion over the hard-won victory of music, harmony, temperance and 're-education'. Finally, there is the 'our revels now are ended' speech (4.1.148–63), in which human life and 'the great globe itself' are likened to a masque, but from a counter-masque standpoint in which vision collapses into its 'baseless fabric' and prophecy shrinks into a dream. We are left, then, with the *aporia,* the figure of unknowing. We can, however, say two things. First, the ambition to raise human

---

8. *Le Nouveau Petit Robert* (Paris, 1993) loosely defines *remords* as 'anguish accompanied by shame caused by consciousness of wrongdoing'. This is shown as having derived in 1170 from *re+mordre*. *Remordre* is defined as (1) 'to inflict suffering by means of remorse' (2) *mordre de nouveau* or 'bite once more'.

nature to some prelapsarian yet millennial status is exposed as 'utopian' (an effect reinforced by the prayerful entreaty of the Epilogue). Second, Caliban's intrusion is in some way material to this new humility, this grounded refusal of the language of vision.

What this building-up and emptying-out of utopia also suggests is that there is no going back. The dream of renewal, once entertained within history—that of Prospero's island or Caliban's nature or the New World—is irreversible. The haunted utopia is still utopia. The ground once having been cleared will never revert to forest. The New World, once having been conjured forth, will never collapse back into the Old. It is in the depth at which this most romance-like of Shakespeare's plays encodes the metahistorical logic of the New World trope as a process of continual historical becoming that it out-stares (out-bites?) the remorseful and nostalgic archaeologies of the twentieth century.

MICHAEL NEILL

"Noises, / Sounds, and sweet airs": The Burden of Shakespeare's *Tempest*†

When Caliban, responding to his companions' terror at the sound of an invisible pipe and tabor, reassures them that "the isle is full of noises" (3.2.128),[1] he draws attention to an aspect of Shakespeare's dramaturgy that is easily disregarded: uniquely among the plays of its time, *The Tempest* is equipped with an elaborate sound track, in which episodes of violent, discordant, and chaotic noise are set against the harmonious songs and instrumental music performed by Ariel and his consort of spirits.[2] Following the work of Enid Welsford and, more recently, Stephen Orgel, it has been usual to connect these effects to the play's conspicuous affiliations with the masque.[3] But insofar as *The Tempest* constitutes a challenge to the spectacular attractions of this courtly genre, it does so not by offering to

---

† From *Shakespeare Quarterly* 59: 1 (2008): 36–59. Reprinted by permission of the author. Notes are by the author unless otherwise specified.

1. Citations from *The Tempest* will be from the edition prepared by Stephen Orgel (Oxford: Clarendon Press, 1987). For the quotation in the title of this essay, see 3.2.133–34. Throughout, emphases added to quotations (in boldface italic type for stage directions or in italic type for running text) are my own.

2. For a good analysis of the play's elaborately patterned aesthetic, see Mark Rose, *Shakespearean Design* (Cambridge, MA: Belknap Press of Harvard UP, 1972).

3. See Enid Welsford, *The Court Masque: A Study in the Relationship between Poetry and the Revels* (Cambridge: Cambridge UP, 1927); Stephen Orgel, *The Jonsonian Masque* (Cambridge, MA: Harvard UP, 1961); and David Lindley, ed., *The Court Masque* (Manchester: Manchester UP, 1984).

meet the court theater on its own ground—the Blackfriars could never hope to match the extravagant resources that Inigo Jones was able to exploit at court—but by insisting on the superiority of the aural tradition. Early modern playgoers, after all, went to "hear" a play rather than to see it; they were "auditors" or "audience" before they were "spectators." Instead of seeking to gratify the eyes of its public, *The Tempest* reasserts the primacy of their ears.

It is not, of course, that this play entirely eschews spectacle; indeed, *The Tempest* begins with a scene of storm and shipwreck that might appear calculated to vie with the scenic extravagance of masque. The storm called for in the opening stage direction—one for which there are very few precedents in the canon[4]—can easily seem to be ushering in a display of spectacular theatricality; however, in a printed text that is unusually punctilious in its attentiveness to stage effects, what is particularly striking about the wording is its emphasis upon the aural: "*A tempestuous **noise** of thunder and lightning **heard**"* (1.1.0 SD). In stark contrast to the lavish evocations of visual magnificence that preface Ben Jonson's masque texts, for example, this direction imagines a storm primarily in acoustic terms—so that even lightning is something to be *heard* rather than seen.[5] It is true that we have no means of knowing for certain to what extent the stage directions in the Folio were scripted by the dramatist himself; it seems likely that in their present form they were supplied by the scribe—probably Ralph Crane—who prepared the *Tempest* manuscript for the printer. But, whatever their origin, there is general agreement that the stage directions consistently attempt to recreate the experience of actual performance.[6] The island world

4. Typically, Shakespeare's plays begin with a simple entry for the characters who are to initiate the dialogue: apart from the martial music that introduces *Coriolanus* and several of the history plays and the "dying fall" of the consort that opens *Twelfth Night* (1.1.4), the only precedent for such a nonverbal opening is provided by the "*Thunder and lightning*" at the beginning of *Macbeth* (1.1 SD). With the exception of *The Tempest* (see n. 1 above), quotations from Shakespeare's works follow *The Riverside Shakespeare*, 2d ed., gen. ed. G. Blakemore Evans (Boston: Houghton Mifflin, 1997)

5. Orgel's note in the Oxford edition insists that the wording "need not imply that no visual effects accompanied the sound of thunder," since we know that "Jacobean theatres had lightning machines" (97n); so that here, as in *Macbeth*, the spectacle of the storm was to be as important as its sound. It is difficult to believe, however, that such machines can have been particularly effective in a theater where darkness had to be imagined by the audience; and Lindley (citing Andrew Gurr) suggests that "the SD's *heard* may accurately reflect a performance in which only off-stage noise was employed." See *The Tempest*, New Cambridge Shakespeare, ed. David Lindley (Cambridge: Cambridge UP, 2002), 1.1 SD note.

6. See Orgel, ed., 56–58; and Peter Holland, "The Shapeliness of *The Tempest*," *Essays in Criticism* 45 (1995): 208–29, esp. 208. In their Arden3 edition of *The Tempest* (Walton-on-Thames: Thomas Nelson, 1999), Virginia Mason Vaughan and Alden T. Vaughan discuss Crane's role and conclude that, while the directions appear to be the work of someone less familiar with theatrical technicalities than Shakespeare must have been, they nevertheless give a good sense of the play's original staging (126–30).

they evoke is one whose landscape is, as it were, mapped by sound. As though advertising the superior power of hearing over seeing, Shakespeare's language repeatedly calls attention to acoustic effects, underlining the extent to which the meaning of his play—what, to use its own terminology, we might call its "burden"—is expressed through the orchestration of inarticulate sound as much as through the eloquence of speech.[7]

I

> She tries a test that seems to work when she is writing: to send out a word into the darkness and listen for what kind of sound comes back. Like a foundryman tapping a bell.
> —J. M. Coetzee, *Elizabeth Costello*[8]

In the final scene of *The Tempest,* as he prepares to "discase" himself before his erstwhile enemies (5.1.85), Prospero famously renounces the "rough magic" (l. 50) that has sustained his authority on the island:

> I'll break my staff,
> Bury it certain fathoms in the earth,
> And deeper than did ever plummet sound
> I'll drown my book.
>   (ll. 54–57)

The sheer familiarity of these lines, combined with their apparent simplicity, easily disguises the complex allusiveness of their verbal play: as the carefully placed "bury" suggests, Prospero's promise to break his staff, while it involves the symbolic evacuation of its magical power, also recalls the ritual performed by the officers of great households at their masters' interment, when, breaking their staffs of office over their heads, they would throw them into the grave to signify release from the burden of office and the surrender of their authority to the power of death.[9] Thus, the promised gesture emphasizes how, even as he prepares to resume the weight of his ducal responsibilities, Prospero simultaneously engages in an act of unburdening, readying himself for the self-mortification of an old age in which "Every third thought shall be my grave" (l. 313). At the same time, his use of "fathoms" (a measurement more usually applied to water than to earth) anticipates the "plummet" and "drown" of the following lines, setting up a cluster of associations that reaches back

---

7. For further commentary on the play's sound effects, see Vaughan and Vaughan, ed., 9, 17–18; and Lindley, ed., *The Tempest,* 18–25.
8. J. M. Coetzee, *Elizabeth Costello* (New York: Penguin Books, 2003), 219.
9. Michael Neill, *Issues of Death: Mortality and Identity in English Renaissance Tragedy* (Oxford: Clarendon Press, 1997), 279.

to the shipboard world of the opening scene, to the apparent drowning of its frantic passengers and crew and to the transformative magic wrought in the mysterious aquatic depths of Ariel's "Full fathom five" (1.2.395–401). That song, as it plumbs the depth of Ferdinand's grief, "sounds" in the same double sense that may be glimpsed when the "deeper . . . sound[ing]" of Prospero's plummet gives way to the deep sound of the *"Solemn music"* that ushers the "spell-stopped" courtiers into Prospero's charmed circle (ll. 387, 404; 5.1.56, 57 SD, 61).[1] The elaborate braiding of puns and quibbles that links these episodes does not stop there; for Ariel's song, as it "remember[s]" Ferdinand's "drowned father," imitates the tolling of Alonso's death knell (1.2.403–06), its heavy note anticipating the weight of the king's own grief for his lost son in the following scene (2.1). It is from this sorrow, and the guilt that precipitated it, that Prospero will finally liberate his penitent captive:

ALONSO   But O, how oddly will it sound that I
            Must ask my child forgiveness!
PROSPERO   There, sir, stop.
            Let us not burden our remembrances with
            A heaviness that's gone.
                                            (5.1.197–200)

The unburdening that Prospero offers to his former enemy is inseparable from that which he plans for himself: only when Alonso is released from the "heaviness" of his past crime can Prospero himself be freed from the weight of his "sea-sorrow" (1.2.170) and from the burden of vindictive remembrance that he—like those revenge protagonists whose plots he at once repeats and redirects—has carried through the play. Thus, the unburdening of Alonso looks forward to the final release for which Prospero will appeal in the epilogue, where his longing to be *"relieved* by prayer" (Epilogue 16) involves not merely the "free[ing] . . . from sorrow" with which *The Oxford English Dictionary* glosses this passage, but the "[freeing] from . . . any task or burden" which is another meaning of "relieve."[2]

The seemingly accidental conjunction of "sound" and "burden" in Prospero's exchange with Alonso picks up a conspicuous, but largely unremarked, piece of wordplay from the first three acts. The motif of burdens and unburdening is given particular prominence in two scenes (2.2 and 3.1), one carefully mirroring the other, that are at the exact center of the play's action. In these scenes, Caliban

---

1. For a general account of the relationship between sound, sounding, and "deep subjectivity" in early modern culture, see Wes Folkerth, *The Sound of Shakespeare* (London: Routledge, 2002), 25–33.

2. *The Oxford English Dictionary*, 2nd ed. (Oxford: Oxford UP, 1989), s.v. "relieve, v.," 3a, 4c. *OED Online*, http://dictionary.oed.com (accessed 7 January 2008).

and Ferdinand (characters linked by their common desire for
Miranda) are shown laboring under the penitential tasks that Prospero has imposed upon them. Each hefts a bundle of logs, firewood
designed for their master's cell; each receives unexpected succor in
his labors; and each concludes his scene by claiming a species of
enfranchisement. Act 2, scene 2, opens with the entry of Caliban,
bowed under *"a burden of wood"* (2.2.0 SD) and ends with his defiant
repudiation of bondage in a song that, in performance, traditionally
announces the discarding of his load:

> A plague upon the tyrant that I serve!
> I'll bear him no more sticks. . . .
> No more dams I'll make for fish,
> Nor fetch in firing
> At requiring,
> . . .'Ban, 'Ban, Ca-Caliban
> Has a new master—get a new man!
> Freedom, high-day! High-day, freedom! Freedom, high-day,
>   freedom!
>
> (ll. 153–54, 170–72, 174–77)

If Caliban's burden is imposed on him as a penance for his rebellion against Prospero's authority and his attempted violation of
Miranda's maidenhead, Ferdinand also suffers under the weight of
past crime and present desire: his father's complicity in Antonio's
palace coup opens him to the charge of being a usurper and a traitor
(1.2.452, 459, 468), while his fascination with Miranda's virgin body
(ll. 426, 446) exposes him to the suspicion that he may be no better
than his monstrous counterpart: "To th' most of men this is a Caliban," declares Prospero, "And they to him are angels" (ll. 479–80).
Ferdinand enters at the beginning of 3.1 visibly bound in the same
condition of "wooden slavery" (l. 62) as Caliban, *"bearing a log"*
(3.1.0 SD)—a "mean task" that would be "heavy" to him (in both
senses of the word), did not Miranda's sympathetic tears lighten its
"baseness" (ll. 4, 5, 12). Just as Caliban claims his "freedom" by
transferring his allegiance to the "wondrous" Stephano (2.2.176–
77, 155), so Ferdinand plights his troth to the "wonder," Miranda,
"with a heart as willing / As bondage e'er of freedom" (1.2.425,
3.1.88–89).

The significance of these two carefully juxtaposed episodes seems
to answer (at first sight, anyway) to a straightforwardly emblematic
reading. Such a reading is suggested partly by the recollection of an
Old Testament episode in which another powerful patriarch, Joshua,
condemned the deceitful inhabitants of Gibeon, who had offered
themselves as his "servants," to become "hewers of wood, & drawers
of water" (Josh. 9:8–27, esp. 11, 23); it is reinforced by Shakespeare's

self-conscious troping of the Christian paradox of freedom-in-service.[3] This paradox is turned on its head when Caliban's determination to free himself from "the tyrant that I serve" (2.2.153) results in his subjection to an even more humiliating servitude, as he swears to follow the drunken Stephano, minister to his needs, and "get [him] wood enough" (l. 152). Ferdinand yields to a different form of subordination, but the parallel between the two logbearers is emphasized when the prince makes a "humble" gesture of submission, kneeling before his chosen "mistress" (3.1.87, 86) in a repetition of Caliban's gesture of subservience to his "new master" (2.2.173). However, Ferdinand's loving submission to Miranda transforms the degrading servitude imposed on him by Prospero into an expression of the voluntary self-abasement that a chivalric lover owed to his lady—a form of "service" resembling the "perfect freedom" promised to the faithful by the Book of Common Prayer:

> The very instant that I saw you did
> My heart fly to your service, there resides
> To make me slave to it, and for your sake
> Am I this patient log-man.
>   (3.1.64–67)

The prince's insistence on Miranda's ability to transmute his "heavy . . . labours" into "pleasures" (ll. 5–7) recalls Christ's reassurance that "my yoke is easie, and my burden light" (Matt. 11:30), while her reciprocal determination to "be [his] servant" and to "bear [his] logs the while" (ll. 85, 24) is reminiscent of St. Paul's injunction that the faithful should "beare . . . one anothers burden" (Gal. 6:2).[4]

If the contrasting liberations of Caliban and Ferdinand look forward to the decisive manumissions and psychological unburdenings of the final scene, they also glance back at Prospero's account of his initial deliverance after he and his small daughter were cast adrift by his usurping brother. In the course of his protracted exposition, Prospero remembers the near despair from which the young Miranda saved him, as the winds drove their "rotten carcase of a butt" (1.2.146) toward the island:

3. Michael Neill, *Putting History to the Question: Power, Politics, and Society in English Renaissance Drama* (New York: Columbia UP, 2000), 13–48, esp. 24. The paradox of service as "perfect freedom," which received its classic expression in the Second Collect for Morning Prayer from Cranmer's prayer book, is discussed at length by David Evett in *Discourses of Service in Shakespeare's England* (London: Palgrave Macmillan, 2005), 1–16; and David Schalkwyk in "Between Historicism and Presentism: Love and Service in *Antony and Cleopatra* and *The Tempest*," *Shakespeare in Southern Africa* 17 (2005): 1–17, esp. 13–15.
4. All biblical citations are taken from the Geneva Bible, the version best known to Shakespeare, and are made parenthetically in the text. See *The Geneva Bible: A Facsimile of the 1560 Edition*, intro. Lloyd E. Berry (Madison: U of Wisconsin P, 1969).

> Thou didst smile,
> Infusèd with a fortitude from heaven,
> When I have decked the sea with drops full salt,
> *Under my burden groaned,* which raised in me
> An *undergoing* stomach to *bear up*
> Against what should ensue.
>
> (ll. 153–58)

"Undergoing" here has the double sense of "suffering" or "enduring," as well as "bearing" a load;[5] if the metaphoric "burden" recalls the burdens of sin and punishment so frequently invoked in scripture,[6] Prospero's wording suggests that their rescue by "providence divine" (l. 159) fulfills the promise announced in the Geneva Bible's headnote to the first epistle of John: "God will bee mercifull unto the faithfull, if *groning under the burden of their sinnes,* they learne to flee unto his mercie."

So far, at least, these interlaced tropes appear to conform to the emblematic interpretation I have been outlining. Their significance is complicated, however, by the way in which Prospero's talk of burdens willingly borne is punningly echoed by Ariel's song later in 1.2, with its call for "sweet sprites [to] bear / The burden" (ll. 379–80). As the ensuing stage direction—*"Burden, dispersedly"* (l. 381 SD)—makes clear, Ariel's intention is that his fellow spirits should take up the chorus, or "burden," of his song; but in the context of a music that allays the fury both of the wild waves and of Ferdinand's passionate grief for his father (ll. 376–77, 392–94), a recollection of Prospero's burden of grief is unavoidable. Although etymologically distinct, these two senses of "burden" had long been assimilated: "burden" in the musical sense (otherwise *bourdon* or *burdoun*) could still carry its original meaning as the bass or undersong accompanying the melody in a choral work. Because this low undersong usually continued when the main singer paused at the end of a stanza, it typically supplied the tune for any chorus or refrain, so that "burden" was extended to refer to the refrain itself; and since the undersong was thought to be "heavier" than the air, the vocal chorus, like Ariel's sprites, was said to "bear the burden" of a song, as though carrying the weight of it.[7] Moreover, because the words of the refrain so often paraphrased the pervading sentiment of the lyric, "burden" also came to mean the "'gist' or essential contents" of a work.[8] With

---

5. *OED Online,* s.v. "undergo, *v.,*" 5.
6. See, e.g., Ps. 38:4; Is. 13:1; and Gal. 6:4–5.
7. *OED Online,* s.vv. "burden, burthen, *n.,*" IV, 9; and "bourdon[2], burdoun, *n.,*" 1. See Margaret's wordplay in *Much Ado About Nothing:* "Clap 's into 'Light a' love'; that goes without a burden" (3.4.44–45); the joke is elaborated later in the play when the dirge sung at Hero's supposed tomb is given the burden "Heavily, heavily" (5.3.18, 21). See also *The Two Gentlemen of Verona,* 1.2.79–81.
8. *OED Online,* s.v. "burden, burthen, *n.,*" IV.9–11.

these punning connections in mind, it is easy to see how the tolling of the funeral bell that concludes Ariel's second song, "Full fathom five" (ll. 395–401), constitutes its "burden" in a triple sense, as a refrain or undersong whose deep notes match both the watery depths of Alonso's supposed tomb, as well as the emotional depths of his son's grief, thereby concentrating the meaning of the entire lyric and the scene of mourning on which it comments. "The ditty," responds Ferdinand (using a word that could mean "burden" or "theme," as well as "the words of a song"[9]) "does remember my drowned father" (l. 404).

The low register of the sounds that typically express human misery makes low notes in music seem a natural correlative for the "heaviness" of "deep" mourning; thus, the diverse burdens borne by the groaning Prospero, the enslaved Caliban and Ferdinand, and the bereaved Alonso resonate with the play's emotional and somatic vocabulary, linking that language to an extensive sequence of musical episodes through the "burden" borne by Ariel's spirit chorus. In 2.1, for example, Ariel's *solemn music* transforms the heaviness of Alonso's grief into the "wondrous heavy" drowsiness into which the shipwrecked King and his loyal followers "sink" (ll. 177 SD, 190, 193). As a result, it is impossible to escape the suggestion that the task of Ariel's spirit chorus, like Miranda's effect on Prospero in the earlier storm described in 1.2, is to assist in an emotional unburdening—so that, by some mysterious transfiguration, the bearing of one "burden" will assist in the lightening of the other, just as this second "sinking" undoes the first.

A further, more oblique version of this musical wordplay occurs in the scene where Ariel, in harpy guise, removes the magical banquet set before Alonso and his entourage: disrupting the scene's *"Solemn and strange music"* with the threatening noise of *"Thunder and lightning,"* the harpy claps its wings and causes the banquet to vanish *"with a quaint device"* before the astonished eyes of the courtiers (3.3.18 SD, l. 53 SD). After a speech in which Ariel, as the harpy, urges "heart's sorrow" upon Prospero's enemies, the spirit disappears amid peals of thunder that give way to *"soft music,"* as the *"strange shapes"* of his "living drollery" return (ll. 82, 83 SD, 20 SD, 22). The contrast here between thunder and music belongs to the pattern of alternating discord and concord around which the play is structured. In this case, however, the simple contrast between cacophony and polyphony is confused by the ironic *"mocks and mows"* (l. 83 SD) of the spirits' eldritch ballet, and by the way in which the peals of thunder resound in Alonso's ear like music—albeit an ominous "Musick of

9. *OED Online*, s.v. "ditty, n.," 3.

Division,"[1] whose notes serve only to remind the king of his exclusion
from the harmony that music exemplifies:

> Methought the billows spoke and told me of it,
> The winds did *sing* it to me; and the thunder,
> That *deep* and dreadful *organ-pipe*, pronounced
> The name of Prosper: it did *bass* my trespass.
>   (ll. 97–100)

For its complete effect, Alonso's vocabulary depends upon its
subtle resonance with the "burdens" exemplified in Ariel's first
musical performance—the two lyrics he sings for Ferdinand, with
their accompanying spirit choruses. Properly speaking, the deep
organ pipe that basses Alonso's trespass, like the spirit choruses of
Ariel's lyrics, should be called a "bourdon" (variously rendered *burdoun, burden,* and *burthen*). Originally denoting the low drone of a
bagpipe or hurdy-gurdy and apparently cognate with the term for
bass, undersong, or refrain—by the seventeenth century the word
bourdon had come to refer to the bass stop on an organ.[2] So the
thunder's harsh music of accusation punningly articulates the burden of the king's offense.

A more intricate version of the same pun occurs in Prospero's
masque, where Ceres' song calls down the blessings of fertility
upon the betrothed couple, including the benison of "Plants with
goodly *burden* bowing" (4.1.113). Since the burden imagined here is
that of laden branches, "bowing" (doing obeisance) evidently plays
on "boughing" (sending out branches);[3] but the juxtaposition with
"burden" in a context of Orphic invocation, suggests that—as in
Sonnet 102's "wild music burthens every bough" (102.11)—musical
"bowing" (as of a stringed instrument) is also involved. The implication here, as in Caliban's description of an island "full of noises,
/ Sounds, and sweet airs" (3.2.128–29), is of a harmony intrinsic to
the very order of nature itself, one that Prospero's masque identifies
with the providence incarnated in Juno and Ceres, who "sings her
blessings" (4.1.109) on the betrothed couple.

Of course, Alonso responds to the bass notes of the thunder's
bourdon, as they sound the base depth of his trespass, as if they too
were expressions of a providential design; they are linked, by a

---

1. The phrase is borrowed from Sir Walter Raleigh's grimly witty descant on death, "The
   Life of Man"; see *The Poems of Sir Walter Ralegh: A Historical Edition,* ed. Michael
   Rudick (Tempe: Arizona Center for Medieval and Renaissance Studies, 1999), 70
   (poem 29c, l. 2).
2. *OED Online,* s.vv. "bourdon²," burdoun," 1–2; and "burden, burthen, *n.*," 9–10. See also
   New Grove Dictionary of Music and Musicians, ed. Stanley Sadie (London: Macmillan,
   2001), vol. 3, s.vv. "bourdon," 1; and "organ stop," 2.
3. *OED Online,* s.vv. "bow, *n.*¹," 6; and "bough, *v.*¹."

further chain of puns, to what Alonso feels must serve as the necessary expiation for his crime—"I'll seek him *deeper* than e'er plummet *sounded,* / And with him there lie mudded" (3.3.102–03). His
words will be echoed, like a refrain repeated in some musical composition, in another speech full of both "rattling thunder" and
"heavenly music" (5.1.44, 52)—Prospero's farewell to his magic,
with which I began this essay. The wordplay in that speech con-
signs the magician's arts (as it will ultimately consign the contrivances of his enemies) to a realm of profound silence, beyond
sounding, which is another way of describing the play's movement
from the vindictive or remorseful torments of memory to the
blessed oblivion announced by Prospero when Alonso prepares to
humble himself before his new daughter-in-law: "Let us not burden
our remembrances with / A heaviness that's gone" (ll. 199–200). In
terms of the recurrent variations on the motif of the Fortunate Fall
to which the wondering Gonzalo now returns his interlocutors—
"Was Milan thrust from Milan that his issue / Should become kings
of Naples?" (ll. 205–06)—it is evident how such intimations of a
harmony lying deep within the apparent confusion of the natural
world fit with a providential understanding of the protagonist's
plotting. Although analyses of the play's music have often addressed
the providential aspect of its symbolic design, it is not always easy
to separate this kind of providence from the more politic "provision
in mine art" (1.2.28) of which Prospero boasts. While the patterns
I have been tracing make complete sense only within the context of
the play's larger treatment of concord and discord, they invite a less
univocal interpretation than Prospero seeks to impose.

II

> Freedom is a word, less than a word, a noise.
> —J. M. Coetzee, *Foe*[4]

If the island world of *The Tempest* is given its sensuous immediacy
and physical presence primarily by the dramatist's manipulation of
sound effects, the idea for such a soundscape[5] may have been planted
in Shakespeare's mind by a contemporary text which has been widely
proposed as a partial inspiration for his play, William Strachey's *True
Repertory of the Wreck and Redemption of Sir Thomas Gates,* an
account of the catastrophic hurricane experienced off the Bermudas

---

4. J. M. Coetzee, *Foe* (London: Secker & Warburg, 1986), 100.
5. For a discussion of the Shakespearean "soundscape" and the need to "listen . . . closely
   to Shakespeare himself listening to the world around him," see Folkerth, 7–11, 14–25,
   esp. 9.

by an English fleet headed to the newly established Virginia colony in 1609.[6] Strachey's narrative stresses above all the terrible clamor of this tempest, its dire assault upon the mariners' hearing:

> *swelling and roaring* as it were by fits, . . . [the storm produced] horror and fear . . . to overrun the troubled and overmastered senses of all, which, taken up with amazement, the *ears* lay so sensible to the terrible *cries and murmurs* of the winds . . . as who was most armed and best prepared was not a little shaken. . . . [F]ury added to fury. . . . Sometimes strikes in our ship amongst women and passengers, not used to such *hurly* and discomfort, . . . [that] our *clamours* drowned in the winds, and the winds in *thunder*. Prayers might well be in the hearts and lips, but drowned in the *outcries* of the officers; nothing *heard* that could give comfort. . . . [T]he glut of water, as if throttling the wind erewhile, was no sooner a little emptied . . . but instantly the winds, as having gotten their *mouths* now free and at liberty, *spake more loud* and grew more *tumultuous* and malignant. . . . Winds and seas were as mad as fury and rage could make them.[7]

Things were little better when the survivors of the shipwreck struggled ashore in the Bermudas, islands that were reported to "be so terrible to all that ever touched on them, [because] such tempests, *thunders*, and other fearful objects are seen and *heard* about

---

6. Strachey's letter was not published until Purchas included it in his *Hakluytus Posthumus* (1625), and there is no way of being certain that a manuscript version was accessible to Shakespeare. As a result, some scholars, including Lindley (*The Tempest*, ed., 31) have recently questioned its plausibility as a source. The fullest of these attacks has been mounted by Roger Stritmatter and Lynne Kositsky in "Shakespeare and the Voyagers Revisited," *Review of English Studies* 58 (2007): 447–72. The authors argue that the *Repertory* uses material that cannot have been available to Strachey until after the supposed arrival of his letter with Sir Thomas Gates's ship in July 1610, but a forthcoming article by Alden C. Vaughan challenges the alleged historical grounds for Stritmatter and Kositsky's conclusions. The only significant textual parallels in the Bermuda section of Strachey's narrative are with Silvester Jourdain's *Discovery of the Barmvdas* (London, 1610). Stritmatter and Kositsky think that Strachey must have copied this material at a later date from Jourdain's published work; but since Jourdain himself returned from Virginia with Gates, there is every reason to suppose that he would have had access to any material sent home by Strachey, elements of which he could then have incorporated into his own text. There is, of course, good evidence that Shakespeare was familiar with a number of New World texts, including Montaigne's "Of the Cannibals" and Peter Martyr's *De Orbe Novo* in Richard Eden's 1555 translation, *The Decades of the Newe Worlde*. (Stritmatter and Kositsky's as-yet-unpublished essay, "'O Brave New World': *The Tempest* and Peter Martyr's *De Orbe Novo*" gives a detailed analysis of important parallels.) However, no other account of storm and shipwreck seems as close to Shakespeare's as Strachey's. Stritmatter and Kositsky, in another unpublished essay, argue for the influence of Erasmus's *Naufragium*, while Arthur F. Kinney, in "Revisiting *The Tempest*," *Modern Philology* 93 (1995): 161–77, identifies James Rosier's voyage narrative *A Trve Relation* (London, 1605) as a probable alternative to Strachey's text, noting that Rosier's narrative too begins with a storm. However, no proposed source gives so much emphasis as Strachey's to the terrifying sound of the storm, nor does any other offer so rich a collection of verbal parallels with *The Tempest*.

7. Strachey, quoted in Orgel, ed., 209–10.

them that they may be called commonly the Devil's Islands."[8] Not
only was their precarious refuge "often afflicted and rent with tempests, *great strokes of thunder, lightning, and rain in the extremity of
violence*,"[9] but to its dreadful hubbub were added the weird cries of
seamews—the very birds whose fledglings Caliban gathers from
the rocks (2.2.163).[1] The birds made a *"strange hollow and harsh
howling"*—one that the castaways themselves learned to mimic,
"holloing, laughing and making the strangest outcry that possibly
they could," in their efforts to trap the birds.[2]

Strachey's is the same *"strange hollow and confused noise"* (4 1 138
SD) with which Shakespeare fills his Mediterranean island: the
"assaultive" cacophony described by Bruce R. Smith that begins
with the wild tumult of a hurricane in which "all the physical attributes that make speech possible . . . are dissolved in a loud, inflec-
tionless confusion"[3] and concludes with the hollowing *"noise of
hunters . . . dogs and hounds"* (l. 251 SD) as Caliban and his fellow
conspirators are driven roaring from the stage. In the opening scene,
Smith suggests, these chaotic sounds are pitched against the vain
efforts of Alonso and his courtiers to reassert the ordered regimen
of speech, efforts that are finally overwhelmed by the fury of nature,
when *"A confused noise within"* (1.1.55 SD) announces their vessel's
foundering.[4] This noise itself, however, consists partly of human
cries—"'Mercy on us!'—'We split, we split!'—'Farewell, my wife and
children!'—'Farewell, brother!'—'We split! we split! we split!'" (ll.
56–58)—so that the hollowing of the storm is barely distinguishable
from the "howling" of the terrified passengers which seems "louder
than the weather" itself (l. 33). Indeed, Antonio and Sebastian
denounce the boatswain as a "bawling, blasphemous, incharitable
dog . . . [an] insolent *noise*maker" (ll. 36–40), as if identifying him
with the anarchic frenzy of the elements, whose leveling "roarers"
(crashing breakers punningly imagined as noisy rioters) care nothing "for the name of king" (l. 16).

8. Strachey, quoted in Orgel, ed., 213.
9. Strachey, quoted in Orgel, ed., 213.
1. I follow Malone's orthographically plausible emendation of "scamels" to "sea-mels" (a
   variant of *seamews*), since F's "Scamels," despite the heroic conjectures of editors,
   makes no convincing sense. See Orgel, ed., 2.2.166n; and *The First Folio of Shakespeare*, prep. Charlton Hinman (New York: W. W. Norton 1968) through-line number
   (TLN) 1216.
2. Strachey, quoted in Orgel, ed., 215.
3. Bruce R. Smith, *The Acoustic World of Early Modern England* (Chicago: U of Chicago
   P, 1999), 337, 336.
4. The fullest treatment of noise in Shakespeare is Kenneth Gross's *Shakespeare's Noise*
   (Chicago: U of Chicago p, 2001). However, although he includes an extended discussion of the storm scene in *Lear* (176–84), Gross's primary concern is with noise conceived as "violent or disorderly forms of speaking: slander, defamation, insult,
   vituperation, malediction, and curse" (1); my interest here is in forms of more or less
   inarticulate sound.

The theatrical emphasis upon sound that characterizes the play's opening is underlined in the language of the second scene, where Prospero's reiterated injunctions foreground the importance of hearing: "The very minute bids thee ope thine *ear*. / Obey, and be *attentive*. . . . Dost thou *attend* me? . . . Dost thou *hear* . . . *Hear* a little further" (1.2.37–38, 78, 106, 135). Ultimately, it is Prospero's ability (one that he shares with, and exercises through, Ariel) to "charm" the "ears" of his adversaries (4.1.178) that ensures his success; the subsequent action repeatedly asserts the imaginative power of hearing over the specious seductions of vision—whether these seductions are exemplified by the banquet that tempts and then cheats the Neapolitan courtiers in 3.3 or by the specious "trumpery" (4.1.186) of the *"glistering apparel"* (l. 193 SD) that lures Stephano and Trinculo to their humiliation. By the same token, the one conspicuous check to Prospero's design involves the lavishly staged betrothal masque that he devises for Miranda and Ferdinand, who (he insists) are to become "All eyes" for the performance (l. 59). Even here it is the harmonies of Juno and Ceres, rather than the "majestic vision" itself, to which Ferdinand attributes the magical charm of the performance (ll. 118, 119). The masque comes to a sudden end when its *"graceful dance"* (l. 138 SD) of nymphs and reapers is interrupted by Prospero's recollection of the "foul conspiracy / Of the beast Caliban and his confederates" (ll. 139–40); then, *"to a strange hollow and confused noise,* [the dancers] *heavily vanish"* (l. 138 SD).

Prospero's ensuing remarks about "the baseless fabric of this vision" (l. 151) suggest an unwitting truth in the magician's self-deprecating reference to the "vanity" of his spectacular artifice (l. 41).[5] At the same time, the audible clash between the masque music and the *"confused noise"* (l. 138 SD) into which it disintegrates, with its echo of the *"confused noise within"* (1.1.55 SD) that announced the imminent sinking of the king's ship in the opening scene, serves as a reminder of how the moral conflict here is repeatedly figured and played out in aural terms. Thus, in the second scene, the compelling power of Prospero's tale, which, Miranda insists, "would cure deafness" (1.2.106), is implicitly contrasted both with the insinuating rhetoric of his usurping brother, which "set all hearts i'th' state / To what tune pleased his *ear*," and with the evil spells of Caliban's mother, the "damned witch Sycorax," who was banished from Algiers "For . . . sorceries terrible / To human *hearing*" (ll. 84–85, 263–65). Furthermore, although the scene is quiet by comparison to the chaotic "roar" of "wild waters" that so terrified Miranda (l. 2), or

---

5. Lindley sees the play as "grow[ing] out of [a] general disquiet [with the court masque], and attempt[ing] itself to grapple with the problems it raises." See David Lindley, "Music, Masque and Meaning in *The Tempest*," in *The Court Masque* (see above, p. 256 n. 3), 47–59, esp. 54.

the "thunder-claps" and "cracks / Of sulphurous roaring" of which
Ariel boasts (ll. 202–04),[6] Prospero's didactic narrative is filled
with the remembered noise of the sea and the answering sounds of
his own despair on the voyage to which he and his infant daughter
were abandoned:

> There they hoist us
> To cry to th' sea that roared to us, to sigh
> To th' winds, whose pity, sighing back again,
> Did us but loving wrong. . . .
> When I . . .
> Under my burden groaned.
> (ll. 148–51,155–56)

These inarticulate sounds of woe and terror are echoed not only in
the "sighs" of the bereaved Ferdinand but in the memory of the
"groans" and "howls" vented by Ariel during his imprisonment in
Sycorax's "cloven pine" (ll. 222, 280, 296, 277) and in the "din" and
"roar" of pain that Prospero threatens to extract from the recalci-
trant Caliban (ll. 369–70), as well as the animal incoherence of the
"gabble" attributed to his once-languageless condition (l. 355).

Again and again, the chaotic tumult of the elements and the
inarticulate cries, groans, and sighs of suffering creatures are off-
set by the strange harmonics of The Tempest's several musics: these
include not just the songs of Ariel—whose elemental name puns on
the "airs" he performs—but the melodies played by offstage instruments at key points in the action. Thus, the discordant hubbub of
the storm is counterpointed by the harmony of Ariel's music as he
enters, "playing and singing" (l. 373 SD)—producing a "sound" so
mysteriously powerful that it not only "remember[s]" (and imagina-
tively re-members) Ferdinand's "drowned father" (ll. 404–06) but
overcomes the violence of the elements themselves. "This music,"
Ferdinand wonderingly remarks, "crept by me upon the waters, /
Allaying both their fury and my passion / With its sweet air" (ll.
390–92). On an island governed by "airy charm[s]" (5.1.54), whose
sounds are orchestrated by an "ayrie spirit,"[7] sweet airs are, as both
Ferdinand and Caliban observe, "i'th' air" (1.2.386, 3.2.129), tem-
pering the rough air of ocean tempest.

The magic influence of harmony is felt once more in the following
scene, when Ariel's "solemn music" lulls Alonso and his courtiers to
slumber (2.1.177 SD), and then again when his "music and song" awake

---

6. Holland, 220–25, discusses the noise of the storm and the insistent recurrence of
"roaring" in the play's language, relating the alternation of music and noise to the
order/disorder pattern of masque and antimasque.
7. The description is from the list of characters printed at the end of the Folio text; see
The First Folio of Shakespeare, fol. 19.

the "snoring" sleepers to the conspiracy of Antonio and Sebastian (ll. 289 SD, 293, 300 SD). Its notes are almost immediately followed, however, by a recurrence of the fearful *"noise of thunder"* (2.2.3 SD) and wind that opened the play and that accompanies the early action of 2.2, where the terrified Caliban, his imagination haunted by the tormenting sounds of Prospero's spirits—the chattering of apes and hissing of adders (ll. 9, 13–14)—is discovered cowering beneath his gabardine by Stephano and Trinculo. In 3.2 and 3.3, music reasserts itself twice more, first with the tune that Ariel *"plays . . . on a tabor and pipe"* (3.2.117 SD) to lure this trio of drunken conspirators across the island, and then in the *"Solemn and strange music"* of the banquet scene (3.3.17 SD). Alonso and Gonzalo marvel at the "harmony" of this "Marvellous sweet music," a "sound expressing, / . . . a kind / Of excellent dumb discourse" (ll. 19–20, 38–40), as though it were vehicle to a meaning that transcends mere words; but their musings are almost immediately interrupted by the fresh outburst of *"Thunder and lightning"* (l. 53 SD) that rings so ominously in Alonso's ears.

"Soft music" is called for again in the following scene when Prospero launches his "harmonious" betrothal masque for Miranda and Ferdinand, with its songs and dances (4.1.58 SD, 119, 105 SD, 109, 138 SD), only for the performance to be cut short by that *"strange hollow and confused noise"* to which the masquers *"vanish"* (l. 138 SD)—an alarming sound later matched by the noise of the hunt that reduces Caliban and his confederates to howling animality (ll. 252 SD, 258). In the final scene, Prospero's great farewell to magic recollects the "roaring war" and "dread rattling thunder" of the storms he has conjured, before he abjures their violence in favor of an appeal for "heavenly music" (5.1.44, 52)—a harmony realized in the "solemn air" with which he ministers to the tormented minds of his "spell-stopped" enemies (ll. 58, 61) and in the song that accompanies Ariel's reinvestiture of Prospero in his ducal attire (l. 87 SD). With that final lyric, the play's sound track effectively comes to an end, although the chaotic noise of the opening is remembered one last time in the boatswain's account of his miraculous release from his shipboard prison:

> . . . even now with strange and several noises
> Of roaring, shrieking, howling, jingling chains,
> And more diversity of sounds, all horrible,
> We were awaked, straightway at liberty.
>
> (ll. 235–38)

Where he was once terrorized by the story of his "monstrous . . . trespass" against Prospero, of which "the billows spoke and told me" (3.3.96, 100, 97), Alonso now looks forward to hearing his former adversary rehearse the story of his life—a narrative that, like *The Tempest* itself, promises to "take the ear strangely" (5.1.316).

Then, in the epilogue, the "heavenly music" of his courtiers' release has its faint, theater-bound equivalent in the sounds of intercession which Prospero begs from the audience—not only the rhythmic sound of clapping that takes the place of the storm's "dreadful thunder-claps" (1.2.202) and the threatening "claps" of Ariel's wings on the banqueting table (3.3.53 SD), but the "gentle breath" (Epilogue 11) of prayer, a last air that must replace the tormented sighing and whistling of the island winds.

This sequence of contrasting acoustic effects has typically been explained by reference to the early modern habit of imagining the created order of things in musical terms.[8] According to this Neoplatonic tradition, the principles of harmony that governed the macrocosm should be mirrored in every aspect of creation, the sublime music of the spheres, to which the planets themselves danced, forming the ideal pattern to which the orders of society and government, like those of the human microcosm itself, were intended to conform. In the discord of a fallen world, it is the constant task of government to strive for the restoration of harmony to the body politic. Thus, Sir John Davies, whose poem *Orchestra* is perhaps the best-known contemporary expression of such ideas, imagined the regulation of colonial disorder in language that Prospero would immediately understand. In his reformatory tract on Ireland, Davies looked forward to a future in which the wild "hubbub" of which Spenser and others complained would be reduced to musical perfection: "The strings of this Irish Harpe, which the Ciuill Magistrate doth finger, are all in tune . . . and make a good Harmony in this Commonweale: So as we may well conceiue a hope, that *Ireland* (which heertofore might properly be called the *Land of Ire* . . .) will from henceforth proeue a Land of *Peace* and *Concorde*."[9] The same figure is elaborated in Ben Jonson's 1613–14 *Irish Masque,* where "*a solemne musique*

8. See, for example, John P. Cutts, "Music and the Supernatural in 'The Tempest': A Study in Interpretation," *Music and Letters* 39 (1958): 347–58; Theresa Coletti, "Music and *The Tempest*," in *Shakespeare's Late Plays*, ed. Richard C. Tobias and Paul G. Zolbrod (Athens: Ohio UP, 1974), 185–99; and Robin Headlam Wells, *Elizabethan Mythologies: Studies in Poetry, Drama and Music* (Cambridge: Cambridge UP, 1994), 63–80, esp. 63. In his essay on "Music in Shakespeare," by contrast, W. H. Auden insists that while "*The Tempest* is full of music of all kinds, . . . it is not one of the plays in which, in a symbolic sense, harmony and concord finally triumph over dissonant disorder." See *The Dyer's Hand and Other Essays* (New York: Random House, 1962), 500–27, esp. 526.
9. Edmund Spenser, *A View of the Present State of Ireland*, ed. W. L. Renwick (London: Eric Partridge, 1970), 70, 72. Sir John Davies, *A Discoverie of the Trve Cavses Why Ireland Was Neuer Entirely Subdued* . . . (London, 1612), sig. Nn3ᵛ. See also Richard Hooker, *Of the Laws of Ecclesiastical Polity:* "Where the King doth guide the state and the lawe the King, that commonwealth is like an harpe or melodious instrument, the stringes whereof are tuned and handled all by one hand, following as lawes the rules and canons of Musicall science." See *The Folger Library Edition of the Works of Richard Hooker*, gen. ed. W. Speed Hill, 4 vols. (Cambridge, MA: Belknap Press for Harvard UP, 1977–82), 3:342. For the possibility that Prospero's island was conceived as a figure for Ireland, and Caliban for the so-called "wild Irish," see Paul Brown, "'This thing of darkness I acknowledge mine': *The Tempest* and the Discourse of Colonialism," in

of harpes," replacing the wild racket of bagpipes, represents the harmonious order to which the king's uncivil subjects are brought by the magic of his regal authority.[1] James here becomes a royal Orpheus—the power of whose lute to command nature itself Shakespeare remembered in the lyric "Orpheus with his lute made trees" (*Henry VIII*, 3.1.3–14)—or he resembles Amphion, founder of Thebes, the sound of whose harp was sufficient to raise the mighty walls of his city.

It is obviously no accident that Antonio should be made to parody these ancient allegories of political harmony when he sarcastically compares Gonzalo's consolatory speeches (designed as they are to rescue his king from the discord of grief) to the music of Amphion's "miraculous harp" (2.1.82);[2] Prospero can indeed be seen as the civil[izing] magistrate of Shakespeare's drama, conjuring concord out of the chaotic violence of the storm and replacing the false "tune" to which his usurping brother "set all hearts i'th' state" (1.2.85, 84) with the *"solemn music"* (5.1.57 SD) that announces his own imminent restoration. As "the best comforter / To an unsettled fancy," he promises to settle the tumult that "boil[s] within [the king's] skull" (ll. 58–59, 60). The magus whose "art" summons the harmonies of a betrothal masque to banish "discord" (4.1.20) from his daughter's marriage bed implicitly offers himself as the Orphic conductor of the play's music. If his score stands for the political, social, and psychological harmony for which he yearns, the storm with which he opens the play bodies forth both the political chaos resulting from his brother's usurpation and the turbulent passions stirred up by that disorder—notably, of course, the vindictive emotion by which he himself is tormented. This is the tumult that Prospero attempts to "still" in his *"beating* mind" after Caliban's conspiracy has disrupted the music of his carefully orchestrated masque (l. 163)—an inner storm that recalls the "tempest" that "beats" in Lear's head even as its pelting violence "invades [him] to the skin" (*King Lear*, 3.4.12, 14, 7). The same punning trope is deployed when Miranda feels the "sea-storm" "still . . . *beating* in [her] mind" (1.2.177, 176) and when Alonso's experiences "infest

---

Political Shakespeare: New Essays in Cultural Materialism, ed. Jonathan Dollimore and Alan Sinfield (Ithaca: Cornell UP, 1985), 48–71; and David J. Baker, "Where Is Ireland in *The Tempest?*," in *Shakespeare and Ireland: History, Politics, Culture*, ed. Mark Thornton Burnett and Ramona Wray (London: Macmillan, 1997), 68–88.

1. *The Irish Masque at Court* in *Ben Jonson: The Complete Works*, ed. C. H. Herford, Percy Simpson, and Evelyn Simpson, 11 vols. (Oxford: Clarendon Press, 1925–52), 7:403, l. 141 SD. See also Michael Neill, "Broken English and Broken Irish: Nation, Language, and the Optic of Power in Shakespeare's Histories," *Shakespeare Quarterly* 45 (1994): 1–32.

2. For parallels between Prospero, Amphion, and Orpheus as orchestrators of a music that has power to conjure harmonious order out of the wild confusion of nature, see Lindley, ed., *The Tempest*, 19.

[his] mind with *beating* on / The strangeness of this business"
(5.1.249–50).

Unlike Lear's storm, however, the "direful" roaring of the island's
"wild waters" (1.2.26, 2) proves to be less a direct expression of the
disordered violence of unregulated nature, than a kind of antimasque
(as Orgel's approach has enabled us to see),[3] merely mimicking such
chaos, since all its effects have been so "safely *ordered*" by its presenter
that there is "Not a hair perished" among those creatures whose terrified cries appeared to signal their mortal destruction (ll. 29, 217). The
fierce "beating" of winds and waves (l. 176) may be echoed in the desperate force of Ferdinand's struggle to "beat the surges under him"
(2.1.109) and in the slapstick violence of the various blows and beat-
ings meted out to Trinculo in 3.2. But the distempered noise of the
drunken Stephano, Trinculo, and Caliban "beat[ing] the ground / For
kissing of their feet" (4.1.173–74) is immediately followed by the sound
of Ariel "beat[ing his] tabor" (l. 175)—the same rhythmic percussion
that accompanied his piping in 3.2—which makes them "lift . . . up
their noses / As they smelt music" (4.1.177–78). There appears to be a
strange consonance between the choreographed movements of the
betrothal masque and the chaotic flight that leaves these rebels "*dancing* up to th' chins" "I' th' filthy-mantled pool beyond [Prospero's] cell"
(ll. 182–83). Moreover, Ariel's beating of musical time has its somatic
echo in the "beat" of the human pulses to which he draws Prospero's
attention (5.1.103, 113–14)—the rhythm with which the human body
keeps its own time—underlining the suggestive etymological link
between "tempest," *tempus,* and musical tempo explored by Douglas L. Peterson.[4]

In details of this kind, the simple opposition between music and
noise, concord and discord seems deliberately blurred, as though
Shakespeare were elaborating a set of more profound variations on
the paradox of "musical confusion" with which he had played in *A
Midsummer Night's Dream* (4.1.110, 118; 5.1.60).[5] If there is a musical tempo to be discovered even in the most distempered noise,
music itself can sometimes threaten to disintegrate into mere
clamor, contrasting with ideal harmony just as the rough bagpipes
of the wild Irish contrast with the civilizing notes of the harp in
Jonson's masque. The "scurvy tune[s]" of the drunken Stephano
and Caliban in 2.2, for example, lie somewhere between music and
noise, Caliban's song of freedom sounding to Trinculo like mere
"howling" (ll. 41, 169), while the raucous catch they share with

3. Orgel, ed., 47.
4. See Douglas L. Peterson, *Time, Tide and Tempest: A Study of Shakespeare's Romances*
   (San Marino, CA: Huntington Library, 1973), 3–70, 214–54.
5. See also *All's Well That Ends Well*, 1.1.172: "His jarring concord, and his discord
   dulcet."

Trinculo provokes even the musically challenged Caliban to complain "That's not the tune" (3.2.117), until an invisible Ariel sounds out its true melody on his *"tabor and pipe"* (l. 117 SD).

It is Caliban himself, however, who is made to draw attention to the soothing effect of a very different island music—"noises, / Sounds, and sweet airs" that, as he explains to the alarmed Stephano and Trinculo, "give delight and hurt not. / Sometimes a thousand twangling instruments / Will hum about mine ears; and sometimes voices" (ll. 129–31). Commenting upon Caliban's response to the soundscape of his island, Bruce Smith suggests that "within the broad acoustic horizons of *The Tempest*, between noise and music, Caliban stands dead center."[6] But it is telling that, despite the lyrical language in which he evokes the sounds that haunt him, Caliban himself does not really seem to distinguish between the island's different kinds of sound—"noise" on the one hand, and music's "sweet airs" on the other. In this context, it is probably significant that among the available meanings of "noise" in Shakespeare's time—a clamor or din, a "loud, harsh, or unpleasant" sound—were "a pleasant or melodious sound" and "a company or band of musicians."[7]

But, while *The Tempest* may capitalize on this paradoxical semantic, its repeated blurring of the distinction between the orchestrated concord of music and the discordant confusion of mere "noise" also seems likely to represent Shakespeare's imaginative response to a detail from Strachey's *Repertory*. In Strachey, the arrival of the storm is heralded by winds that are described as "singing and whistling" around the ship.[8] It is a casual touch, but one that nevertheless appears to color the moment at which Trinculo recognizes "another storm brewing" as soon as he hears it "sing i' th' wind" (2.2.19–20), just as it seems to be recalled later when "The winds did sing" "The name of Prosper" to the despairing Alonso (3.3.98, 100). This last episode, in particular, suggests that Shakespeare may have found in Strachey's metaphor the suggestion of an unexpected consonance between the terrifying uproar of the storm and the mysterious providence by which "it pleased our merciful God to make even this hideous and hated place both the place of our safety and means of our deliverance."[9] This consonance is mirrored in the "loving wrong" (1.2.151) that Prospero and Miranda suffer from the winds that lash the rotten boat carrying them to the island, as well as in Ferdinand's recognition that "Though the seas threaten, they are merciful" (5.1.178). So, just as hellish suffering can be the instrument of redemption, it is as if some mysterious melody were hidden in the

6. Smith, 337.
7. *OED Online*, s.v. "noise, *n.*," 2b, 3.
8. Strachey, quoted in Orgel, ed., 209.
9. Strachey, quoted in Orgel, ed., 213.

wildest, most incoherent racket—a melody that, like the music of the spheres, is either inaudible to fallen creatures or, if heard at all, perceived only by the dispensation of grace.

Some such intuition appears to underlie the differing accounts of the mysterious *"music and song"* (2.1.289 SD) by which Alonso and his loyal followers are awakened, just in time to save them from assassination by Antonio and Sebastian. To the virtuous Gonzalo this ethereal music resembles a melodious "humming" (l. 310); but the conspirators claim to have been terrorized by a very different kind of noise.

> SEBASTIAN ... we heard a hollow burst of bellowing,
> Like bulls, or rather lions—did't not wake you?
> It struck mine ear most terribly.
>
> ALONSO I heard nothing.
>
> ANTONIO O, 'twas a din to fright a monster's ear,
> To make an earthquake. Sure, it was the roar
> Of a whole herd of lions.
>
> (ll. 304–09)

If music can be presented as a monstrous din or else be drowned out by chaotic hubbub, by the same token, the most inharmonious uproar can sometimes appear to resolve itself into mysterious harmony.[1] Thus, the "sweet air" of Ariel's first song, in which the dancing feet of his fellow sprites "kissed / The wild waves" into silence, is accompanied by a chorus of harsh animal noises, the barking of dogs and crowing of cocks (1.2.392, 376–77).[2] The burden of Ariel's second song imitates the grim tolling of a funeral bell, while his last resounds with the cry of owls (5.1.90). For Aristotle, Lucretius, and other classical theorists it was the rational, ordering power of human speech—as opposed to the purely emotive force of the inchoate sounds uttered by animals—on which the very existence of the *polis* and its social order depended.[3] But in *The Tempest* that distinction

---

1. The role of music becomes even more ambiguous, as David Lindley argues in "Music, Masque and Meaning," in *The Court Masque* (see p. 256, n. 3 above), when it is remembered that, according to contemporary theories, music had the capacity to "delude or spur illicit passions as well as cure, heal, and restore" (47). Lindley writes that the play "exploits and explores the tensions" between the conventions of the court masque, in which the symbolic power of music was "firmly controlled and directed" (47), and those of the playhouse, where its function was more varied and unpredictable. See also his discussion of audience response in *Shakespeare and Music* (London: Thomson Learning, 2006), 218–33.
2. Here, I assume that Orgel and other editors are correct in assigning the cockcrow at 1.2.385 (like the barking at ll. 381–82) to the chorus of sprites indicated by F's earlier stage direction *"Burthen dispersedly"* (First Folio, TLN 525 SD). Howell Chickering, "Hearing Ariel's Songs," *Journal of Medieval and Renaissance Studies* 24 (1994): 131–72, esp. 155, suggests that the raucous chorus of these songs links them with the discordant catches of Stephano and Trinculo.
3. For a full discussion, see Deborah Levine Gera, *Ancient Greek Ideas on Speech, Language, and Civilization* (Oxford: Oxford UP, 2003).

is less secure. Thus, in the first and last of Ariel's songs—depending on how they are performed—we might think of the bestial chorus either as being absorbed into a music that allays both the fury of the waves and Ferdinand's passion of despair, or (contrariwise) as a residue of confusion that resists all such comforting reconciliation.[4]

The ways in which musical order itself sometimes threatens to disintegrate into acoustic confusion—as, for example, when the consort that accompanies the "graceful dance" of nymphs and reapers in the betrothal masque gives way to *"confused noise"* (4.1.138 SD)—seem to suggest that the reforming power of art, by some entropic principle, is in constant danger of reverting to the disorder of fallen nature. Prospero's magic, moreover, is always tainted by the suspicion that it traffics in the forbidden, and that for all its benevolent professions, it may constitute a kind of Faustian overreaching—something that in the end will have to be renounced, like his magician's staff and book, and consigned to the oblivious silence, "deeper than did ever plummet sound," of that "abyss of time" from which his vindictive memories first surfaced (5.1.56, 1.2.50). From this perspective, the animal chorus of barking and crowing that constitutes the burden of Ariel's first song can seem to resemble the lunatic cacophony of birds and beasts that erupts in Middleton and Rowley's *The Changeling*,[5] vocalizing the violently discordant passions that seethe beneath the ordered surface of society.

The ambivalence of such an episode, combined with the uncertain status of his magical practice, may encourage the conjecture that, far from being a transcendent sage whose studies have put him in tune with the deep harmonies of nature, Prospero has merely mastered the arts of politic manipulation more effectively than the brother who, by controlling "the *key* / Of officer and office," once contrived to "set all hearts i' th' state / To what *tune* pleased his *ear*" (1.2.83–85). Prospero's metaphors, after all, give a more sinister valency to music, seeming to endow Antonio with the power to effect his own baleful metamorphoses, "new creat[ing]" the "creatures" of Prospero's court (ll. 81–82) in parodic anticipation of the transformations wrought by the art of the magician-prince at the end of the play. Striking a

---

4. For Lindley, the barking and crowing of the choric sprites creates a discomfort with the sublime metamorphoses of Ariel's "sea-change," to "make . . . us uneasily conscious of the compromise with truth that Prospero's designs necessitate." What Shakespeare dramatizes is a clash between the traditional Neoplatonic view of music as an instrument of transcendental harmony and a newer account of it as primarily rhetorical in its effects. The audience is left, Lindley suggests, divided between skepticism and a nostalgic regret at the dissolution of those Platonic theories that once sustained "a Sidneyan belief in art's golden world" ("Music, Masque and Meaning," 49, 58).

5. After the entry of "MADMEN *above, some as birds, others as beasts*," Isabella explains, "Sometimes they imitate the beasts and birds, / Singing, or howling, braying, barking— all / As their wild fancies prompt 'em." See Thomas Middleton and William Rowley, *The Changeling*, 3d rev. ed., ed. Michael Neill (London: A. and C. Black, 2006), 3.2.184 SD, 189–91.

similar note, Ferdinand primly remembers a time when "Th' harmony of [ladies'] tongues" sounded a dangerous siren song that "into
bondage / Brought my too diligent ear" (3.1.41–42). In a play where
bondage (whether for Ariel, Caliban, or Ferdinand himself) typically
follows transgression, this seemingly casual conceit carries a more
powerful resonance than it otherwise might—especially coming, as
it does, in a scene where this "patient log-man" interprets his "wooden
slavery" as a form of chivalric service to Miranda, a "bondage" more
desirable than "freedom" (ll. 67, 62, 89).

From one perspective, as we have seen, Ferdinand's experience
amounts to a profane yet mysteriously consoling version of the Christian paradox of freedom-in-service; but the tune that seduces Stephano and Trinculo with the prospect of "a brave kingdom . . . where I
shall have my music for nothing" (3.2.137–38) is a different matter.
"[C]harm[ing] their ears" with its "lowing," only to lure them "calf-
like" into "Toothed briars, sharp furzes, pricking gorse, and thorns"
and then into a "foul lake [that] / O'er-stunk their feet," it finally
betrays the rebels to the threatening *noise of hunters . . . dogs and
hounds,*" who pursue them until they "roar" at the "cramps" and "dry
convulsions" that "grind their joints" (4.1.178–80, 183–84, 251 SD,
255–58), consigning them to humiliating subjection even as their
principal tormentor is promised that he may "have the air at freedom"
(l. 262). In contrast to the curative "heavenly music" (5.1.52) that her-
alds the release of the "spell-stopped" courtiers (l. 61), Prospero's
music is exposed here as an agent of sensual deception and an instrument of oppressive discipline.[6] Once the orchestrating power of the
magician's "potent art" (l. 50) is questioned in this way, it raises the
possibility that, deeper than the sounding measure of his plummet,
there are other measures that he cannot hear: the noises and sounds,
to which Caliban responds with such uncharacteristically tender lyricism, may be of quite another order than those that "rough magic"
(l. 50) can summon, just as the "sweet air[s]" (1.2.392) of Ariel's real
music will sound only when he achieves the liberty suggested by his
name, becoming free as air. Caliban's song of liberation, significantly
enough, ends in a pair of chanted lines that are surely designed as its
"burden"—"'Ban, 'Ban, Ca-Caliban / Has a new master—get a new
man!" (2.2.174–75)—in which his very name fragments into inarticulate cries that resemble cursing ("'Ban, 'ban"). This is perhaps how
freedom sounds, when the slave casts off the burden of his imposed
language ("my profit on't / Is I know how to curse" [1.2.362–63]).

6. Observing these contradictions, Lindley argues that "by stressing the essentially rhetorical nature of music and dramatising the way in which it is used to manipulate and
control, Shakespeare questions the traditional view of its God-derived power. . . . The
music of the island is not Prospero's . . . but Ariel's [and] in this respect the play seems
to suggest that music is of itself morally neutral" (*The Tempest*, Lindley, ed., 19, 22).

The implications of such a conclusion for our understanding of Prospero are, of course, entirely in accord with postcolonial readings of the play—most conspicuously with that offered in Aimé Césaire's *Une tempête*. In this irreverent reworking of *The Tempest*, Prospero is a ruthless agent of empire, an "old colonial addict" who justifies his appropriation of Caliban's and Ariel's island by presenting himself, in exactly Shakespeare's metaphor, as the orchestrator of sublime order, although the real music of the play belongs to the creatures of the island, above all to Caliban and the African spirit beings of his disorderly pantheon:

> Understand me well.
> I am not, in the ordinary sense,
> the master, as this savage thinks,
> but rather the conductor of a boundless score:
> this island.
> Drawing out voices, myself alone,
> and mingling them at my pleasure,
> arranging out of confusion
> the sole intelligible line.
> Without me, who would be able
> to draw music from all this?
> Without me, the island is dumb.[7]

In Shakespeare's play, it is difficult to avoid the self-reflexive implications of the patterns I have described. These implications, needless to say, expose the author as complicit in the very hubris that the magician's farewell to his art ("Ye elves of hills, and brooks" [5.1.33]) at once renounces and celebrates. The "burden" under which the tempest-tossed Prospero groans, as a laboring mother might groan under the "burden" of her pregnancy,[8] is not simply the weight of his past sins, but the burden of revenge with which his history has charged him—a burden linked not just to the "fardels" of tormented memory in Hamlet's "weary life" (*Hamlet*, 3.1.75, 76) but to the "monstrous birth" of Iago's vindictive scheming (*Othello*, 1.3.404). By extension, however, it is also the burden of the dramatic narrative itself; if we take it in that sense, it may be colored by the use of "burden" in the English Bible to translate the Hebrew *massā*, meaning "lifting up (of the voice), utterance, oracle" or "prophecy" or "heavy doom"[9]—the use suggestively exemplified by "The burden of Tyrus

---

7. My own translation, adapted from Aimé Césaire, *A Tempest* (*Based on Shakespeare's "The Tempest"; Adaptation for a Black Theater*), trans. Richard Miller (New York: Ubu Repertory Theater Publications, 1992), 73. [An excerpt from Césaire's play appears on pp. 343–47 of this volume.—*Editors*]

8. *OED Online*, s.v. "burden, burthen, *n.*," 4a. See also Orgel, ed., 1.2.156–57n.

9. *OED Online*, s.v. "burden, burthen, *n.*," III.8; and Alexander Cruden, *A Complete Concordance to the Holy Scriptures of the Old and New Testament . . .* (New York: M. W. Dodd, 1854), s.v. "burden."

[and Zidón]" as the prophet Isaiah announced it: "for the sea hathe spoken, *euen* the strength of the sea. . . . Howle . . . ye that dwell in the yles" (Is. 23:1, 4, 6). Steeped as it is in the language and motifs of scripture, *The Tempest* is a play that might easily be read as trespassing on sacred ground; it is partly for this reason that the magician-dramatist who orchestrates its action is required to abjure his art. At this moment of ceremonious unburdening, as Prospero flourishes his magic staff one last time before breaking it, we may wish to remember (as the more alert members of Shakespeare's audience might have done) that an old but still extant synonym for "staff" was "bourdon," "burdon," or "burdoun," and that—perhaps significantly for a poet who never tired of punning on his own name—the word could also mean "spear or spear-shaft."[1]

In the light of this wordplay, Sir John Gielgud's famous *coup de théâtre* in Peter Hall's 1973 production may deserve revisiting, as something more than a mere throwback to sentimental Victorian fantasy. Just as he prepared to speak the epilogue, Gielgud's Prospero doffed his ducal bonnet to reveal a startling resemblance to the Droeshout engraving of Shakespeare. Spoken by an actor who has performed the role of a playwright-magician, one whose "charms" (Epilogue, 1) have visibly shaped the plot of the play the audience has just witnessed, the epilogue is largely responsible for the long-lived reading of the play as Shakespeare's public farewell to his craft.[2] The burden that Prospero seeks to discard, when—like Caliban, Ferdinand, and Ariel before him—he claims the indulgence of freedom, resembles that of the theatrical artist seeking manumission as one of His Majesty's Servants. That, too, is part of the "burden" of *The Tempest*.

WILLIAM H. SHERMAN

Shakespearean Somniloquy: Sleep and Transformation in *The Tempest*†

In 1989, the *Guardian*'s tireless theatre critic Michael Billington chaired a roundtable discussion with a group of famous actors and

---

1. *OED Online*, s.v. "bourdon¹, burdoun, n.," 2.
2. This approach goes back to at least 1838, when Thomas Campbell declared *The Tempest* marked by "a sort of sacredness as the last work of the mighty workman. Shakespeare, as if conscious that it would be his last, and as if inspired to typify himself, has made its hero a natural, a dignified, and benevolent magician." See the *New Variorum* edition of *The Tempest*, ed. Horace Howard Furness (Philadelphia: J. B. Lippincott, 1892), 356.

† From *Renaissance Transformations: The Making of English Writing, 1500–1650*, ed. Margaret Healy and Thomas Healy (Edinburgh: Edinburgh UP, 2009), pp. 177–91. © William H. Sherman. Reproduced with permission of Edinburgh University Press via PLSclear. Notes are by the author unless otherwise specified.

directors. The event was part of a series of public conversations on Shakespeare's place in contemporary culture, and the question posed to the panel (and their audience) on this particular day was 'Does Shakespeare's Verse Send You to Sleep?'[1] After each of the speakers confessed that they had once or twice found their heads nodding at a play, they took turns blaming other people for their lapses in concentration. Most of them charged bad actors or tone-deaf directors with failing to convey the dynamic energies of Shakespeare's texts. As Tony Church put it,

> If you just blandly trot through and hope, as Peter Brook once said, that the verse will go on by itself, like a railway train on tracks, then it can become boring . . . It's possible to get away with Shakespeare by just letting the train run on its tracks, because the rhythm will go on, the shapes, the melodies will go on; and for years, from when I [first] started going to the theatre, that's how people spoke Shakespeare—and I did go to sleep for parts of it. (p. 101)

In his introduction to the published discussion, the editor John Elsom offered the intriguing theory that the soporific effects of Shakespeare's verse might not be the result of performers on auto-pilot but rather the inevitable side effect of changes in pronunciation since Shakespeare's day:

> Modern pronunciation flattens and lightens the vowel sounds, leaving a blander sound to the verse and quickening the speed of delivery. Under those circumstances, the metrical stress become[s] a barely conscious hidden beat, blurring verse and prose, and sometimes sounding like a hypnotic throb. (p. 99)

Billington, for his part, blamed the tourism industry: 'My belief is [that] it's not Shakespeare's verse that sends you to sleep, but those horrendous package tours where you do Oxford in the afternoon and Stratford in the evening' (p. 113).

But everyone was in complete agreement about two points: first, that when Shakespeare's verse sends us to sleep it is a bad thing, and, secondly, that Shakespeare himself has no share in the blame. Everyone, that is, but an anonymous member of the audience who, in the brief question-and-answer session, wondered if it might be possible to 'construe [the question posed by the title] as a compliment' (p. 112), reminding the panellists that we sometimes find ourselves lulled by the beauty of speeches or scenes that we may not be properly taking in. What makes us so sure, then, that Shakespeare

---

1. The conversations were later published in John Elsom (ed.), *Is Shakespeare Still Our Contemporary?* (London: Routledge, 1989), ch. 5. Billington's panelists included Sheila Allen, Alexander Anikst, Tony Church and David Thacker.

and his contemporaries would have seen sleepiness as an inappropriate response to the patterns of sound and imagery they presented to viewers and readers? Do we know enough about the place of sleep in Elizabethan somatics and aesthetics to assume that early modern playgoers (like modern ones) would consider vigilant wakefulness the hallmark of successful appreciation of great art?

We do know, after all, that sleep was the subject of a wide range of artistic representation in classical, medieval and Renaissance Europe. Andy Warhol may have broken new ground with his infamous film *Sleep* (which hovers for more than five hours over the sleeping figure of John Giorno), but he was hardly the first artist to exploit the surprising potential of slumbering lovers or gods: the 'sleeping cupid' was a favourite theme of ancient sculptors, revived by Michelangelo and made most famous, perhaps, by the painter Caravaggio.[2] We know that Elizabethan writers of and on music praised that art for having the power to transport, instruct and heal its hearers by bringing on an actual or metaphorical slumber—a state explicitly invoked in a conspicuously high proportion of the period's songs. In 1609, Robert Jones gave his entire 'Fourth Booke of Ayres' the title *A Musicall Dreame*, explaining his conceit in the dedicatory epistle:

> I betooke me to the ease of my Pillow, where *Somnus* hauing taken possession of my eyes, and *Morpheus* the charge of my senses; it happened mee to fall into a Musical dreame, wherein I chanced to haue many opinions and extrauagant humors of diuers Natures and Conditions, some of modest mirth, some of amorous Loue, and some of most diuine contemplation; all these I hope, shall not giue any distaste to the eares, or dislike to the mind, eyther in their words, or in their seuerall sounds, although it is not necessarie to relate or diuulge all Dreames or Phantasies that Opinion begets in sleepe.[3]

Such visions—at once playful and profound, and under the aegis of both classical and biblical models—also provided the framing

---

2. David Roberts makes a similar observation at the beginning of his essay, 'Sleeping beauties: Shakespeare, sleep and the stage', comparing Shakespeare's interest in sleeping women to the British artist Cornelia Parker's 1995 exhibition, *The Maybe*. Parker filled the Serpentine Gallery with glass cases full of 'relics of the famous and the dead', and in the largest case of all she installed the actress Tilda Swinton, sound asleep (*Cambridge Quarterly*, 35:3 (2003), pp. 231–54).

3. Edward Doughtie (ed.), *Lyrics from English Airs, 1596–1622* (Cambridge, MA: Harvard University Press, 1970), pp. 316–17. On music, magic and sleep in the Renaissance see Gary Tomlinson, *Music in Renaissance Magic: Toward a Historiography of Others* (Chicago: University of Chicago Press, 1993); and for sensitive readings of *The Tempest*'s soundscape, see Michael Neill, '"Noises, / Sounds, and sweet airs": The burden of Shakespeare's *Tempest*', *Shakespeare Quarterly*, 59:1 (Spring 2008), pp. 36–59 [pp. 256–79 in this volume—Editors], and Bruce R. Smith, *The Acoustic World of Early Modern England: Attending to the O-Factor* (Chicago: University of Chicago Press, 1999).

device for the 'medieval dream poem', one of the period's most popular genres (featuring some of the best-known work by Chaucer, Langland and Gower).[4]

And we know, above all, that Shakespeare's entire corpus testifies to a deep and enduring preoccupation with sleep and dreams. In his suggestive essay 'Sleeping through Shakespeare', Ronald Hall reports that

> Shakespeare's works contain about a thousand references to sleep. If you put together all the passages where a character is asleep onstage, you get a total performance time equal to one-and-a-half plays. This excludes all of the offstage sleepers that we only hear of . . . Even in plays with no onstage sleep at all, images of sleep can exercise and accumulate considerable force. Sleep on- or offstage, speeches on sleep or [the] lack of it, incidental images of sleep [and] dreams: these are not confined to one period of the works or to one type of play.[5]

In a comprehensive survey of onstage sleepers in medieval and Renaissance plays, David Bevington reminds us that even in the first half of Shakespeare's career he was already using sleep 'as a metaphor for the fluid boundaries between reality and illusion, life and art, theater and dream'.[6]

As Shakespeare's life and art were coming to an end, this metaphor became more rather than less potent, culminating in a speech, towards the end of *The Tempest*, that is often read as Shakespeare's farewell to the stage:

> Our revels now are ended. These our actors,
> As I foretold you, were all spirits and
> Are melted into air, into thin air;
> And like the baseless fabric of this vision,
> The cloud-capped towers, the gorgeous palaces,
> The solemn temples, the great globe itself,
> Yea, all which it inherit, shall dissolve,
> And, like this insubstantial pageant faded,
> Leave not a rack behind. We are such stuff

4. Useful overviews include A. C. Spearing, *Medieval Dream Poetry* (Cambridge: Cambridge University Press, 1976); Peter Brown (ed.), *Reading Dreams: The Interpretation of Dreams from Chaucer to Shakespeare* (Oxford: Oxford University Press, 1999); and Helen Phillips, 'Medieval dream poems', in Peter Brown (ed.), *A Companion to Medieval English Literature and Culture, c. 1350–1500* (Oxford: Blackwell, 2007), pp. 374–86.
5. Ronald Hall, 'Sleeping through Shakespeare', *Shakespeare in Southern Africa*, 12 (1999/2000), pp. 24–32, p. 24.
6. David Bevington, 'Asleep onstage', in John A. Alford (ed.), *From Page to Performance: Essays in Early English Drama* (East Lansing: Michigan State University Press, 1995), pp. 51–83, p. 68.

As dreams are made on, and our little life
Is rounded with a sleep.[7]

D. G. James observed that 'the words "sleep" . . . and "dream" recur again and again' in *The Tempest*—though, in fact, 'dream' appears only four times in the play, twelve fewer than *A Midsummer Night's Dream* and thirteen fewer than *Richard III*, and *The Tempest*'s twelve uses of 'sleep' are matched by four other plays and surpassed by *A Midsummer Night's Dream*, *Richard III* and *Macbeth* (with twenty-six).[8] What James described as the play's 'pervasive dreamlike quality' emerges from other features—from the story's strange and shifting setting, its conspicuous use of music, its frequent jumps in logic, and above all from the fact that (as Hall put it) 'virtually every character in the play apart from the spirits is at some point associated literally or figuratively with sleep'.[9] To be more precise, if we include the Master, the Boatswain and a mariner or two (all of whom fall asleep after the opening storm and are not roused until the closing moments of the play), well over half of the play's characters spend part of the play in an actual—and often visible—state of slumber. The only major characters whose sleep is not depicted or described are Antonio, Sebastian, Trinculo and Stephano, all of whom are involved in conspiracies enabled by the sleep of others. This must be the highest tally of sleepers in any single play (and this in the second shortest text in the canon), and it is all the more remarkable since the action explicitly takes place not at night but, more or less in real time for the standard theatrical performance in the period, between two and five or six in the afternoon.

If Shakespeare can be said to have written a dream poem, it may be *The Tempest* rather than *A Midsummer Night's Dream*: indeed, some modern productions have gone so far as to set the play as an elaborate psychodrama taking place within the mind of Prospero. And if *Hamlet* marks Shakespeare's most potent experiments with the soliloquy, *The Tempest* offers his final and most profound exploration of somniloquy, plumbing the power of what one of the play's own characters calls 'sleepy language'—language about sleep, language in sleep, and even language that brings on sleep.[1] In this essay I will argue, first, that the play has much to teach us about the place

7. Shakespeare, *The Tempest*, in Peter Hulme and William H. Sherman (eds.), *The Norton Critical Edition*, 2nd ed. (New York: W. W. Norton, 2019), 4.1.148–58. All citations are of this edition.
8. D. G. James, *The Dream of Prospero* (Oxford: Clarendon Press, 1967), p. 148.
9. Hall, 'Sleeping through Shakespeare', p. 30.
1. 'Somniloquy', or 'somniloquism', is in fact the technical term psychologists use for sleep-talking (as a companion to the better-known term used for sleep-walking, 'somnambulism'). Arthur M. Arkin, *Sleep-Talking: Psychology and Psychophysiology* (Hillsdale, NJ: Erlbaum, 1981), p. 10.

of sleep in the artistic and ethical designs of Renaissance texts, and, secondly, that sleep can paradoxically help us to account for the peculiar restlessness of *The Tempest*'s critical and creative afterlife.

Sleep may strike us as the action farthest removed from thinking, speaking, writing or indeed acting—as such, perhaps the most unpromising state of all for dramatic representation. Most Renaissance medical theory considered sleep to be the categorical opposite of waking, with which it formed one of the so-called 'non-naturals' necessary for maintaining the balance of humours within the body. It was typically defined as a lack of everything associated with being awake. 'Sleepe,' explained Thomas Cogan in his *Haven of Health* (1584):

> Is defined to be an impotencie of the senses. Because in sleepe the senses be unable to execute their office, as the eye to see, the eare to heare, the nose to smell, the mouth to tast, and all sinowy parts to feele. So that the senses for a time may seeme to be tyed or bound, and therefore sleepe is called of some the bond of the senses.[2]

Levinus Lemnius's *The Touchstone of Complexions* (1581) described sleep as:

> nothing els but a resting of the Animal faculty, and a pawsing from the actions and busines of the day, whereby the vertues of the bodies being faynt . . . are reuiued and made fresh againe, and all the weary members & Senses recomforted. (sig.G8v)

As this passage suggests, sleep was generally praised (when part of a properly regulated regime) for its restorative or recuperative powers: in other words, it was not just part of what makes us human but played an important role in keeping us so. According to Cogan, in fact, sleep is the perfect natural therapy for the various conditions from which the characters in *The Tempest* suffer: 'it refresheth the body, it reviveth the minde, it pacifieth anger, it driveth away sorowe'.[3]

It is this approach to sleep that Renaissance poets most often turned to in voicing the complaints of their unhappy courtiers and lovers. For instance, sonnet 45 in Daniel's 1592 sequence, *Delia*, begins,

---

2. Cited in Garrett A. Sullivan, Jr, *Memory and Forgetting in English Renaissance Drama: Shakespeare, Marlowe, Webster* (Cambridge: Cambridge University Press, 2005), p. 33.
3. Cited in Marcus Noll, *An Anatomy of Sleep: Die Schlafbildlichkeit in den Dramen William Shakespeares* (Würzburg: Königshausen and Neumann, 1994), p. 24; compare Karl H. Dannenfeldt, 'Sleep: Theory and practice in the late Renaissance', *Journal of the History of Medicine and Allied Sciences*, 41 (October 1986), pp. 415–41.

Care-charmer Sleep, son of the sable Night,
Brother to Death, in silent darkness born,
Relieve my languish, and restore the light;
With dark forgetting of my care return,
And let the day be time enough to mourn
The shipwreck of my ill-adventured youth.

It ends, in the final couplet, with 'Still let me sleep, embracing
clouds in vain, / And never wake to feel the day's disdain.' One of
Drummond of Hawthornden's sonnets from his 1616 *Poems* imagines sleep as an even safer haven:

Sleep, Silence' child, sweet father of soft rest,
Prince whose approach peace to all mortals brings,
Indifferent host to shepherds and to kings,
Sole comforter of minds with grief opprest;
Lo, by thy charming-rod all breathing things
Lie slumbering, with forgetfulness possest.[4]

In other contexts, too, sleep offered its miraculous powers of restoration in the face of traumatic experiences—including tempests.
John Cook's pamphlet describing his voyage to Ireland during the
'great storm' of 5 January 1650 described the deepest of dreams in
the unlikeliest of circumstances:

The storm still increased, and I grew exceeding heavy and
sleepy . . . so it pleased God, that sitting as upright as I could,
I fell into as fast a sleep as ever I was in all my life. And in my
sleep I dreamed. That I was in an upper chamber with my
sweet Redeemer Christ Jesus, and that there were many suit-
ers attended to speak with him; to beseech him to save their
Ships and Barks that they might not perish by the storme.[5]

The storm that occupies the opening scene of *The Tempest* has similar effects on those who experience and witness it—including Prospero's daughter, Miranda, who sinks into a deep sleep some 200 lines
after watching the wreck of what must be the first ship she has ever
seen, with the apparent loss of the first human visitors to the island
in her lifetime. During those lines, in which Prospero recounts the

4. I cite the Daniel and Drummond poems from Peter Washington (ed.), *Poems of Sleep
and Dreams*, Everyman Library (New York: Random House, 2004), p. 48 (Daniel) and
p. 49 (Drummond). On the connections between sleep and forgetting, see Sullivan,
Memory and Forgetting, and Christopher Ivic and Grant Williams (eds.), *Forgetting in
Early Modern English Literature and Culture: Lethe's Legacies* (London: Routledge,
2004).
5. John Cook, *A True Relation of Mr. Iohn Cook's Passage by Sea from Wexford to Kinsale
in that great Storm Ianuary 5. Wherein is Related the Strangeness of the Storm, and the
Frame of his Spirit in it. ALSO, The Vision that he saw in his sleep, and how it was
Revealed that he should be preserved, which came to pass very miraculously. All written
by himself* (Cork and London: for T. Brewster and G. Moule, 1650), pp. 8–9.

actions that led to their exile from Milan and identifies the noblemen
who have just been washed up on their shore, Miranda finds it sur-
prisingly difficult to stay awake: three times Prospero breaks off to
ask her if she is paying attention before acknowledging (or is it com-
manding?), 'Thou art inclined to sleep. 'Tis a good dullness, / And
give it way. I know thou canst not choose' (1.2.185–86).[6]

Miranda's fit of narcolepsy, like Cook's dream, suggests that
Renaissance sleep could be strikingly different from our own, testifying to causes and effects that are richer and stranger than anything the medical texts would lead us to expect. And when we turn to
Shakespeare's plays, we find that sleep is almost never simply or
straightforwardly therapeutic: indeed, it is very rarely a positive force
of any kind in his plays, or (for that matter) in the romance texts with
which *The Tempest* is closely affiliated. As in Sidney's *Arcadia* and
Spenser's *Faerie Queene*, sleep is associated with the loss of control
over one's passions and with vulnerability to a wide range of physical
and moral dangers. Far from being a simple state of passive repose,
sleep was often a charged site of potentially radical transformation.
From the Middle Ages onwards, romance fictions are concerned
above all with altered states, in the various senses of that phrase,
disorientations and reorientations that are at once physical, geographical and political. These altered states are brought about, in
Cymbeline, Pericles and *The Winter's Tale*, through disguises, drugs,
prophecies, marriages and travel. But in *The Tempest* Shakespeare
turned (or returned) to sleep as his agent of transport.[7]

When we first meet Ferdinand in act 1 scene 2, after he has been
led around the island by Ariel's disembodied music and has suc-
cumbed to the respective charms of Miranda and Prospero, he has
been possessed by a kind of waking sleep: 'My spirits, as in a dream,
are all bound up' by 'My father's loss, the weakness which I feel, /
The wreck of all my friends, [and] this man's threats / To whom
I am subdued' (1.2.485–88). Similarly, sleep comes to the seamen
after their extraordinary exertions and to the Neapolitan courtiers
after trauma and grief—combined, once again, with the musical

6. It is not clear from the text that Prospero puts Miranda to sleep—though virtually all
productions play it that way and most editors add a stage direction to that effect. But
even if Miranda's sleep is caused by Prospero, its timing and purpose are open to many
different interpretations: see Jennifer Lewin, '"Your actions are my dreams": Sleepy
minds in Shakespeare's last plays', *Shakespeare Studies*, 31 (2003), pp. 180–200, p. 187.
7. Both Mary Baine Campbell and Garrett Sullivan see sleep and dreams as doing similar
work to metaphor (defined by George Puttenham, in 1589, as 'an inversion of sense
by transport'): see Campbell, 'Dreaming, motion, meaning: Oneiric transport in
seventeenth-century Europe', in Katharine Hodgkin, Michelle O'Callaghan and S. J.
Wiseman (eds.), *Reading the Early Modern Dream: The Terrors of the Night* (London:
Routledge, 2008), pp. 15–30, and Sullivan, 'Romance, sleep, and the passions in Sir
Philip Sidney's *The Old Arcadia*', *ELH*, 74 (2007), pp. 735–57, pp. 752–3.

enchantments of Ariel.[8] These are the same sounds, perhaps, that inspire Caliban's dreams of clouds opening to pour riches on him:

> Be not afeard: the isle is full of noises,
> Sounds and sweet airs that give delight and hurt not.
> Sometimes a thousand twangling instruments
> Will hum about mine ears; and sometimes voices,
> That, if I then had waked after long sleep,
> Will make me sleep again; and then, in dreaming,
> The clouds methought would open and show riches
> Ready to drop upon me, that when I waked
> I cried to dream again.
>
> (3.2.128–36)

This may be the most moving—and certainly the most memorable—description of sleep in the play; but for Prospero's purposes, the most significant scene occurs in act 2, scene 1. In that scene Prospero makes Ariel send the Neapolitan king Alonso and his courtly entourage selectively to sleep. In order of their innocence, they give into what they describe as a 'wondrous heav[iness]' (190) and a 'strange drowsiness' (191)—the loyal old councillor Gonzalo first, then the passive noblemen Adrian and Francisco, and finally Alonso himself. Again, the slumber is sudden: as the others fall dead asleep around him, the king muses, 'What, all so soon asleep? I wish mine eyes would, with themselves, shut up my thoughts. I find they are inclined to do so' (183–85). Alonso's brother Sebastian and Prospero's brother Antonio remain awake and assure the king that they will stand guard over him. Looking at the sleeping figure of the king, Antonio urges Sebastian to follow his lead and usurp his brother's position:

ANTONIO
 Th'occasion speaks thee, and
My strong imagination sees a crown
Dropping upon thy head.
SEBASTIAN   What? Art thou waking?
ANTONIO
Do you not hear me speak?
SEBASTIAN   I do, and surely
It is a sleepy language, and thou speak'st
Out of thy sleep. What is it thou didst say?

---

8. Sarah F. Williams considers the relationship between music and enchanted sleep in a number of Elizabethan plays, but does not discuss the example of *The Tempest*, in '"Singe the enchantment for sleepe": Music and bewitched sleep in early modern English drama', in Christine Göttler and Wolfgang Neuber (eds.), *Spirits Unseen: The Representation of Subtle Bodies in Early Modern European Culture* (Leiden: Brill, 2008), pp. 179–94. Our best guide to Ariel's music is David Lindley, *Shakespeare and Music*, Arden Shakespeare (London: Methuen, 2006).

This is a strange repose, to be asleep
With eyes wide open; standing, speaking, moving,
And yet so fast asleep.
ANTONIO   Noble Sebastian,
Thou lett'st thy fortune sleep—die rather; wink'st
Whiles thou art waking.
SEBASTIAN   Thou dost snore distinctly;
There's meaning in thy snores.

                                        (2.1.200–11)

In this case, onstage sleep is both a sign of the sleepers' virtue and
a lesson about their vulnerability to the political machinations of
those who are not virtuous.

Similarly, Prospero's customary afternoon naps give Caliban and
his co-conspirators the opportunity for political machinations of
their own. Caliban punctuates the drunken banter of Stephano and
Trinculo with desperate urgings to take advantage of his master's
apparent vulnerability:

                I'll yield him thee asleep,
Where thou mayst knock a nail into his head.

                                        (3.2.57–58)

    as I told thee, 'tis a custom with him
I'th' afternoon to sleep. There thou mayst brain him

                                        (3.2.81–82)

Within this half hour will he be asleep.
Wilt thou destroy him then?

                                        (3.2.106–07)

                                speak softly;
All's hushed as midnight yet.

                                        (4.1.205–06)

                        If he awake,
From toe to crown he'll fill our skins with pinches,
Make us strange stuff.

                                        (4.1.230–32)

Once again, Prospero is using sleep to stage-manage a lesson in
virtue. But his sleep may have been bound up in another lesson in
virtue, one in which he himself served as the negative exemplar.
Renaissance writers unanimously warned against sleeping during
the day—on both medical and moral grounds. Cogan's *Haven of
Health* was unequivocal on this matter:

after[-]noone sleepe maketh undigested and rawe humours, whereof groweth oppilations, which oppilations engender fevers. Also it maketh a man slouthfull . . . Again, it causeth head ache, because grosse and undigested meate, remaining yet in the stomacke, sendeth up grosse vapours to the braine. And last of all, it breedeth rheumes. (sig.Gg4r)

So it is possible that Prospero's own afternoon sleep may well have struck *The Tempest*'s early audiences as an emblem for the abdication of princely duty, and therefore as a sign that he has not yet learned the lesson that landed him on the island in the first place.

Traditional approaches to *The Tempest* have tended to find not just in its closing speeches of forgiveness and release but in its very sleepiness a comforting note of resolution. While *The Tempest* has probably been subjected to more political readings than any other Shakespeare play, those critics who have considered the play's use of sleep and dreams have tended to take a different tack from the political readers, generally reinforcing the traditional interpretations that see Prospero as ultimately benign and his plot as moving towards contrition and reconciliation. Even Marjorie Garber, who is as sensitive to the play's unsettling qualities as anyone, describes Prospero's closing speeches as a 'calm resolution', concluding that 'imagination and the dream world give way in the half-light of morning to "clearer reason"' and that in act 5 of the play we are presented with a 'series of awakenings which will culminate in reconciliation'.[9] But in his essay on *The Tempest*, 'Miraculous harp', Harry Berger, Jr, challenged just this sort of reading of the play: 'The renunciation pattern is there', he concedes,

> but only as a general tendency against which the play strains. Too many cues and clues, too many quirky details, point in other directions, and critics have been able to make renunciation in this simple form the central action only by ignoring those details.[1]

To Berger's list of quirky details we can add one that has taken on new importance in the light of recent work on the history of sleep: in the closing scenes of the play, many characters express confusion about whether or not they are awake. The courtiers are finally released from the agonising spell that has them wandering around the island in a waking nightmare for the second half of the play, but

9. Marjorie B. Garber, *Dream in Shakespeare: From Metaphor to Metamorphosis* (New Haven: Yale University Press, 1974), pp. 209–12.
1. Harry Berger, Jr, 'Miraculous harp: A reading of Shakespeare's *Tempest*', in *Second World and Green World: Studies in Renaissance Fiction-Making* (Berkeley: University of California Press, 1988), pp. 147–85, p. 150.

we are given repeated indications throughout act 5 that they never
return to their senses. As Ariel delivers the dazed Neapolitans into
the magic circle, Prospero observes that

> The charm dissolves apace
> And, as the morning steals upon the night,
> Melting the darkness, so their rising senses
> Begin to chase the ignorant fumes that mantle
> Their clearer reason.
>
> (5.1.64–68)

And several lines later he promises that

> Their understanding
> Begins to swell, and the approaching tide
> Will shortly fill the reasonable shore
> That now lies foul and muddy.
>
> (5.1.79–82)

But we never see it happen. He spends most of his remaining words
trying to convince the courtiers that he is flesh and blood and not
another product of the 'subtleties o'th' isle, that will not let you
believe things certain' (5.1.124–25). Postcolonial critics have pointed
out that Prospero never really relinquishes the control he uses to
keep the other characters under his tyrannical spell (except, perhaps, in the epilogue where he turns that power over to the members of the audience).[2] Prospero promises Ariel, 'My charms I'll
break, their senses I'll restore, / And they shall be themselves'
(5.1.31–32)—but we never see it happen. We are told that he will
break his staff and drown his book, but we never witness it. We are
told that Ariel will be freed after performing one final task—but we
can only assume it happens. We are told that there will be forgiveness all around, but there are some significant exceptions when the
time comes to deliver. When the Boatswain is summoned to court in
the play's closing moments, and asked by Alonso what miracle has
delivered him and their ship, he responds, 'If I did think, sir, that I
were well awake, / I'd strive to tell you' (5.1.232–33). He explains
how they were roused from their sleep by 'strange and several noises
/ Of roaring, shrieking, howling, jingling chains', and 'Even in a
dream . . . brought moping hither' (235–43). So perhaps, in the end,
it is not the language and logic of the dream that pervade this play
but rather that 'strange repose' between waking and sleep.

If the historian A. Roger Ekirch is right in his extraordinary work
on 'Pre-industrial slumber in the British Isles', this hypnagogic state
was, in fact, much less strange in Shakespeare's day. Reminding us

---

2. See, for instance, Peter Hulme, 'Prospero and Caliban', in *Colonial Encounters: Europe
and the Native Caribbean, 1492–1797* (London: Methuen, 1986).

that early modern sleepers tended to have an hour or more of drowsy wakefulness between what was explicitly called 'first sleep' and 'second sleep', Ekirch argues that 'segmented sleep' was the norm before the advent of electricity and the dawning of artificial lighting, and suggests that it played an important role in both domestic and imaginative life:

> Until the modern era, up to an hour or more of quiet wakefulness midway through the night interrupted the rest of most Western Europeans, not just napping shepherds and slumbering woodsmen. Families rose from their beds to urinate, smoke tobacco, and even visit close neighbors. Remaining abed, many persons also made love, prayed, and, most importantly, reflected on the dreams that typically preceded waking from their 'first sleep'. Not only were these visions unusually vivid, but their images would have intruded far less on conscious thought had sleepers not stirred until dawn . . . In addition to suggesting that consolidated sleep, such as we today experience, is unnatural, segmented slumber afforded the unconscious an expanded avenue to the waking world that has remained closed for most of the Industrial Age.[3]

The relative tranquillity and continuity of modern slumber have allowed us to forget, in other words, that the border between wakefulness and sleep was a less stable and more active zone in the premodern imagination. And this in turn suggests that it may be the shifting, 'tricksy' charms of Ariel as much as Prospero's rough magic or Caliban's dreams of revenge that account for the play's uncanny ability to transport and be transported.

If we survey *The Tempest*'s later adaptations and appropriations, from the seventeenth century onwards, it quickly becomes clear that they have continued to explore the play's somniloquent power—even when the focus is far from sleepy. Fred McLeod Wilcox's pioneering film *Forbidden Planet* (1956) may be best remembered for taking *The Tempest* into the future and into outer space, where Ariel is transformed into the multilingual robot Robby. But it also takes us into the past and into the inner space of the dreaming mind. Prospero appears as Dr Morbius; he and his daughter are the only surviving members of an expedition for the exploration and colonisation of other planets. The name 'Morbius' combines Morpheus (the god of dreams) and *morbus* (Latin for 'illness'), and he accidentally unleashes the monstrously destructive psychic force

---

3. A. Roger Ekirch, 'Sleep we have lost: Pre-industrial slumber in the British Isles', *American Historical Review*, 106:2 (April 2001), pp. 342–85.

that stands in for Caliban in the film.[4] In what may be the most explicit Freudian parable in popular cinematic history, he realises too late that the sleep-learning exercises he has been using to absorb the superior intelligence of the original inhabitants of Altair-4 have given deadly, physical form to the fears and desires of his own unconscious mind. And where Prospero renounces his 'rough magic', Morbius abjures his 'id'—saving his daughter and her new love by sacrificing his uncontrollable passions.

In 1996, when the time came for the popular fantasy writer Neil Gaiman to conclude his long-running *Sandman* comic-book series, he turned to the text that has traditionally been read as Shakespeare's farewell to his art. The seventy-fifth and final issue of *The Sandman* is an almost word-for-word adaptation of *The Tempest*— but with a long epilogue in which Shakespeare meets none other than Morpheus himself (the story-giving Sandman of the series title). As they talk, and visit the otherwise uninhabited island that Morpheus lives on in a state of permanent exile, we discover that, at the beginning of his career, Shakespeare had signed a Faustian pact, receiving from the Sandman a pool of stories 'to give men dreams that would live on long after I was dead'.[5]

Perhaps the most interesting example of all is Derek Jarman's 1979 film of *The Tempest*. In *Jubilee*, Jarman had transported Queen Elizabeth I to the punk London of the 1970s, with the help of the magician John Dee and the spirit Ariel, and he later offered a queer take on the Renaissance with his *Caravaggio* and *Edward II*. But none of these projects prepares us for the sophistication with which Jarman approaches Shakespeare's play on sleep. Jarman had originally designed a stage production of the play, where Prospero turned out to be insane, imagining all of the parts from the asylum his brother had placed him in.[6] But the film production translates Prospero's seething imagination to the equally disturbing world of the dream: in the original press-kit Jarman described the setting as 'A film of the night—or one night, any night . . . a twilight never-never land'.[7] The film opens with the deep and rhythmic breathing of the sleeping Prospero, face covered by a gauzy scarf, thrashing and murmuring as he dreams up a cinematic flashback of a storm at sea. As with *Forbidden Planet*'s Morbius, Jarman's storm is a projection of Prospero's sleeping fantasies that casts a shadow over the entire film. The characters are both figments of a dream and projected images who vanish into thin air. Like Prospero's metatheatrical play-within-a-play in act 4, this

4. Tim Youngs, 'Cruising against the id: The transformation of Caliban in *Forbidden Planet*', in Nadia Lie and Theo D'haen (eds.), *Constellation Caliban: Figurations of a Character* (Amsterdam: Rodopi, 1997), pp. 211–29.
5. *Sandman* 75 (DC Comics, March 1996), p. 32.
6. Michael O'Pray, *Derek Jarman: Dreams of England* (London: BFI, 1996), p. 110.
7. *The Tempest*. Dir. Derek Jarman. 1979. DVD. Kino, 2000.

opening film-within-a-film calls attention to Prospero's own insubstantial status. And the use of candlelight for the Gothic interior scenes and of dusky blue filters outdoors keeps the viewers (literally and figuratively) in the dark, making us wonder if Prospero has ever woken up from his cinematic dream and who, for that matter, is calling the shots. With these techniques Jarman comes very close to what David Bevington sees as Shakespeare's most mature use of sleep:

> Sleep becomes a more ambiguous state . . . it grows more difficult to 'read' as a theatrical signifier, and more consciously connected . . . with the very business of writing and acting plays. As sleep becomes more metatheatrical, it serves as an apt vehicle for explorations of carnival inversion, indeterminacy of meaning, uncertainty as to the will of Providence, and the ironies of human lack of self-awareness.[8]

And finally, in the most audacious of the film's many textual rearrangements, Jarman forgives the courtiers and frees Ariel before falling asleep again. 'We are such stuff / As dreams are made on, and our little life / Is rounded with a sleep' is heard over the deep and rhythmic breathing that began the film, which then closes with a blackout and a dedication to the memory of Jarman's recently deceased mother.

Jarman is being true to the play's dramatic effect and intellectual background. Almost everyone remembers these lines as coming at the end of the play rather than (as they actually do) in the middle of a speech from the middle of act 4. And he is effectively reviving the Renaissance association between sleep and death—and between voyages (especially by sea) and mortality. But the scenario gives Prospero's dreams of death the kind of last word that they never quite achieve, and puts him in absolute control of his sleepy magic—however rough it turns out to be. Despite Prospero's—and Jarman's—desire to round things off with the ultimate slumber, *The Tempest* keeps talking in its sleep.

PETER HULME AND WILLIAM H. SHERMAN

Performances and Productions[†]

One of the peculiar features of *The Tempest* is that after the early performances the "original" play wasn't seen again until 1838: for nearly 200 years of its history, to see *The Tempest* performed meant watching the version of the play as rewritten by John Dryden and

---

8. Bevington, 'Asleep onstage', p. 53.
† Written for this Norton Critical Edition. All notes are by the authors.

William Davenant as *The Enchanted Island* (see below, pp. 314–20). This version, particularly when adapted as an opera, emphasized the play's theatricality: *The Tempest* has more music than most of Shakespeare's plays, and more spectacle. Indeed, the spectacles are crucial elements of the plot—whether they are the magical illusions that entrap and tantalize Prospero's enemies or the celebratory masque Prospero organizes to mark the betrothal of Miranda and Ferdinand. For that reason, the play continues to generate productions and performances that cross generic boundaries and push the limits of technology. Perhaps fittingly, the temptations and dangers of both science and illusion are key themes of the play, its finale seeing Prospero renounce his own technology—magic—and start to pay attention to the importance of human relationships. In the essay that follows, we describe some of the most significant productions from the last century or so in order to give a sense of the variety of forms in which the play has been seen, the range of artistic responses that keep making this old text relevant to new audiences.[1]

The early twentieth century saw a classic modern production of the play and the earliest film version, not to mention the most ambitious performance ever "staged": Percy MacKaye's community masque called *Caliban by the Yellow Sands*, a huge outdoor show involving over 1,500 chiefly amateur participants, watched in 1916 by tens of thousands of spectators in New York (see below, pp. 330–43). Powerful actor-managers could always choose their roles, and in many ways Prospero was an obvious choice—being himself the actor-manager *par excellence*. So the decision by Herbert Beerbohm Tree (1852–1917) to play Caliban in his 1904 production at Her Majesty's Theatre in London was of great significance. Although Tree retained some of the monstrous characteristics of late nineteenth-century productions that had represented Caliban as a kind of "missing link"—the pointed ears, the overgrown fingernails, the unkempt hair—he played the character as a creature struggling to become human. In his notes on the play Tree recalled that, contrary to misreadings, Prospero's lines "Then was this island— / Save for the son that she did litter here, / A freckled whelp, hag-born—not honored with / a human shape" (1.2.281–84) state unequivocally that Caliban was human, which is how Tree played him.

In particular, Tree placed great emphasis on the ending of the play. He omitted the play's epilogue and moved Prospero's renunciation of

1. For more extensive studies, see Virginia Mason Vaughan, *The Tempest: Shakespeare in Performance* (Manchester: Manchester UP, 2011), and the editions of the play by Christine Dymkowski, *The Tempest*, Shakespeare in Production (Cambridge: Cambridge UP, 2000), and David Lindley, *The Tempest*, Shakespeare at Stratford Series (London: Arden Shakespeare, 2003).

his magic ("Ye elves of hills") to the final scene, rearranging matters so that Caliban was seen creeping out of his cave as the ship bearing Prospero and his companions disappeared over the horizon. Crouched on a lonely rock, Caliban stretched out his arms before the final curtain triggered tumultuous applause. In the souvenir program issued for the fiftieth performance, Tree offered his own explanation of the play's final tableau:

> Prospero breaks his staff, at which there is lightning and thunder, followed by darkness. Through the darkness we gradually see once more a picture of the Yellow Sands enveloped in a purple haze. The Nymphs are again singing 'Come unto these yellow sands.' But their music is broken by the homing-song of the sailors, and we see the ship sailing away, carrying Prospero and the lovers, and all their train. Caliban creeps from his cave, and watches the departing ship bearing away the freight of humanity which for a brief spell has gladdened and saddened his island home, and taught him to 'seek for grace.' For the last time Ariel appears, singing the song of the bee. Taking flight at the words 'Merrily, merrily shall I live now,' the voice of the sprite rises higher and higher until it is merged into the note of the lark—Ariel is now free as a bird. Caliban listens for the last time to the sweet air, then turns sadly in the direction of the departing ship. The play is ended. As the curtain rises again, the ship is seen on the horizon, Caliban stretching out his arms towards it in mute despair. The night falls, and Caliban is left on the lonely rock. He is a King once more.[2]

This offers a nice indication of how directors can make meaning of the play's silences—in this case, just how all the actors leave the stage at the end of the action. All the actors except for Tree himself, so that Caliban is allowed to take center stage.

Lasting less than twelve minutes and using the most primitive cinematic technology, the 1908 *Tempest* directed by Percy Stow (1876–1919) is the earliest surviving presentation of the entire play on the silver screen. *The Tempest*'s first foray into the world of film had come a few years earlier, when Charles Urban's cameras captured the opening storm and shipwreck from Tree's stage production: it was made for a regional tour by Tree's company and intended to replace the cumbersome and expensive apparatus needed to produce the scene, with the two-minute film giving way to a live rendition of the rest of the performance. But Stow's adaptation for the

2. Tree's souvenir program and his "A Personal Explanation" can be found at David Lindley, *Beerbohm Tree's 1904 Version of Shakespeare's Tempest*, University of Leeds, 2010, http://eprints.whiterose.ac.uk/10743/. See also Mary N. Nilan, "'The Tempest' at the Turn of the Century: Cross-currents in Production," *Shakespeare Survey* 25 (1972): 113–23.

Clarendon Film Company stands out not only as the first attempt to capture the entire plot (including several pieces of reported action from the story's pre-history) but indeed as the first time cinematic effects were used to liberate its characters from the conventions of theatrical staging.

The opening minutes introduced viewers to the new medium's brave new world; and while the compressions of the plot are sometimes jarring and the acting often looks silly to twenty-first-century eyes, the effects must have charmed the film's original audience and still carry a quaint magic today. Stow's outdoor settings, stop-motion shooting, double exposures, and jump cuts more than made up for the lack of speech to deliver pictures that were moving in both senses of the word. Walter Benjamin argued that one of the functions of art is to create a demand that can only be satisfied later: as he put it in his landmark essay "The Work of Art in the Age of Mechanical Reproduction" (1936), there are "critical epochs in which a certain art form aspires to effects which could be fully obtained only with a changed technical standard, that is to say, in a new art form."[3] Watching Stow's short *Tempest*—and knowing the play's peculiar appeal to film directors throughout the twentieth century—it's easy to see how Shakespeare calls forth artistic techniques that only became possible with the invention of cinema.

Three of the most highly regarded twentieth-century theatrical productions of *The Tempest* were those directed by Giorgio Strehler, Peter Brook, and Jonathan Miller. Strehler's *La tempesta* is often referred to as the most visually impressive modern production of the play. Strehler (1921–1997) had mounted the very first Italian theatrical production of *The Tempest* in 1948 in Florence, but the renowned version—in a translation by Agostino Lombardi—was made for his Piccolo Teatro in Milan in 1978, and then revived in Paris, Rome, and Milan in 1983–84, touring also to New York and Los Angeles. The production is particularly remembered for its scenography, designed by Luciano Damiani, which produced spectacular effects, though with simple materials. When the audience entered the theater, a white curtain—a simple large sheet—hid the stage. Voices could be heard and the shadows of actors seen moving around, while thunder growled in the background. Then, as the house lights were turned off, flashing backlights signaled the start of the tempest, which grew to a crescendo of screams and musical effects. The stage seemed covered in waves as stagehands moved around under a huge blue silk sheet. The top-mast fell. The sailors

---

3. Walter Benjamin, "The Work of Art in the Age of Mechanical Reproduction," in *Illuminations*, ed. Hannah Arendt, trans. Harry Zohn (New York: Schocken Books, 1969), p. 237.

and courtiers appeared and disappeared in the waves. A final high-pitched scream marked the end of the scene. Gradually the noise of the tempest faded, replaced by whispered voices, the sound of bells, and the music of a viola and a flute. The large white sheet dropped at the foot of the proscenium—from where it would intermittently rise at moments of turbulence—revealing a stage dusted with sand where an old man was talking to a girl. The ending of the play was equally spectacular. When Ariel was freed, he clambered over the folded sheet and ran up the central aisle, escaping the play and the theater itself. Prospero then broke his staff, causing the whole stage set to collapse around him. This was a metatheatrical *Tempest*, underscoring Prospero's power as dramatist and stage manager. The characterization in Strehler's production was largely traditional, though Caliban was clearly played as a black slave, an early indication of the "colonial" reading of the play that would soon find its clearest form in Jonathan Miller's production. In this respect, Strehler was following practice in the United States, where African American actors had been cast as Caliban in several postwar productions.[4]

Peter Brook (b. 1925) has directed *The Tempest* more times than any other text by any other author. And few directors working in any period or medium have gone through such dramatic changes of approach to the same source material. Brook's first production of the play, which closed the 1957 season at the Memorial Theatre in Stratford-upon-Avon, was relatively traditional. While it established John Gielgud as one of the twentieth century's great Prosperos, it marked a crisis in Brook's relationship with Shakespeare. In an open letter to the playwright, published in *The Times* on September 1, 1957, he explained that in the course of the production he came to realize that *The Tempest* was Shakespeare's "gravest mistake" and apologized to him for failing to disguise its weakness more thoroughly.[5] By 1968, however, Brook's relationship to both author and play had recovered. That year Brook published his seminal study *The Empty Space* in which he described *The Tempest* as a successful example of "how a metaphysical play can find a natural idiom that is holy, comic and rough."[6] And despite his claim (in the same essay) that the text is "unplayable today," he chose it for his contribution to the 1968 Théâtre des Nations Festival in Paris.

The student riots of May 1968 forced this festival to close, and Brook's "experiment" (as he called it) was relocated to London's

4. See Giorgio Strehler, "Notes on *The Tempest*," trans. Thomas Simpson, *PAJ: A Journal of Performance and Art* 24:3 (2002): 1–17.

5. Peter Brook, *The Shifting Point: Theatre, Film, Opera 1946–1987* (New York: Harper & Row, 1987), p. 4.

6. Peter Brook, *The Empty Space* (London: MacGibbon & Kee, 1968), p. 95.

Round House. More provocation than production, it marked a radical departure in both scenography and dramaturgy. Just as the students on the streets were challenging the capitalism and puritanism of their parents, Brook called for an approach to the play that purged it of the smug and sentimental Englishness that had come to stifle it. He broke down the divisions between actors and audience and (anticipating his epoch-making *Midsummer Night's Dream* of 1970) provided only the most minimal structure for the stage—with both characters and spectators moving freely around a set of bare platforms on industrial scaffolding. And he shattered the text into pieces, subordinating its poetry to physical and sexual violence, putting what language remained into the mouths of performers who not only came from different countries but invoked theatrical traditions very remote from the Elizabethan stage.

Contemporary postcolonial approaches to *The Tempest* are often dated from Octave Mannoni's *Psychologie de la colonisation* (1950), translated into English in 1956 (see above, pp. 146–54). The 1970 production at the Mermaid Theatre by Jonathan Miller (b. 1934) had already made use of Mannoni's ideas, and the 1988 Old Vic revival was nicely timed in the light of growing academic interest in what was becoming known as postcolonial studies. Miller's 1988 program contained extensive quotations from Mannoni. Andrzej Krauze's striking image (used on the cover of this Norton Critical Edition) was on the program, as well as being an advertising poster. Krauze (b. 1947) had honed his skills as a cartoonist and an illustrator under the Communist regime of his native Poland, and his characteristically strong lines are here put to good use, with the cracked birdlike skull suggestive of the predatory violence just below the surface finery of the white courtiers. In keeping with the implications of Miller's production, the animalistic imagery usually associated with Caliban is turned back on the play's European noblemen. By contrast, and against previous British practice, Ariel and Caliban were cast and played simply as black humans, Caliban as a field hand, Ariel as a house servant—perhaps indicating the influence of Aimé Césaire's 1969 version of the play, *Une tempête* (A Tempest; see below, pp. 343–47). The last scene of Beerbohm Tree's 1904 production had Caliban surveying the island on which he had been left, alone. In a gesture to Frantz Fanon's warnings in *The Wretched of the Earth* about the pitfalls of national consciousness, Miller's production similarly ended on the island, but now with Ariel picking up the pieces of Prospero's broken staff, holding them together, and pointing them threateningly at Caliban.[7]

---

7. Frantz Fanon, *The Wretched of the Earth* (1961), trans. Richard Philcox (New York: Grove Press, 2004).

Fully operatic and balletic versions of the play inevitably emphasize movement and music, expanding the original but also sometimes offering genuine insights into the play. Two examples stand out from the last half-century, by the Ballet Rambert and by the composer Thomas Adès.

Rambert (as it's now called) is Britain's oldest dance company, begun in 1916 by Marie Rambert, a Polish refugee. The Ballet Rambert was a full-time touring company during World War II but returned in the 1960s to its original, more adventurous ethos, introducing US choreographers such as Glen Tetley (1926–2007), who mounted productions like *Pierrot Lunaire*, *Ricercare*, and (in 1979) *The Tempest*, his only full-evening work, with Christopher Bruce as Prospero. It was later performed by the Norwegian National Ballet as part of Tetley's eightieth-birthday celebrations. Tetley is renowned for having combined the previously quite separate traditions of ballet and modern dance. Once other choreographers seized on the range of movement vocabulary he had opened up, the distinctions between ballet and contemporary dance became forever optional.

Ballet has *none* of Shakespeare's words to work with and therefore needs to find the spirit of the play in completely different ways. Tetley's *Tempest* was primarily visual in impact, with—as in Strehler's landmark production—physical material playing an important part. His designer, Nadine Baylis, provided costumes with yards of trailing silk, like those seen in Japanese Kabuki theater. In the opening scene dancers emerged from great waves of silk symbolizing the sea. At one point Ariel entered the stage trailing huge flowing wings, like a gigantic butterfly. Kabuki-style figures and martial arts sequences added to the evident rapprochement Tetley was suggesting between the play and Chinese philosophy. As Tetley wrote, "Prospero's speeches link with the thoughts of Heraclitus and Lao-tse: life is a paradox; in life we must accept death; to lose everything is to regain everything; our world is change; everything flows." In conclusion, he appended a quotation from Lao-tse: "Going far is returning."[8]

Critics noted that the play's family drama was enhanced in the ballet. Ferdinand and Miranda celebrated their love inside a magic square, quite separate from the rest of the action. Sycorax made an early appearance giving birth to Caliban, her presence on the island perhaps hinting that Prospero is the father. Certainly Caliban and Ariel (as danced by Thomas Yang and Gianfranco Paoluzi) looked like

8. Quoted from Tetley's program notes for the New York premiere of the Norwegian National Ballet's production in Anna Kisselgoff, "Dance View: Tetley Looks to the Orient in His 'Tempest,'" *New York Times*, October 24, 1982, p. 72.

brothers under the domination of Prospero's father figure, rather than like opposing forces. Prospero resembled a young sage preaching reconciliation, not a magician acting as an agent of providence. Some critics thought that Tetley's most inventive choreography was inspired by the subtly homoerotic encounters between Prospero, Ariel, and Caliban—adding yet another dimension to the relationships between Shakespeare's characters.

Many composers have written incidental music for *The Tempest*, including Tchaikovsky, Sibelius, Michael Tippett, and Michael Nyman, but attempts to produce a fully fledged opera based on the play have resulted in only one marked contemporary success: the 2004 version by Thomas Adès (b. 1971) premiered at the Royal Opera House, London, with Simon Keenlyside as Prospero and Cynthia Sieden as Ariel. Adès's music was described by critics with adjectives such as incandescent, ravishing, lush, and evocative. In operatic terms, Adès's *Tempest* is quite traditional in form: the play's five acts become the opera's conventional three, with the music mostly tonal or modal. There are clearly identified duets and ensembles, and the kinds of dances often found in Baroque-period operas.

The libretto by Meredith Oakes closely follows the Shakespearean narrative while reducing and paraphrasing the text into a half-rhymed vernacular. So, for example, the original "Full fathom five thy father lies / Of his bones are coral made; / Those are pearls that were his eyes" (1.2.395–97) becomes in the libretto "Five fathoms deep / Your father lies / Those are pearls / That were his eyes." Small but significant changes of emphasis tend to heighten the play's dramatic conflicts. Antonio and Sebastian have sharper disagreements. Prospero is humanized by limiting his power over the other characters so that, for example, Miranda's relationship with Ferdinand is developed against his will, though with his ultimate blessing, and Antonio snubs his final offer of forgiveness, saying, "Your life has been my death." As in Jonathan Miller's production, at the end of the opera Caliban and Ariel are left together on the island.

The high soprano vocal part written for Ariel is considered one of the most difficult vocal parts ever written for a coloratura. Prospero is a high baritone; Caliban, Ferdinand, and Antonio all tenors, breaking the operatic tradition that would have seen rivals and opposites Ferdinand and Caliban distinguished vocally. Stefano (bass baritone) and Trinculo (countertenor) might seem ill matched vocally, yet Stefano is allowed a measure of the seriousness that comes with that range. As with Oakes's libretto, Adès's musical decisions tend to emphasize the complexity of the play's psychology and politics.

In recent decades, some of *The Tempest*'s most adventurous travels have been on screen rather than on stage—though few productions in any medium have taken the play as far as the pioneering sci-fi film *Forbidden Planet* (1956), which transposed the action to outer space and accompanied it with history's first electronic-music film score.[9] Closer to home, two of Britain's most avant garde filmmakers, Derek Jarman (1942–1994) and Peter Greenaway (b. 1942), would turn back to the Renaissance at key points in their careers, and the text that both of them of them chose was *The Tempest*. In 1978, Jarman had marked the twenty-fifth year of the reign of the second Queen Elizabeth with a punk fantasia called *Jubilee*. The anarchic film offered a prescient portrait of the Margaret Thatcher era; but it was set in the sixteenth century rather than the twentieth, and the action that occupies most of the film is a dark glimpse of the distant future revealed to Queen Elizabeth I. The conjuror responsible for this time-traveling spectacle was John Dee (1527–1609), sometimes thought to be a model for Prospero, and like the stage magician in Shakespeare's play he calls on Ariel to deliver the vision to the Queen (and to us).

One year later, Jarman produced a full-length film of *The Tempest* itself, giving the singer Toyah Wilcox and blind mime artist Jack Birkett—both of whom had appeared in *Jubilee*—the roles of Miranda and Caliban, and casting the radical poet-actor Heathcote Williams as Prospero. If *Jubilee* used the Renaissance to hold the mirror up to modern Britain, Jarman's *Tempest* used a range of modern technologies to travel back and forth in time, producing some of his oeuvre's most sensitive meditations on history and even mortality. In one of the production's many rearrangements of Shakespeare's text, he closed the film with Prospero's soliloquy from Act 4, concluding not with reconciliation or a return to home but with the philosophical frame of the play's most resonant lines—"We are such stuff / As dreams are made on, and our little life / Is rounded with a sleep."

After *The Tempest*, Jarman would go on to produce *The Angelic Conversation* (an experimental collage set to readings of Shakespeare's sonnets), a film of Christopher Marlowe's play *Edward II*, and a meditation on the life of Caravaggio. Like Jarman, Greenaway has often found his center of gravity in the sixteenth and seventeenth centuries. More at home in Dutch art and Italian architecture than in English literature, however, his film of *The*

9. See Lisa Hopkins, *Screen Adaptations of "The Tempest"* (London: Methuen Drama, 2008); Judith Buchanan, *Shakespeare on Film* (London: Routledge, 2005); and Simon Ryle, "Re-nascences: The Tempest and New Media," in his *Shakespeare, Cinema and Desire* (Basingstoke: Palgrave Macmillan, 2014), pp. 174–211.

Tempest—1990's *Prospero's Books*—looks at the play through the eyes of a Renaissance art historian, with many of its tableaux taken directly from the period's paintings and illustrations. But as the title suggests, Greenaway's central conceit is the small library of books that Gonzalo smuggles into Prospero's boat—the volumes that the exiled duke "prized above my dukedom" and which he would need (as Greenaway imagined) to find his way to the island, subdue the natives, raise his daughter, and continue his studies. These twenty-four fanciful volumes are introduced one by one as interludes in, or glosses on, the action. They conclude with a volume containing thirty-six plays—none other than the First Folio preserving the first printing of *The Tempest*, suggesting that Prospero's art and Shakespeare's are inextricably linked.

In casting John Gielgud as Prospero, in fact, Greenaway not only provided a fitting swan song to the twentieth century's greatest player of that role but also played on the idea that the character stands in for Shakespeare himself—as author more than orchestrator of the play's plot. Perhaps the most audacious (if also tedious) aspect of Greenaway's film is that Prospero writes the story as it unfolds, with Gielgud speaking all of the lines of all of the characters until he renounces his art toward the end of the play. As if to compensate for the silenced voices of the other characters, Greenaway's inspired casting of Caliban gave the role to the experimental dancer Michael Clark, who says more with his movements than most actors manage with words, making this production a play of the body as much as of the mind.

Finally, and unusually, the U.S. director Julie Taymor (b. 1952) has shown herself equally adept with stage and screen—taking us full circle to the proto-cinematic stagings with which we began. In 1986, Taymor directed her first Shakespeare play, *The Tempest*, for Theatre for a New Audience in New York, followed by *The Taming of the Shrew* and *Titus Andronicus*. She later received considerable acclaim for her stage direction of the musical *The Lion King* (1997), adapted from the animated film, and she has also directed both classical and contemporary operas. Taymor's first major film was *Titus* (1999), based on Shakespeare's *Titus Andronicus* and starring Anthony Hopkins. Its opening scene surprised viewers by introducing the ancient battles that frame the play through a modern boy playing with toy soldiers. Her film of *The Tempest* (2010) took chances of a different kind: it is probably the first, and certainly the highest-profile, version to turn Prospero into Prospera, with Helen Mirren garnering considerable acclaim for her performance.

The film's screenplay is "adapted from" the play, but narrative changes are in fact minor. Prospera's backstory is inevitably slightly

different, with Glen Berger seamlessly providing new "Shakespearean" lines; some scenes, like the masque, are cut to allow for cinematic equivalents; and Ferdinand is given Feste's song from *Twelfth
Night*, "O Mistress Mine," with which to serenade Miranda. The
volcanic beaches of Lān'ai, where much of the filming was done,
leads to the "yellow sands" becoming the "darkened sands."

The change of gender at the center of the film makes slight but
significant shifts to many of the relationships between the characters. As mother, Prospera is closer and warmer than usual to
Miranda. Although Ariel and Caliban are well contrasted—Ariel
almost translucent, Caliban half covered in mud—both are male,
and their exchanges with Prospera carry subtle erotic charges. At
the end of the film, Prospera and Caliban stare at each other in
close-up, a powerful moment of the kind that only film can provide.
Most interesting, though, is the sense that, for Prospera, the island
has provided freedom more than exile: freedom to conduct her
alchemical experiments far from the disapproving eyes of Milanese
men. Antonio has accused her of killing her husband by witchcraft—
strengthening the implicit parallel with Sycorax—so revenge is certainly a motive, but there is a sense that if it were not for her
daughter, this Prospera would feel no urgency to go back to Italy.
Laced into her tight-fitting dress for the confrontation with the
courtiers, she is on the cusp of returning to a world where women's
options are much more restricted than on the island of her exile.

REWRITINGS AND
APPROPRIATIONS

Plays

JOHN FLETCHER AND PHILIP MASSINGER

John Fletcher (1579–1625), one of the most prolific writers for the Renaissance stage, is best known for his collaborations with Francis Beaumont, Philip Massinger (1583–1640), and William Shakespeare himself (on two or more of the plays he had a hand in after *The Tempest*). Fletcher consistently explored the tragicomic and romantic possibilities suggested by *The Tempest*, and many of his plays featured travel and trade in exotic settings. In the opening scenes from *The Sea Voyage* (written in 1622 and published in 1647), Fletcher and Massinger offer their own version of a dramatic tempest off the coast of a "desert island."

From The Sea Voyage[†]

Act 1, Scene 1

The scene: first at sea, then in the desert islands

A *tempest, thunder and lightning. Enter* MASTER *and two* SAILORS.

MASTER
    Lay her aloof,[1] the sea grows dangerous:
    How it spits against the clouds, how it capers,
    And how the fiery element frights it back!
    There be devils dancing in the air, I think.
    I saw a dolphin hang i' th' horns of the moon,
    Shot from a wave: hey day, hey day!
    How she kicks and yerks?[2]
    Down with'e main mast, lay her at hull,[3]
    Fardel up all her linens,[4] and let her ride it out.

[†] From *The Sea Voyage* [1622], first printed in Francis Beaumont and John Fletcher, *Comedies and Tragedies* (London: Humphrey Robinson and Humphrey Mosely, 1647). All notes are by the editors of this Norton Critical Edition.
1. Clear of the shore.
2. Jerks.
3. With all sails furled.
4. Furl all her sails.

1 SAILOR

She'll never brook[5] it, Master.

She's so deep laden that she'll bulge.

MASTER   Hang her.

Can she not buffet[6] with the storm a little?

How it tosses her! She reels like a drunkard.

2 SAILOR

We have discovered the land, sir.

Pray let's make in, she's so drunk; else,

She may chance to cast up all her lading.

1 SAILOR

Stand in,[7] stand in, we are all lost else,

Lost and perished.

MASTER   Steer her a-starboard there.

2 SAILOR

Bear in[8] with all the sail we can. See Master,

See, what a clap of thunder there is,

What a face of heaven, how dreadfully it looks?

MASTER

Thou rascal, thou fearful rogue, thou hast been praying;

I see't in thy face, thou hast been mumbling,

When we are split,[9] you slave. Is this a time,

To discourage our friends with your cold orisons?[1]

Call up the Boatswain. How it storms! Holla!

      [*Enter* BOATSWAIN.]

BOATSWAIN

What shall we do, Master?

Cast over all her lading?[2] she will not swim

An hour else.

MASTER   The storm is loud,

We cannot hear one another. What's the coast?

BOATSWAIN

We know not yet; shall we make in?[3]

            Enter ALBERT, FRANVILE, LA-MURE, TIBALT DU-PONT, MORILLAT.

ALBERT

What comfort, sailors?

I never saw, since I have known the sea

---

5. Endure.
6. Struggle.
7. Head for the shore.
8. Head for the shore
9. Broken.
1. Prayers.
2. Throw overboard the cargo.
3. Head for the shore.

(Which has been this twenty years) so rude a tempest.
In what state are we?

MASTER   Dangerous enough, Captain.
We have sprung five leaks, and no little ones;
Still rage; besides her ribs are open;
Her rudder almost spent; prepare yourselves;
And have good courages, death comes but once,
And let him come in all his frights.

ALBERT   Is't not possible
To make in to th' land? 'Tis here before us.

MORILLAT
Here, hard by, sir.

MASTER   Death is nearer, gentlemen.
Yet do not cry, let's die like men.

TIBALT
Shall's hoist the boat out
And go all at one cast?[4] The more the merrier.

MASTER
You are too hasty, Monsieur.
Do ye long to be i' th' fish-market before your time?
Hold her up there.

Act 1, Scene 4

* * *

Enter SEBASTIAN *and* NICUSA.

AMINTA
But ha! What things are these?
Are they human creatures?

TIBALT   I have heard of sea-calves.

ALBERT
They are no shadows, sure: they have legs and arms.

TIBALT
They hang but lightly on, though.

AMINTA
How they look! Are they men's faces?

TIBALT
They have horse-tails growing to 'em, goodly long manes.

AMINTA
Alas, what sunk eyes they have!
How they crept in, as if they had been frightened!
Sure they are wretched men.

4. All at once.

TIBALT   Where are their wardrobes?
   Look ye, Franvile, here are a couple of courtiers.
AMINTA
   They kneel, alas, poor souls.
ALBERT
   What are ye? Speak: are ye alive,
   Or wand'ring shadows, that find no place on earth
   Till ye reveal some hidden secret?
SEBASTIAN
   We are men as you are;
   Only our miseries make us seem monsters.
   If ever pity dwelt in noble hearts—
ALBERT
   We understand 'em, too: pray mark 'em, gentlemen.
SEBASTIAN
   Or that heaven is pleased with human charity;
   If ever ye have heard the name of friendship;
   Or suffered in yourselves the least afflictions;
   Have gentle fathers that have bred ye tenderly,
   And mothers that have wept for your misfortunes,
   Have mercy on our miseries.
ALBERT   Stand up, wretches;
   Speak boldly, and have release.
NICUSA   If ye be Christians,
   And by that blessed name, bound to relieve us,
   Convey us from this island.
ALBERT   Speak: what are ye?
SEBASTIAN
   As you are, gentle born. To tell ye more
   Were but to number up our own calamities,
   And turn your eyes wild with perpetual weepings.
   These many years in this most wretched island
   We two have lived, the scorn and game of fortune.
   Bless yourselves from it, noble gentlemen;
   The greatest plagues that human nature suffers
   Are seated here, wildness, and wants innumerable.
ALBERT
   How came ye hither?
NICUSA
   In a ship, as you do, and as you might have been
   Had not heaven preserved ye for some more noble use;
   Wracked desperately; our men and all consumed
   But we two, that still live and spin out
   The thin and ragged threads of our misfortunes.

ALBERT
  Is there no meat above?
SEBASTIAN   Nor meat nor quiet;
  No summer here, to promise anything;
  Nor autumn, to make full the reapers hands;
  The earth obdurate to the tears of heaven,
  Let's nothing shoot but poisoned weeds.
  No rivers, nor no pleasant groves, no beasts;
  All that were made for man's use fly this desert;
  No airy fowl dares make his flight over it,
  It is so ominous.
  Serpents and ugly things, the shames of nature,
  Roots of malignant tastes, foul standing waters;
  Sometimes we find a fulsome sea-root,
  And that's a delicate; a rat sometimes,
  And that we hunt like princes in their pleasure;
  And when we take a toad, we make a banquet.

THOMAS HEYWOOD

In an unusually long and varied career as a writer, Thomas Heywood
(1573?–1641) captured the vital energies of English writing in an age
that saw both the revival of classical learning and the expansion of
geographical horizons. *The English Traveller* (first performed around
1625 and first printed in 1633) takes a skeptical look at the period's
vogue for travel and draws heavily on the themes and vocabularies of
The Tempest, as in this scene comparing the Gallants' drunken revelry
to the experience of a shipwreck.

From The English Traveller†

From *Act 2, Scene 2*

  Enter YOUNG LIONEL, RIOTER, BLANDA, SCAPHA, *two* GAL-
  LANTS, *and two* WENCHES, *as newly waked from sleep.*
YOUNG LIONEL. We had a stormy night on't.
BLANDA.   The wine still works,
  And with the little rest they have took tonight
  They are scarce come to themselves.

---

† From *The English Traveller* [c. 1625] (London: Robert Raworth, 1633). All notes are by
the editors of this Norton Critical Edition.

YOUNG LIONEL.   Now 'tis a calm,
   Thanks to those gentle sea-gods that have brought us
   To this safe harbour. Can you tell their names?
SCAPHA.   He with the painted staff I heard you call
   Neptune.
YOUNG LIONEL.   The dreadful god of seas,
   Upon whose back ne'er stuck March fleas.[1]
FIRST GALLANT.   One with the bill keeps Neptune's porpoises,
   So Ovid says in's *Metamorphoses*.
SECOND GALLANT.   A third the learned poets write on,
   And as they say, his name is Triton.[2]
YOUNG LIONEL.   These are the marine gods to whom my father
   In his long voyage prays, too. Cannot they,
   That brought us to our haven, bury him
   In their abyss? For if he safe arrive,
   I, with these sailors, sirens and what not,
   Am sure here to be shipwracked!
FIRST WENCH.   [*To* RIOTER.]   Stand up stiff.
RIOTER.   But that the ship so totters; I shall fall.
FIRST WENCH.   If thou fall, I'll fall with thee.
RIOTER.   Now I sink,
   And, as I dive and drown, thus by degrees
   I'll pluck thee to the bottom.   *They fall.*
         Enter REIGNALD.
YOUNG LIONEL.   Amain[3] for England! See, see,
   The Spaniard now strikes[4] sail.
REIGNALD.   So must you all.
FIRST GALLANT.   Whence is your ship? From the Bermoothes?[5]
REIGNALD.   Worse, I think: from Hell.
   We are all lost, split, shipwracked and undone;
   This place is a mere quicksands.
SECOND GALLANT.   So we feared.
REIGNALD.   Where's my young master?
YOUNG LIONEL.   Here man. Speak. The news?
REIGNALD.   The news is, I, and you—
YOUNG LIONEL.   What?
REIGNALD.   She, and all these—
BLANDA.   I?

1. Fleas are particularly active in spring.
2. A sea god, half man, half fish.
3. Full speed.
4. Lowers.
5. Bermuda; but also an infamous haunt of prostitutes in London.

REIGNALD.   We, and all ours, are in one turbulent sea
   Of fear, despair, disaster and mischance
   Swallowed. Your father, sir—
YOUNG LIONEL.   Why, what of him?
REIGNALD.   He is—
   O, I want breath—
YOUNG LIONEL.   Where?
REIGNALD.   Landed, and at hand.
YOUNG LIONEL.   Upon what coast? Who saw him?
REIGNALD.   I, these eyes.
YOUNG LIONEL.   O Heaven, what shall I do, then?
REIGNALD.   Ask ye me
   What shall become of you that have not yet
   Had time of study to dispose myself?
   I say again, I was upon the quay,
   I saw him land and this way bend his course.
   What drunkard's this, that can outsleep a storm
   Which threatens all our ruins? Wake him.
BLANDA.   Ho, Rioter, awake!
RIOTER.   Yes, I am wake.
   How dry hath this salt water made me. Boy,
   Give me th'other glass.
YOUNG LIONEL.   Arise, I say.
   My father's come from sea.
RIOTER.   If he be come,
   Bid him be gone again.
REIGNALD.   Can you trifle
   At such a time, when your inventions, brains,
   Wits, plots, devices, stratagems and all
   Should be at one in action? Each of you
   That love your safeties, lend your helping hands,
   Women and all, to take this drunkard hence
   And to bestow him elsewhere.
BLANDA.   Lift, for heaven's sake!
   They carry him in.
REIGNALD.   But what am I the nearer? Were all these
   Conveyed to sundry places, and unseen,
   The stain of our disorders still remain,
   Of which the house will witness, and the old man
   Must find when he enters; and for these
   I am left here to answer.
      Enter again [YOUNG LIONEL *and the others*].
                         What, is he gone?
YOUNG LIONEL.   But whither? But into the self-same house

That harbours him, my father's, where we all
Attend from him surprisal.[6]

REIGNALD.   I will make
That prison of your fears your sanctuary.
Go, get you in together.

YOUNG LIONEL.   To this house?

REIGNALD.   Your father's, with your sweetheart, these and all.
Nay, no more words, but do't.

BLANDA.   That were
To betray us to his fury.

REIGNALD.   I have't here
To bail you hence at pleasure. And in th'interim
I'll make this supposed gaol to you as safe
From th'injured old man's just incensèd spleen
As were you now together i'the Low Countries,
Virginia, or i'th'Indies.

BLANDA.   Present fear
Bids us to yield unto the faint belief
Of the least hopèd safety.

REIGNALD.   Will you in?

ALL.   By thee we will be counselled.
    [*All except* YOUNG LIONEL *and* REIGNALD *go in.*]

JOHN DRYDEN AND WILLIAM DAVENANT

Many of Shakespeare's plays were revived for the Restoration stage, and
the author and critic John Dryden (1631–1700) and the playwright and
theater manager William Davenant (1606–1668) were responsible for
several of the most successful adaptations. As a play (first staged in
1667) and an opera (first produced in 1674, with additions by Thomas
Shadwell and music by some of the period's greatest composers), this
version of *The Tempest* all but displaced Shakespeare's from the stage
for nearly two centuries. Dryden and Davenant simplified Shakespeare's
language, updated the political nuances, and put new emphasis on dramatic spectacle; and they added several new characters, giving Miranda
both a sister (Dorinda) and a counterpart in Hippolito—a young man,
also raised by Prospero, who has never seen a woman.

---

6. Await his surprise appearance.

From The Enchanted Island[†]

From *Act 2, Scene 3*

Enter PROSPERO *alone.*

PROSP.

'Tis not yet fit to let my Daughters know I kept
The infant Duke of *Mantua* so near them in this Isle,
Whose Father dying bequeath'd him to my care,
Till my false Brother (when he design'd t'usurp
My Dukedom from me) expos'd him to that fate
He meant for me. By calculation[1] of his birth
I saw death threat'ning him, if, till some time were
Past, he should behold the face of any Woman:
And now the danger's nigh: *Hippolito!*
        [*Enter* HIPPOLITO.

HIP.

Sir, I attend your pleasure.

PROSP.

How I have lov'd thee from thy infancy,
Heav'n knows, and thou thy self canst bear me witness,
Therefore accuse not me for thy restraint.

HIP.

Since I knew life, you've kept me in a Rock,
And you this day have hurry'd me from thence,
Only to change my Prison, not to free me.
I murmur not, but I may wonder at it.

PROSP.

O gentle Youth, Fate waits for thee abroad,
A black Star threatens thee, and death unseen
Stands ready to devour thee.

HIP.

You taught me not to fear him in any of his shapes:
Let me meet death rather than be a Prisoner.

PROSP.

'Tis pity he should seize thy tender youth.

HIP.

Sir, I have often heard you say, no creature liv'd
Within this Isle, but those which Man was Lord of;
Why then should I fear?

PROSP.

But here are creatures which I nam'd not to thee,

---

† From *The Tempest or The Enchanted Island* [1667] (London: Printed by J. M. for Henry
  Herringman at the Blew Anchor in the Lower-walk of the New-Exchange, 1670),
  pp. 24–28. All notes are by the editors of this Norton Critical Edition.
1. I.e., astrological reckoning.

Who share man's soveraignty by Nature's Laws,
And oft depose him from it.

HIP.

What are those Creatures, Sir?

PROSP.

Those dangerous enemies of men call'd women.

HIP.

Women! I never heard of them before.
But have I Enemies within this Isle, and do you
Keep me from them? do you think that I want
Courage to encounter 'em?

PROSP.

No courage can resist 'em.

HIP.

How then have you, Sir,
Liv'd so long unharm'd among them?

PROSP.

O they despise old age, and spare it for that reason:
It is below their conquest, their fury falls
Alone upon the young.

HIP.

Why then the fury of the young should fall on them again.
Pray turn me loose upon 'em: but, good Sir,
What are women like?

PROSP.

Imagine something between young men and Angels:
Fatally beauteous, and have killing Eyes,
Their voices charm beyond the Nightingales,
They are all enchantment; those who once behold 'em,
Are made their slaves for ever.

HIP.

Then I will wink and fight with 'em.

PROSP.

'Tis but in vain, for when your eyes are shut,
They through the lids will shine, and pierce your soul;
Absent, they will be present to you.
They'l haunt you in your very sleep.

HIP.

Then I'le revenge it on 'em when I wake.

PROSP.

You are without all possibility of revenge,
They are so beautiful that you can ne're attempt,
Nor wish to hurt them.

HIP.

Are they so beautiful?

PROSP.

    Calm sleep is not so soft, nor Winter Suns,
    Nor Summer Shades so pleasant.

HIP.

    Can they be fairer than the Plumes of Swans?
    Or more delightful than the Peacocks Feathers?
    Or than the gloss upon the necks of Doves?
    Or have more various beauty than the Rain-bow?
    These I have seen, and without danger wondred at.

PROSP.

    All these are far below 'em· Nature made
    Nothing but Woman dangerous and fair:
    Therefore if you should chance to see 'em,
    Avoid 'em streight, I charge you.

HIP.

    Well, since you say they are so dangerous,
    I'le so far shun 'em as I may with safety of the
    Unblemish'd honour which you taught me.
    But let 'em not provoke me, for I'm sure I shall
    Not then forbear them.

PROSP.

    Go in and read the Book I gave you last.
    Tomorrow I may bring you better news.

HIP.

    I shall obey you, Sir.

                                [*Exit* HIPPOLITO.

PROSP.

    So, so; I hope this lesson has secur'd him,
    For I have been constrain'd to change his Lodging
    From yonder Rock where first I bred him up,
    And here have brought him home to my own Cell,
    Because the Shipwrack happen'd near his Mansion.
    I hope he will not stir beyond his limits,
    For hitherto he hath been all obedience:
    The Planets seem to smile on my designs,
    And yet there is one sullen cloud behind,
    I would it were disperst.

        [*Enter* MIRANDA *and* DORINDA.

    How, my daughters! I thought I had instructed
    Them enough: Children! retire;
    Why do you walk this way?

MIR.

    It is within our bounds, Sir.

PROSP.

    But both take heed, that path is very dangerous.

Remember what I told you.

DOR.

Is the man that way, Sir?

PROSP.

All that you can imagine is ill there,
The curled Lyon, and the rugged Bear
Are not so dreadful as that man.

MIR.

Oh me, why stay we here then?

DOR.

I'le keep far enough from his Den, I warrant him.

MIR.

But you have told me, Sir, you are a man;
And yet you are not dreadful.

PROSP.

I child! but I am a tame man; old men are tame
By Nature, but all the danger lies in a wild
Young man.

DOR.

Do they run wild about the Woods?

PROSP.

No, they are wild within Doors, in Chambers,
And in Closets.

DOR.

But Father, I would stroak 'em and make 'em gentle,
Then sure they would not hurt me.

PROSP.

You must not trust them, Child: no woman can come
Neer 'em but she feels a pain full nine Months:
Well I must in; for new affairs require my
Presence: be you, *Miranda*, your Sister's Guardian.

                                 [*Exit* PROSPERO.

DOR.

Come, Sister, shall we walk the other way,
The man will catch us else, we have but two legs,
And he perhaps has four.

MIR.

Well, Sister, though he have; yet look about you
And we shall spy him e're he comes too near us.

DOR.

Come back, that way is towards his Den.

MIR.

Let me alone; I'le venture first, for sure he can
Devour but one of us at once.

DOR.

How dare you venture?

MIR.

We'll find him sitting like a Hare in's[2] Form,
And he shall not see us.

DOR.

I, but you know my Father charg'd us both.

MIR.

But who shall tell him on't? we'll keep each
Others Counsel

DOR.

I dare not for the world.

MIR.

But how shall we hereafter shun him, if we do not
Know him first?

DOR.

Nay I confess I would fain[3] see him too. I find it in my
Nature, because my Father has forbidden me.

MIR.

I, there's it, Sister, if he had said nothing I had been quiet. Go
softly, and if you see him first, be quick and becken me away.

DOR.

Well, if he does catch me, I le humble my self to him,
And ask him pardon, as I do my Father,
When I have done a fault.

MIR.

And if I can but scape with life, I had rather be in pain
nine Months, as my Father threatn'd, than lose my longing.

[Exeunt.

The Scene changes, and discovers HIPPOLITO *in a Cave walking, his face from the Audience.*

HIP.

Prospero has often said that Nature makes
Nothing in vain: why then are women made?
Are they to suck the poyson of the Earth,
As gaudy colour'd Serpents are? I'le ask that
Question, when next I see him here.

Enter MIRANDA *and* DORINDA *peeping.*

DOR.

O Sister, there it is, it walks about like one of us.

2. In his.
3. Gladly.

MIR.

I, just so, and has legs as we have too.

HIP.

It strangely puzzles me: yet 'tis most likely
Women are somewhat between men and spirits.

DOR.

Heark! it talks, sure this is not it my Father meant,
For this is just like one of us: methinks I am not half
So much afraid on't as I was; see, now it turns this way.

MIR.

Heaven! what a goodly thing it is!

DOR.

I'le go nearer it.

MIR.

O no, 'tis dangerous, Sister! I'le go to it.

* * *

THOMAS DUFFETT

The Dryden/Davenant *Tempest* (see above, pp. 314–20) was a box-office
hit for Davenant's Duke's Company, and in 1675 the rival theater company (Thomas Killigrew's King's Company) commissioned a parody by
Thomas Duffett (fl. 1672–1684). Duffett's irreverent *Mock-Tempest* not
only mocked the style of Restoration adaptations but also anticipated the
Shakespearean burlesques of the eighteenth and nineteenth centuries,
shifting the play to the London underworld and turning Prospero into
the Keeper of Bridewell (the chief prison for prostitutes).

From The Mock-Tempest[†]

Act 1, Scene 2

The Scene changed to Bridewell.

Enter PROSPERO *and* MIRANDA.

PROSPERO   Miranda, where's your sister?

MIRANDA   I left her on the dust-cart-top, gaping after the huge
noise that went by.—

PROSPERO   It was a dreadful show.

MIRANDA   O woe, and alas, ho, ho, ho! I'm glad I did not see it though.

---

† From *The Mock-Tempest: or, The Enchanted Castle. Acted at the Theatre Royal* (London: for William Cademan, 1675), pp. 9–12. All notes are by the editors of this Norton
Critical Edition.

PROSPERO   Hold in thy breath, and tell thy virtuous body there's no harm done, they're all reserved for thine and thy sister Dorinda's private use.

MIRANDA   And shall we have 'em all, a-ha! That will be fine i'fads;[1] but if you don't keep 'em close, pray father, we shall never have 'em long to ourselves, pray; for now ev'ry gentlewoman runs huckst'ring[2] to market, the youth are bought up so fast that poor publicans[3] are almost starved, so they are so.

PROSPERO   Leave that to my fatherly care.

MIRANDA   And shall we have 'em all, ha, ha, he! O good dear how, how the citizens' wives will curse us.—

PROSPERO   Miranda, you must now leave this tom-rigging[4] and learn to behave yourself with a grandeur and state befitting your illustrious birth and quality.—Thy father, Miranda, was 50 years ago a man of great power, Duke of my Lord Mayor's dog-kennel.—

MIRANDA   O lo, why father, father, are not I Miranda Whiff, sooth, and aren't you Prospero Whiff, sooth, Keeper of Bridewell, my father?

PROSPERO   Thy mother was all mettle.[5]—As true as stell,[6] as right's my leg, and she said thou wert my daughter. Canst thou remember when thou wert born? Sure thou canst not, for then thou wert but three days old.

MIRANDA   I'fads, I do remember it father, as well as 'twere but yesterday.

PROSPERO   Then scratch thy tenacious poll,[7] and tell me what thou findest backward in the misty black and bottomless pit of time.

MIRANDA   Pray father, had I not four or five women waiting upon top of me, at my mother's groaning, pray?

PROSPERO   Thou hadst, and more, Miranda, for then I had a tub of humming stuff[8] would make a cat speak.

MIRANDA   O Gemine![9] Father, how came we hither?

PROSPERO   While I despising mean and worldly bus'ness, as misbecoming my grave place and quality, did for the bett'ring of my mind apply myself to the secret and laudable study of nine-pins,[1] shuffleboard, and pigeon-holes[2]—dost thou give ear, infant?

MIRANDA   I do, most prudent sir.

---

1. In faith, truly.
2. Haggling.
3. Collectors of tolls.
4. Immodest behavior.
5. Character, spirit.
6. Steel.
7. Top of the head.
8. Strong liquor.
9. A mild oath.
1. Skittles, an English bowling game
2. A game in which balls are bowled at arched compartments.

PROSPERO   My brother, to whom I left the manage of my weighty
state, having learned the mysterious craft of coupling dogs and of
untying them, and by strict observation of their jilting carriage,
found the time when Venus, Countess, Lady, Beauty, and the rest
of my she-subjects were to be obliged, by full allowance of their
sports, soon grew too popular, stole the hearts of my currish vas-
sals, and so became the ivy-leaf which covered my princely issue
and sucked out all my juice. Dost observe me, child?

MIRANDA   Yes, forsooth father, this story would cure kibed-heels.[3]

PROSPERO   This miscreant, so dry[4] he was for sway, betrayed me to
Alonso, Duke of Newgate;[5] and in a stormy and dreadful night
opened my kennel gates, and forced me thence with thy young
sister and thy howling self.

MIRANDA   Father! did they kill us then, pray, father?

PROSPERO   Near the kennel they dared not for the love my dogged
subjects bore me.—In short to Newgate we were carried,—And
thence all in a cart, without a cov'ring or a pad of straw, to Hyde
Park Corner, we were hurried there on the stubbed carcass of a
leafless tree, they hoisted us aloft to pipe to winds,[6] whose
murm'ring pity whistling back again did seem to show us cursed
kindness.

MIRANDA   O poor father!—But whereof, how did we 'scape, father?

PROSPERO   Some friends we had, and some money, which gained the
assistance of a great man called Gregoria Dunn, appointed master
of that black design. Now luck begins to turn.—But ask no more; I
see thou grow'st pink-eyed, go in and let the nurse lay thee to sleep.

MIRANDA   And shall she give me some bread and butter father?

PROSPERO   Ay, my child,—go in.—   *Exit* MIRANDA.
So, she's fast.—Ariel, what ho my Ariel?
        Enter ARIEL *flying down.*

ARIEL   Hail most potent master, I come to serve thy pleasure, be it
to lie, swear, steal, pick pockets, or creep in at windows—

PROSPERO   How didst thou perform the last task I set thee?

ARIEL   I gathered the rabble together, showed them the bawdy
house, told 'em they used to kill prentices, and make mutton pies
of 'em—I led them to the windows, doors, backward, forward,
now to the cellar, now to the house top—Then I ran and called
the constable, who came just as the rabble broke in, and the
defendants were leaping from the balcony, like sailors from a
sinking ship. The Duke and his train I clapped into a coach.

3. Heels afflicted with chilblains.
4. Desirous.
5. A London prison.
6. I.e., hung us on the gallows at Tyburn, the place of execution for convicts from Newgate Prison.

PROSPERO   Are they all taken and safe?
ARIEL   All safe in several parts of this thy enchanted castle of
Bridewell; and not a hair of 'em lost.
PROSPERO   'Twas bravely done, my Ariel! What's o-clock?
ARIEL   Great Tom[7] already has struck ten:
Now blessed are women that have men,
To tell fine tale, and warm cold feet,
While lonely lass lies gnawing sheet.
PROSPERO   We have much to do ere morning come: follow me, I'll
instruct thee within.
Before the gorgeous sun upon house top doth sneer,
The Laud knows what is to be done, the Laud knows where.

Exeunt.

ROBERT AND WILLIAM BROUGH

The Brough brothers were part of a lively reaction against the high literary culture of Victorian England: Robert (1826–1860) and William (fl.
1848) sent up not just *The Tempest* but a wide range of European plays,
operas, and novels. Their *Enchanted Isle*, first performed in August 1848,
engaged in a light-hearted way with the curious political upheavals of
that year: both Prospero and Alonso are deposed monarchs; Caliban
moves from down-trodden slave to Marxist revolutionary; and Ariel
leads a group of constables called in to suppress protests and rebellions.

From The Enchanted Isle[†]

SCENE IV. *Before* PROSPERO's *Cell, a combination of a Cave
and a modern Dwelling, being a rock,* L. [*left*], *with a street
door and a window let into it. On the door a plate, with 'Sig.
Prospero'. A board,* R. [*right*], *on which is pasted a poster, with
'Blaze of Triumph!! Positively the last week of Sig. Prospero,
the celebrated Wizard of the Isle!! who is about to Break his
Staff and Drown his Book!!!'*
         A Landscape and Sea View in the back.

Enter MIRANDA *from door,* L.

---

7. The bell that rang the hour in the clock-tower at the Palace of Westminster.
† From *The Enchanted Isle, or 'Raising the Wind' on the Most Approved Principles. A
drama without the smallest claim to legitimacy, consistency, probability, or anything else
but absurdity; in which will be found much that is unaccountably coincident with Shak-
speare's 'Tempest'* (London: National Acting Drama Office, 1848), pp. 14–19. First performed at the Royal Amphitheatre, Liverpool, August 7, 1848, and at the Adelphi
Theatre, London, November 20, 1848. All notes are by the editors of this Norton Critical Edition.

MIRANDA.   Now he may come as soon as e'er he pleases.
I think this style—as fast men say—'the cheese'[1] is.
                                        [*Looking at her dress.*]
I wonder who he is, and what he's like,
And if his fancy I may chance to strike.
But where's that Caliban! He's never near
When wanted. Caliban, where are you?

CALIBAN.   [*Within.*]   Here!

MIRANDA.   Come here, slave!
        Enter CALIBAN, *with a Wellington boot on one arm and a*
        brush in his hand.

CALIBAN.   Slave! Come, drop that sort of bother;
Just let me ax, 'Ain't I a man and a brother?'[2]

MIRANDA.   The airs that servants give themselves just now,
They are the 'Greatest Plague in Life',[3] I vow.
Don't answer me, but work, you gaping swine;
Polish those boots, or else there'll be a shine.
Then come to me.   [*Exit.*

CALIBAN.   There, now; her dander's riz[4]—
It's jolly hard upon a cove,[5] it is.
List to my story; when it meets your ears
I'm sure the *Boxes*[6] will be all in *tears*,
And in the *gentle pit*[7] each *gent'll pity* me.
I'm plain, straightforward, honest, every *bit* o' me;
And though in polished articles I deal,
'A round unvarnished tale'[8] I will reveal.

        TUNE—'*Georgy Barnwell, good and pious*'.

Sons of freedom, hear my story,
    Pity and protect the slave;
Of my wrongs the inventory
    I'll just tip you in a stave.[9]
                                Tiddle ol, &c.
                        [*Brushes the boot to the chorus.*
From morn till night I work like winkin',[1]
    Yet I'm kicked and cuffed about,

1. Exemplary.
2. "Am I not a man and a brother?" was the motto engraved on the anti-slavery medallion made by the potter Josiah Wedgwood.
3. I.e., the maidservant, according to the popular novel of that title (pub. 1847) by Augustus and Henry Mayhew.
4. Temper's risen.
5. Chap.
6. Special boxed seats in a theater.
7. Humble area for audience.
8. A phrase spoken by Shakespeare's Othello.
9. Sing you a song.
1. Flat out.

With scarce half time for grub or drinkin',
   And they never lets me have a Sunday out.
                         Tiddle ol, &c.

And if jaw to the gov'nor I gives vent to,
   He calls up his spirits in a trice,[2]
Who grip, squeeze, bite, sting, and torment—oh!
   Such friends at a *pinch* are by no means nice.
                         Tiddle ol, &c.

But I'll not stand it longer, that I'll not,
I'll strike at once, now that my *mettle's* hot.
Ha, here he comes! Now soon I'll make things better;
'Hereditary Bondsmen',[3] hem! Et cetera.
                    [*Folds his arms and looks dignified.*

   Enter PROSPERO.

PROSPERO.   Well, sir, why don't you work?
CALIBAN.   [*Giving the boot a single rub.*] Ay, there's the rub.[4]
PROSPERO.   What, mutinous! Out, vile, rebellious cub!
CALIBAN.   [*With sudden vigour.*] Oh, who's afraid? Blow you and
   your boots together!   [*Throws boot down.*
   My soul's above your paltry upper leather.
PROSPERO.   [*Aside.*] That's democratic, and by no means morall
   [*To* CALIBAN.] Pick up that boot, unless you'd pick a quarrel.
   You'd best not raise a breeze.
CALIBAN.   Oh, blow your breezes!
   The love of liberty upon me seizes;
   My bosom's filled with freedom's pure emotions,
   And on the 'Rights of Labour'[5] I've strong notions.
PROSPERO.   You want work, then?
CALIBAN.   No—up for my rights I'll stick;
   I've long enough been driven—now I'll kick.

    TUNE—'*When the Heart of a Man*'.

When the back of a donkey's oppress'd with wares,
Which weigh rather more than his strength well bears,
   Instead of submitting he stoutly—stoutly
Plucks up a spirit and shows some airs.
   Stripes are administer'd—kicks also,

---

2. Instantly.
3. From Byron's *Childe Harold's Pilgrimage* (1812–18): "Hereditary bondsmen! Know ye
   not / Who would be free themselves must strike the blow?"
4. That's the problem. From Hamlet's "To be or not to be" soliloquy.
5. Title of several popular tracts published in the 1840s, a time of industrial unrest.

But his stout ribs no emotion show.
        Press him,
        Caress him,
        Try kicking
        Or licking,
The more he is wallop'd the more he won't go.

PROSPERO.   This sort of thing at once I'd better crush;
I'll stand no more—pick up that boot, then brush.

                                    [Pointing off with staff.

CALIBAN.   Never—I swear.

PROSPERO.   Oh, very good; we'll see, sir.

   Taps his wand on the stage. FAIRY SPECIALS[6] *appear from all parts, and commence laying on to* CALIBAN *with their staves, chasing him round the stage.*

CALIBAN.   [*Picks up the boot.*] Oh no, sir—don't sir—please, sir—
twasn't me, sir!   [*Runs off, followed by* FAIRIES.

PROSPERO.   Thus disaffection should be timely checked.
Now for the prince, whom shortly I expect;
He little thinks, in his perambulations,
How soon he'll drop upon some blood relations,
Nor that he stands on matrimony's edge;
For at his *uncle's* he must leave a *pledge*—
His heart; Miranda from his breast must pick it,
And on it lend her own—ay, that's the ticket.[7]
I have a plan their passion to ensure—
All sorts of trouble I'll make him endure;
And on their intercourse I'll lay restriction,
So that they'll fall in love from contradiction.

MIRANDA.   [*From door.*] Pa!

PROSPERO.   Yes, dear!

MIRANDA.   Come, and put some tidy things on.

PROSPERO.   Well, look me out a collar, one with strings on.   [*Exit.*

   Railway music; a bell and steam whistle. A FAIRY SPECIAL *rises through trap,* C. [center] *with a flag, and holds it out as Railway policemen do. A noise of an approaching Train is heard. Shortly after enter a fairy Locomotive,* R. *with* ARIEL *and a* SPECIAL *as engineer and stoker, attached to a car, in which sits* FERDINAND, *attended by* FAIRY SPECIALS. *Train stops at* C. ARIEL *and* FERDINAND *get out.*

6. I.e., special constables.
7. What's wanted.

ARIEL.   Now then, sir, for the Wizard Cavern Station;
  Your ticket, please—this is your destination.
      [*Jumps into train.*
FERDINAND.   [*Looking round amazed.*] Nay, pray explain—just say
      why here you bring me.   [*Train drives off,* L.
  Gone, like the baseless fabric of a thing' me![8]
  The train has vanished into sheer vacuity;
  That engine shows the greatest ingenuity.
  The very line's gone. Oh, it's clear as day
  That line was but a 'Pencilling by the way';[9]
  And something's rubbed it out; or 'tis perhaps
  One of those airy atmospheric chaps.   [*Sees the door.*
  But ho! What's here? 'A local habitation?'
  Ay, 'and a name'. Now for some explanation.
                                        [*Reads the bill.*
  'Um! 'Blaze of triumph!' That's a flaming placard;
  I'll knock, and boldly; yes, egad, I'll whack hard   [*He knocks.*

PROSPERO *comes out suddenly followed by* MIRANDA.

PROSPERO.   [*Fiercely.*] 'Who am dat a knocking at de door?'[1]
FERDINAND.   It's me!
PROSPERO.   And pray, sir what may your intentions be?
FERDINAND.   Pity the sorrows of a poor young man,
  Whom fairy sprites have brought unto your door,
  Who wishes you to give him—if you can,
  A simple explanation—nothing more.
MIRANDA. [*Aside.*] 'Tis he, I know; with Cupid's darts I'm struck.
FERDINAND.   [*Seeing* MIRANDA.] Good Heavens! What a captivating
      duck!
PROSPERO.   [*Aside.*] They're smitten. [*Aloud and sternly.*] For the
      questions you have put,
  I've but one answer, which is simply 'Cut!' [*Motioning his wand.*
FERDINAND.   [*Astonished.*] Cut?
MIRANDA.   Cut?
PROSPERO.   Yes, cut!
MIRANDA.   Well really, Pa, I call
  That cut the most unkindest cut of all.[2]
PROSPERO.   Silence, bold minx! Now, once for all, sir—hook it!
  This is no inn—was it for such you took it?

8. Thingummy.
9. *Pencillings By The Way* was the title of a popular 1835 book by the U.S. author Nathaniel
   P. Willis.
1. Title of a popular contemporary minstrel song. The speaker of the line is a brothel
   keeper.
2. Antony's description of Brutus's stabbing of Caesar in Shakespeare's *Julius Caesar*.

FERDINAND.   An inn your house by me was never *thought* to be,
　Tho' I confess I really think it *ought* to be.
　It might accommodation find at least
　For man, since it accommodates a beast.
MIRANDA.   Pa, I'm ashamed of you. [*To* FERDINAND.] Sir, don't
　suppose
　That rudeness such as that my father shows
　Runs in the family. I've none of it;
　I don't take after him.
FERDINAND.   You don't, a bit.
　All I can say is—if from him you came,
　'Deny thy father and refuse thy name',[3]
　And in return please to accept of me.   [*Opens his arms.*
MIRANDA.   I like the barter, most amazingly.
                              [*About to rush into his arms.*
PROSPERO.   [*Stopping her.*] Back, forward puss! Egad, 'twas time to
　stop her;
　Advances such as these are most improper.
FERDINAND.   Our passion's sudden, but the style's not new,
　We're 'Romeo and Juliet' number two.
　Maiden, I swear—
PROSPERO.   Pooh, pooh! Your vows are *hollow* as
　Drums. And besides, we don't allow no *followers*,
　Save men whose minds are honorably bent—
　Not such as you—a trickster and a gent.
FERDINAND.   [*Drawing his sword à la De Mauprat in 'Richelieu'.*[4]]
　Gent! Zounds[5]—Sir Conjuror!
PROSPERO.   Ho, my angry child!
　You've drawn your sword—you'd best have drawn it mild.

　　　[*Waves his wand.* FERDINAND *is transfixed and unable to move.*

FERDINAND.   Holloa! What's this? Quite powerless I'm grown;
　From a real *brick*[6] I'm changed into a *stone.*
　I don't half like it—it quite spoils one's pleasure;
　This is a most unfair Coercive Measure.
　Come, please to set me free, old fellow, will you?
　And 'pon my word, I'll promise not to kill you.
PROSPERO.   You plead in vain; no, there take up your dwelling,
　A fatal column of my magic spelling.
MIRANDA.   You can't be such a brute, Pa, surely no;
　I'll be his bail, if you will let him go.

---

3. Juliet's words to Romeo in Shakespeare's *Romeo and Juliet.*
4. Popular play written in 1839 by Edward Bulwer-Lytton.
5. God's wounds (a mild oath).
6. Good fellow.

FERDINAND.   Thou art my *bale* of precious goods the rarest,
  Within my heart locked up, and safely ware'us'd.[7]
  How I'd embrace thee, were I only free!
MIRANDA.   'More free than welcome'[8] you could never be.
PROSPERO.   [*Aside.*] All right! I've changed my mind another way;
  I'll punish you; therefore be free, I say.

      [FERDINAND *goes through pantomime expressive of being free.*

FERDINAND.   As the first sign of liberty I seize
  The freedom of the *press*, or rather squeeze. [*Embraces* MIRANDA.
PROSPERO.   Phew! Here's an open armed and public meeting.
  Egad! It's time that the *rappel*[9] was beating.

      *Knocks his wand on the stage as policemen do. The sound is
      answered, and* FAIRY SPECIALS *flock in from all parts and
      group around.*

[*To* FERDINAND *and* MIRANDA.] Now then, disperse.
FERDINAND.   Divide us if you can.
  I s'pose you call yourself a loyal man.
  And here you're getting up an agitation,
  Our union to repeal by separation.
MIRANDA.   Though as in Parliament, on every side
  They stun our ears and cry 'Divide, divide',
  Yet we'll not part.
PROSPERO.   You won't?
FERDINAND.   No!
PROSPERO.   Then, of course.
  The law's authority I must enforce.
  Tear them asunder! [*The* SPECIALS *pull them apart.*] Now, my
      loving pair,
  I'll teach you both my mighty power to dare.
  [*To* MIRANDA.] You, miss, I sentence, ere the moon is full,
  To work six ottomans in Berlin wool.
  [*Turning to* FERDINAND.] And as for him, who'd 'steal what isn't
      his'n,'   [*Indicating* MIRANDA.
  Now that he's 'cotched',[1] of course 'he goes to pris'n'.
  Off with him—let him have some bread—nought richer;
  His bed some straw; his only friend a pitcher.

      SONG—PROSPERO *and* CHORUS.
      TUNE—'*Nix my Dolly*'.

---

7. Warehoused.
8. A phrase then associated with anti-Catholic or anti-Irish sentiment.
9. Call-to-arms.
1. Scotched, caught.

In a box of the stone-jug all forlorn,
Whose walls your efforts will treat with scorn,
                    To break away,

All covered with irons, you'll have to lay,
Which will put a stop to your capers gay.
    Fixed,[2] my jolly pal, there you'll stay,
    Fixed, my jolly pal, there you'll stay.
[*Exit into house.* FAIRIES *march to music of the chorus, one detach-
    ment taking* MIRANDA *off by the door,* L., *the others taking*
                        FERDINAND *off,* R.

PERCY MacKAYE

Percy MacKaye (1875–1956) was a U.S. dramatist and poet particularly associated with the notion of "civic theater," in which the public
would be involved not merely as spectators. His most ambitious project, *Caliban by the Yellow Sands*, is discussed in the essay by Coppélia
Kahn in this volume (see above, pp. 188–211). The extracts that follow
offer MacKaye's own explanation of his intentions and an indication of
the size of the undertaking.

From Caliban by the Yellow Sands[†]

Preface

Three hundred years alive on the 23rd of April, 1916, the memory
of Shakespeare calls creatively upon a self-destroying world to do
him honor by honoring that world-constructive art of which he is a
master architect.

Over seas, the choral hymns of cannon acclaim his death; in
battle-trenches artists are turned subtly ingenious to inter his art;
War, Lust, and Death are risen in power to restore the primeval
reign of Setebos.

Here in America, where the neighboring waters of his "vexed
Bermoothes" lie more calm than those about his own native isle,
here only is given some practical opportunity for his uniterable[1]
spirit to create new splendid symbols for peace through harmonious international expression.

As one means of serving such expression, and so, if possible, of
paying tribute to that creative spirit in forms of his own art, I have

2. Secured.
† From *Caliban by the Yellow Sands* (Garden City, NY: Doubleday, Page & Co., 1916), pp.
    xiii–xxviii, 159–65. All notes are by the author unless otherwise specified.
1. Incomparable [*Editors*].

devised and written this Masque, at the invitation of the Shakespeare Celebration Committee of New York City.

The dramatic-symbolic motive[2] of the Masque I have taken from
Shakespeare's own play "The Tempest," Act I, Scene 2. There,
speaking to Ariel, Prospero says:

> "Hast thou forgot
> The foul witch Sycorax, who with age and envy
> Was grown into a hoop?   .   This damn'd witch Sycorax,
> For mischiefs manifold and sorceries terrible
> To enter human hearing   .   was hither brought with child
> And there was left by the sailors. Thou   .   ,
> Wast then her servant;
> And, for thou wast a spirit too delicate
> To act her earthly and abhorred commands,
> Refusing her grand hests, she did confine thee,
> By help of her most potent ministers
> And in her most unmitigable rage,
> Into a cloven pine, within which rift
> Imprisoned thou didst painfully remain   .   .
> Then was this island—
> Save for the son that she did litter here,
> A freckled whelp hag-born—not honor'd with
> A human shape   .   .   .   that Caliban
> Whom now I keep in service. Thou best know'st
> What torment I did find thee in,   .   . it was a torment
> To lay upon the damn'd   .   .   *It was mine art,*
> When I arrived and heard thee, that made gape
> The pine and let thee out."

"It was mine art"   .   .   There—in Prospero's words [and Shakespeare's]—is the text of this Masque.

The art of Prospero I have conceived as the art of Shakespeare in
its universal scope: that many-visioned art of the theatre which, age
after age, has come to liberate the imprisoned imagination of mankind from the fetters of brute force and ignorance; that same art
which, being usurped or stifled by groping part-knowledge, prud-
ery, or lust, has been botched in its ideal aims and—like fire ill
handled or ill-hidden by a passionate child—has wrought havoc,
hypocrisy, and decadence.

Caliban, then, in this Masque, is that passionate child-curious
part of us all [whether as individuals or as races], grovelling close to
his aboriginal origins, yet groping up and staggering—with almost
rhythmic falls and back-slidings—toward that serener plane of pity

2. Theme [Editors].

and love, reason and disciplined will, where Miranda and Prospero commune with Ariel and his Spirits.

In deference to the master-originator of these characters and their names, it is, I think, incumbent on me to point out that these four characters, derived—but reimagined—from Shakespeare's "The Tempest," become, for the purposes of my Masque, the presiding symbolic *Dramatis Personæ* of a plot and conflict which are my own conception. They are thus no longer Shakespeare's characters of "The Tempest," though born of them and bearing their names.

Their words [save for a very few song-snatches and sentences] and their actions are those which I have given them; the development of their characters accords with the theme—not of Shakespeare's play but of this Masque, in which Caliban's nature is developed to become the protagonist of aspiring humanity, not simply its butt of shame and ridicule.

My conception and treatment also of Setebos [whose name is but a passing reference in Shakespeare's play], the fanged idol [substituted by me for the "cloven pine"]; of Sycorax, as Setebos' mate [in form a super-puppet, an earth-spirit rather than "witch"], from both of whom Caliban has sprung; of the Shakespearian Inner Scenes, as brief-flashing visions in the mind of Prospero; of the "Yellow Sands" as his magic isle, the world; these are not liberties taken with text or characters of Shakespeare; they are simply the means of dramatic license whereby my Masque aims to accord its theme with the art and spirit of Shakespeare.

Shakespeare's own characters, that use his words[3] in scenes of his plays, have then no part in my Masque, except in the Inner Scenes,[4] where they are conceived as being conjured by Prospero and enacted by the Spirits of Ariel.

The theme of the Masque—Caliban seeking to learn the art of Prospero—is, of course, the slow education of mankind through the influences of coöperative art, that is, of the art of the theatre in its full social scope. This theme of coöperation is expressed earliest in the Masque through the lyric of Ariel's Spirits taken from "The Tempest"; it is sounded, with central stress, in the chorus of peace when the kings clasp hands on the Field of the Cloth of Gold; and, with final emphasis, in the gathering together of the creative forces of dramatic art in the Epilogue. Thus its motto is the one printed on the title page, in Shakespeare's words:

---

3. The words of Shakespeare used in this Masque are quoted from the Tudor Edition of Shakespeare's Works, edited by Neilson and Thorndike (Macmillan). The stage directions and cuts, however, are not taken from any edition, but have been made by me for purposes of the Inner Scenes.
4. In this book these Inner Scenes are printed in black-faced type.

> "Come unto these yellow sands
> And then take hands."

So much for my Masque in its relationship to Shakespeare's work and his art. Its contribution to the modern development of a form of dramatic art unpractised by him requires some brief comment.

This work is not a pageant, in the sense that the festivals excellently devised by Mr. Louis N. Parker in England, Mr. Lascelles in Canada, or Mr. Thomas Wood Stevens in America have been called pageants.[5] Though of necessity it involves aspects of pageantry, its form is more closely related to the forms of Greek drama and of opera. Yet it is neither of these. It is a new form to meet new needs.

I have called this work a Masque, because—like other works so named in the past—it is a dramatic work of symbolism involving, in its structure, pageantry, poetry, and the dance. Yet I have by no means sought to relate its structure to an historic form; I have simply sought by its structure to solve a modern [and a future] problem of the art of the theatre. That problem is the new one of creating a focussed dramatic technique for the growing but groping movement vaguely called "pageantry," which is itself a vital sign of social evolution—the half-desire of the people not merely to remain receptive to a popular art created by specialists, but to take part themselves in creating it; the desire, that is, of democracy consistently to seek expression through a drama *of* and *by* the people, not merely *for* the people.

For some ten years that potential drama of democracy has interested me as a fascinating goal for both dramatist and citizen, in seeking solution for the vast problem of leisure.[6] Two years ago at Saint Louis I had my first technical opportunity, on a large scale, to experiment in devising a dramatic structure for its many-sided requirements. There, during five performances, witnessed by half a million people, about seven thousand citizens of Saint Louis took part in my Masque [in association with the Pageant by Thomas Wood Stevens]. In the appendix of this volume a photograph gives a suggestion of one of those audiences, gathered in their public park [in seats half of which were free, half pay-seats] to witness the production.[7]

---

5. During the first two decades of the twentieth century, these three dramatists all staged popular pageants involving many hundreds of participants [*Editors*].
6. An outline of suggestions on this subject I published in a volume, "The Civic Theatre, in Relation to the Redemption of Leisure" [1912]. Further ideas and their applications are contained in the prefaces and dramatic texts of my Bird Masque "Sanctuary," "Saint Louis: A Civic Masque," and "The New Citizenship," a Civic Ritual.
7. The outgoing cost of the Saint Louis production was $122,000; the income $139,000. The balance of $17,000 has been devoted to a fund for civic art. The cost of producing a single play by Sophocles at Athens was $500,000.

That production was truly a drama of, for, and by the people—a true Community Masque; and it was largely with the thought of that successful civic precedent that the Shakespeare Celebration first looked to Central Park as the appropriate site to produce their Community Festival, the present Masque, as the central popular expression of some hundreds of supplementary Shakespearean celebrations.

In so doing, they conceived the function of a public park—as it is conceived almost universally west of the Eastern States, and almost everywhere in Europe—to be that of providing outdoor space for the people's expression in civic art-forms.

The sincere opposition of a portion of the community to this use of Central Park would never, I think, have arisen, if New York could have taken counsel with Saint Louis's experience, and its wonderfully happy civic and social reactions. The opposition, however, was strong and conscientious; so that, on the same principle of community solidarity which was the *raison d'etre* for their informal application to use Central Park, the Shakespeare Celebration withdrew their wish to use it. To split community feeling by acrimonious discussion was contrary to the basic idea and function of the Celebration, which are to help unite all classes and all beliefs in a great coöperative movement for civic expression through dramatic art.

One very important public service, however, was performed by this Central Park discussion; it served clearly to point out a colossal lack in the democratic equipment of the largest and richest metropolis of the western hemisphere: namely, the total lack of any public place of meeting, where representative numbers of New York citizens can unite in seeing, hearing, and taking part in a festival or civic communion of their own. New York, a city of five million inhabitants, possesses no public stadium or community theatre. Little Athens, a mere village in comparison, had for its heart such a community theatre, which became the heart of civilization. Without such an instrument, our own democracy cannot hope to develop that coöperative art which is the expression of true civilization in all ages.

Happily for the Shakespeare Celebration and its aims, a large measure of solution has, at the date of this preface, been attained by the gracious offer of the New York City College authorities, through President Mezes, to permit the use of the Lewisohn Stadium and athletic field, temporarily to be converted into a sort of miniature Yale Bowl, for the production of the Shakespeare Masque on the night of May 23rd and the following four nights.

By the brilliant conception and technical plans of Mr. Joseph Urban for joining to the present concrete stadium of Mr. Arnold Brunner its duplicate in wood, on the east side of the field, and so placing the stage on its narrower width to the north, there will be

created a practical outdoor theatre, remarkable in acoustics, qualified to accommodate in excellent seats about twenty thousand spectators, and some two or three thousand participants in the festival.

If such a consummation shall eventually become permanent there,
it will complete the realization of a practicable dream already rendered partly complete by Mr. Adolf Lewisohn's public spirited donation of the present concrete structure. Referring to that practicable
dream, I wrote four years ago in my volume "The Civic Theatre":[8]
"One day last spring, traversing with President John Finley the
grounds lately appropriated, through his fine efforts, by the City of
New York for a great stadium at the City College, I discussed with
him the splendid opportunity there presented for focussing the popular enthusiasm toward athletic games in an art dramatic and nobly
spectacular."

This new dramatic art-form, then—a technique of the theatre
adapted to democratic expression and dedicated to public service—I
have called by the name Community Masque, and have sought to
exemplify it on a large scale in two instances, at Saint Louis and at
New York.

The occasion of this preface is not one to discuss the details of that
new technique further than to suggest to the public, and to those critics who might be interested to make its implications clearer than the
author and director of a production has time or opportunity to do,
that the exacting time limits of presenting dramatically a theme
involving many dissociated ages, through many hundreds of symbolic
participants and leaders, are conditions which themselves impel the
imagination toward creating a technique as architectural as music,
as colorful as the pageant, as dramatic as the play, as plastic as the
dance.

That my own work has attained to such a technique I am very far
from supposing. I have, however, clearly seen the need for attaining
to it, whatever the difficulties, if a great opportunity for democracy
is not to be lost. To see that much, at a time when the vagueness of
amateurs, however idealistic in desire, is obscuring the austere outlines of a noble technical art looming just beyond us, may perhaps
be of some service.

As visual hints to the structure (Inner and Outer) of the present
Masque, the charts here published may be suggestive to the reader.
To the reader as such it remains to point out one vital matter of
technique, namely, the relation of the dramatic dialogue to the
Masque's production.

Even more than a play [if more be possible], a Masque is not a
realized work of art until it is adequately produced. To the casual

8. Page 71, on Constructive Leisure (Mitchell Kennerley, 1912).

reader, this Masque, as visualized merely on these printed pages, may appear to be a structure simply of written words: in reality it is a structure of potential interrelated pantomime, music, dance, lighting, acting, song [choral and lyric], scene values, stage management and *spoken* words.

Words spoken, then, constitute in this work but one of numerous elements, all relatively important. If no word of the Masque be heard by the audience, the plot, action, and symbolism will still remain understandable and, if properly produced, dramatically interesting. Synchronous with every speech occur, in production, effects of pantomime, lighting, music, and movement with due proportion and emphasis. Such, at least, is the nature of the technique sought, whether or not this particular work attains to it.

A Masque must appeal as emphatically to the eye as a moving picture, though with a different appeal to the imagination.

Because of this only relative value of the spoken word, there are many producers [theoretical and practical] who believe that the spoken word should be eliminated entirely from this special art of the theatre.

Artists as eminent and constructive in ideas as Gordon Craig,[9] and many whom his genius has inspired, advocate indeed this total elimination of speech from the theatre's art as a whole. For them that art ideally is the compound of only light and music and movement. The reason for this, I think, is because the sensibility of those artists is preëminently visual. Moreover, they are relatively inexpert, as artists, in the knowledge of the technique and values of the spoken word. Being visually expert and creative, they have, by their practical genius, established a world-wide school of independent, visual art [assisted only by mass sounds of music].

For them this art has well nigh become *the* art of the theatre. Yet it is not so, I think, and can never be so, to that watching and listening sensibility for which all dramatic art is created—the soul of the audience. That soul, our soul, is a composite flowering of all the senses, and the life-long record of the spoken word [reiterated from childhood] is an integral, yes, the most intimate, element of our consciousness.

The association of ideas and emotions which only the spoken word can evoke is, therefore, a dramatic value which the art of the theatre cannot consistently ignore. It is chiefly because those artist-experts in word values, the poets, who might contribute their special technique to the theatre's art, turn elsewhere creatively, that the field is left unchallenged and open to the gifted school of the visualists. The true dramatic art—which involves ideally a total coöperation—does

9. Edward Gordon Craig (1872–1966), prominent modernist theater practitioner [*Editors*].

not, and cannot, exclude the poet-dramatist. Shakespeare and Sophocles lived before electric light; if they had lived after, they would have set a different pace for Bakst and Reinhardt,[1] and established a creative school more nobly poised in technique, more deeply human in appeal.

Now, therefore, when the poets are awaking to a new power and control of expression, here especially in our own country, if they will both learn and teach in this larger school, there rises before us the promise of an art more sensuous, sane, and communal than the theatre has ever known.

So, in the pioneering adventure of this Masque, which seeks by experiment to relate the spoken word to its larger coöperation with the visual arts, I have devised a structure in which the English language, spoken by actors, is an essential dramatic value.

Why, then, take pains [as I have done] to make it relatively non-essential in case it should *not* be heard?

For this reason: that now—at the present temporary and still groping stage of development of community Masque organization and production—there can be, in the nature of the case, no complete assurance beforehand of adequate acoustics in setting, or of voices trained to large-scale outdoor speech.

But, if this be so, would it not be the wiser part of creative valor to adapt my structure wholly to these elementary conditions, risk nothing, and devise simply pantomime?

No, for by that principle no forward step for the spoken word could ever be taken. *If we are to progress in this new art, we must seek to make producing conditions conform to the spoken play, even more than the play to those conditions.*

And this can be done; it has been done.

At Saint Louis the vast amphitheatre for my Masque was at first considered, by nearly all who saw it, to be utterly unsuited to the spoken word; yet, after careful study, experiment and technical provision for its use, the speech of actors was heard each night by at least two-thirds of the hundred and fifty thousand listeners. Of the seven thousand actors only about fifteen spoke, but these conveyed the spoken symbolism and drama of the action.

In the present Masque I have focussed the spoken word on the raised constructed stage of wood confined it to the speech of eight principal acting parts, and about twenty other subordinate parts, whose speaking lines [from Shakespeare's plays] are still further focussed at the narrower inner stage, provided with special sounding boards.

---

1. Max Reinhardt (1873–1943), Austrian theater director and producer. Léon Bakst (1866–1924), Russian scene and costume designer [*Editors*].

On the other hand, for the ground-circle of the "Yellow Sands," where the thousands of participants in the Interludes take part under an open sky, I have provided no spoken words, but only pantomime, mass movements, dances and choruses.

To the reader, then, I would repeat, that the words of this printed Masque are an essential, though not an exclusive, part of its structure, and are meant primarily to be spoken, not primarily to be read.

As in the case of my Civic Ritual "The New Citizenship"[2] this Masque can only have its completely adequate production on a large and elaborate scale. Like the Civic Ritual, however, which—originally designed for the New York stadium—is being performed on an adapted scale in many parts of the country, in schools and elsewhere, this Masque may perhaps serve some good purpose in being made available for performance in a smaller, simpler manner, adapted to the purposes of festivals during this year of Shakespeare's Tercentenary. At the invitation, therefore, of Mr. Percival Chubb, President of the Drama League of America, who first suggested to me the writing of a Memorial Masque to Shakespeare, the publishers have made arrangements with officers of the Drama League for making known its availability as stated in their announcement printed at the back of this volume.

The accompanying stage-designs are the work of Mr. Joseph Urban, the eminent Viennese artist and producer [who has recently become an American], and of Mr. Robert Edmond Jones, designer of the scenes and costumes for Mr. Granville Barker's production of "The Man Who Married a Dumb Wife."

At the date of this preface, Mr. Arthur Farwell has nearly completed his compositions for the lyric choruses and incidental music of the Masque. The choruses will shortly be made available, published by G. Schirmer, New York.

With all three of these artists I am fortunate in being associated in preparations for the Masque's New York production next May.

These preparations have met with many complex difficulties of launching and organization; the time remaining is very brief to accomplish the many-sided community task for which the Masque is designed; only the merest beginnings of so vast a movement can be attempted; but, with coöperation and support from those who believe in that task, the producers look forward hopefully to serving, in some pioneering degree, the great cause of community expression through the art of the theatre.   PERCY MACKAYE.
New York, February 22, 1916.

* * *

2. New York, 1915, Macmillan.

PERSONS AND PRESENCES
OF THE TEN INNER SCENES

[Enacted by the Spirits of Ariel.]

FIRST INNER SCENE

SPEAKING PERSONS

Antony
Cleopatra
Charmian
Eros

PANTOMIME GROUPS

Roman Soldiers
Egyptian Populace
Flutists
Harpists
Wine Bearers

SECOND INNER SCENE

SPEAKING PERSONS

Cressida
Her Attendant
Pandarus
Boy
Troilus

MUTE PERSONS

Hecuba
Helen
Æneas
Antenor
Hector
Paris
Helenus

PANTOMIME GROUPS

Trojan Warriors
Trojan Populace

THIRD INNER SCENE

SPEAKING PERSONS

Brutus

Lucius, a boy
Ghost of Cæsar

MUTE PRESENCES

Shapes in the Darkness

FOURTH INNER SCENE

SPEAKING PERSONS

SAINT AGNES [An Image]
A SHEPHERD [Impersonated by Prospero]
A SHEPHERD BOY [Impersonated by Ariel]
OTHER SHEPHERDS

FIFTH INNER SCENE

SPEAKING PERSONS

Hamlet
Horatio
Marcellus

MUTE PERSONS

The Ghost of Hamlet's Father

SIXTH INNER SCENE
[Derivative from Shakespeare]

PANTOMIME PERSONS AND GROUPS

King Henry the Eighth, of England
King Francis the First, of France
Their Soldiers and Followers

SEVENTH INNER SCENE

SPEAKING PERSONS

Benvolio
Mercutio
Romeo
Juliet
Lorenzo
Florizel
Perdita

MUTE PERSONS

Jessica

EIGHTH INNER SCENE

SPEAKING PERSONS

Orlando
Jacques
Duke
Adam

PANTOMIME GROUPS

Foresters of Arden

NINTH INNER SCENE

SPEAKING PERSONS

Sir Hugh Evans [as Fairy]
Sir John Falstaff
Mistress Ford
Mistress Page
Mistress Quickly [as Fairy]
Pistol [as Hobgoblin]

PANTOMIME GROUPS

Fairies [Counterfeited by Followers of Sir Hugh]

TENTH INNER SCENE

SPEAKING PERSONS AND GROUPS

King Henry the Fifth
His Soldiers and Followers

INTERLUDE I
FIRST ACTION: EGYPTIAN
COMMUNITY ACTORS [148]

Comprise

PARTICIPANTS [75]
FIGURANTS [73]

Osiris, the god of summer and fecundity.
Worshippers of Osiris [Men and Women].

7 Groups, each group comprising
15 Dancers [Parts & Figs.]
5 Drum-players, Followers [Parts and Figs.]
1 Priest Leader [Participant]
Total Dancers. 105
    "   Drum-players. 35

                                                        140
    "   Leaders 7

                                                        147
Osiris 1

                                                        148

THEME

Egyptian Worshippers of the god Osiris, B. C. 1000, celebrate his resurrection from death by a dramatic ritual, symbolizing how the seven portions of his rended body unite again at his rebirth.

ACTION

At the deep pealing of gongs, from each of the three entrances to the ground-circle, two diverging Processions issue forth, a seventh issuing from the cell of Caliban. All are dressed in robes and concealing masks of black.

Slowly, to the rhythmic beat of Egyptian drums [borne by the last five in each procession], by seven separate routes, they move out upon the Yellow Sands, and so converge toward the altar at the centre.

Within about a rod of the altar they pause, while their seven Priest-Leaders move forward—each bearing a fire urn—to the altar, on which an immense circular disk lies. On the disk, a prone Shape lies concealed beneath a black cloth.

Bowing before the altar, the seven Priests then rise and, mounting the steps, extend their arms to touch the rim of the disk. Thus— their black masks turned skyward—they raise their shrill voices in a mournful Egyptian chant.

Moving then backward to the ground, they drop incense within their seven urns, from which rise seven pillars of smoke, lighted by the glow of fire beneath.

In this increasing glow, the black Shape on the disk stirs, slowly rises beneath its dark cloth, and extends upward its hidden arms. During this, the drums beat from a low muffled cadence increasingly to a loud rolling rhythm, to which now—at a shrill choral cry from all the worshippers—the black cloth on the central Shape sloughs to its feet, revealing—in a burst of radiant splendor—the flame-bright form of the god Osiris.

In tall shining mitre, he raises his ox-herd's whip and shepherd's crook. With these, to the joyous cries of his Worshippers, he bestows with archaic gesture a seven-fold sign of benediction.

Once more then mounting the altar steps, the Priests step forth from their black robes and masks in their own garments of yellow gold. Thus, touching again the rim of the disk, they begin to revolve it—at first slowly.[3]

And now at its first motion, Osiris begins to dance.

In this dance he expresses the former beneficence of his life, the sufferings of his death, the rending of his body into seven parts and finally the joy of his resurrection.[4]

In rhythm to the primitive music, the Priests revolve the disk to the dancing movement of the god.

In this revolving movement his Worshippers below join in a dance on the ground (expressive of the blending of the seven parts of his body), where one by one successively the seven Processions encircle the altar and the dancing Osiris. As they do so, they slough off their dark garments, weaving thus a whirling movement in which the proportion of black ever diminishes while the golden yellow increases, until finally—in a blaze only of gold-yellow radiance—the Priests raise aloft on its pedestal the disk, still spinning, while the flame-red god, still dancing, is borne away in procession by his joyous Worshippers, shouting aloud their shrill cries of "Osiris!"

When all have disappeared through the south gate of the circle, Prospero on his throne speaks to Ariel,[5] announcing the Second Action of the Interlude—his art of the drama in Greece.

*   *   *

AIMÉ CÉSAIRE

From A Tempest[†]

Born in Martinique, Aimé Césaire (1913–2008) was equally distinguished as a poet and a playwright. His Une tempête—with its indefinite article—was written in 1969 and first performed in Tunisia. Subtitled "Adaptation for a Black Theatre," it highlights matters of race, specifying a black Caliban and a mulatto Ariel, although the

---

3. The revolving of the disk, of course, is apparent only, not real. Actually, the disk remains motionless; it appears to revolve because of the motion of the Priests around it.
4. See "Kings and Gods of Egypt," Alexandre Moret; pp. 69–108.
5. Similarly before each of the Actions of each Interlude, Prospero makes a brief explanatory comment to Ariel (and thus to the audience).
† From A Tempest [1969], trans. Philip Crispin (London: Oberon Books, 2000), pp. 57–61. © Aimé Césaire, translated by Philip Crispin, 2002. Reprinted by permission of Oberon Books Ltd. All notes are by the editors of this Norton Critical Edition.

opening stage direction has actors choosing masks in "the ambiance of
a psychodrama." Despite the play's being more overtly about colonial
and racial issues than Shakespeare's original, the exchanges between
Caliban and Prospero are written with lyricism and humor.

*　　*　　*

CALIBAN:
　　You must understand, Prospero:
　　for years I bowed my head,
　　for years I stomached it,
　　stomached all of it:
　　your insults, your ingratitude,
　　and worst of all, more degrading than all the rest,
　　your condescension.
　　But now it's over!
　　Over, do you hear!
　　Of course, for the moment you're still
　　the stronger.
　　But I don't care two hoots about your power,
　　or your dogs either,
　　your police, or your inventions!
　　And do you know why I don't care?
　　Do you want to know?
　　It's because I know I'll have you!
　　You'll be impaled! And on a stake
　　you'll have sharpened yourself!
　　You'll have impaled yourself!
　　Prospero you're a great illusionist:
　　you know all about lies.
　　And you lied to me so much,
　　lied about the world, lied about yourself,
　　that you ended up by imposing on me
　　an image of myself:
　　underdeveloped, in your words,
　　incompetent,
　　that's how you forced me to see myself,
　　and I hate that image! And it is false!
　　But now I know you, you old cancer,
　　and I also know myself!

　　And I know that one day
　　my bare fist, my bare fist alone
　　will be enough to crush your world!
　　The old world is falling apart!

Isn't it true? Just look!
It even bores you to death!
And by the way, you have a chance to finish it off:
You can get the hell out.
You can go back to Europe.
But there's no hope of that!
I'm sure you won't leave!
That makes me laugh—your 'mission',
your 'vocation'!
Your vocation is to get on my wick![1]
And that's why you'll stay,
like those men who established the colonies
and can no longer live elsewhere.
An old addict, that's what you are.

PROSPERO: Poor Caliban! You're well aware that you're heading toward your own perdition. That you're rushing toward suicide! That I will be the stronger, and stronger each time! I pity you!

CALIBAN: And I hate you!

PROSPERO: Beware! My generosity has limits.

CALIBAN: (*Chanting.*)
Shango[2] marches with strength
across the sky, his covered way!
Shango is a fire-bearer,
each step he treads shakes the heavens
shakes the earth
Shango, Shango oh!

PROSPERO:
I have uprooted the oak, roused the sea,
shaken the mountain, and baring
my breast against adversity,
I have exchanged thunder with Jupiter, bolt for bolt.
Better still! From the brute monster I made man!
But oh!
To have failed to find the path
to the man's heart, if that really is where man
is to be found.
    To CALIBAN.
Well, I hate you as well!
For you are the one who
made me doubt myself
for the first time.

1. On my nerves.
2. A major Yoruba deity.

Addressing the Lords.

. . . My friends, come closer. I take my leave of you. I am going
no longer. My fate is here: I shall not flee it.

ANTONIO: What, Your Grace!

PROSPERO:

Understand me well.
I am not, in the ordinary sense
the master, as this savage thinks,
but rather the conductor of a vast score:
this isle.
Teasing out voices, myself alone,
and coupling them at my pleasure,
arranging out of the confusion
the sole intelligible line.
Without me, who would be able
to derive music from all this?
Without me, this island is dumb.
Here then, my duty.
I will remain.

GONZALO: Oh miraculous day to the end!

PROSPERO: Do not be distressed. Antonio, remain lieutenant of my
estates and use them as regent until Ferdinand and Miranda may
take effective possession of them, joining them with the Kingdom
of Naples. Nothing that has been ordained for them must be postponed: let their marriage be celebrated in Naples with due royal
splendour. Honest Gonzalo, I place my trust in your good faith. At
this ceremony, you shall stand as father to our Princess.

GONZALO: You may rely on me, Your Grace.

PROSPERO: Gentlemen, farewell.

They exit.

And now, Caliban, there's only us!
What I have to tell you will be brief:
Ten times, a hundred times, I've tried to save you,
above all from yourself.
But you have always answered me with rage
and venom, like
the opossum that hoists itself up by its own tail
the better to bite the hand
that pulls it from the darkness.
Well, boy, I shall spurn my indulgent nature
and, from now on, I will answer your violence
with violence!

*Time passes by, symbolised by the curtain's being lowered half-
way and then being taken up again. In semi-darkness,* PROSPERO

appears, aged and weary. His gestures are stiff and automatic, his speech weak and listless.

Funny, for some time now, we've been invaded by opossums. They're everywhere. . . Peccaries,[3] wild boar, all those unclean beasts! But, above all, opossums. Oh, those eyes! And that hideous leer! You'd swear the jungle wanted to invade the cave . . . But I'll defend myself . . . I will not let my work perish . . . (*Roaring.*) I will defend civilisation! (*He fires in all directions.*) They've got what was coming to them . . . Now, this way, I'll have some peace for a blessed while . . . But it's cold . . . Funny, the climate's changed . . . Cold on this island . . . Have to think about making a fire . . . Ah well, my old Caliban, we're the only two left on this island, just you and me. You and me! You-me! Me-you! But what the hell's he up to? (*Roaring.*) Caliban!

In the distance, above the sound of the surf and the mewing of birds, snatches of CALIBAN's *song can be heard.*

LIBERTY, OH-AY! LIBERTY!

---

3. Medium-sized hoofed animals mainly found in Central and South America.

Poems

PERCY BYSSHE SHELLEY

The Tempest was the favorite play of English Romantic poet Percy Bysshe Shelley (1792–1822), and *Ariel* was his choice of name for the ill-fated sailboat upon which he drowned in July 1822. Here Shelley casts himself in the role of Ariel, to the Miranda and Ferdinand of Jane and Edward Ellerker Williams. In the summer of 1822, Percy and his wife, author Mary, shared with them the Casa Magni, near the bay of San Terenzo in Italy; and Edward drowned along with Shelley in the boating accident. The guitar that accompanied Shelley's poem can now be found at the Bodleian Library, Oxford.

With a Guitar, to Jane[†]

Ariel to Miranda.—Take
This slave of Music, for the sake
Of him who is the slave of thee,
And teach it all the harmony
In which thou canst, and only thou,
Make the delighted spirit glow,
Till joy denies itself again,
And, too intense, is turned to pain;
For by permission and command
Of thine own Prince Ferdinand,
Poor Ariel sends this silent token
Of love that never can be spoken;
Your guardian spirit, Ariel, who,
From life to life, must still pursue
Your happiness;—for thus alone
Can Ariel ever find his own.
From Prospero's inchanted cell,
As the mighty verses tell,

† From *The Poems of Percy Bysshe Shelley*, ed. C. D. Lodock, vol. 2 (London: Methuen & Co., 1911), pp. 278–79. All notes are by the editors of this Norton Critical Edition.

To the throne of Naples, he
Lit you o'er the trackless sea,
Flitting on, your prow before,
Like a living meteor.
When you die, the silent Moon,
In her interlunar swoon,
Is not sadder in her cell
Than deserted Ariel.
When you live again on earth,
Like an unseen star of birth
Ariel guides you o'er the sea
Of life from your nativity.
Many changes have been run,
Since Ferdinand and you begun
Your course of love, and Ariel still
Has tracked your steps, and served your will;
Now, in humbler, happier lot,
This is all remembered not;
And now, alas! the poor sprite is
Imprisoned, for some fault of his,
In a body like a grave;—
From you he only dares to crave,
For his service and his sorrow,
A smile to-day, a song to-morrow.
The artist who this idol wrought,
To echo all harmonious thought,
Felled a tree, while on the steep
The woods were in their winter sleep,
Rocked in that repose divine
On the wind-swept Apennine;[1]
And dreaming, some of Autumn past,
And some of Spring approaching fast.
And some of April buds and showers,
And some of songs in July bowers,
And all of love; and so this tree,—
Oh that such our death may be!—
Died in sleep, and felt no pain,
To live in happier form again:
From which, beneath Heaven's fairest star,
The artist wrought this loved Guitar,
And taught it justly to reply,
To all who question skilfully,
In language gentle as thine own;

1. The Apennine mountains extend the length of peninsular Italy.

Whispering in enamoured tone
Sweet oracles of woods and dells,
And summer winds in sylvan cells;
For it had learnt all harmonies
Of the plains and of the skies,
Of the forests and the mountains,
And the many-voicèd fountains;
The clearest echoes of the hills,
The softest notes of falling rills,
The melodies of birds and bees,
The murmuring of summer seas,
And pattering rain, and breathing dew,
And airs of evening; and it knew
That seldom-heard mysterious sound,
Which, driven on its diurnal round,
As it floats through boundless day,
Our world enkindles on its way.
All this it knows, but will not tell
To those who cannot question well
The Spirit that inhabits it;
It talks according to the wit
Of its companions; and no more
Is heard than has been felt before
By those who tempt it to betray
These secrets of an elder day.
But sweetly as its answers will
Flatter hands of perfect skill,
It keeps its highest, hollest tone
For our belovèd Jane alone.

ROBERT BROWNING

Robert Browning (1812–1889) was one of Victorian England's most influential poets. First published in his *Dramatis Personae* of 1864, Browning's dramatic monologue "Caliban upon Setebos" was primarily intended as a satire of Victorian theologians, but it also offers a strikingly original meditation on Caliban's peculiar language and his vexed relationship to creation and power.

From Caliban upon Setebos; or,
Natural Theology in the Island[†]

'Thou thoughtest that I was altogether such a one as thyself.'[1]

['Will sprawl, now that the heat of day is best,
Flat on his belly in the pit's much mire,
With elbows wide, fists clenched to prop his chin.
And, while he kicks both feet in the cool slush,
And feels about his spine small eft-things[2] course,
Run in and out each arm, and make him laugh:
And while above his head a pompion-plant,[3]
Coating the cave-top as a brow its eye,
Creeps down to touch and tickle hair and beard,
And now a flower drops with a bee inside,
And now a fruit to snap at, catch and crunch,—
He looks out o'er yon sea which sunbeams cross
And recross till they weave a spider-web
(Meshes of fire, some great fish breaks at times)
And talks to his own self, howe'er he please,
Touching that other, whom his dam called God.
Because to talk about Him, vexes—ha,
Could He but know! and time to vex is now,
When talk is safer than in winter-time.
Moreover Prosper and Miranda sleep
In confidence he drudges at their task,
And it is good to cheat the pair, and gibe,
Letting the rank tongue blossom into speech.]

Setebos, Setebos, and Setebos!
'Thinketh, He dwelleth i' the cold o' the moon.

'Thinketh He made it, with the sun to match,
But not the stars; the stars came otherwise;
Only made clouds, winds, meteors, such as that:
Also this isle, what lives and grows thereon,
And snaky sea which rounds and ends the same.

'Thinketh, it came of being ill at ease:
He hated that He cannot change His cold,

---

† From *The Poetical Works of Robert Browning* (London: Smith, Elder, & Company,
1889), 7:149–50, 161. All notes are by the editors of this Norton Critical Edition. The
brackets are Browning's.
1. David, *Psalms* 50.21.
2. Small lizards; newts.
3. Pumpkin.

Nor cure its ache, 'Hath spied an icy fish
That longed to 'scape the rock-stream where she lived,
And thaw herself within the lukewarm brine
O' the lazy sea her stream thrusts far amid,
A crystal spike 'twixt two warm walls of wave;
Only, she ever sickened, found repulse
At the other kind of water, not her life,
(Green-dense and dim-delicious, bred o' the sun)
Flounced back from bliss she was not born to breathe,
And in her old bounds buried her despair,
Hating and loving warmth alike: so He.

* * *

[What, what? A curtain o'er the world at once!
Crickets stop hissing; not a bird—or, yes,
There scuds His raven that has told Him all!
It was fool's play, this prattling! Ha! The wind
Shoulders the pillared dust, death's house o' the move,
And fast invading fires begin! White blaze—
A tree's head snaps—and there, there, there, there, there,
His thunder follows! Fool to gibe at Him!
Lo! 'Lieth flat and loveth Setebos!
'Maketh his teeth meet through his upper lip,
Will let those quails fly, will not eat this month
One little mess of whelks, so he may 'scape!]

JOAQUIM MARIA MACHADO DE ASSIS

The Brazilian Joaquim Maria Machado de Assis (1839–1908) is best
known as one of Latin America's finest and most subtle novelists, but
he was also a distinguished poet. "No alto" (At the Top) is, perhaps
significantly, the final poem in his collection called *Occidentales*,
"western" poems first published in his *Poesias completas* (1901). The
hand of "the other one" (Caliban) held out to the poet prefigures the
twentieth-century interest in Caliban throughout the Americas.

At the Top†

A poet had reached the mountain peak;
wending his way down the western slope,

---

† Translated from the Portuguese by Lúcia Sá and Gordon Brotherston. Reprinted by
permission of the translators.

he saw a strange thing,
a fell figure.

He turns his eyes to the subtle, sky-born,
delightful Ariel, his companion from the start,
and fearfully asks
who or what is that?

Like a merry sweet sound lost in the air
or as it were
a vain thought

Ariel dissolved without further word.
To help him down the hill
the other one held out his hand.

RAINER MARIA RILKE

Rainer Maria Rilke (1875–1926) is regarded as the finest German
modernist poet, one of the creators of new forms of lyricism and sensu-
ality. Born in Prague, but a restless traveler across Europe, Rilke left a
large body of work that culminated in the *Duino Elegies* and the *Sonnets to Orpheus*, both published in 1923. "The Spirit Ariel," perhaps
another meditation on the role of the artist, belongs to this late period.

The Spirit Ariel†

(After reading Shakespeare's *Tempest*)

Sometime, somewhere, it had set him free,
that jerk with which you flung yourself in youth
full upon greatness, far from all respect.
Then he grew willing: and since then a servant,
after each service waiting for his freedom.
Half-domineering, half almost ashamed,
you make excuses, that for this and this
you still require him, and insist, alas!
how you have helped him. Though you feel yourself
how everything detained by his detention
is missing from the air. Sweet and seductive,

† From *Selected Works, Volume II: Poetry*, trans. J. B. Leishman (New York: New Directions, 1960), p. 292. Copyright © 1960 by New Directions Publishing Corp. Reprinted by
permission of New Directions Publishing Corp.

to let him go, and then, abjuring magic,
entering into destiny like others,
to know that henceforth his most gentle friendship,
without all tension, nowhere bound by duty,
a something added to the space we breathe,
is busied heedless in the element.
Dependent now, having no more the gift
to form the dull mouth to that conjuration
that brought him headlong. Powerless, ageing, poor,
yet breathing *him*, incomprehensibly
far-scattered fragrance, making the Invisible
at last complete. Smiling, to think you'd been
on nodding terms with that, such great acquaintance
so soon familiar. Perhaps weeping, too,
when you remember how it loved you and
would yet be going, always both at once.

(And there I left it? Now he terrifies me,
this man who's duke again.—The ways he draws
the wire into his head, and hangs himself
beside the other puppets, and henceforth
begs mercy of the play! . . . What epilogue
of achieved mastery! Putting off, standing there
with only one's own strength: "which is most faint.")

H.D.

The U.S. expatriate Hilda Doolittle (1886–1961), known as H.D., was
one of the founders of the Imagist school of poetry. Her allusive and
musical writing intertwined female identity, literary history, and personal psychology. H.D.'s poem on *The Tempest* (part of her 1949 tribute to Shakespeare, *By Avon River*) emerged from visits to
Stratford-upon-Avon in the wake of a personal breakdown and the collective trauma of World War II; it is one of the few creative responses
to *The Tempest* to focus on the figure of Claribel.

From By Avon River[†]

I

Come as you will, but I came home
Driven by *The Tempest*; you may come,

† From *By Avon River* (New York: Macmillan, 1949), pp. 5–7, 9.

With banner or the beat of the drum;
You may come with laughing friends,

Or tired, alone; you may come
In triumph, many kings have come

And queens and ladies with their lords,
To lay their lilies in this place,

Where others, known for wit and song,
Have left their laurel; you may come,

Remembering how your young love wept
With Montague long ago and Capulet.

II

I came home driven by *The Tempest*;
That was after the wedding-feast;
'Twas a sweet marriage, we are told;
And she *a paragon . . . who is now queen,
And the rarest that e'er came there*;

We know little of *the king's fair daughter
Claribel*; her father was Alonso,
King of Naples, her brother, Ferdinand,
And we read later, *in one voyage
Did Claribel her husband find at Tunis*:

Claribel was outside all of this,
The Tempest came after they left her;
Read for yourself, *Dramatis Personae*.

III

Read for yourself, *Dramatis Personae*,
Alonso, Sebastian, Prospero,
Antonio, Ferdinand, Gonzalo,
Adrian, Francisco, Caliban
(Whom some call Pan),
Trinculo, Stephano, Miranda,
Ariel, Iris, Ceres, Juno;

These are the players, chiefly,
Caliban, a savage and deformed slave,
Ariel, an airy Spirit, Miranda,

The magician's lovely daughter,
The magician—ah indeed, I had forgot
Boatswain, Mariners, Nymphs and Reapers,

And among these, are other
Spirits attending on Prospero.

IV

Read through again, *Dramatis Personae*,
She is not there at all, but Claribel,
Claribel, the birds shrill, Claribel,
Claribel echoes from this rainbow-shell,
I stooped just now to gather from the sand;

Where? From an island somewhere . . .
Some say the *Sea-Adventure* set out,
(In May, 1609, to be exact)
For the new colony, Virginia;
Some say the *Sea-Adventure* ran aground
On the Bermudas; but all on board
Were saved, built new ships
And sailed on, a year later;

It is all written in an old pamphlet,
Did he read of her there, Claribel?

*   *   *

VIII

Awkwardly, tenderly,
We stand with our flowers,
Separate, self-consciously,
Shyly or in child-like
Delicate simplicity;

Each one waits patiently,
Now we are near the door;
Till sudden, wondrously,
All shyness drops away,
Awkwardness, complacency;

Ring, ring and ring again,
'Twas a sweet marriage,
So they say, *my beloved is mine*

And I am his; Claribel
The chimes peel;

Claribel, the chimes say,
The king's fair daughter
Marries Tunis; O spikenard,
Myrrh and myrtle-spray,
'Twas a sweet marriage;

Tenderly, tenderly,
We stand with our flowers,
Our belovèd is ours,
Our belovèd is ours,
To-day? Yesterday?

KAMAU BRATHWAITE

Born in Barbados in 1930, poet and critic Kamau Brathwaite, like his
compatriot George Lamming (see above, pp. 154–74), has had a long
and fruitful relationship with *The Tempest*. This early poem, written in
1969, speaks with the voice of a modern Caliban. More recently Brathwaite has adopted the figure of Sycorax to name his unique combination of customized typefaces and spellings.

From Caliban†

Ninety-five per cent of my people poor
ninety-five per cent of my people black
ninety-five per cent of my people dead
you have heard it all before O Leviticus O Jeremiah O Jean-Paul
    Sartre

and now I see that these modern palaces have grown
out of the soil, out of the bad habits of their crippled owners
the Chrysler stirs but does not produce cotton
the Jupiter purrs but does not produce bread

out of the living stone, out of the living bone
of coral, these dead

† From *The Arrivants: A New World Trilogy* (Oxford: Oxford UP, 1973), pp. 191–92.
    © Edward Brathwaite 1967, 1968, 1969, 1973. Reprinted by permission of the publisher.
    All notes are by the editors of this Norton Critical Edition.

towers; out of the coney
islands of our mind-

less architects, this death
of sons, of songs, of sunshine;
out of this dearth of coo ru coos,[1] home-
less pigeons, this perturbation that does not signal health.

In Havana that morning, as every morning,
the police toured the gambling houses
wearing their dark glasses
and collected tribute;

salute blackjack, salute backgammon, salute the
    one-armed bandit
Vieux Fort and Andros Island, the Isle of Pines;
the morals squadron fleeced the whores
Mary and Mary Magdalene;

newspapers spoke of Wall Street and the social set
who was with who, what medals did the Consulate's
Assistant wear. The sky was cloudy, a strong breeze;
maximum temperature eighty-two degrees.

It was December second, nineteen fifty-six.[2]
It was the first of August eighteen thirty-eight.[3]
It was the twelfth October fourteen ninety-two.[4]

How many bangs how many revolutions?

*   *   *

SUNITI NAMJOSHI

Suniti Namjoshi (b. 1941) is a Canadian writer of Indian origin, living
and teaching in England. Her poetry and prose "fables" combine her
Hindu background with her position as a lesbian and feminist. In her
sequence "Snapshots of Caliban," Namjoshi shifts freely between voices
and identities, exploring alternative and repressed gender dynamics
among Miranda, Caliban, and Prospero.

1. Curucui, tropical birds.
2. The day Fidel Castro (1926–2016) and his companions landed in eastern Cuba to begin
   their guerrilla campaign against the corrupt regime of Fulgencio Batista (president
   1940–44 and 1952–59).
3. The day of full slave emancipation in all British colonies.
4. The date of Christopher Columbus's landfall in the New World.

From Snapshots of Caliban†

VI

There's something wrong with Caliban.
    Is it her shape? Is it her size?
If I could say that Caliban is stupid,
then that might help, but she can read and write
    and sometimes her speech is so lucid.
She does not feel? But I've heard her howling:
she howls like a dog or some tiresome animal,
    and she sobs at night.
Yet she is Caliban. I've seen her gaping
    at the blue heavens, or at me,
and I fear her dream. For there is something
I dislike so thoroughly about Caliban:
if she had her way, she would rule the island,
    and I will not have it.

VII *From Caliban's Notebook*

They dreamed it. There was no storm,
no shipwreck, nobody came. Prince Ferdinand
was a rock or a tree. M dreamed it.
She said to the tree, "Bow gracefully,"
and the tree bowed with Ariel in it.
As for revenge—the old man's dream—
even in his dream he could not change them,
not utterly; they still plotted, still schemed—
as though in a play—until Ariel once again
was sent to intervene.
        And they never got away,
for here we all are, M and myself
and doddering P, still islanded,
still ailing, looking seaward
            for company.

* * *

† From *Because of India* (London: Onlywomen Press, 1989), pp. 91, 92, 94. First pub-lished in *From the Bedside Book of Nightmares* (Fredericton, Canada: Fiddlehead, 1984). Reprinted by permission of the author.

IX Prospero's Meditations

Two monsters are crawling out of my eyes
and onto the sand, scrabbling and scuttling,
climbing and sliding on top of one another,
tipping over stones, doing themselves,
and one another too, some damage perhaps.
Of the two crabs which is more dainty?
Which one of the two least crab-like?
Most graceful? Is there a lovelier sheen
on one curved carapace, a subtler shine?
Their function escapes me.
　　　　　　　They have broken their claws.
Oh my pretty playthings,
　　　　　　　my shining instruments!

LEMUEL JOHNSON

Lemuel Johnson (1942–2002) was brought up in Freetown, Sierra Leone, and later lived in France, Austria, and the United States, where he taught English. His collection of poems, *Highlife for Caliban*, addresses the colonial history of West Africa very much in the spirit of George Lamming's essay (see above, pp. 154–74), the author identifying with Caliban at the same time as recasting the play's events. Johnson also wrote the important critical work *Shakespeare in Africa (and Other Venues): Import and the Appropriation of Culture* (1998).

Calypso for Caliban†

ackee rice salt fish is nice

as when I set down to substance
and to sum, but, seduced, think
to be elf with printless foot
is admiration and nice

this is the place
my inheritance
a chain of leached bones
my inheritance

---

† From *Highlife for Caliban* (Trenton, NJ: Africa World Press, Inc., 1995), pp. 39–42. Reprinted by permission of the Estate of Lemuel Johnson. All notes are by the editors of this Norton Critical Edition.

mother this
chain of leached stones
airless quays
dust that rises
to coast on water

but they walk on water
for you
they walk on water
papa prospero
atibo legba[1]
the whores
with water will
walk on water

papa prospero
jig me mama
an' jig she mama
papa prospero jig
jig me mama
to born the beast

prospero
atibo legba
is him goin to make
all so, and thee,
prosperous so;

to make the beast
is him goin to kiss
in his own true-true name
the whores
until the red part white
more so than black can
white in she certain parts.

Mary-Miranda and mother
and holy virgin,
so come to us
so pray for us
in all your own
true-true name—that the will
be done too for dem mamas with

---

1. Traditional vodou invocation to Legba, the guardian of the crossroads.

the derelict vaginas,
though defunct; that they be
holy maid and ready
now to make the beast
with two backs
with atibo prospero
even till the kingdom.

come, keep too the air
out of Sycorax hole:

let this, that I am
set to be, choke unborn
where she think to born
me black; lacking
in air that is light,

for is so things happen,
prospero,
if a whore put
to black lips, sir,
on her private vagina, sir.

but, you, virgin
daughter of god's
own true self,
admired so in
your body's own self,
keep open the carnival,
this feast of ashes,
and Lent (this dance
of flex knee
and tight thigh)
for when the black
beast to come
prowls so about
the derelict pasture
that is man's
braincase sometimes;

when I will prowl
these quays,
dissatisfied, with my face
prospero
against the face

prospero
of your daughter
prospero
prowling the fringes
of the tempest.
god's own daughter,
ora pro nobis,[2]
and again be admired

when I turn the corners
of these my eyes
for a vision of hulks
and black flesh
drugged in vomit and fart,
ora pro nobis

when I set down to substance
and to sum and think to be
elf with printless foot
is admiration and nice;

when the wind breaks
in derelict places,
and I grow to be at last
not ariel-spirit
not daughter-flesh,
but prey for us,

be present at the table,
and in your own
true-true admiration;
when I am myself again
only in this or that corner
of a dissatisfied face;

be present
while and still I am ready,
if the revel end,
to wake and cry to dream again.

2. Pray for us (Latin).

HEINER MÜLLER

The East German playwright Heiner Müller (1929–1995) was best known in the English-speaking world for his radical adaptation of *Hamlet, Hamletmachine* (1978). His rewritings of Shakespeare are dislocated and provocative, drawing on Marx's political philosophies and Brecht's theatrical strategies in an attempt to unsettle our relationship to Shakespearean authority.

[Go Ariel]†

Go Ariel silence the tempest and
throw the dazed ones on the beach
            I need them
living so I can kill them
For me   Father
      Why

EDWIN MORGAN

The Scottish poet Edwin Morgan (1920–2010) was the first Poet Laureate of Glasgow, where he spent his entire life. His playful, learned, and moving work ranges from sonnets and libretti to concrete poetry and translations of continental classics (often into Scots rather than English). For Morgan, poetry was a space for linguistic invention and imaginative travel—through the literary and historical figures of the past and our everyday experiences and aspirations.

Ariel Freed‡

I lifted my wings at midnight.
Moonlit pines, empty paths,
broochlike lagoons dwindled below me.
Oh I was electric: my wingtips
winked like stars through the real stars.
Cold, brisk, tingling that journey,

---

† Translation by Carl Weber, from *PAJ: A Journal of Performance and Art* 65 (2000): 110. Reprinted by permission of the Estate of Carl Weber.
‡ From *Virtual and Other Realities* (Manchester: Carcanet Press Ltd., 1997), p. 101. Reprinted by permission of the publisher.

voyage more than journey, the night
had waves, pressures I had to breast,
thrust aside, I had a figurehead or
perhaps I was a figurehead with
dolphins of the darkness as companions.
Only to have no shore, no landfall,
no runway, no eyrie, no goal and no fall!

TED HUGHES

One of twentieth-century Britain's most celebrated writers, Ted Hughes (1930–1998) engaged with Shakespeare as both a critic and a poet. His final collection of poems, *Birthday Letters* (1998), offered an unexpectedly intimate poetic account of his marriage to the U.S. poet Sylvia Plath (who committed suicide in 1963, and who herself borrowed names and themes from *The Tempest* for her major collection of poems, *Ariel*). In "Setebos," Hughes maps the characters of *The Tempest* onto the drama of his life with Plath.

Setebos[†]

Who could play Miranda?
Only you. Ferdinand—only me.
And it was like that, yes, it was like that.
I never questioned. Your mother
Played Prospero, flying her magic in
To stage the Masque, and bless the marriage,
Eavesdropping on the undervoices
Of the honeymooners in Paris
And smiling on the stair at her reflection
In the dark wall. My wreckage
Was all of a sudden a new wardrobe, unworn,
Even gold in my teeth. Ariel
Entertained us night and day.
The voices and sounds and sweet airs
Were our aura. Ariel was our aura.
Both of us alternated

† From *Birthday Letters* (London: Faber & Faber Ltd., 1998), pp. 132–33. Copyright © 1998 by Ted Hughes. Reprinted by permission of Faber & Faber Ltd. and Farrar, Straus & Giroux.

Caliban our secret, who showed us
The sweetest, the freshest, the wildest
And loved us as we loved. Sycorax,
The rind of our garden's emptied quince,
Bobbed in the hazy surf at the horizon
Offshore, in the wings
Of the heavens, like a director
Studying the scenes to come.

Then the script overtook us. Caliban
Reverted to type. I heard
The bellow in your voice
That made my nape-hair prickle when you sang
How you were freed from the Elm. I lay
In the labyrinth of a cowslip
Without a clue. I heard the Minotaur
Coming down its tunnel-groove
Of old faults deep and bitter. King Minos,
Alias Otto—his bellow
Winding into murderous music. Which play
Were we in? Too late to find you
And get to my ship. The moon, off her moorings,
Tossed in tempest. Your bellowing song
Was a scream inside a bronze
Bull being roasted. The laughter
Of Sycorax was thunder and lightning
And black downpour. She hurled
Prospero's head at me.
A bounding thunderbolt, a jumping cracker.
The moon's horns
Plunged and tossed. I heard your cries
Bugling through the hot bronze:
'Who has dismembered us?' I crawled
Under a gabardine, hugging tight
All I could of me, hearing the cry
Now of hounds.

ROBIN KIRKPATRICK

Poet and distinguished scholar and translator of Dante, Robin Kirkpatrick (b. 1943) is Emeritus Professor of Italian and English Literature at the University of Cambridge, where he is a Life Fellow of Robinson College.

Envoi[†]

Turning (no word: these words are none as yet)
who draws new born from indigo—those bruised
    lagoons, all breathing nebulae!—a white
more white as, tightening round its ogee, hands
    stitch finely old and needle-eyed the lines
that mark the mirror brow and tell time gone?

Arc down (those bright steel brushes being wings)
    to ask, when silence sings you to an end,
whose voice that is, young still beyond the mask.

† From *A Collection* (Cambridge: The Chaddesden Press, 2013), p. 30. Copyright © Robin Kirkpatrick, 2013. Reprinted by permission of the author.

Selected Bibliography

Sound introductions to Shakespeare and to Shakespearean studies can be found in *The New Cambridge Companion to Shakespeare*, ed. Margreta De Grazia and Stanley Wells (Cambridge: Cambridge UP, 2010); *The Oxford Companion to Shakespeare*, ed. Michael Dobson and Stanley Wells, 2nd ed., revising eds. Will Sharpe and Erin Sullivan (Oxford: Oxford UP, 2015); *The Bedford Companion to Shakespeare: An Introduction with Documents*, ed. Russ McDonald (Boston: Bedford Books, 1996); and Stanley Wells and Gary Taylor, with John Jowett and William Montgomery, *William Shakespeare: A Textual Companion* (New York: W. W. Norton, 1997).

Essay Collections

Bigliazzi, Silvia, and Lisanna Calvi, eds. *Revisiting* The Tempest: *The Capacity to Signify*. Basingstoke: Palgrave Macmillan, 2014.

Döring, Tobias, and Virginia Mason Vaughan, eds. *Critical and Cultural Transformations: Shakespeare's* The Tempest, *1611 to the Present. REAL—Yearbook of Research in English and American Literature* 29. Tübingen: Narr Verlag, 2013.

Graff, Gerald, and James Phelan, eds. *The Tempest: A Case Study in Critical Controversy*. Boston: Bedford, 2000.

Hulme, Peter, and William H. Sherman, eds. *"The Tempest" and Its Travels*. London: Reaktion Books, 2000.

Lie, Nadia, and Theo D'haen, eds. *Constellation Caliban: Figurations of a Character*. Amsterdam and Atlanta, GA: Rodopi, 1997.

Murphy, Patrick M., ed. The Tempest: *Critical Essays*. New York: Routledge, 2001.

Palmer, D. J., ed. *Shakespeare:* The Tempest. Basingstoke: Macmillan, 1991.

Vaughan, Virginia Mason, and Alden T. Vaughan, eds. *Critical Essays on Shakespeare's "The Tempest."* New York: G. K. Hall & Co., 1997.

———, The Tempest: *A Critical Reader*. London: Bloomsbury, 2014.

White, R. S., ed. The Tempest: *Contemporary Critical Essays*. London: Macmillan, 1999.

Wood, Nigel, ed. *The Tempest*. Buckingham: Open UP, 1995.

Other Works

• indicates works included or excerpted in this Norton Critical Edition.

Baker, David J. "Where Is Ireland in *The Tempest*?" In Mark Thornton Burnett and Ramona Wray, eds., *Shakespeare and Ireland*. Basingstoke: Macmillan, 1997. 68–88.

Baldo, Jonathan. "Exporting Oblivion in *The Tempest*." *Modern Language Quarterly* 56 (1995). 111–44.

Barker, Francis, and Peter Hulme. "'Nymphs and reapers heavily vanish': The Discursive Contexts of *The Tempest.*" In John Drakakis, ed., *Alternative Shakespeares.* London: Methuen, 1985. 191–205.

Barton, Anne. Introduction to William Shakespeare, *The Tempest.* The New Penguin Shakespeare. London: Penguin, 1968. 7–51.

Bate, Jonathan. *Shakespeare and Ovid.* Oxford: Clarendon P, 1993.

Bender, John. "The Day of *The Tempest.*" *ELH* 47 (1980): 235–58.

Berger, Harry, Jr. "Miraculous Harp: A Reading of Shakespeare's *Tempest.*" *Shakespeare Studies* 5 (1969): 253–83.

Berger, Karol. "Prospero's Art." *Shakespeare Studies* 10 (1977): 211–39.

Black, James. "The Latter End of Prospero's Commonwealth." *Shakespeare Survey* 43 (1991): 29–41.

Borlik, Todd Andrew. "Caliban and the Fen Demons of Lincolnshire: The Englishness of Shakespeare's *Tempest.*" *Shakespeare* 9:1 (2013): 21–51.

Breight, Curt. "'Treason doth never prosper': *The Tempest* and the Discourse of Treason." *Shakespeare Quarterly* 41 (1990): 1–28.

Brockbank, Philip. "*The Tempest*: Conventions of Art and Empire." In J. R. Brown and B. Harris, eds., *Later Shakespeare.* London: Edward Arnold, 1966. 183–201.

Brotton, Jerry. "'This Tunis, sir, was Carthage': Contesting Colonialism." In Ania Loomba and Martin Orkin, eds., *Post-Colonial Shakespeares.* London: Routledge, 1998. 23–42.

Brown, Paul. "'This thing of darkness I acknowledge mine': *The Tempest* and the Discourse of Colonialism." In Jonathan Dollimore and Alan Sinfield, eds., *Political Shakespeare: New Essays in Cultural Materialism.* Manchester: Manchester UP, 1985. 48–71.

Bruster, Douglas. "Local *Tempest*: Shakespeare and the Work of the Early Modern Playhouse." *Journal of Medieval and Renaissance Studies* 25:1 (1995): 33–53.

Brydon, Diana. "Re-writing *The Tempest.*" *World Literature Written in English* 23:1 (1984): 75–88.

———. "Sister Letters: Miranda's *Tempest* in Canada." In Marianne Novy, ed., *Cross-Cultural Performances: Differences in Women's Re-Visions of Shakespeare.* Urbana: U of Illinois P, 1993. 165–84.

Bullough, Geoffrey, ed. *Narrative and Dramatic Sources of Shakespeare.* London: Routledge & Kegan Paul, 1975. 8: 275–339.

Burnett, Mark Thornton. "'Strange and Woonderfull Syghts': *The Tempest* and the Discourses of Monstrosity." *Shakespeare Survey* 50 (1997): 187–99.

Busia, Abena P. A. "Silencing Sycorax: On African Colonial Discourse and the Unvoiced Female." *Cultural Critique* 14 (1989–90): 81–104.

Callaghan, Dympna. "Irish Memories in *The Tempest.*" In her *Shakespeare without Women: Representing Gender and Race on the Renaissance Stage.* London: Routledge, 2000. 97–138.

Cartelli, Thomas. *Repositioning Shakespeare: National Formations, Postcolonial Appropriations.* London: Routledge, 1999.

Chedgzoy, Kate. *Shakespeare's Queer Children: Sexual Politics and Contemporary Culture.* Manchester: Manchester UP, 1995.

Chickering, Howell. "Hearing Ariel's Songs." *Journal of Medieval and Renaissance Studies* 14:1 (1994): 132–72.

Cholij, Irena. "'A Thousand Twangling Instruments': Music and *The Tempest* on the Eighteenth-Century London Stage." *Shakespeare Survey* 51 (1998): 79–94.

Clare, Janet. "Tracings and Data in *The Tempest*: Author, World, and Representation." *Shakespeare Survey* 68 (2015): 109–17.

• Coleridge, Samuel Taylor. "Notes on *The Tempest.*" In *The Literary Remains of Samuel Taylor Coleridge*, coll. and ed. Henry Nelson Coleridge. London: W. Pickering, 1836. 2: 92–102.

Diala, Isidore. "(De)Stabilising the European Classic: Sycorax, Esiaba Irobi's *The Tempest.*" *Shakespeare in Southern Africa* 24 (2012): 25–43.

Dobson, Michael. "'Remember / First to possess his books': The Appropriation of *The Tempest.*" *Shakespeare Survey* 43 (1991): 99–107.

———. *The Making of the National Poet: Shakespeare, Adaptation, and Authorship, 1660–1769.* Oxford: Clarendon P, 1992.

Dolan, Frances E. "The Subordinate('s) Plot: Petty Treason and the Forms of Domestic Rebellion." *Shakespeare Quarterly* 43 (1992): 317–40.

· Dryden, John. "[The Character of Caliban]." From the Preface to *Troilus and Cressida, or, Truth found too late* (1679). In *Dryden: The Dramatic Works,* ed. Montague Summers. London: Nonesuch P, 1932. 5: 21–22.

Dymkowski, Christine, ed. *The Tempest.* Shakespeare in Production. Cambridge. Cambridge UP, 2000.

Esolen, Anthony M. "'The Isles Shall Wait for His Law': Isaiah and *The Tempest.*" *Studies in Philology* 94:2 (1997): 221–47.

Evans, Malcolm. "Some Subtleties of the Isle." In his *Signifying Nothing: Truth's True Contents in Shakespeare's Text.* Brighton: Harvester P, 1996. 17–38.

Fernández Retamar, Roberto. *Caliban and Other Essays.* Trans. Edward Baker et al. Minneapolis: U of Minnesota P, 1989.

Fiedler, Leslie. *The Stranger in Shakespeare.* New York: Stein and Day, 1972.

Frey, Charles. "*The Tempest* and the New World." *Shakespeare Quarterly* 30 (1979): 29–41.

Fuchs, Barbara. "Conquering Islands: Contextualizing *The Tempest.*" *Shakespeare Quarterly* 48 (1997): 45–62.

Gibbons, Brian. "*The Tempest* and Interruptions." *Cahiers Élisabéthains* 45 (1994): 47 58.

Gilbert, A. H. "*The Tempest*: Parallelism in Characters and Situation." *Journal of English and German Philology* 14 (1915): 63–74.

Gillies, John. "Shakespeare's Virginian Masque." *ELH* 53 (1986): 673–707.

———. *Shakespeare and the Geography of Difference.* Cambridge UP: Cambridge, 1994.

· ———. "The Figure of the New World in *The Tempest.*" In Peter Hulme and William H. Sherman, eds., *"The Tempest" and Its Travels.* London: Reaktion Books, 2000. 180–200.

Goldberg, Jonathan. *Tempest in the Caribbean.* Minneapolis: U of Minnesota P, 2004.

Greenblatt, Stephen. "Learning to Curse: Aspects of Linguistic Colonialism in the Sixteenth Century." In his *Learning to Curse: Essays in Early Modern Culture.* New York: Routledge, 1990. 16–39.

———. "Martial Law in the Land of Cockaigne." In his *Shakespearean Negotiations: The Circulation of Social Energy in Renaissance England.* Oxford: Clarendon P, 1988. 142–63.

———. *Marvellous Possessions: The Wonder of the New World.* Oxford: Oxford UP, 1992.

Griffiths, Trevor R. "'This island's mine': Caliban and Colonialism." *Yearbook of English Studies* 13 (1983): 159–80.

Guffey, George Robert, ed. *After "The Tempest."* Berkeley: U of California P, 1969.

Gunther, Genevieve. "The End of Magic: Instrumental Aesthetics in *The Tempest.*" In her *Magical Imaginations: Instrumental Aesthetics in the English Renaissance.* Toronto: U of Toronto P, 2012. 86–106.

Gurr, Andrew. "*The Tempest*'s Tempest at Blackfriars." *Shakespeare Survey* 41 (1989): 91–102.

Hadfield, Andrew. *Literature, Travel, and Colonial Writing in the English Renaissance, 1545–1625.* Oxford: Oxford UP, 1998.

Hall, Kim F. *Things of Darkness: Economies of Race and Gender in Early Modern England.* Ithaca: Cornell UP, 1995.

Halpern, Richard. "'The Picture of Nobody': White Cannibalism in *The Tempest*." In David Lee Miller et al., eds., *The Production of English Renaissance Culture*. Ithaca: Cornell UP, 1994. 262–92.

Hamilton, Donna B. *Virgil and "The Tempest": The Politics of Imitation*. Columbus: Ohio State UP, 1990.

Hamlin, William M. "Men of Inde: Renaissance Ethnography and *The Tempest*." *Shakespeare Studies* 22 (1994): 15–44.

Hawkes, Terry. "*The Tempest*: Speaking Your Language." In his *Shakespeare's Talking Animals*. London: Edward Arnold, 1973. 194–214.

———. "Swisser-Swatter: Making a Man of English Letters." In John Drakakis, ed., *Alternative Shakespeares*. London: Methuen, 1985. 26–46.

Hendricks, Margo, and Patricia Parker, eds. *Women, 'Race', and Writing in the Early Modern Period*. London: Routledge, 1994.

Holderness, Graham. "*The Tempest*: Spectacles of Disenchantment." In Graham Holderness, Nick Potter, and John Turner, *Shakespeare: Out of Court*. London: Macmillan, 1990. 136–94.

Holland, Norman. "Caliban's Dream." *Psychoanalytical Quarterly* 37 (1968): 114–25.

Holland, Peter. "The Shapeliness of *The Tempest*." *Essays in Criticism* 45:3 (1995): 208–29.

———. "Modernizing Shakespeare: Nicholas Rowe and *The Tempest*." *Shakespeare Quarterly* 51 (2000): 24–32.

———. Introduction to William Shakespeare, *The Tempest*. The Pelican Shakespeare. New York: Penguin Books, 1999. xxvii–xli.

Hopkins, Lisa. *Screen Adaptations of* The Tempest. London: Methuen Drama, 2008.

Horowitz, Arthur. *Prospero's "True Preservers": Peter Brook, Yukio Ninagawa, and Giorgio Strehler—Twentieth-Century Directors Approach Shakespeare's "The Tempest."* Newark: U of Delaware P, 2004.

Hulme, Peter. "Prospero and Caliban." In his *Colonial Encounters: Europe and the Native Caribbean, 1492–1797*. London: Methuen, 1986. 89–134.

Irobi, Esiaba. *Sycorax: Esiaba Irobi's Adaptation of William Shakespeare's* The Tempest, *a Comedy*. Enugu, Nigeria: ABIC Books, 2013.

• James, Henry. "[Surrendering to *The Tempest*]." From Introduction to *The Tempest*. In Sidney Lee, ed., *The Complete Works of William Shakespeare*. New York: George D. Sproul, 1907. 16: ix–xxxii.

Jameson, Anna. "Miranda." In her *Shakespeare's Heroines* [1832]. London: George Newnes, 1897. 148–55.

Johnson, Lemuel A. *Shakespeare in Africa (and Other Venues): Import and the Appropriation of Culture*. Trenton, NJ: Africa World Press, 1998.

Johnson, Nora. "Body and Spirit, Stage and Sexuality in *The Tempest*." *ELH* 64 (1997): 683–700.

Joseph, May. "The Scream of Sycorax." In her *Nomadic Identities: The Performance of Citizenship*. Minneapolis: U of Minnesota P, 1999. 127–39.

Kahn, Coppélia. "The Providential Tempest and the Shakespearean Family." In Murray M. Schwartz and Coppélia Kahn, eds., *Representing Shakespeare: New Psychoanalytic Essays*. Baltimore: Johns Hopkins UP, 1980. 217–43.

• ———. "Caliban at the Stadium: Shakespeare and the Making of Americans." *Massachusetts Review* 41:2 (2000): 256–84.

• Kemble, Fanny. "Some Notes on *The Tempest* (Parts I, II, and III)." In her *Notes upon some of Shakespeare's Plays*. London: Richard Bentley & Sons, 1882. Repr. in Ann Thompson and Sasha Roberts, eds., *Women Reading Shakespeare, 1660–1900: An Anthology of Criticism*. Manchester: Manchester UP, 1997. 121–25.

Kermode, Frank. Introduction to William Shakespeare, *The Tempest*. The Arden Shakespeare. London: Methuen & Co., 1954. xi–xciii.

Kingsley-Smith, Jane. "*The Tempest*'s Forgotten Exile." *Shakespeare Survey* 54 (2001): 223–33.

Knapp, Jeffrey. *An Empire Nowhere: England, America, and Literature from "Utopia" to "The Tempest."* Berkeley: U of California P, 1992.
- Knight, G. Wilson. *The Shakespearean Tempest, with a Chart of Shakespeare's Dramatic Universe.* Oxford: Oxford UP, 1932.
———. "The Shakespearian Superman: A Study of *The Tempest*." In his *The Crown of Life: Essays in Interpretation of Shakespeare's Final Plays* [1947]. London: Methuen & Co., 1964, 203–55.
Kott, Jan. *The Bottom Translation: Marlowe and Shakespeare and the Carnival Tradition.* Trans. Daniela Miedzyrzecka and Lillian Vallee. Evanston: Northwestern UP, 1987.
- Lamming, George. "A Monster, a Child, a Slave." In his *The Pleasures of Exile* [1960]. London: Allison & Busby, 1984; Ann Arbor: U of Michigan P, 2004. 95–117.
Lanier, Douglas. "Drowning the Book: Prospero's Books and the Textual Shakespeare." In James C. Bulman, ed., *Shakespeare, Theory, and Performance.* London: Routledge, 1996. 187–209.
Latham, Jacqueline E. M. "*The Tempest* and King James's *Daemonologie*." *Shakespeare Survey* 28 (1975): 117–23.
Lindley, David. "Music, Masque, and Meaning in *The Tempest*." In David Lindley, ed., *The Court Masque.* Manchester: Manchester UP, 1984. 47–59.
———. Introduction to William Shakespeare, *The Tempest.* The New Cambridge Shakespeare. Cambridge: Cambridge UP, 2013. 1–101.
Loomba, Ania. "Seizing the Book." In her *Gender, Race, and Renaissance Drama.* Manchester: Manchester UP, 1989. 142–58.
———. "Shakespeare and Cultural Difference." In Terence Hawkes, ed., *Alternative Shakespeares.* London: Routledge, 1996. 2: 164–91.
- Lupton, Julia Reinhard. "Creature Caliban." *Shakespeare Quarterly* 51 (2000): 1–23.
Mackenthun, Gesa. "A Monstrous Race for Possession: Discourses of Monstrosity in *The Tempest* and Early British America." In Tim Youngs, ed., *Writing and Race.* London: Longman, 1997. 52–79.
Magnusson, A. Lynne. "Interruption in *The Tempest*." *Shakespeare Quarterly* 37 (1986): 52–65.
- Mannoni, Octave. *Prospero and Caliban: The Psychology of Colonization* [1950]. Trans. Pamela Powesland. Ann Arbor: U of Michigan P, 1990.
Maquerlot, Jean-Pierre, and Michèle Willems, eds. *Travel and Drama in Shakespeare's Time.* Cambridge: Cambridge UP, 1996.
Marcus, Leah. "The Blue-Eyed Witch." In her *Unediting the Renaissance: Shakespeare, Marlowe, Milton.* London: Routledge, 1996. 1–37.
Marienstras, Richard. "Prospero ou le machiavélisme du bien." *Bulletin de la Faculté des Lettres de Strasbourg* 43 (1965): 899–917.
———. "Elizabethan Travel Writing and Shakespeare's *The Tempest*." In his *New Perspectives on the Shakespearean World* [1981]. Trans. Janet Lloyd. Cambridge: Cambridge UP, 1985. 160–85.
Marx, Leo. "Shakespeare's American Fable." In his *The Machine in the Garden: Technology and the Pastoral Ideal in America.* New York: Oxford UP, 1964. 37–72.
McDonald, Russ. "Reading *The Tempest*." *Shakespeare Survey* 43 (1991): 15–28.
Miko, Stephen J. "Tempest." *ELH* 49 (1982): 1–17.
Mowat, Barbara A. "Prospero, Agrippa, and Hocus Pocus." *English Literary Renaissance* 11 (1981): 281–303.
———. "Prospero's Book." *Shakespeare Quarterly* 52 (2001): 1–33.
———. "*The Tempest*: A Modern Perspective." In Barbara A. Mowat and Paul Werstine, eds., *The Tempest.* The New Folger Library Shakespeare. New York: Washington Square P, 1994. 185–99.
Muñoz Simonds, Peggy. "'Sweet Power of Music': The Political Magic of 'the Miraculous Harp' in Shakespeare's *The Tempest*." *Comparative Drama* 29 (1995): 61–90.

• Neill, Michael. "'Noises, / Sounds, and sweet airs': The Burden of Shakespeare's Tempest." *Shakespeare Quarterly* 59:1 (2008): 36–59.

Nilan, Mary M. "'The Tempest' at the Turn of the Century: Cross-currents in Production." *Shakespeare Survey* 25 (1972): 113–23.

Nixon, Rob. "Caribbean and African Appropriations of *The Tempest*." *Critical Inquiry* 13 (1987): 557–78.

Norbrook, David. "'What Cares These Roarers for the Name of King?': Language and Utopia in *The Tempest*." In Gordon McMullan and Jonathan Hope, eds., *The Politics of Tragicomedy*. London: Routledge, 1992. 21–54.

• Orgel, Stephen. "Prospero's Wife." *Representations* 8 (1985): 1–13.

———. Introduction to William Shakespeare, *The Tempest*. Oxford: Oxford UP, 1987. 1–87.

Pasternak Slater, Ann. "Variations within a Source: From Isaiah XXIX to *The Tempest*." *Shakespeare Survey* 25 (1972): 125–35.

Patterson, Annabel. "'Thought Is Free': *The Tempest*." In her *Shakespeare and the Popular Voice*. Oxford: Basil Blackwell, 1989. 154–62.

Potter, Lois. "A Brave New *Tempest*." *Shakespeare Quarterly* 43 (1992): 450–55.

Powell, Jocelyn. "*The Tempest, or The Enchanted Island*." In his *Restoration Theatre Production*. London: Routledge & Kegan Paul, 1984. 62–83.

Purkiss, Diane. "The Witch on the Margins of 'Race': Sycorax and Others." In her *The Witch in History: Early Modern and Twentieth-Century Representations*. London: Routledge, 1996. 251–75.

Raley, Marjorie. "Claribel's Husband." In Joyce Green MacDonald, ed., *Race, Ethnicity, and Power in the Renaissance*. Cranbury, NJ: Associated University Presses, 1997. 95–119.

• Rowe, Nicholas. "[The Magic of *The Tempest*]." In *The Works of Mr. William Shakespear*. London: for Jacob Tonson, 1709. 1: xxiii–xxvi.

Ryle, Simon. "Re-nascences: *The Tempest* and New Media." In his *Shakespeare, Cinema and Desire*. Basingstoke: Palgrave Macmillan, 2014. 174–211.

Sachdev, Rachana. "Sycorax in Algiers: Cultural Politics and Gynecology in Early Modern England." In Dympna Callaghan, ed., *A Feminist Companion to Shakespeare*. Oxford: Blackwell, 2000. 208–25.

Schmidgall, Gary. "*The Tempest* and *Primaleon*: A New Source." *Shakespeare Quarterly* 37 (1986): 423–39.

• Sherman, William H. "Shakespearean Somniloquy: Sleep and Transformation in *The Tempest*." In Margaret Healy and Thomas Healy, eds., *Renaissance Transformations: The Making of English Writing, 1500–1650*. Edinburgh: Edinburgh UP, 2009. 177–91.

Skura, Meredith Anne. "Discourse and the Individual: The Case of Colonialism in *The Tempest*." *Shakespeare Quarterly* 40 (1989): 42–69.

Smith, James. "The Tempest." In his *Shakespearian and Other Essays*. Cambridge: Cambridge UP, 1974. 159–261.

Sokol, B. J. "*The Tempest*: 'All Torment, Trouble, Wonder and Amazement': A Kleinian Reading." In B. J. Sokol, ed., *The Undiscover'd Country: New Essays on Psychoanalysis and Shakespeare*. London: Free Association Books, 1993. 179–216.

Sokol, B. J., and Mary Sokol. "*The Tempest* and Legal Justification of Plantation in Virginia." In Holger Klein and Péter Dávidházi, eds., *Shakespeare Yearbook* 4 (1997): 353–80.

Solomon, Julie Robin. "Going Places: Absolutism and Movement in Shakespeare's *The Tempest*." *Renaissance Drama* n.s. 22 (1991): 3–45.

Spiller, Elizabeth. "Shakespeare and the Making of Early Modern Science: Resituating Prospero's Art." *South Central Review* 26 (2009): 24–41.

• Strachey, Lytton. "Shakespeare's Final Period." In his *Books and Characters*. London: Chatto & Windus, 1922. 60–64.

Strehler, Giorgio. "Notes on *The Tempest*." Trans. Thomas Simpson. *PAJ: A Journal of Performance and Art* 24:3 (2002): 1–17.

Stritmatter, Roger, and Lynne Kositsky. "Shakespeare and the Voyagers Revisited." *Review of English Studies* n.s. 58, no. 236 (September 2007): 447–72.
———. *On the Date, Sources and Design of Shakespeare's "The Tempest."* Jefferson, NC: McFarland, 2013.
Sturgess, Keith. "'A Quaint Device': *The Tempest* at the Blackfriars." In his *Jacobean Private Theatre.* London: Routledge & Kegan Paul, 1987. 73–96.
Summers, Joseph H. "The Anger of Prospero." *Modern Quarterly Review* 12 (1973): 116–35.
Sundelson, David. "So Rare a Wondered Father: Prospero's *Tempest.*" In Murray M. Schwartz and Coppélia Kahn, eds., *Representing Shakespeare: New Psychoanalytic Essays.* Baltimore: Johns Hopkins UP, 1980. 33–53.
Taylor, David Francis. "The Disenchanted Island: A Political History of *The Tempest,* 1760–1830." *Shakespeare Quarterly* 63:4 (2012): 487–517.
Taylor, Mark. "Prospero's Books and Stephano's Bottle: Colonial Experience in *The Tempest.*" *Clio* 22:2 (1993): 101–13.
Test, Edward M. "*The Tempest* and the Newfoundland Cod Fishery." In Barbara Sebek and Stephen Deng, eds. *Global Traffic: Discourses and Practices of Trade in English Literature and Culture from 1550 to 1700.* London: Palgrave Macmillan, 2008. 201–20.
Thompson, Ann. "'Miranda, Where's Your Sister?': Reading Shakespeare's *Tempest.*" In Susan Sellers, ed., *Feminist Criticism: Theory and Practice.* London: Harvester Wheatsheaf, 1991. 45–56.
• Tieck, Ludwig. "Shakespeare's Treatment of the Marvellous" [1793]. Trans. Louise Adey. In Jonathan Bate, ed., *The Romantics on Shakespeare.* Harmondsworth: Penguin, 1992. 60–66.
Tudeau-Clayton, Margaret. "Shaking Neptune's 'Dread Trident': *The Tempest* and Figures of Virgil." In her *Jonson, Shakespeare and Early Modern Virgil.* Cambridge: Cambridge UP, 1998. 194–244.
Vaughan, Alden T. "William Strachey's 'True Reportory' and Shakespeare: A Closer Look at the Evidence." *Shakespeare Quarterly* 59:3 (2008): 245–73.
Vaughan, Alden T., and Virginia Mason Vaughan. *Caliban: A Cultural History.* New York: Cambridge UP, 1992.
Vaughan, Virginia Mason. "Literary Invocations of *The Tempest.*" In Catherine M. S. Alexander, ed., *The Cambridge Companion to Shakespeare's Last Plays.* Cambridge: Cambridge UP, 2009. 155–72.
———. *The Tempest: Shakespeare in Performance.* Manchester: Manchester UP, 2011.
Vaughan, Virginia Mason, and Alden T. Vaughan. Introduction to *The Tempest.* The Arden Shakespeare. London: Thomas Nelson and Sons, 2011. 1–160.
Warren, Roger. "Rough Magic and Heavenly Music: *The Tempest.*" In his *Staging Shakespeare's Late Plays.* Oxford: Clarendon P, 1990. 158–207.
Wickham, Glynne. "Masque and Anti-Masque in *The Tempest.*" *Essays and Studies* n.s. 28 (1975): 1–14.
Wikander, Matthew H. "'The Duke my Father's Wrack': The Innocence of the Restoration *Tempest.*" *Shakespeare Survey* 43 (1991): 91–98.
Wilcox, Helen. "Vengeance and Virtue: *The Tempest* and the Triumph of Tragicomedy." In her *1611: Authority, Gender and the World of Early Modern England.* Malden, MA: Wiley-Blackwell, 2014. 192–210.
Williams, Deanne. "Prospero's Girls." *Borrowers and Lenders: The Journal of Shakespeare and Appropriation* 9:1 (2014). http://www.borrowers.uga.edu/1382/show
Wilson, Richard. "Voyage to Tunis: New History and the Old World of *The Tempest.*" *ELH* 64: 2 (1997): 333–57.
Witmore, Michael. "Spinoza and *The Tempest*: An Island of One." In his *Shakespearean Metaphysics.* London: Continuum, 2008. 90–127.
Yates, Frances A. "Prospero: The Shakespearean Magus." In her *The Occult Philosophy in the Elizabethan Age.* London: Routledge, 1979. 159–63.
Zabus, Chantal. *Tempests after Shakespeare.* New York: Palgrave, 2002.